The Kiss of Peace

A Contemporary Exploration into
Song of Solomon

Diane Virginia

M Zion Ridge Press LLC

Mt Zion Ridge Press LLC
295 Gum Springs Rd, NW
Georgetown, TN 37366

https://www.mtzionridgepress.com

ISBN 13: 978-1-955838-02-3

Published in the United States of America
Publication Date: October 1, 2021

Editor: Sara Foust
Editor-In-Chief: Michelle Levigne
Executive Editor: Tamera Lynn Kraft

Cover art design by Tamera Lynn Kraft
Cover Art Copyright by Mt Zion Ridge Press LLC © 2021

ENDORSEMENTS

Are you yearning for a deeper, more intimate relationship with Jesus Christ? Throughout the pages of *The Kiss of Peace: A Contemporary Exploration into Song of Solomon*, Diane comes alongside you as a friend as she unveils the depths of love and peace tucked into the play, Song of Solomon. This anointed book can change your life and unite you to your Bridegroom Jesus Christ, whose stage name is Beloved Solomon. Read it for yourself, and then consider blessing others by hosting a *Kiss of Peace* small group study.

Jan Coates
Author of *Set Free: God's Healing Power for Abuse Survivors and Those Who Love Them*,
Television and Radio Speaker, Conference Speaker

Diane invites us on a fascinating and deeply intimate journey of exploration of our relationship with the Groom of the Church with her study, *The Kiss of Peace: A Contemporary Exploration into Song of Solomon*. With compelling vignettes and well-researched and doctrinally sound analysis, we work our way through the Book of Song of Solomon and garner wisdom along the path. Each chapter offers an opportunity for us to grow deeper in our relationship with Christ. What a gift this book is for the believer looking for an oft-understudied, yet important part of the Holy Bible.

Alynda Long, M.L.S., Creative Writing
Founder and Editor of Faith Beyond Fear
Contributing Author to *Dear Wife: 10 Minute Invitations to Practice Connection with Your Husband*
and *Stories of Roaring Faith: Vol 3*.

In *The Kiss of Peace: A Contemporary Exploration into Song of Solomon*, Diane seeks to restore a biblical understanding of Song of Solomon as an allegorical representation of the divine love the Groom, Jesus Christ, has for us, His cherished Bride. She compels us to seek more of His presence. It is with respect and admiration that I endorse this book.

Victor Marcos
Pastor/Missionary to Lima, Peru, Artist, Virginia Beach, Virginia

The Kiss of Peace: A Contemporary Exploration into Song of Solomon will bring many to a fresh awareness of God's love and His desire to have an intimate relationship and fellowship with His people. Song of Solomon is in the Old Testament, but Diane excellently brings out that this is a picture of Jesus Christ and His Bride, His Church, and God's overwhelming desire for His intimacy to be accepted and reciprocated.

Dr. Tony McCanless, D.D.
Senior Pastor, Faith and Healing Worship Center, Sofia, North Carolina
Speaker, Author of *Thirty-five Years of Divine Health*

In *The Kiss of Peace: A Contemporary Exploration into Song of Solomon*, Diane takes the reader on a journey that brings Song of Solomon to life. A must-read for those who long to go deeper in their intimacy with Christ.

Brandie J. Muncaster
Speaker, Blogger, Devotion Writer, Author of *Garden Tales: A Seed's Story*

The Kiss of Peace: An Exploration into Song of Solomon, transforms our thinking, broadening the scope of biblical truths—turning all other misinterpretations of Song of Solomon on their axis. Diane Virginia writes with passion, purpose, and genius creativity. Her special way of bringing Scripture to life offers fresh understanding of God's unending love for His church. Diane's beautifully poetic, theologically sound teaching makes *The Kiss of Peace* a must-read for anyone desiring the unconditional, redeeming love of God—the lover of our souls.

LaTan Roland Murphy
Award Winning Author of *Courageous Women of the Bible*
Writer, Speaker, Decorator, Lover of people and strong coffee

The Kiss of Peace: An Exploration into Song of Solomon is an easy reading exploration of a unique book in the Bible, Song of Solomon, that first found approval with audiences in the author's speaking ministry. This intriguing approach should find favor, especially with women hungry for a deeper relationship with our Savior.

Leslie H. Stobbe
Author, Editor, Writing Coach, Ghostwriter
Recipient of Five Lifetime Achievement Awards

In *The Kiss of Peace: A Contemporary Exploration into Song of Solomon* Diane has opened this often-misunderstood book, and brought understanding, with sensitivity to the reader. *The Kiss of Peace* is not only informative, it is enjoyable as the reader realizes Song of Solomon is an allegorical love story written by Jesus Christ to His bride. I wholeheartedly recommend this book to anyone who wants to deepen their understanding of the Bridegroom Jesus Christ.

Evelyn Mason Wells
Speaker, Missionary
Contributing Author to Award winning *Heart Renovations, Breaking the Chains,* and other books

In *The Kiss of Peace: A Contemporary Exploration into Song of Solomon,* Diane eloquently narrates the love story, Song of Solomon, in such a way that you feel as if you were cast into the lead role. She pulls back the veil for a glimpse into what the inner chamber holds if you dare to drink the wedding cup and say "yes" to Jesus Christ's marriage proposal. Diane bravely trumpets this love story with such honor and love for the Author. Her knowledge and wisdom will inspire you to hold on because wedding night intimacy with your Beloved Groom is worth learning to embrace His name for you, as "Love."

Maria C. Wingard
Founder of Hope Will Arise Ministry
Blogger, Conservative Activist, Motivational Speaker

Inspired by the Holy Spirit, Solomon's allegory tells the greatest love story ever. Each chapter in *The Kiss of Peace: A Contemporary Exploration into Song of Solomon* allows readers to intimately experience the depth of Christ's love for His bride—the church—by inviting them into this biblical story. In reading each vignette scene, I gained a deeper understanding of the relationship Christ desires to have with me personally. Whenever this world attempts to separate me from my faith in my Beloved, I will reach for this book.

J.D. Wininger
Follower of God, Writer, Speaker, and Friend

In *The Kiss of Peace: An Exploration into Song of Solomon*, Diane gives us an opportunity to glean insights that will enhance our lives. She helps us embrace the divine love we witness in the Bride and Bridegroom, who allegorically represent Jesus Christ and His church. This book will inspire you to experience your Heavenly Bridegroom's love.

Bishop Harry L. Wood, B.Th., M.Th., D.D.
Administrative Bishop of United Community Bible Churches, Inc.
Founder of Foundational Faith Ministries
Author of *The Great Revelation to Mankind*

A MESSAGE FROM GLENDA SHOUSE

What a joy it has been to watch the progress of *The Kiss of Peace: A Contemporary Exploration into Song of Solomon*. From the beginning, when God dropped this idea into my spiritual sister Diane's heart, and then through the rewrites, edits and on to publishing, I have had the pleasure of reading this amazing work.

It has been a tremendous blessing to witness the conception, birth, and growth of a work of God. And then to finally see it become reality is my delight. Congratulations, Diane, for holding onto and pursuing your God-given dream.

The Kiss of Peace is an intimate look into the Savior's divine love for each of us individually, and for His church, corporately. As you read this beautiful story of the Song of Solomon, your love for Beloved Jesus will grow and your understanding of the depth of His love will be revealed, allowing you to experience Him at a deeper level of intimacy.

Ahead of you is a marvelous journey. From Sharon's Valley, to Mt. Bethel, where you as the Bride yield your struggles, and then onward to the Father's banqueting table where you commune, and ultimately behind the veil of the enclosed garden at Mt. Hermon, where you and your Beloved Groom's romance find its completion, you will experience divine peace and love as never before. Prepare to be blessed by the One who gave His life to make you complete!

Glenda Shouse
Founder of Three-Strand Cord Ministry
Devotion Writer, Intercessor
Contributing Author to *Love Knots: Stories of Faith, Family, and Friendships, Volumes 1 and 2*

ACKNOWLEDGEMENTS

This list of acknowledgments would not be complete without first thanking you, the reader, for journeying with me through Song of Solomon. God has a message for you, and I thank you for taking the time to discover Jesus Christ's bridal message in this vignette.

Prepare to be swept off your feet and become starry-eyed in love with your Bridegroom. Prepare also to realize the depth of love He has for you, His Bride, which the Scripture says is like a strong root, anchoring us in the fullness of God (see Ephesians 3:14-18).

Thanks go to my husband Phil, who supported this book when it was only a concept. From the first day I was smitten by my Savior's kiss of peace, to the last rewrite, and even today, he has supported this writing journey, never wavering in the knowledge this book would be royalty published.

Phil delivered chocolates, crackers 'n cheese, and beverages whenever he noticed I was burning the midnight oil. He never complained about peanut butter for dinner — or no dinner — so I could stay in "the writer's zone," even keeping an eye on tornadic weather, permitting me to stay focused and prioritize writing.

He stood with me through my many computer woes, replacing the shift key, followed by the entire keyboard, and the fan — twice. When I finally "fired" my computer due to screen-freeze, he found a monitor I could hook up to so I could keep writing while he found a laptop replacement.

When I got discouraged because the Lord had instructed me to wait for royalty publishing, but I read the statistics of a new writer being picked up by a royalty publisher was 5 percent, my husband redirected my thoughts to penning the message and letting God work out the details.

I would love to say the support I received from my husband was because he loves me — which he does — but he had an additional motivation. He recognized that the spiritual romance of the Bridegroom Jesus Christ, to you, His Bride, needed to be revealed. He continues to pray with me that you will be transformed by this message.

Thanks go to my spiritual sister, Glenda Shouse. She read every version of *The Kiss of Peace* from its conception, and loved its developmental stages. Glenda sent Scriptures, encouraging notes, offered prayer often, gave sound advice, and stood fast, believing I would see the fulfillment of this publishing goal. She got a pen for me to sign the book contract because she knew I would need this reminder to hold onto God's promise, as it was ten long years of waiting.

Thanks go to Pastor/Missionary Victor Marcos. He prayed often as I developed this work, and each prayer was a blessing, but one instance stands out best. When we placed the manuscript on the altar of the CBN chapel and dedicated *The Kiss of Peace* there, I felt it was at that precise moment the promise was sealed. In that picturesque little chapel, as Victor and his wife Angela, and my husband and I bowed before the Lord, His tangible presence came into the room. I knew then that God would set up the right chain of events to bring this book to royalty publication.

Thanks go to my spiritual sister, Stephanie Pavlantos. She believed in the book's message, looking on it with scholarly excellence, encouraging me to submit the manuscript to the very publishing house that picked it up.

Thanks go to my writing coach, Leslie H. Stobbe. He believed in my unique approach to this biblical vignette, knowing this would help a modern-day reader relate to its timeless message. Having done his own research and writing on Song of Solomon, he was the perfect wordsmith to do a doctrinal vetting as he edited through the manuscript. Les became a friend through the process, and a gentleman I greatly admire.

Thanks go to Founder/Executive Editor Tamera Kraft of Mt. Zion Ridge Press, and to her amazing team. Tamera recognized this work on its merits alone. Sara Foust edited the manuscript, making it sparkle. Through this Spirit-led publishing house, the dream has taken shape, crafting the manuscript into book form. Because Tamera listened to the Holy Spirit, knowing this book will give you a glimpse into Beloved's bridal message, we have walked through the publishing door.

I cannot express the joy I feel in partnering with this particular publishing house. The goals of Mount Zion Ridge Press met what I was looking for in a publishing company in full measure. May the Lord bless Tamera and the entire Mount Zion Ridge Press family. Thanks, Tamera, for bringing forth *The Kiss of Peace* into published form.

In closing, I'd like to thank my Bridegroom Jesus Christ, allegorically Beloved Solomon, whose spiritual kiss of peace He imparted to me one morning while I was reading Song of Solomon. This started my writing journey. For years, my Beloved took me into the wedding chamber and revealed Song of Solomon with such depth I could not — *not* — write this book. My Bridegroom's kiss of peace continued to be transforming, so I knew I must obey His calling to pen this work, and in doing so, to reveal your story and His, for you truly are the Bride and He is the Bridegroom of this spiritual romance.

It is my prayer that you will use *The Kiss of Peace* to springboard into a realm of marital bliss with the Lord of Glory that we can only dream of as being possible. Embrace your story and fully receive your Bridegroom's divine kiss of peace.

Shalom,
Diane Virginia

✦✦✦✦✦✦

To Phil, Glenda, and Victor, who believed this divine romance should be revealed.

And to you, His Bride.

And to my Lord Jesus Christ.

Thanks, my Beloved, for Your kiss of peace.

✦✦✦✦✦✦

TABLE OF CONTENTS

PREFACE

What's in a kiss? Love is in a kiss, especially if it's from your Bridegroom Jesus Christ.

Song of Solomon is a misunderstood book, and rarely read, because we don't know how to interpret its passionate phrases and subject matter. And yet, here it is—smack dab in the middle of our Bibles. This mystery unravels when we realize Song of Solomon is an allegory whose poetic vernacular represents only spiritual truths. All is spiritual; nothing within the vignette is to be received as literal. Once we see this, we can begin to grasp its truths. This is where my journey began, and I pray it will become yours as well.

In ancient biblical times, the bridegroom would offer a cup to his bride. If she sipped, she was signaling her willingness for him to betroth her. So, in this vignette, you need only say "yes" to receive your Groom's kiss and become His Bride.

Think of the cup—it is filled with the blood of your Savior's veins. This marriage cup cost Him His very life, for this cup not only represents His marriage proposal, it represents the Communion cup of His shed blood and the sacrifice He made to redeem His Bride by going to Calvary's cross. Your Beloved Bridegroom knows you are worth this bridal price, and He has no regrets in proposing marriage to you. In fact, He is so certain about His decision to betroth you He offers not one, but multiple kisses.

Do you sense His nearness? Do you smell the sweet-oil aroma of the Spirit as He ushers divine love into your prayer room? Don't be in a rush. Settle in and rest a while. Tarry as long as you can in your Beloved Savior's holy embrace. Receive each of His kisses—don't miss any of them—for each is tailored for you, the Bride of Christ, whom He loves.

Oh, I haven't even told you the good part yet. "Beloved Solomon," which means "Beloved Peacemaker," calls you "Love." That's right. Your bridal name is "Love." Let that sink in for a good while, because if you're like me, you're thinking about your flaws about now. No worries…Your Beloved has overcome them for you, every shortcoming having been erased by His divine embrace.

Are you ready to come behind the veil and into the marriage chamber, which represents the Holy of Holies, to unite your spirit with the Spirit of the Bridegroom Jesus Christ? Your journey begins with a spiritual kiss. And it gets more glorious from there.

Receive your Groom's kisses of divine peace as we begin the adventure.

Shalom,
Diane Virginia

Chapter One
The Kiss

Let him kiss me with the kisses of his mouth —
For your love is better than wine.
~Song of Solomon 1:2

Greet one another with a kiss of love.
Peace to you all who are in Christ Jesus. Amen
~1 Peter 5:14

A kiss…

Does the memory of a kiss hold special meaning to you? Perhaps you remember your fiancé expressing newfound love with a trembling first kiss. Or is it the moment when your child was born? You took your cherished bundle into your arms and kissed her sweet, soft head? Is it a grandmother you remember, and the kisses she lavished upon your cheeks and brow? Oh, what depths of love and heights of joy one kiss can create! One kiss can become an eternal memory.

I remember my friend Charles standing at the altar of the church. When his bride Elizabeth appeared, he gasped at her entrance. The couple smiled with a knowing look. What did they know? They believed only death could dissolve their marriage bond.

They celebrated by singing a duet. As Charles lifted a tear from his bride's lashes, I realized everyone, including the groom, was crying. But the love this couple felt induced more than emotion — their bond was spiritual.

Promises of love spoken through faltering lips, starry-eyed gazes, and tender smiles — these brought joy to the onlookers — but there was one expression the congregation still yearned to witness.

It was the long-awaited kiss…

The bride and groom's story was penned that day, their covenant of love having been sealed through the groom's kiss and his bride's response. Love declared through this kiss was the crescendo to remember!

The ceremony was beautiful, but the kiss sealed their vows.

It was a beautiful kiss.

It was a holy kiss.

Arms were entwined, and love was declared through an embrace and a kiss. As Elizabeth reclined in her groom's arms, this marked a new beginning for her and a completion of all that was missing within her.

I knew this marriage would last. Their future was written in the kiss…

I remember my own wedding day. My husband follows all the rules. He is quite reserved. And yet, his kiss was so exceptional I will treasure it forever.

The pastor asked us to light a unity candle. Two flames became one. Then, we knelt before the Lord in quiet reflection and received Holy Communion. Rising, we joined hands and faced each other. We spoke our vows of commitment and exchanged rings with intense devotion to the promises we were making in the sight of our God.

And then, there was the blessing. It was a beautiful blessing; truly, it was.

My veil — it was already lifted.

Pastor spoke one blessing after another…

I saw it in my beloved's eyes. He just couldn't wait! The love boiling within him had to find an expression. My fiancé swept me into his strong embrace, lifted me off my feet, and kissed me!

3

Our pastor, still praying blessings over us, opened his eyes just in time to witness this unrehearsed explosion of affection. Pastor then said, matter-of-factly, "By the way, you may kiss your bride."

Giggles and applause erupted as we stepped into life as one.

How did we know? We knew it by the kiss...

Now, step into a century of long ago. The stage is set, and you are an actor in a play called *Song of Solomon.* You are cast as a Shulamite woman from the country of Israel. By profession, you are a shepherdess and a keeper of the vines. But you leave this mundane life and search for the One you hope will complete you. He does not disappoint! He becomes your Groom.

What happens then?

Your future transforms by a kiss...

We would think this vignette would start with backstory, but instead, it opens with the kiss of your Groom. Scene after scene then plays out, revealing how your love story began and how your Groom's first and subsequent kisses worked completion in you.

There's something unusual about your Groom's kiss. Although the vignette is written in ordinary language, the expression is spiritual—not physical. This vignette is an allegory of divine love. And so, as you enter this romance, reach higher than the human dimension and into the spiritual realm. The vignette is an awakening into divine love by your Groom's kisses of peace. His allegorical name is Beloved Solomon, but His identity as Jesus Christ is revealed in every scene. Yes, dear reader, you are the Bride of Christ.

You and Beloved Solomon have nicknames for each other. He calls you "Love," and you call Him "Beloved." There is security in His identification of you, for this gives you the assurance He loves you with a passion unlimited by human enterprise. Therefore, before you ever understand your Groom's divine kisses of peace, you receive your bridal name, as "Love."

In the vignette scenes that follow, I've taken the liberty to capitalize names and pronouns in order to honor Beloved and you, His Bride. Other than that, they are as they appear in the New King James Version of the Bible. Take time to experience these scenes. It is your Bridegroom's intention that you personalize this romance.

Song of Solomon is a true love story. You truly are "Love," and your Betrothed truly is Jesus Christ, allegorically represented as Beloved Solomon, but this is an exploration into Song of Solomon, so for now, let's pretend we are actors in a play.

Let the journey begin:

*****

SONG OF SOLOMON 1:1-4
Scene One: The Kiss

SETTING: Wedding-day flashback at the curtain of the marriage chamber; the Holy of Holies.

AT RISE: LOVE stands outside BELOVED'S chamber reminiscing with her MAIDENS. She is starry-eyed in love.

(Curtain rises)

NARRATOR

[1]The song of songs, which *is* Solomon's.

LOVE
(Touching her cheek as if applying soothing ointment)

[2]Let Him kiss me with the kisses of His mouth—for Your love *is* better than wine. [3]Because of the

fragrance of Your good ointments, Your Name *is* ointment poured forth; therefore the virgins love You. ⁴Draw me away! We will run after You. The King has brought me into His chambers: (Closing her eyes, Love draws her fingertips to her lips, and lifts her chin in remembrance of Beloved's kisses.)

MAIDENS
⁵ᵃWe will be glad and rejoice in You. We will remember Your love more than wine.

LOVE
(Speaking to her unseen Beloved with confidence)
⁵ᵇRightly do they love You.
(Looks over her shoulder longingly as the music crescendos)

NARRATOR
Love's countenance speaks of contentment and oneness within her Bridegroom-King's embrace.

*****

Hello, Love. Does it seem curious to you, as it does to me, that this opening act is an accounting of—there is no way to say this gently—a bedroom scene? You receive the first kiss of your Groom behind the veiled wedding chamber. There is no story development, no courtship as a lead-in, no historical progression, and no description of physical touch.

We do not see you walking down an aisle, as in a traditional wedding. Instead, the vignette begins with the reminiscence of your Groom's first kiss and the intimacy you have experienced behind the wedding veil. It is hot, passionate lovemaking emanating from the holiest of places—the secluded wedding chamber—that the Lord starts with to demonstrate His romance of His cherished Bride, and this opening scene entails His most zealous expression—your consummation. This truly is an unusual way to begin a book.

It takes little imagination to envision your blushing face as you recall to your lady friends who wait for you outside the wedding chamber the kisses of your Husband-King. You say no more to the maidens except to share the kisses—for the rest is exclusive intimacy only you and your Groom partake of. Even a single kiss you have received is an intimacy you can scarcely express, but you try.

I can tell you honestly, the first time I read these opening lines of Song of Solomon, I closed my Bible, set it on the table and said, "Later, God." But the more I thought about this scene, I understood the reason for this unprecedented beginning.

Perhaps the Lord's intent is to emphasize the mind-boggling spiritual intimacy available to every believer. Beloved whets our appetite with His best—which are His divine kisses of love and peace that await the Bride of Christ behind the veil of the Holy of Holies. From this point of entry, the Groom reveals to us throughout the rest of the play how we can attain this focused, pure, divine love He desires to impart to us as His Bride.

THE GROOM'S SIGNATURE
Thus, the intensity of Beloved's divine love becomes the signature of His authorship of Song of Solomon. It is as if the Lord wants us to understand this first, "I love you with a divine love that is boiling in its expression, and I am not ashamed of My love's intensity." He wants us to recognize this before we come to know Him experientially.

THE ALLEGORICAL ALLURE OF ROMANCE
This vignette is written as an allegory because this format gives us an opportunity to discover the otherwise undiscoverable realm of the Spirit. Simply stated, your Groom's love is expressed as a romance because divine love has no human equivalence. Therefore, your Groom chooses mankind's

most passionate expression — sex within the marriage covenant — as an approximation of His intended communication. Keep this in mind as you read the ardent lovemaking portrayed in Song of Solomon. Unless we recognize this as an allegory, we will entirely miss the play's intended meaning. Nothing is to be taken literally — the entire vignette is an allegorical representation of the spiritual realm.

ALTERNATE VIEWS

Should we throw out commentaries that portray Song of Solomon as a book that will enhance our marriages? I don't think so. Although limited, there is definitive value in this interpretation. For instance, this year, my husband presented me with a ring with the Hebraic words, *I am my beloved's and my beloved is mine,* taken from Song of Solomon 6:3. I faithfully wear it adjacent to my wedding ring, knowing my covenant with Beloved Solomon — allegorically, Jesus Christ — enhances my marriage bond with my earthly husband. My husband even asked me to prioritize my spiritual Groom, and he acknowledged we both should aim to become more like our spiritual Bridegroom. Therefore, I can affirm that by reading Song of Solomon as a married couple, this will definitely enhance marriages, but even more so when we acknowledge Song of Solomon is primarily about our divine marriage to the Lord Jesus Christ.

Some commentaries describe Song of Solomon purely in sexual terms. After all, even a casual read through reveals these obvious sexual undertones. All generations have seen this. These books read it amiss, manufacturing conclusions that are not intended or implied.

H. A. Ironside speaks about the restrictions placed on families in Jewish homes because of this error: "The Jews did not allow a young man to read the book until he was thirty years of age, lest he might read into it mere human voluptuousness and misuse its beautiful phrases."[1] The Jewish community respected Song of Solomon as an allegorical expression of divine truths, and guarded it from being interpreted as a book about sex. We, too, must guard the integrity of this sacred text.

CANONIZATION

Scholars have long debated the canonicity of Song of Solomon due to its inclusion of sexual content. At the Council of Jamnia in 90 A.D., Rabbi Akiba argued for Song of Solomon to be canonized.[2] What motivated him to fight for its inclusion in the Tanakh (Jewish Bible) is this opening scene, where the Bride experiences her Groom's kisses. He presented Song of Solomon as an allegory of God's divine love within the Holy of Holies. Akiba wrote, "The whole world attained its supreme value only on the day when the Song of Songs was given to Israel."[3]

Other ancient biblical commentators agreed with Rabbi Akiba, such as Origen of the third century and Theodore of Cyr of the fifth century. These scholars went a step further by noting the messianic interplay between the Groom Jesus Christ, and His Bride, the Church.

Unfortunately, there has been a paradigm shift in today's culture. Books that purport the vignette as a celebration of erotic and sexual love abound. This is the very error the Jewish fathers guarded their children from! Modern-day writers are prone to misrepresent Song of Solomon because they do not recognize it as an allegory.

This is why it is imperative we keep Rabbi Akiba's wisdom alive.

The allegory, Song of Solomon, is a holy book of divine love the Lord extends to you, His cherished Bride. Through this venue, He is showing you secrets of the heavenly realm that transcend the natural dimension. With this perspective, let's return to our discussion of Scene One.

---

[1] Ironside, H. A., LITT. D. *Addresses on the Song of Solomon.* Chicago: Loizeaux Brothers, Inc. Bible Truth Depot. 1933. Chapt. One, pg. 7. http://www.baptistbelievers.com/
[2] W.M. Christie (July 1925). "The Jamnia Period in Jewish History" http://www.biblicalstudies.org.uk/pdf/jts/026_347.pdf (PDF). *The Journal of Theological Studies,* Biblical Studies.org.uk
[3] Blech, Benjamin, Rabbi. *The Complete Idiot's Guide to Understanding Judaism, 2nd Edition: A Guided Tour Through the Beliefs, Laws, and Traditions of Judaism.* Penguin. Chapter Seven, p. 89. (August 1, 1999).

SCENE ONE: THE FLASHBACK

Scene One is a flashback of your wedding chamber experience. You are a newlywed, remembering your wedding day and the blissful honeymoon that you experienced behind the veil of the Holy of Holies. Although Beloved makes no appearance, His kisses have become a memory that you cherish. The daughters of Jerusalem meet you outside the wedding chamber, and they rejoice with you there as you come from behind the veil.

So, what do you share? You begin by saying, *Let him kiss me with the kisses of his mouth…* (Song 1:2a), but you become so captivated by this joyous memory that your friends' inquiring faces fade from your view, and you speak as if only your Husband-King is listening, *…for your love is better than wine* (Song 1:2b). You are so caught up with this memory that you mention only three rudiments about your experience: 1) the touch of your Groom's lips upon your own, 2) the cup of wine He offers you, and 3) the Name associated with your Groom's fragrant oils. Let's examine these.

THE GROOM'S KISS

The definition of the word *kisses* (Song 1:2) in its original language carries the meaning of being "fastened up, touched, armed, equipped, or attached."[4] In the physical realm, as lips fasten together, they induce pleasure receptors. In the spiritual realm, they represent the same pleasant fastening up.

Two become one with the kiss…

Beloved's kisses exude wet marks upon your face. As you touch your cheeks, you remember the essence of your Lord's passion. You draw your fingers to your lips and taste your Husband-King's oils. They are fragrant, rich, and calming. You can go into this remembrance and bask in the nearness of His presence at all times and in all places.

The spiritual deposits of Beloved's kisses are as intentional as the wet deposits of the physical kisses that you feel, smell, taste, and reminisce about. You receive His kisses within the Holy of Holies; the very dwelling-place of the Lord Most High, and this experience is only available within the covenant of marriage.

THE CUP OF WINE

You say that your Lover's kisses are more satisfying than a sip of sweet sanguine wine. You recall this detail because it was customary for a prospective groom to propose marriage by offering his lady a cup of wine, to which, if she sipped, she was agreeing to marry her suitor.

As a believer, you recognize this as the Communion cup. This is a costly gift, for the wine represents His shed blood. This is the purchase price for you, His comely Bride. We are two lines into the vignette, and already we recognize the messianic symbolism that runs through its entirety. The identity of your Groom as Jesus Christ is undeniable.

You state that Beloved's kisses are better than the Communion cup. What can possibly be more significant than Christ's shed blood? Consider this: Salvation is available to every person, and yet some individuals choose to not receive the gift of salvation. In like manner, some individuals choose to not receive Beloved's marriage invitation. What is better than the Communion kiss? The "yes" that you speak to your Beloved regarding His marriage proposal affirms your Groom's Communion kiss. Until you say "yes" to His bridal invitation, it is only a symbol, and not a personal revelation. As you sip from the Communion cup, this gives you the right to become Beloved's Bride.

THE TORN VEIL

Let's look at a New Testament comparison to the wedding scene of the vignette as you come

---

[4] James Strong, LL.D., S.T.D. *The New Strong's Expanded Exhaustive Concordance of the Bible*. Nashville: Thomas Nelson Publishers, 1995. OT #5401, *nashaq*

behind the veil of the Holy of Holies.

On Calvary's cross, Beloved Jesus won the victory as He shouted, *"Father, into thy hands I commit my spirit"* (Luke 23:46b). At that exact moment, an eclipse darkened the sun and the veil of the Temple was torn from top to bottom, opening the way into the Holy of Holies. Because the veil has been opened to you by your Savior's blood atonement, you have access into the Holy of Holies of Heaven.

How is it that you, a mere mortal, can enter into this most holy place? It is because you have sipped from the Communion cup, and by doing so, you have accepted your Husband's marriage proposal to become the Bride of Christ.

One sip seals your destiny, writes your story, and betroths you as Bride, and yet, Beloved offers you an eternal number of sips from His cup of blessing as well as an eternal number of kisses.

WORDS OF LIFE

When we memorize Scripture, every word is like a kiss from our Groom, in written form. During this blessed Communion with your Beloved, He imparts wisdom to you through conversation. In Psalm 119, you say, *I will delight myself in Your statutes; I will not forget Your word* (Psalm 119:16). Remember this as you read and memorize the Word — each verse to the Bride is like a kiss from the Groom.

THE OILS; THE NAME; THE VEILED CHAMBER

As you step from behind the veil, you mention the fragrances of Beloved's ointments that have invaded your being. These oils are identified later as being myrrh and frankincense. Thus, your Lover's identity as the Anointed High Priest and the King of Kings is represented in this opening scene.

The fragrances you willingly inhale are the oils of His love. These become your essential oils. How do they get on your cheeks and lips? They come from close contact as you press into your Husband-King's embrace. Time spent in undistracted worship is the key to experiencing these oils. Your Husband-King rewards you with the oils of His love as you worship Him. Holiness comes upon you simply because you make the choice to tarry.

Let's be honest about this commitment — if you're like me, it's a struggle. I fight getting up at 'o'dark-thirty' to spend time with my Husband-King. But I've learned I must prioritize my time with Him above other activities.

Beloved comes first. No excuses.

And then, when my Beloved's presence does come upon me, the struggle seems silly. I love Him! There is no goodness within me outside of my connection to the True Vine, Jesus Christ, so I must be purposeful in my commitment to spend time with Him.

The most intimate spiritual experiences we can have are the times we spend in private communion, exclusively with our Groom. This is when we experience the marital chamber of the Holy of Holies in its deepest expression.

BEHIND THE VEIL

Where do you fit into this vignette, Love? This is your story of intimacy with your Beloved Groom. He loves you, His cherished Bride. It is you who has been face-to-face and cheek-to-cheek with the King of Glory, and it is you who has allegorically consummated this marriage within the holy wedding chamber. In this, the most holy of all places, you have the exclusive attention of your Husband-King. You discover a love you could only dream of in part, that you now experience in full measure.

You are loved, truly loved — and now, you experience the depth of your Husband's love. There is nothing within this holiest of places but love. You experience a love that is pure, unadulterated, perfect, and holy. Furthermore, the divine love you experience within the wedding chamber is not merely a substance; it has become the person, Jesus Christ, whose allegorical name is Beloved Solomon.

THE GROOM'S NAMES
BELOVED

Your Groom's nickname, "Beloved" translates as the word, *dowd*.[5] This comes from an unused root word which means "to boil." Let's look at this word picture.

If we were to take a snapshot of a boiling pot of liquid, would this photo adequately describe the liquid within it? No, it would not because it would miss the dynamic nature intrinsic within the bubbling liquid. In like manner, Beloved's love is intense, consuming, and alive.

This word *dowd* is used in Song of Solomon as a unique term. In other places, it usually translates as an "uncle" or a close relative. But, exclusively in Song of Solomon, it is used to describe marital love. What do we learn from this? Think of the role of an uncle. This shows the positional relationship of your Husband-King. An uncle would protect and shelter you, gather you into His bosom, and keep you safe. In the book of Ruth, Beloved is your "Boaz," the Kinsman-Redeemer, who rescues you when no relative is willing to do so.

In the vignette, your Beloved is like this Kinsman-Redeemer, but as your Husband-King, His role extends beyond the role of an uncle or redeemer. Therefore, translating the close bond you have with Him as "marital love" instead of "uncle" is appropriate.

"Divine marital love" comes close to the intended meaning of Beloved's name, *Dowd*. In two biblical passages in the New Testament, your Groom is described in three simple but profound words, *God is love* (1 John 4:8b, 16b). Think of the significance — the God of love is divine love personified. This is Beloved's identification.

SOLOMON

Your Groom's name, "Solomon," translates as the Hebrew word, *Shelomoh*,[6] which means "peaceful." The root word is *shalom*, which means "prosperity, peace, or completeness." It is "a harmonious state of the soul and mind," which signifies "a prosperous relationship."[7] Solomon means "peace" in its completed form. It is the perfection of peace, and, just as we see His nickname, Beloved, meaning love personified, His name, Solomon, means peace personified.

Does your Groom typify this peace? In both the Old and New Testament, we see that He does. Ezekiel speaks of the covenant of peace, as he writes, *"Moreover I will make a covenant of peace [shalom] with them"* (Ezekiel 37:26a). Isaiah prophesizes about Messiah as he writes, *For unto us a Child is born, unto us a Son is given … and His name will be called … The Prince of Peace [shalom]* (Isaiah 9:6, in part). The shepherds receive the good news of the birth of Messiah as an angelic choir proclaims, *"Glory to God in the highest, and on earth, peace [eirne],[8] good will toward men"* (Luke 2:14)! Jesus often reveals His allegorical identity as "Solomon." On one passage He declares, *"These things I have spoken to you, that in Me you may have peace [eirne][9]"* (John 16:33a).

BELOVED SOLOMON: AN ENCODED TRUTH

"Beloved Solomon," your *Dowd Sheloma*, is equivalent to saying, "Beloved Peacemaker." This is the identity of the Groom. Meditate on this, Love. Our Groom, who lavishes you with His kisses is divine love and peace personified. This is the treasure-trove encoded within His vignette name.

---

5 Strong. OT #1730 *dowd*; beloved, wellbeloved; from an unused root meaning "to boil."
6 Strong. OT #8010, *Shelomah*
7 Strong. OT #7965, *shalom*
8 Strong. NT #1515, *eirene*
9 Strong. NT #1515, *eirene*

THE BRIDE'S NAMES
LOVE

Let's look at your names. Beloved uses many terms, so we will recap only the most frequently used.

Your name, "Love," and His nickname, "Beloved," both translate into the word, "love," but His is a weightier version because it is in the plural form,[10] whereas yours is singular. We see from this that while Your Beloved gives infinite quantities of divine love, your nickname is singular because your love is finite. But there is one location where your love is as limitless as your Spouse's. Let's examine this.

DOWD; DIVINE LOVE

Your Beloved calls you to frequent His secluded mountaintop garden and the wedding chamber therein—allegorically again representative of the Holy of Holies. As you respond to His calling to come away with Him, you attain your highest love potential.

Twice in a single passage entry, your Beloved calls the love you offer to him, "*dowd*."[11] This is the holy love your Groom possesses, while your love is finite, so how is this possible? In the mountains of Lebanon, you become as Beloved during times of ascent because unity with Him permits this. Beloved does not demand you to possess divine love, but at these times, you do. So, there are times within the marriage chamber that you get it—you become so united with your Spouse that you also possess the divine *dowd*-love of your Beloved and you are identified as "Beloved." These instances are rare—only two references are in the vignette—but that this unity is possible should compel us to spend time worshipping our Savior in seclusion and with focused intensity.

SISTER-SPOUSE

Your Groom calls you, *my spouse* (Song 4:8, for example) in many instances of the vignette. We learn something interesting when we look at these passages in both the King James and the New King James versions. These verses are rendered, "my sister, *my* spouse." These terms are used in conjunction, but the second "*my*" in these phrases is added by the translators, so a more accurate rendering would be the compound word, "my sister-spouse."

Beloved is expressing here your positional relationship. Siblings have a unique relationship because they are equals. You are to Beloved as close as a sister, but your relationship is even closer because you are His spouse. Thus, the term "sister-spouse" is the closest English translation of this bridal name. This shows how unified Beloved desires to be with us, that He, the King of all kings, would call us "sister." He permits unity.

FAIREST AMONG WOMEN; COMPLETED AND GLORIOUS WITHIN

The maidens often echo Beloved's endearment, *fairest among women* (compare Song 1:8 with 1:15, for example). This tells us that even when we feel like a mess, Beloved sees us as completed by His love. Tie this into a love-knot and wave it in front of the enemy the next time he tries to harass you! Beloved loves us at all times, not just when we have ourselves pulled together. Whether we are feeling broken or complete, His love for us is the same. From His heavenly perspective, He has carved a path for completeness, which will be worked within us over time, so He already sees the end result.

Receive this compliment, Love. You are the fairest Bride, and you are Beloved's chosen. You are enough, not because of your abilities but because you have decided to unite with Him, and as you do so, His love completes you.

---

[10] *Gesenius' Lexicon. Blue Letter Bible.* "Dictionary and Word Search for *dowd (Strong's 1730)*". Blue Letter Bible. 1996-2013. 19 Mar 2013. www.blueletterbible.org/lang/lexicon/lexicon.cfm?strongs=H1730

[11] Ibid.

Let's delve further. Beloved's title for you, *my fair one*, (Song 2:13) translates as "comely, beautiful, and bright."[12] This indicates the glory of your Beloved that shines through you, making you lovely to behold. You are a glory carrier! As the kisses of peace rest within you and you press into an intimate embrace, the fragrant oils of frankincense and myrrh come upon you and you become Beloved's radiant Bride; you reflect Beloved's glory. Just as Moses' face shone when he tarried in the Lord's presence, your kissed face sparkles with the most beautiful sheen imaginable.

LOVE; WIFE OF PASSION

Your Groom's favorite and most frequently used name for you is "Love." In fact, He uses it as a nickname. It is used in two distinct ways:

The first usage translates as *rayah,*[13] which means "beloved companion" or "lover." Its root word indicates your position as Beloved's marriage partner.[14] Genesis 2:24 records marriage partners as being one flesh. Because your spirit is one with Beloved's Spirit, represented in the vignette as the joining of marriage partners, His strength becomes your strength, and this union erases your weaknesses.

The second usage of "Love" translates as *ahabah.*[15] It means "to desire; to breathe after," or "to have longing for." It carries with it the association of running after your Groom in a hot, passionate pursuit. It refers to the sentimental aspect of your marriage. It is your choice to pursue Him, and because you do, He calls you Love.

RECEIVE BELOVED'S KISSES

Sharing in Beloved's kisses is gratifying and makes you long for more. You are full of love, and yet you want to drink of the kisses of your Husband's endless supply. It is as if eternity is embedded in each kiss.

Do you want to know a secret? Beloved is listening to the longings of your heart right now, and He longs for you. Truly, He does! You are the comely Bride whom He pursues with the passionate, boiling love of His divine nature called *dowd.* Permit your Groom's love to become a reality as we explore each scene.

THE PIVOTAL SCENE

This opening scene is a flashback of the pivotal event to which we will compare all other scenes of the vignette. In four verses, in this first scene, you understand Beloved Solomon is Jesus Christ, your Beloved Peacemaker, and you are His chosen Bride.

AUTHORSHIP; POINT OF VIEW

Beloved could have recorded Scene One Himself, but instead, it is your words of remembrance that He records as you emerge from behind the veil. In fact, the entire vignette is written from your point-of-view. You are that important to your Groom. It is as if you have a ghost-writer.

Even so, the vignette's opening lines answer the question of authorship, *The song of songs, which* is *Solomon's* (Song 1:1). Your Beloved Jesus Christ is the Author of this vignette. Your part, therefore, is to fully receive the love song penned by the Author of authors.

---

[12] Strong. OT #3302 *yaphah*

[13] Strong. OT #7474, *rayah*; root word OT #7453, *rea*

[14] In the *Gesenius's Lexicon, rea* is defined as "a companion… with whom one has intercourse." Obviously, *rayah* and *rea* reference a married couple.

[15] Strong. OT #157, *ahab,* masculine tense; OT #160, *ahabah,* feminine tense

THE PROTOTYPE

Where does the earthly King Solomon fit in? God inspired him to write the vignette, but it is a typology of your divine King Jesus Christ. The earthly Solomon was wise, but as a human he was flawed, particularly in his thoughts about romance. In contrast, the divine Solomon is perfect in every way, and He is the true Author of the vignette.

THE SONG

The vignette is written as a song to be sung. Matthew Henry writes, "It is the song of songs, a most excellent song, not only above any human composition, or above all other songs which Solomon penned, but above any other of the Scripture-songs ... It is not the song of fools ... but the song of the wisest of men."[16]

Henry points out Song of Solomon is the only one of King Solomon's songs that exists today,[17] and canonized within the pages of our Bible; "Solomon's songs were a thousand and five; those that were of other subjects are lost, but this of seraphic love remains, and will to the end of time."[18] Beloved has preserved this song as His gift to you.

CANONICAL LOCATION

Notice Song of Solomon's canonical location. Smack-dab in the middle of our Bibles, we have this slender and often misunderstood book, with its theme being the pursuit of God, represented by a romancing couple singing the love song of the ages, and of the transforming power of divine covenantal love.

Why is it in the center of our Bibles? Its location is central so we can't help but notice it.

THE VIGNETTE FORMAT

What spiritual connection awaits as you step into this vignette? As you declare, *Let him kiss me with the kisses of his mouth: for your love* is *better than wine* (Song 1:2), this opening statement is a call for Beloved Solomon, who is love and peace personified, to kiss you with the boiling hot love-force that only His Spirit embodies. And yet, the wedding chamber the Lord of Glory draws you into is filled with this divine love.

If I were to be plunged into a boiling pot, what would the results be? I'd be killed, so it would have no draw or appeal to it at all. But what if this boiling pot were that of Beloved Jesus Christ's love? This boiling pot, my friend, is a realm of face-to-face intimacy that is truly desirable. This boiling pot permeates us until we are completely pure! I don't want to plunge into a boiling pot in the natural, and I'm sure you don't either, but the boiling pot of our Bridegroom's divine love is a supernatural realm we should willingly desire.

APPLYING THE TRUTHS

Let these words sink deep into your spirit: You are Beloved's Bride, and He loves you. In fact, your Bridegroom boils with divine love for you. Let's take action:

First, put on your Groom's love as a garment. Wear His love each day as a soft blanket.

Next, put on your name, as "Love," His passionate wife. Your very name, as you embark on this journey, identifies the depth of your Groom's love for you and that He considers you to be His most intimate companion.

Receive the awakening He imparts to you as your Groom kisses you with peace. Once you have received one kiss from your Husband-King, you will be transformed forever. But remember,

---

[16] Henry, Matthew. *Matthew Henry's Commentary on the Whole Bible*. 6 vols. USA: Hendrickson Publishers, Inc., 1994. Vol 3. pg 867.
[17] Henry references 1 Kings 4:32
[18] Ibid

there is an endless supply.

Finally, reciprocate His spiritual kisses, with the assurance that He receives you no matter how frail your love is compared to His own, knowing that as you participate with Him, your love will become divine. You are pictured as having the same nearness as John, the disciple whom Jesus loved, who leaned upon Jesus' breast the night before the crucifixion (see John 13:25, 21:20). John asked for his Lord's divine embrace, and Jesus did not deny him. Neither will Beloved deny you, for Song of Solomon 8:5a reads, *Who is this coming up from the wilderness, leaning upon her beloved?* It is you, His Bride, pressing into the spiritual embrace of your willing Bridegroom.

DRAW ME

If you are like me, peering into the wedding chamber is a bit overwhelming. You may say, as I did when I first read this scene, "My Beloved, I don't know how to be Your Bride. I desire for my Beloved to draw me, but I struggle with the fact that I don't deserve the boiling hot love You desire to lavish upon me. And the kisses! The very thought of Your kisses is somewhat unfathomable."

I desired this face-to-face intimacy, and I longed for Him to draw me, but I did not know the practical steps this involved. The answer is revealed in Scene One. As you ask Beloved to draw you to Him, you say, *Draw me away* (Song 1:4)! Speak these words aloud, as I did, "Draw me." This is a request for you to desire Him. Now add, the word "away." As you say, "Draw me away," you are inviting your Beloved to sweep you into His wedding chamber, and to place within your spirit the passion He needs you to have. He will draw you as He did me, and He will satisfy your deepest longings to know Him.

CONCLUSION

In Scene One, Beloved Solomon reveals the end results of your love song, which are the kisses of peace you receive within the holy wedding chamber. He desires to covenant with you, but the choice to accept Beloved's marriage proposal is yours alone. Will you say "yes" to your suitor's marriage proposal? If so, say it aloud, to seal your decision to receive your Groom.

Before your Bridegroom came on the scene, the enemy tried to define you by a genealogical scar. I call it Kedar's scar. But then, you searched for Beloved, and your life took on a whole new dimension. This next scene will help you to determine how your love song began and how Beloved drew you into the wedding chamber embrace.

I invite you to read on. But first, let's talk to our Groom. I'll pen some words, but I encourage you to make this your very own expression. Let's seal the romance that is beginning to bubble within your spirit. Pray these words, or your very own, to your Beloved Solomon—your *Dowd Sheloma*—your Beloved Peacemaker:

My Bridegroom,

I acknowledge Your allegorical Name, Beloved Solomon, identifies You as my Beloved Peacemaker, but Your true identity is Jesus Christ. Draw me into a covenantal marriage relationship and into wedding room bliss. I say, "yes" to your marriage proposal, and I choose to sip from the cup of wine that represents the Communion covenant You signed in blood on Calvary's cross.

As I experience this next scene, take me back to my beginnings where I first accepted You. Help me to navigate these torrid circumstances, knowing You have chosen me. And now, my Beloved Solomon — my Dowd Shelomah — my Beloved Peacemaker Jesus Christ, I pledge my allegiance exclusively to You, and I sign this with my newfound name, the bridal name You have chosen to call me in the most excellent of songs — that of "Love."

Your Bride,
Love

BRIDAL REFLECTION

1) Think of a kiss that caused remembrance. Why is a groom's kiss more intimate than any natural kiss? How does Beloved's divine kiss of peace compare to/differ from a groom's kiss?

2) Why is Song of Solomon written as a vignette (play)? How does this format help you to experience Beloved Jesus Christ's divine message?

3) Who are the two main actors in Song of Solomon, and who do they represent?

4) Why is it important to keep Rabbi Akiba's wisdom alive regarding the vignette, Song of Solomon? Discuss the canonization of Song of Solomon.

5) Why is Beloved's divine love—*dowd*—like a boiling pot?

6) You, as Bride, say to Beloved Jesus Christ, "Draw me away!" How does this statement help to create marital intimacy in the spiritual realm?

7) In the vignette, what is the bridal name your Groom Beloved Solomon, allegorically Jesus Christ, calls you most often? In your fanciest writing, write your bridal name in the blank: _____

Chapter Two
Kedar's Scar

I am dark, but lovely, O daughters of Jerusalem,
like the tents of Kedar, like the curtains of Solomon.
~Song of Solomon 1:5

For you were like sheep going astray, but have now returned
to the Shepherd and Overseer of your souls.
~1 Peter 2:25

(RRRing!)
"Children, report to your classrooms. The school day is about to begin."
"White Socks! Julia's wearing white socks!"
"She'll look great in mud socks! She's a...."
(Tee hee hee!)
I'm a...? Wha...?
"Hey, White Socks, wanna play with us at recess?"
(RRRRRRRing!)
"Eeek, we're late!"
(Tweet!) "Walk!"
"Run! Don't let that safety patrol catch you!"
"Good morning, boys and girls. We're going to have a great day because we are paying attention. Oh! Look at Julia! She's supporting the new dress code by wearing white socks with her saddleback shoes. Everybody, remember to wear white socks tomorrow."
(Whispers and giggles.)
"Open your spelling books to Lesson Five."
"White Socks follows all the rules."
(Tee hee!)
"Who's talking? Boys and girls, pay attention."
Lesson Five. White Socks is having a great day because she's paying attention. Wait, I'm not "White Socks!" I'm definitely not a... What did they call me?
"Pay attention, sweetie. We're in Reading Circles now."
*****

Labels! They're like gum on a sidewalk. The more we try to escape their grip, the stronger they stick. Julia doesn't recall much of her first-grade year, but she does remember, in vivid detail, the teasing she received about her bleach-white, dress-code-proper ankle socks. She'd roll them down, squat to try to cover them—she'd do anything to make them disappear. But, despite her efforts, there they were. Bleach-white ankle socks. Her mind would race; *I'm "White Socks," and I don't fit in.* For years after the "White Socks" incident, Julia would wear socks of any color—except white. Fluorescent green and purple striped toe-socks were fun to wear, but white socks? Never! Even into high school, she avoided wearing white socks. We all remember "the bully" and "the bullied," and if we were one of those two, the recollection is more vivid.

As we grow up, we stop labeling others, right? Oh, wait. Do I hear you saying you have painful memories of your teenage years? If so, you're not alone. For many of us, the teasing we endured then was worse. These recollections can be painful if we hold onto them, so Beloved shows us, through the vignette, the solution to the pain.

It is your turn to tell the Lover of your soul your story. Transport yourself into our romantic Old-World setting, and although I cannot hear your exact memory, Beloved can. Speak the memory and permit Him to turn your tragedy into triumph. Your Groom understands you so well He has portrayed you in His book.

In this scene, you are an adolescent of marrying age, and you live with your mother and stepfather. You've participated in religious rituals, but you sense there must be more than this form of religion that denies the power and presence of the living King.

Memories surface from the teasing from your peers…

A label haunts you. Your friends and family call you, "Dark!" You know all too well the destructive power of words. How does this label come about? It is a reference to your heritage. Your birthfather, Kedar, has scarred the present for you, but you still love him. Today, you may have a heritage that also leads to feeling unaccepted. Beloved deliberates this issue in the vignette.

In Scene Two, you feel compelled to learn of the Shepherd-King. It is a wise choice, for as you do so, you exchange the false labels for the true identifiers your Groom calls you.

Step into the vignette:

*****

SONG OF SOLOMON 1:5-8
Scene Two: Kedar's Scar

SETTING:	Foreground: The toppling walls of LOVE'S vineyard; falling trellises; rows of oiled raisins drying on the sunny patio.
	Background: Pastures; Lebanon's mountain range.
AT RISE:	Foreground: The HECKLING MAIDENS carelessly weave through the trellises, knocking vines off the trellises as they go. One KIND MAIDEN refrains, secretly re-tying as many of the toppling vines as she can reach.
	Background: LOVE is walking her flock of sheep and goats in for the night. Her dark-olive skin is sunburned, and she is exhausted.

LOVE
(Center stage)
(LOVE arrives at the vineyard; she begins to re-tie the vines onto the trellises. The KIND MAIDEN assists her. LOVE wipes sweat from her brow and avoids eye contact with the HECKLING MAIDENS.)

NARRATOR
Atop Love's crumbling fortress, the heckling maidens play a spontaneous game of tag. Love knows her peers disapprove of her.

HECKLING MAIDENS
(Laughing. Whispering. Pointing at Love.)
Ha! You're dark!
(LOVE tidies her clothing and continues her chores. KIND MAIDEN smiles at her; LOVE avoids eye contact.)

16

NARRATOR

Love knows all too well she is unkempt. One maiden is different from the others. She cringes at the ridicule Love is enduring. This maiden must know the King.

    (KIND MAIDEN kneels in a praying position, facing Lebanon.)

HECKLING MAIDENS

    (Shouting, laughing, and taunting continues)

Dark! You're the dark one!

LOVE

    (Lifts head; strokes arms; eyes brimming with tears; cheeks flushed)

[5]I am dark, but lovely, O daughters of Jerusalem, like the tents of Kedar, like the curtains of Solomon.

    (Eyes brim with tears)

NARRATOR

What had its beginnings as secretive backbiting has become a cruel game. Some of these maidens ridiculing Love are her blood relatives. As if it were alive, their label "dark" hits her as a low blow. Love totters between opposing worlds. Will she listen to these taunting voices of unified consternation, or will she search for truth? Her pain, as a wet wall, mounts. As if she can deny gravity, she holds onto this brimming wall of heartache. A single tear escapes her brave façade and traces her sunburned cheek.

LOVE

    (Tears brimming; one tear traces LOVE's cheek.)

    (Spotlight on LOVE's tear.)

[6]Do not look upon me, because I *am* dark, because the sun has tanned me. My mother's sons were angry with me; they made me the keeper of the vineyards, *but* my own vineyard I have not kept.

    (KIND MAIDEN weaves her way through the crowd; she catches LOVE'S tear.)

NARRATOR

Look at the kind maiden. She also is crying! This maiden's gaze is upon Lebanon's stately mountain range.

    (The KIND MAIDEN touches LOVE'S arm and motions for her to kneel. LOVE kneels, tentatively, trembling, searching for truth. The KIND MAIDEN prays with LOVE.)

Love speaks, yet now to an unseen acquaintance. Upon King Solomon she will focus, and only upon Him.

    (LOVE rises. The KIND MAIDEN continues to kneel in prayer.)

LOVE

    (LOVE addresses her unseen King)

[7]Tell me, O You whom I love, where You feed *Your flock,* where You make *it* rest at noon. For why should I be as one who veils herself by the flocks of Your companions?"

KIND MAIDEN

    (Rises from prayer; points to the sand)

[8]If you do not know, O fairest among women, follow in the footsteps of the flock, and feed your little

goats beside the shepherds' tents."
>   (Spotlight on sand; LOVE'S tear falls on her toe)

NARRATOR

Does this maiden speak the truth? Love's tear teeters. It falls! As the splashes of liquid pain kiss Love's toe, she steps out. No longer will she leave her spiritual vineyard untended. By acknowledging that she needs to find the King, she is releasing her soul from endless toil.
>   (LOVE falls to the ground, weeping, sifting the sand, searching the horizon. The KIND
>   MAIDEN points to footsteps in the sand)

Could it be that the King has passed this way? Love's tears are freely flowing now. They have outlined the footprint of the Shepherd, with the dot of His staff beside it. Could it be the King was looking for her? He is a Shepherd, so He must have frequented the same valley in search of lost sheep.
>   (Spotlight on footprint and staff imprint)
>   (LOVE traces the footprint with her fingers. Rising, she follows the tracks.)

Amidst the cleansing tears that stain Love's dusty face, she wonders if she will find the Shepherd-King. She is journeying to the Sharon Valley located at the base of the stately Lebanon mountain range where she has heard the Shepherd-King pastures His sheep. As she chooses to embark on this search, she is stepping out of her past and into a brand-new future.

*****

What is happening in Scene Two? As you embark on a spiritual pilgrimage, you are, in fact, searching for labels, but you are learning to discern truth from deception. Isn't this the universal search—to know our identity and purpose? But then, when we get hit with the enemy's ammunition—false labels—we unknowingly accept these lies as truth.

LABELS THAT LIE

What are the lies your peers have used to shame you? They taunt you, saying, "You are dark!" With this label, they reference you as inferior and your work tending the vineyards and the flocks as undignified. In effect, they are saying, "Your sunburned body is worn out!"

Your friends also imply, "If your stepfather cares about you, why doesn't he protect you?" Your stepfather, like your birthfather Kedar, may also be an absentee, so you have no father figure to look up to.

In order to compensate for this confusion of identity, you adopt a work-hard mentality. Even so, emptiness looms within your soul. The false label, "dark," distorts your thoughts. Like our protagonists, you repeat their false narrative, saying to yourself, *I'm ugly, and my tanned color proves I don't belong!*

LABELS OF TRUTH

God gives us just enough information in the vignette that we can relate to brokenness, but He leaves out the details. Why is this so? The truth is, no matter what situation we find ourselves in, Beloved identifies with our pain, and He loves us through it.

What is your true identity? The truth is you are the apple of Beloved's eye (see Psalm 17:8). There is nothing you have done or ever will do that can take His love away. Beloved shows you this in the vignette so you will know this applies to your life today.

You. Are. Loved.

The King of Glory has removed your shame, and He embraces you as His Bride of choice. He sees you as perfected because He is perfect, and the Perfect One receives you as you come behind the veil of the Holy of Holies. But here in the vignette, you have not yet learned of your new identity.

Consider your current situation. Are you the one who is shamed in your family? Beloved has a promise for you. He says, *When my father and my mother forsake me, then the LORD will take care of me*

(Psalm 27:10). Beloved values you deeply, and He wants to fellowship with you. He is here today, and He writes your future. Permit Him to rewrite your script.

DECISIONS

"You're a _____."

Be honest, Love, what would be written in the blank for you? This is the dark skin and sunburn from toil that has scarred you, and it hurts! But take heart. Beloved will set things right, because you are to Him the fairest lady He has ever set eyes on. Therefore, make the decision that His labels override any "dark" labels. The truth is you are the apple of Beloved's eye and He loves you with a divine love that will never fade.

THE GROOM'S SCARS

Beloved wears your injuries as scars that He alone should bear. He wears the sunburn of disappointment, rejection, pain, and ridicule on your behalf. These are engraved on His hands, feet, brow, back, and side. After He arose, and could have looked perfect, He chose to keep enough scars to assure you of His sacrificial love. In the vignette, the kind maiden shows you Beloved wants to bear your burdens.

THE LABEL, DARK

You are burnt three ways: 1) Physically, you are dark in color as well as sunburned from toil. 2) Emotionally, you are burnt from the rejection you've endured. 3) Your spiritual neglect indicates you believe the lie that Beloved is not available for you.

This last injury is the deepest wound. But the truth is, Beloved loves you deeply. The first step in relationship building is to acknowledge you need Him. When you respond to the kind maiden, you are in essence saying, "I need You, my King, and I won't stop searching until I find You." Beloved uses this resolve as the balm that heals all three scars.

The lie the enemy would have us believe is that we have to be perfect before Beloved will accept us. Nothing could be further from the truth! Beloved accepts us just the way we are. This is why He shows us our completion in Scene One before He helps us tackle our deficiencies. As we come to Him, His love perfects and heals us over time. We cannot spoil the love He eternally has for us.

THE BRIDE'S MOTHER

Your lineage is from *the tents of Kedar* (Song 1:5b). This gives us a glimpse into your mother's involvement with your birthfather, whose illegitimate faith lineage marks you as an outcast.

Absent from this scenario is how this relationship plays out. Was your mother abducted? Did she have an affair? We are not told. We do know the rejection you suffer is a result of your family's displaced anger against your birthfather.

Your mother never wed Kedar, because in order for her to be accepted in her culture, she would not have married a foreigner.[19] The probable indiscretion could have gone unnoticed except for your skin color—you are darker than your family.

As is the case with most secrets, somebody told it. Your family knows all about the situation, and they blame you, labeling you a spiritual outcast, with a "dark" soul. As utterly absurd as this may seem, you partially believe the false label assigned to you.

And isn't this the way it is with labels? They are senseless, but when we believe them, they hold power over us. This is why the enemy uses repetition, via badgering speech, to do his level best

---

[19] Rich, Tracey R. "Marriage: Prohibited Marriages and Illegitimate Children." *Judaism 101*. N.P., 2011. Web. 2012. www.jewfaq.org/marriage.htm.

to persuade you to believe the lie.

THE BRIDE'S BIRTHFATHER, KEDAR

Your birthfather Kedar's absenteeism indicates he does not value you. That you still feel a tie to this man of absence makes no sense to your half-kin. If this were not so, you would have let go of your dark feelings long ago. Yet, you accept the label as truth, openly acknowledging you are the dark one.

The reason your kin blame you instead of your mother, is because you still love Kedar, even though they treat him as the outcast they will not talk about. They despise your decision to acknowledge and love him. Kedar has a past we must uncover in order for this to make sense.

THE BRIDE'S STEPFATHER AND SIBLINGS

Does your stepfather model a love that protects all his children, whether they are his blood-kin or adopted? He does not. Instead, he allows your siblings to rule the roost.

And rule, they do.

You do not need to work two jobs, but you reason that hard work will make you measure up to your family's expectations. Because you are not pure kindred, they justify this caste system. Why not shove all the servile jobs on the dark one? They have a slaver's mentality! You are rejected by your mother, birthfather, stepfather, siblings, and kin. Will the shackles ever come off?

THE BRIDE'S RELIGION

By referencing Solomon's curtains (see Song 1:5a), you are denoting the outer curtain of the Tabernacle. This indicates your mother's faith-lineage. She has influenced you positively in this manner. Even so, you have neglected your spiritual life.

Religion, to you, involves mimicking the rules and traditions your mother has taught you. These don't satisfy, and they seem senseless. Consequently, when you make this reference, this implies you've tried religion and it was ineffective in alleviating your pain. Even so, you sense there is more than the shallow belief system she has modeled for you.

THE BRIDE'S JOBS

You are a vinedresser and a shepherdess. We know you favor the shepherding job because you say your mother and siblings make you work the vineyards. Both jobs require physical exertion, and neither is prestigious. And so, out of sheer exhaustion, your performance wanes. The workaholic mentality fails to alleviate your pain.

THE BRIDE AS SHEPHERDESS

To work as a shepherdess is particularly difficult for a young lady. You walk the fields, finding pasture and fresh, running water for your sheep and goats. You watch the lambs and kids, and you carry the sick or lame.[20] Each spring, you tend to the newborn lambs. Periodically, you mend the thorny braided briar sheepfolds where your animals stay overnight. Rather than sleeping soundly, you stay alert to fend off predators who may lurk on the fringes of the fence. During the day, you continue to guard your flocks and you practice your cunning defense skills, including the use of knives and a sling and stone. Predators include bears, wolves, and foxes.[21]

THE BRIDE AS VINEDRESSER

Your job as a vinedresser can be summed in a word: tedious. Because vines only produce

---

[20] Wight, Fred H. "Manners and Customs in Bible Lands." Baptist Bible Believers Website, 1953. Web. 2012.
www.baptistbiblebelievers.com/OTStudies/MannersandCustomsInBibleLands1953
[21] Ibid

grapes on new growth, you prune ninety percent[22] of the vines each fall to ensure an abundant spring harvest. You collect grapes at their optimal sweetness. Then you make several products: You dry them to make raisins, by turning and oiling each one as they bake in the sun.[23] You tread fresh grapes into juice, which you preserve either as sweet or fermented wine. You boil grapes until they reduce to syrupy pulp, and from this, you make jelly.[24] You scatter limestone pebbles as fertilizer under the main trunk of each vine. You maintain a safe boundary wall of heavy, boulder-sized rocks that need to stay stacked to fend off predators.

SPIRITUAL PARALLEL

Let's parallel the above to your spiritual life: You say, *my own vineyard I have not kept* (Song 1:6b). At this point, your opinion of religion is that it is as tedious as vine keeping. You have the know-how, but it's not satisfying. Although you have tended to the spiritual needs of your family with rigorous discipline, by this ritual-keeping you've neglected your own spirituality. In essence, you are trying to work your way into acceptance with your family.

The parallel to this vineyard example is works-based religion. This never works. This is like the deck of cards some of us played with as kids, trying to stack them high. Oh, it would work for a while, but eventually it would tumble. Perhaps the boundary wall of stacked stones resembles the best picture of what you are experiencing. You've tried but failed to keep the walls up. Beloved Jesus wants a relationship with us—not a ritual. He wants to be the one we look to, rather than trying to earn and perform in order to be loved. His love for you has never been performance-based.

There is a paradigm shift when you embark on your spiritual pilgrimage. This is when you mention shepherding, but now, rather than being a shepherdess, you are looking for the True Shepherd. You are no longer looking for a form of religion anymore. Rather, you are searching for a relationship, and the rest that is found exclusively in The Great Shepherd. At this moment of surrender, you are closer to Beloved than you ever were when you put on your brave façade or your works mentality.

You've seen most of your shepherd-friends turn aside from the deep truths of Beloved. They have settled. Your family has settled. They are content with religious dogma. This type of religious busyness has no appeal to you at all.

In contrast, you have observed a few select shepherds who have pastured in Beloved's fields, and they have returned from these spiritual pilgrimages refreshed. This influences you to accept the kind maiden's encouragement to embark on your own spiritual pilgrimage.

You will not settle until you sit at Beloved's feet, feast on His words, and know His most intimate desires. Although broken, you go after your Shepherd-King with a whole heart. And, as we can see from Scene One, your surrender results in marriage, so this approach certainly pays off.

THE KIND MAIDEN'S ADVICE

The kind maiden cautions you to not go on a solo search. You would have done just that, but the wise maiden knows there are shepherds in the valley who can be of genuine help to you. You question how to discern which ones you are to follow. The maiden's advice is twofold:

First, she directs you to *follow in the footsteps of the flock, and feed your little goats beside the shepherds' tents* (Song 1:8). We could camp out in this one verse all day! But let's summarize her advice in a sentence:

Follow in the footsteps of those who follow the True Shepherd.

When we examine the footsteps of the flocks, we are able to discern which shepherds are

---

[22] Bruce, Jim. "Three Stumbling Blocks to Growing Grapes in the Backyard." Pioneer Thinking Company, n.d. Web. 2012. www.pioneerthinking.com/jb_grapes.html.
[23] Ibid
[24] Ibid

sinister and which are peaceable. Sheep will only follow a peaceable shepherd, long-term. They might start following a prideful or angry "shepherd," but eventually they catch on. A peaceable shepherd models genuine care for his flock (see John 10:10-14).

Second, she advises you to follow the shepherds whom the little goats—representative of children and new believers—are comfortable following (see Song 1:8b). If the shepherds have any controlling tendencies, they are not the ones you should follow. These are the false shepherds Jesus talks about in John 10:13. You should not trust these hirelings.

THE GROOM AS SHEPHERD

When the kind maiden identifies your King as the Shepherd, she is revealing the two characteristics that make up His Name as "Beloved Solomon." Remember, Beloved Solomon, *Dowd Shelomah*, means Beloved Peacemaker. These two qualities perfectly describe our Shepherd. He is loving, and He is peaceable.

Perhaps the maiden shows you His peaceable quality first because, at this point, this is your primary need. You want a refuge from the pain and anxiety that angst you. Only after you receive a measure of His peace will you be able to receive the love that is equally found in your Beloved. The peace and love Beloved has are divine, so it is unlike any you've ever experienced. Rather than being a temporary fix, it is the fix for all life's problems, and it only comes through relationship.

THE BRIDE'S GENEOLOGY

Kedar's scar that defines you is a label that must come off. In order to accomplish this, let's delve into your genealogy. To get the best understanding of what we read in Song of Solomon, let's look at the book of Genesis. We will explore Adam and Eve, Cain and Abel, and then move on to Abraham and Sarah, Hagar, Isaac, Ishmael, and lastly, your birthfather Kedar. This might feel like a "bunny trail," but we need this information if we are to get the best understanding of the vignette.

With this in mind, let's hop into their stories…

ADAM AND EVE'S CHOICES

We all know the story of Genesis chapter 3—Satan dupes Eve, she eats the "apple," Adam does too, and they tumble from the godly life of dependence upon the Creator into lofty independence with its consequential feelings of nakedness, shame, self-isolation, and worthlessness.

God sees it all, and foreknows the first couple will fall, but in His mercy, He clothes His son and daughter with lambskins, symbolic of the Lamb of God, Jesus Christ, so that even while they are leaving the Garden of Eden, they know He loves them. The glory robes Adam and Eve once wore dissipate, and they become acutely aware of their nakedness and their need for the Creator, but they are ashamed to come to Him.

If you are a parent, I'm sure you can see God's reasonings for allowing them to sin. There comes a point in a son or daughter's life where we release them. Young adults need to make their decisions, even if this involves them making wrong choices. We hope they will remember their godly upbringing, but the values we've instilled in them are theirs to accept or reject. When they fall, we then, in love, pick up our broken but yielded children, and we help them put their lives back together. If only we could spare them this process! But it is natural, and sometimes learning the hard way helps our children to make wise decisions in the future.

MESSIANIC PROPHECY

When Adam and Eve sin, God allows His children to feel the consequences of their choices, but along with this, He gives them the promise of restoration. Genesis 3:15 reads, *And I [God] will put enmity between you [Adam] and the woman [Eve], and between your seed and her Seed; He shall bruise your head, and you shalt bruise His heel.*

This prophecy is ultimately fulfilled by the coming of Jesus Christ. He is the "Seed" that will come from the woman, Mary. He will be from her natural seed but birthed from the Holy Spirit's divine seed, so the Savior Jesus Christ will be the perfect God-Man and, therefore, the solution to mankind's sinful nature. Jesus the Beloved will bear the sins of mankind in order to redeem them. However, the process will be filled with "enmity," so we need to take particular notice of this word.

ENMITY DEFINED

The word "enmity" means "hatred or hostility,"[25] and it indicates a blood feud. The root word indicates rivaling tribes hating and warring to the death. Not until one party is avenged by death is the enmity satisfied. Enmity rears its ugly head first in Genesis but continues throughout the Bible, into Revelation and into today.

Without original sin, eternity would have been on Earth. But God allows Adam and Eve to make mistakes—even big ones. If He had forced them into a faith relationship, they would have been puppets on a string, not able to have a meaningful, free-will relationship with their Creator. Adam and Eve are responsible for their choices because they are created in God's image and likeness (see Genesis 1:26a), so He expects them to set their own godly path.

How are Adam and Eve duped? Satan coerces them into believing they will become "little gods" if they choose independence rather than dependence upon their Creator (see Genesis 3:5). Since they are created in God's image, and God is a creator, they fall right into Satan's deceptive power trap. They have an innate desire to create, but this cannot be done successfully outside of God's direction.

CAIN'S CHOICE

After the fall, God allows Adam and Eve to procreate. Their sons take two separate paths. Cain is insanely jealous of Abel's choice to follow God wholeheartedly. Ultimately, he is miserable with his choices and the favor God shows his brother Abel, so he murders him. He could have repented, but that would have required him giving up self-will, and he does not want to go there. He likes being a "little god." The divisiveness of enmity gives him a power rush.

CONTRASTING CHOICES

Contrast the enmity that boils in Cain with the boiling-hot God-love, *Dowd*, that makes up Beloved's character. The divergence is remarkable. Love and hate are both commanding forces but are very opposing choices.

Even into the New Testament, we read about Cain's enmity-choice. 1 John 3:11-12 reads, *For this is the message that you heard from the beginning, that we should love one another, not as Cain who was of the wicked one and murdered his brother. And why did he murder him? Because his works were evil and his brother's righteous.*

Jesus Christ, your Beloved, talks about these contrasting choices in The Sermon on the Mountain, saying, *"You have heard that it was said to those of old, 'You shall not murder, and whoever murders will be in danger of the judgment.' But I say to you that whoever is angry with his brother without a cause shall be in danger of the judgment. And whoever says to his brother, 'Raca* [Moron!]*' shall be in danger of the council. But whoever says 'You fool!' shall be in danger of hell fire.* (Matthew 5:21-23). As we read here, Jesus' standards in the New Covenant are more stringent than the Old Covenant. Enmity is a serious matter. Our Beloved confirms this with these and other words.

Jesus gives the greatest two commandments—loving God above all else and loving people— as the principles the entire Word of God hinges upon (see Deuteronomy 6:4; Matthew 22:37-40). Our Beloved considers the choice to love as vital. But just like the stacked vineyard wall that resembles a

---

[25] Strong. OT #H342, enmity, *'eybah*; enmity, hatred; from Strong's OT #H340,*'oyeb*, hostility: --enmity, hatred.

playing card tower that falls quickly, divine love is not in our sinful nature unless we are connected to the True Vine, Jesus Christ. We first must make a faith choice. Then we will be better than Cain in the decisions we make.

THE FAITH CHOICE

Before we start taking pot shots at Adam and Eve or Cain, let's examine our own hearts. Have we made this faith choice? God designed us to be glory-carriers just like our predecessors. We, too, are made in His image, and He is full of glory. We can choose faith by pursuing our peaceable Beloved, or we can choose enmity, and that's what Scene Two in Song of Solomon is all about. When we are independent, we are on the enmity tour. When we are faith-dependent, we can walk alongside Beloved in ministry and be a carrier of His glory.

In today's society, we will face persecution when we choose faith. I remember a relative telling me emphatically that I made my decision for Jesus Christ because I was "weak" and that I'd turn into a "Jesus-freak" if I did not tone things down. He warned me I'd need Jesus every day if I kept messing around with this faith thing. My response was, "If this is weakness, then I choose to be weak, and as for the 'Jesus-freak' title, thanks for the compliment. As for daily dependence, you're wrong on that one—I need Jesus every second of every hour." Then I stormed out of that relative's house and slammed the door. Wham! Oops! Flesh got in there. But the truth is, we need to make a firm choice. Mine is faith. What is yours? I'm guessing yours is faith, too, since you are reading this.

Jesus knows we will face persecution. This is a given. In the vignette, you are being persecuted for not choosing to have enmity against your birthfather. John records Beloved's commentary on the subject, *"Blessed are those who are persecuted for righteousness' sake, for theirs is the kingdom of heaven. Blessed are you when they revile and persecute you, and say all kinds of evil against you falsely for My sake. Rejoice and be exceedingly glad, for great is your reward in heaven, for so they persecuted the prophets who were before you"* (Matthew 5:11-12).

KEDAR'S CHOICE

To gain insight into why your birthfather, Kedar, and being "dark" attracts taunting from your peers, let's look at Isaiah 21:16b-17 MSG. At the end of God's message regarding Arabia, the prophet concludes, *"Within one year—I'll sign a contract on it!—the arrogant brutality of Kedar, those hooligans of the desert, will be over, nothing much left of the Kedar toughs." The God of Israel says so.* This is the backdrop for the Kedar references, and this reveals the reasons for your self-doubt and your Israeli family's rejection of you. Simply stated, your birthfather is a bully who has been disciplined by God Himself. Even though we see this severe judgment falling on his behavior, there is more to his story, and yours, that we need to explore.

Kedar is the grandson of the Patriarch Abraham, and his mother's name is Hagar, not Sarah. Thus, Kedar comes from Cain's line, and he, too, becomes a murderer. Contrast this to your mother's lineage, which comes from the peaceable line of Seth. One of Seth's relatives, named Enoch, is so peaceable that rather than dying, he is translated into God's presence.

What a mixed bag! But, as we will come to discover, God has a reason your genealogy includes both lineages. The dynamics established in these early years of creation affect today's times. Once we understand the sin pattern our forefathers fell into, we can easily discern the solution.

ABRAHAM, FATHER OF NATIONS

God calls Abraham—then named Abram—to go to an unknown destination. He is to father a people who will reverence God (see Genesis 12:1-4; 17:4). God Himself will change his name to Abraham, which means, "Father of a Multitude," or "the Father of Many Nations."[26] But first, he and

---

[26] Strong's OT #H85, *Abraham,* Father of a multitude (Genesis 17)

his predecessors must choose faith instead of enmity.

Abraham has a reputation as being a man of exceptional faith (see Hebrews 11:6-12). Because of this, Abraham's nickname is, "the friend of God" (see James 2:23; Isaiah 41:8). It is Abraham *who contrary to hope, in hope believed, so that he became the father of many nations* (Romans 4:18a). It is Abraham who *calls those things which do not exist as though they did* (Romans 4:17b). Therefore, God establishes His everlasting covenant through this Patriarch (see Genesis 17:7).

The name "Abram" means "High Father,"[27] and comes from words that mean, "father of height,"[28] and "lofty" or "proud."[29] In contrast, "Abraham" means "father of a multitude; father of nations." God's plan is for the covenant-bearer to become High Father. The point is, aside from God's intervention, all Abram would have become was an exalted, lofty father who influenced a few people and was proud about his accomplishments.

God has a better plan, but it comes with a price.

In order for Abram to become Abraham, and for his self-will to be pushed aside so he can be a glory-carrier whose influence is enough for him to be the Father of Nations, he is about to enter the school of hard knocks. God's commission for him to become the Father of Nations means there must be no self-will, no self-exaltation, no self-promotion, no lofty goals, no pride, and — most of all — there must be an absence of enmity.

Let me say that again — there must be no enmity.

Zero. Zilch. Nada. None.

Otherwise, God's will for Abraham's life will not come about at all, and if His had not, neither would yours in the vignette, nor would ours in the here and now.

Furthermore, Abraham must prove himself over a period of time. It's easy to have faith for a day — but God wants His son to have faith that cannot be shaken. And in order for that characteristic to develop, there must be a testing period.

Let's discuss the honing process Abraham goes through.

BREAKING TIES

First, God tells Abram, *"Get out of your country, from your family, and from your father's house to a land that I will show you"* (Genesis 12:1). Why is God calling Abram to be separate? For Abram to resist the sin patterns that are already well established in the people around him, he must leave. Accordingly, when Abram is seventy-five years old, the Lord calls him to leave the city of Haran and go to an unknown destination that God will reveal to him (see Genesis 12:1).

Already, Abram is on a faith-walk.

I remember God calling us to move to North Carolina while our relatives were centrally located in Florida. This was in December of 1995. I clearly heard the Lord telling me we would move "while the earth budded," which indicated spring of that same year. He told me to trust Him with my family members' salvation, but to witness to them one last time and to prepare them for our soon departure.

We hosted a supper. The kids acted out the Christmas story to our entire family (including our non-Jesus-freak relative). My aunt played music on a toy keyboard while our four- and five-year-old children played Joseph and Mary. We commissioned the dog to play the donkey, the angel, the sheep, the cow, and any other creature the kids thought was important. We then explained to our family we felt we would be leaving. Some relatives understood, and — you guessed it — Mr. Independent told us to stop exercising faith in our unseen God.

But we knew...

---

[27] Strong. OT #H87, *Abram*, high father.
[28] Strong. OT #H48, *Abiyriam*, father of height (i.e., lofty); from OT #H7311
[29] Strong. OT #H7311 *ruwm*, rise, raise up, extol, exalt (self), offer (up) presumptuously, promote, etc.

A year later, we moved to North Carolina just as God said. To add zing to God's message, our moving day, which was one day past the final day of spring, puzzled me. Why hadn't we moved in spring? It was officially the first day of summer. God kept His promise to bring forth buds by blanketing our entire two-and-a-half acres with buds from the trees that had sheared off during a tropical storm. Our land was literally covered in tree buds. We could not even rake them up around the property—there were that many.

Abram knew that his unseen God had called him to depart. He, like we, were willing to embark on the faith-walk. And I'm guessing you also have a faith story.

MISTAKE #ONE—PARTIAL OBEDIENCE

Abram obeys. Well, he partially obeys. Lot, Abram's nephew, cannot accept his uncle's explanation that God has called him to travel to an unknown destination, so when the chips fall, Lot travels with him. Let's see this for what it is—it is a mistake. God has called Abram to be separated. Therefore, bringing his nephew is not in the plan.

MIRACLE CHILD

God promises that Abraham's descendants will be from his own "bowels" and they will be as the "stars" or as the "sand" of the seashore or as the "dust of the earth" (see Genesis 13:16; 15:4-6). Abram already knows Sarai is "barren" (see Genesis 11:30). Furthermore, Sarai is old—in fact, she is menopausal. Therefore, from the onset, Abram knows he can only carry out God's plan to conceive an heir by the Lord's miraculous provision. Against all odds, Abram believes God's promise to them.

ALTAR BUILDING; PRAYER DEPENDENCE

Abram goes into the land of Canaan and passes through the plain of Shechem of Moreh and on to Bethel (see Genesis 12:5-8). In both these places, the Lord appears to him and renews the calling as Abram is deep in prayer. Note the significance here; Jesus Christ, in a form we are not told, appears to this patriarch who is known for his faith. This happens several times, so we can see Abram has a well-developed prayer life.

Notice the dependence Abram is developing. Altar building, for the purpose of worshipping God, becomes Abram's habit. Each time he builds an altar, he is learning to have faith, which contrasts the system of enmity the people around him, including his father's family, have modeled. Abram needed this separation to practice holiness and dependence upon his Creator.

So far, we've seen three key traits that enables God to use Abram: 1) Abram obeys God even when he doesn't know the entire plan. 2) Abram has faith in God. For instance, he believes Sarai will miraculously conceive when it is physically impossible. 3) Abram develops the habit of worshipping his Creator.

MISTAKE #TWO—THE LIE

A famine hits the land of Canaan, so Abram moves his family to Egypt (Genesis 12:10). But at this location, there is a problem…

Omitted from the dialogue is the altar building.

We do not see Abram worshipping God or consulting Him regarding this decision. Big mistake! Consequentially, he spends his time fearful of the king due to Sarai's great beauty, and he lies about her being his wife. Instead, Abram tells Sarai to pretend she is his sister. He later repeats this mistake. Nonetheless, God blesses Abram, and when they finally leave Egypt, they are prosperous because of the generous gifts of the king.

CONTINUING THE JOURNEY

When Abram returns to Bethel and the surrounding area of Hai, he calls upon the Lord once again (see Genesis 13:1-9). He is beginning to realize he is sold out, but not 100 percent. God needs him to be totally reliant. God has a national calling on Abram, so He knows to continue the honing process. For that job, Abram needs to be equipped well.

His job description reads: Unshakable. Faith. Required.

This time, Abram needs direction concerning his nephew, Lot. Abram is concerned that the arguments of the herdsmen over the best grazing land for their herds are becoming a poor witness to their Canaanite neighbors. He decides it is best that he and Lot separate. Abram asks his nephew to choose the land he wants. Lot takes the well-watered valley, ignoring the immoral lifestyle common amongst the people of Sodom and Gomorrah.

By default, Abram takes the less-habitable mountains of Canaan.

COVENANT RENEWAL

It is after this separation that God again renews the covenant. Because Abram has finally placed God at the helm of his spiritual ship, he can witness to the surrounding immoral people, while he himself maintains a holy lifestyle.

Abram's calling is recorded in Genesis 13:14b-18, *And the LORD said to Abram, after Lot had separated from him: "Lift your eyes now and look from the place where you are — northward, southward, eastward, and westward; for all the land which you see I give you and your descendants forever. And I will make your descendants as the dust of the earth; so that if a man could number the dust of the earth, then your descendants also could be numbered. Arise, walk in the land through its length and its width, for I give it to you."*

THE HONING PROCESS

Abram travels to the plain of Mamre in Hebron (see Genesis 13:18), builds an altar, and worships God once again. He is deeply surrendered to God's plan, and he worships with his wholehearted devotion.

Time passes, and Abram has conquests, such as saving his nephew Lot from five warring kings; interceding for Lot when God is going to destroy wicked Sodom and Gomorrah; and other such adventures. If only he had left this nephew in Haran! Over time, God works in Abram the character traits He desires.

This honing process works the same way in us. While we are awaiting the fulfillment of a dream, God is working on our character. God wanted us, His chosen vessel, to have the unshakable faith Abram developed. When we apply what Abram knew — to obey God, have faith in Him, and learn the art of worship — our Beloved arises within us, too, as a mighty, unstoppable force. Strife ceases. Enmity is squelched. What remains within us is the holiness of God. Abraham was on a learning curve, and so are we.

LOSING HOPE

After a great while, Abram grows impatient and asks God to give him a child through his servant Eliezer (Genesis 15:1-21). This was a custom of the times, so it makes sense to Abram, but God answers with a "no," and He reassures Abram his heir will come from his own body.

God causes a deep sleep to come upon him as he is worshipping, and the Lord once again renews the covenant. Notice the tenderness here — God does not rebuke Abram for doubting — instead, He fixes him. Abram hasn't plunged into self-will this time, and he stops himself from doing so by surrendering his doubts to his merciful Father.

Abram believes God once again and he trusts God will provide this miracle child, despite the fact that Sarai's womb is infertile (see Genesis 20:17-21:1). The man we know as the Father of Faith, begins to have doubts, but he allows God to work faith in him once again.

MISTAKE #THREE — THE DOOZY

Abram's desire for a male heir takes precedence over obedience to God's plan, and he takes Sarai's handmaiden Hagar as a concubine, which was a custom common to the times. Sarai, who suggested this, thinks this is a good short-cut.

You guessed it; Abram falls for it. Husbands, listen up — wives, myself included, don't always have the best plan. Vet the plans before God, as a couple, before acting.

I wonder how pretty Hagar was. My guess is she was a beauty. Hagar came from the Egyptian line of women, so she was most likely one to swoon over. Sarai did not have to do much convincing for Abram to sleep with Hagar. It's a biological response for men to look, and Abram did so.

Neither Abram nor Sarai ask Hagar to share her thoughts on this arrangement. So, we can predict the results of this doozy. When Hagar conceives, she "despises" Sarai (see Genesis 16:4). "Despise" is a harsh word, but it is descriptive of the bitter truth. Hagar's forced conception creates bitterness in all the family members, not just in Hagar.

By the time Hagar gives birth to Ishmael, the two women are feuding openly. So, the "old nemesis of Cain" named "enmity" renews with a vengeance. Sarai's discipline of Hagar became physically abusive, but even then, Hagar refuses to comply with her leadership. Instead, she runs away.

THE ANGEL AND MORE ALTAR BUILDING

Hagar returns, and explains to Abram that God spoke to her while she was in the desert. She shares that through an angelic visitation, the Lord promises, *"I will multiply your descendants exceedingly, so that they shall not be counted for multitude"* (Genesis 16:10b).

Let's look at the beginning of this verse to see who this angel is: *Then the Angel of the LORD said to her…* I'd like to pause right there. The Angel of the LORD is Jesus Christ. This is no ordinary angel — rather, it is the very Savior of mankind who appears to Hagar. He declares He has a destiny for her people too. They will multiply, and it is God's greatest desire for them to be saved, serve Him, and be filled with peace through the absence of enmity by the choices they make. That's the ideal.

Take particular note that Jesus Christ appears to both Abraham and Hagar. To Abraham, His presence is tangible during altar building, during the deep sleep God causes, and during the intimate prayer conversations where He gives visionary appearances as He establishes the covenant (i.e., Genesis 17:1-5). God truly has a plan for both peoples. Jesus Christ's scarlet thread runs throughout both Testaments from Genesis to Revelation.

Take notice also that although Abraham is flawed, he has such a deep faith in God that the LORD calls him "friend." Wouldn't it be amazing to sit with Abraham during one of his worship sessions? Abraham had deep conversations with his Creator, and he adjusted his thinking according to what he learned during these sessions. Whether the LORD comes as the Angel, or as another form — Spirit or flesh — is not revealed to us. My guess is that He appears as the Angel as He appeared to Hagar.

The point is this: Altar building is the most important activity Abraham learns.

We can learn a lesson from this. Do we toss our worry list on God and walk away, or — like Abraham and Hagar — do we spend time in uninterrupted worship so we will know what is the best plan for our lives? Practice the art of focused, uninterrupted worship.

TEMPORARY TRUCE

Abram is able to establish a temporary truce between the women. Hagar then gives birth to Ishmael. Abram, desperate for God's promise to be fulfilled, reasons Hagar's son will grow up to bring God's peace to the nations. But this is deception. Abram is duped into believing Hagar's son Ishmael, rather than Sarai's son yet-to-be-conceived, is God's intended heir, but he is not. God's promise to Hagar is that her son's lineage will become a great nation. Although this is a similar promise God has given to Abram, God has a separate plan for both nations. Ishmael is Hagar's son, not Sarai's, and deep within Abram's spirit, he knows this, although he is not yet ready to admit this.

By a supernatural act that only God can perform, a nation will be born to Abram and Sarai from whom the blessed Messiah will come. Abram must continue to believe this, but with a toddler at his feet, this is difficult. This is the point Abram is learning — he must believe in God's provision outside of what he can accomplish by his own efforts.

ENMITY RISES

Let's get back to the emotional climate. Can you imagine how Sarai feels as she witnesses the attention Hagar receives after Ishmael's birth? The son of Abram's dreams — or so he surmises — is upon Sarai's handmaiden's bosom. Hagar's role in birthing and nursing Abram's first male heir makes her the center of his world! Sarai is on the sidelines, watching and fuming. It is not a healthy family dynamic. It is a breeding ground for hatred. Enmity rises, boiling, as a power-force of destruction.

FAITH COMES

Recorded in Genesis 17:15-22 is Abram and Sarai's repentance. And this is where the story gets good again. Abram has another conversation with God, and as could be predicted, he once again tries to convince God the infant Ishmael will be the heir by whom the nations are blessed. God counters, affirming that through Ishmael a great nation will come, but holds firm to His original promise, that through Abram's wife Sarai will be born the son they will name Isaac and who will be the heir. He adds that this miracle child will be born the same time next year. Abram believes God. And this makes all the difference.

REPENTANCE/NAME CHANGES

It is at this time that the Lord changes Abram and Sarai's names to Abraham and Sarah (Genesis 20:17-21:3). He does this because they are finally on board with His original plan. No longer do their thoughts wander, and they live by faith rather than by what they can achieve in the natural realm. No longer are they independent — rather, they are dependent. No longer are they prone to the self-made road that leads to enmity.

As a sign of their dependence, Abraham establishes the practice of circumcision, where the procreation flesh on all males is cut as a sign of the contract. Abraham is ninety-nine years old and Ishmael is thirteen years old when they are circumcised.

Abraham and Sarah become the father and mother of nations, and their great faith, which developed over time, is the character we most remember about the patriarch and his wife.

MIRACLE SON, ISAAC

Nine months later, the miraculous happens. Against natural ability, Sarah's womb revives, menstruates, and conceives God's intended heir (see Genesis 17:7, 19, 21). Sarah is ninety years old when she births Isaac. Abraham waits twenty-four years for the fulfilment of the promise! At age one hundred, Abraham holds his miracle-child. When he was initially called, Abram was seventy-five years old (see Genesis 12:4).

MATURING PROCESS

Why do Abraham and Sarah wait twenty-four years for the fulfillment of God's promise? God saw their potential, but He was working a measure of faith in them. This could not be accomplished in a day. It took every bit of this twenty-four-year span for this couple to develop their character to the point that they did not just have faith, but they had unshakable faith.

Enmity needed to be completely eliminated in these faith-walkers, and it was. Obedience to

God's calling took precedence. However, the doozy of a mistake Abraham made early on caused the seed of enmity to be replanted, not in the heir Isaac, but in Ishmael.

Let me say this, and I'll try to not grit my teeth: Waiting for God's promise is good. Oh, it is tough! I've been there! You've been there too, right? But when God says, "Wait," He is working faith and obedience in us just like He worked faith and obedience in the patriarch Abraham. Permit Him to walk with you through the process. Don't take a shortcut. Wait for God's best plan.

THE BRIDE'S SONG

This is where Song of Solomon comes into play. In the vignette, when God works in you, Love, the powerful love force and the divine peace found exclusively in your Beloved, He is equipping you to be the glory-carrier who will change the destiny of mankind. He is preparing you for ministry. The longer the wait, and the tougher the honing process, the greater the calling He has upon your life.

THE SEED OF ENMITY

Let's finish Abraham's story so we can see how the stories in Genesis connect your birthfather, Kedar, to Song of Solomon. At the birth of Isaac, the favor and firstborn rights shift. This breaks all protocol for the younger Isaac, rather than the older Ishmael, to be the heir.

Abraham watches as thirteen-year-old Ishmael mocks the newborn, not once, but continually. His teasing and cursing are not easy to dismiss. The hateful environment is not good for either of Abraham's sons. After much prayer, and at the urging of Sarah, Abraham releases Hagar and her teenage son, Ishmael (see Genesis 21:8-12), and when they leave, peace is restored. However, Hagar holds bitterness in her heart. Peace within the immediate family is restored, but the enmity between Ishmael's and Isaac's genealogy is the byproduct (see Genesis 21:11-12).

Try as he may, Abraham is never able to convince Hagar that this family separation is the best plan. He gives her gifts and supports her dreams, but she remains bitter. Therefore, what started out as a war between two women becomes a war between generational lines that persists even today.

Modern-day Israel is from the lineage of Isaac, and Arabia is from the lineage of Ishmael. Dr. H.L. Wilmington states, "The agony of the world's most troubled hot spot, the Middle East, has been caused in part by Abraham's sin some thirty-nine centuries ago."[30]

KEDAR AS WARRIOR

Kedar is the second of Ishmael's sons. Kedar is so good at teaching his sons fighting skills that his descendants are called the "princes of Kedar."[31] So, who is your birthfather? He is a self-made man, and he is not just a warrior; he is the chief warrior, who teaches his family fighting skills. Warring has become his identity, and along with it, the sin of enmity.

Kedar lives in the shadow of hatred's prejudice, hurls fiery insults, strikes wildly at anyone around him, and he masters the art of war, having learned the pattern of despising the Israelis from his banished father, Ishmael. His sins' origins are idolatry, pride, rebellion, self-reliance, and enmity (see Isaiah 21:16-17, 42:8, 11).

To further exemplify this hatred, Kedar is not Ishmael's firstborn son; he is the second son of four,[32] so as a middle child, he is predisposed to take on rejection. To compensate, he gains a false sense of identity through conquests.

Kedar wants nothing to do with the God of Israel. In fact, he is bent on destroying the nation. Contrast this to the faith and dependence God instilled in Abraham. The best example the Bible gives

---

[30] Wilmington, Dr. H. L. *Wilmington's Guide to the Bible*. Carol Stream, Illinois: Tyndale House Publishers, Inc., 1984. P. 38.
[31] Orr, James, M.A., D.D. General Editor. "Entry for 'Kedar'". "International Standard Bible Encyclopedia". 1915. https://www.biblestudytools.com/dictionary/kedar/
[32] Genesis 25:13 and 1 Chronicles 1:29. Ishmael's four sons, in birth order: Nebajoth, Kedar, Adbel, and Mibsam.

of Kedar's vicious choices is Psalm 120:6. Here we see Kedar and his people insisting on war, when his neighbors are peaceable and pursuing peace.

THE LABEL, DARK

We see, therefore, that in the vignette, your statement, *I am dark…like the tents of Kedar* (Song 1:5) has profound significance. What at first glance seems trivial is actually your way of stating, with choice words, that the family feud of centuries is your heritage. Your mixed bloodline is of the nomadic outcasts of Hagar's son Ishmael. But you also have the Israelite bloodline of your mother's lineage.[33] This is as volatile as Shakespeare's *Romeo and Juliette.*

Remember, Scripture records that when Hagar runs away to the desert, God tells her Ishmael will become "a great nation," but He also warns her he will become "a wild man" (see Genesis 16:12). Because Ishmael's lineage is of nomadic tent people and of animal herders who are the sun-blackened, dark-olive-skinned[34] peoples of the Arabian Desert[35] and occupationally they become warriors, your scar is not merely a sunburn from toil. And so, when you refuse to stop loving your birthfather, Kedar, your mother and siblings project this narrative on you. Your scar is not merely a sunburn from toil; it is this generational scar that is passed on to you through your father that makes you "dark."

THE BRIDE AS AMBASSADOR

It becomes clear, when we know this backstory, why your family despises Kedar. But is this the right decision? To despise Kedar sets your family on the same path as his destructive ways and its consequential enmity. This is where your mission comes in…

You are the bridge between the choices of enmity or love and self-will or faith.

You totter between two worlds: In the vignette the kind maiden tells you that you are *fairest among women* (Genesis 1:8), and of great value to the Shepherd-King, while your mother's family treats you as an abject outcast who is the daughter of a murderer, labeling you "dark." Even your father, Kedar, by his absence, treats you as an outcast.

Who are you? What is your true value?

You surrender this burning fuse to the Lord as you begin your spiritual pilgrimage. In order to accomplish this, you decide to prioritize the pursuit of your Shepherd-King above all other activities. Only your King can make sense of this odd set of circumstances.

INTENTIONALITY

Does Satan win the battle of the centuries? Not. At. All. He is outwitted by a damsel who chooses to love and to have faith in God alone, rejecting enmity even though others are imposing this upon you. Despite all the odds that are stacked against the Arabian people—or any people—they can experience Beloved's peace. But this can only be imparted through a glory-carrier such as yourself, and you are particularly effective because you've personally experienced the sting of enmity.

Your outcast heritage in the vignette is no accident; it is providence. And perhaps it is today as well. Perhaps you are the damsel who is positioned at this moment, in an enmity-filled situation, because of God's providential choosing, so you can be the bridge for a lost friend or family member to enter the peace Beloved provides.

Two peoples present their prejudice in an open feud, and you speak kindness to both peoples.

---

[33]Orr, James, M.A., D.D. General Editor. "Entry for 'Kedar'". "International Standard Bible Encyclopedia". 1915. https://www.biblestudytools.com/dictionary/kedar/
[34] Minister Fortson. Black History in the Bible. Web. Feb 2, 2016. http://www.blackhistoryinthebible.com/blurred-lines/kedar-the-dark-skinned-grandson-of-abraham/
[35] Gill, John. "Exposition of the Book of Solomon's Song Commonly Called Canticles." Providence Baptist Ministries, n.d. Web. 2012. www.pbministries.org/books/gill/Solomons_Song/chapter1/song_01_v05.html

You embrace what your great-grandmother Hagar knew when she met the Angel of the LORD, Jesus Christ, that God has a plan for both nations. This is why you identify with both family lines. You are supposed to love them, and you do.

Here you are, the most unlikely of people — an outcast, illegitimate child — and you speak redemption to both bloodlines. When you accept Beloved's lordship, you set into motion this plan of reconciliation that God has envisioned from the beginning of time. God knew His people would need a rescue, and He provides this through you.

Be unashamedly Beloved's witness.

Perhaps Hagar, Ishmael, and Kedar could not forgive, but centuries later, and even today, redemption continues to be offered by the Savior Jesus Christ, through your marriage covenant as revealed in Song of Solomon. You search not only for your own identity, but also for the identity of Israel, Saudi Arabia, and each nation, tribe, and individual on earth.

THE CENTRAL MESSAGE

The central message is this: God has a destiny for all peoples. There is no nation or person who is unredeemable. The Lord wills all to be saved. This is the Groom's message that you carry within your person. Redemption is possible as we take our position as Bride. Our future is written in 2 Corinthians 5:20a, *Now then, we are ambassadors for Christ, as though God were pleading through us.*

How does this relate to you today? If Beloved can fix this "worst-case, always-been-that-way" scenario, where you are this "dark," rejected damsel, then He can bring peace to your situation today. Just because your present condition has been terrible for a long time does not make an iota of difference. By developing a solid relationship with Beloved, you are changing the course of history for others by your example.

In Acts 10-11, we see Peter witnessing to the Gentile people and the Holy Spirit manifests Himself to them by gifting them with the heavenly language of tongues in the same way He has manifested Himself to the Jews. Peter says, *"In truth I perceive that God shows no partiality. But in every nation whoever fears Him and works righteousness is accepted by Him"* (Acts 10:34b). This principle still applies. You are the ambassador sent to all who are spiritually hungry, whom the Lord will send to you.

As your spiritual journey progresses, you are dressed for this battle. All the characteristics our Beloved possesses, He freely gives you. What is not in the bridal attire? Enmity. Like the patriarch Abraham, we must solely rely on Beloved. This alone breaks the sin pattern of Kedar.

THE BRIDE'S VICTORY

Shake off the labels "dark," "white socks," and any other false labels that have been spoken over you, and receive your true identity as Beloved's ambassador, whose name is "Love," the Bride of Christ.

Receive others in love. No one can be "dark" in your eyes; all peoples are redeemable. We must continue to share God's love and peace, regardless of what we see in the natural realm. We are not accountable for the results of our witness, but we are responsible to be Christ's ambassador. This is our firm and commissioned responsibility.

SPIRITUAL AWAKENING

Let's learn one more life-altering lesson from the patriarch Abraham. His strength is fueled by his ability to worship. Therefore, let's look at your spiritual awakening, and the worshipful spirit Beloved reveals to you that's within you, waiting to emerge within you.

In the vignette, you describe your spiritual condition as a curtain. You say, *"I am dark…like the curtains of Solomon"* (Song 1:5). These reference the animal skin curtains[36] that covered the tent of the Tabernacle. [37] This outermost covering, visible to all, was made from badger skins. It is an impenetrable curtain of ram skins dyed red, followed by a curtain of goats' hair. These three layers are impenetrable to wind, rain, dust, and other natural elements. Although each layer has profound spiritual significance, God also chose them because they form a tough weatherproof exterior that protects the inner curtain.

Beneath is the innermost curtain, which is made of soft, finely woven, cherub-embroidered, colorful linen. It is an artistic tapestry work that can easily be damaged. And so, the tough badger-ram-and-goat-hair skins protect this inner sanctuary.

It is not obvious from the Tabernacle's appearance that there is anything beautiful hidden within, but there is. The most holy place is within this tough exterior.

When you say, *"I am dark...like the curtains of Solomon"* (Song 1:5), this is akin to you saying in today's language, "I am as rough and hard as a roof shingle." But you are also expressing that a place of worship is hidden within your drab-looking exterior. You hope your spirit is pliable enough for Beloved to work into your spirit a beautiful tapestry of His making.

Is your spirit pliable enough for Beloved to create this worship tapestry? My guess is, if you are reading this you are ready for Him to fashion you into a tapestry of His choosing as a worshipper, just like He does in the vignette. Beloved takes your aspirations, and He creates you to become a worshipper that He weds. That's how much confidence He has in your readiness.

Hear Beloved's Spirit as He calls to you today. Above the confusion of false labels and spiritual inefficiencies, He wants you to know you are comely. As you journey ever closer into your Beloved's arms of peace — for truly, He is your Groom — He imparts to you His kisses of peace. These spiritual kisses are how you change the world. And only a worshipper receives them. How do you receive Beloved's kisses? By tending to your own spiritual needs through resting in your Beloved's divine love, you are empowered. It is that simple.

When you decide to step through the boundary of your known world — the vineyard and the pastures — and into the unknown territory of the Sharon Valley, your ultimate destination is the Lebanon mountaintop where Beloved resides. By journeying to the Sharon Valley and from there to Lebanon's mountain, you are showing you are pliable — thus, you are ready to learn about the Groom who loves you and holds your future.

FOOTPRINTS INTO THE BRIDE'S FUTURE

In the vignette, the moment you embark on your spiritual pilgrimage, you see the nearly imperceptible footsteps that have been in the sand. Why had you not seen them? You were focusing on your faults and listening to the jeering of your relatives. Furthermore, you were working the two jobs. Therefore, this robbed your time. You didn't have time to look for these footsteps. You were fooled by others' priorities rather than looking for your own.

Now that you are focusing on Beloved, you see each sand imprint. The false labels slough away as you journey to the King. You are as a sheep, being guided by the unseen Shepherd. You take time to worship, time to rest, and time to dream.

Friend, when we are too busy to pause, we are too busy. Let me say that again — when we are too busy to pause, we are too busy. Beloved wants us to focus on Him. I know when I get to the point that I am overworked and exhausted, I become irritable. These times happen when I have forgotten to practice the art of worship. Therefore, in my busiest times, I make it a point to worship Beloved more, not less. The Bridegroom never wears out His Bride. He moves in peace, equipping us with this rest.

---

[36] Exodus 26:1, 7, 14. The four layers of curtains were as follows: 1) outer curtain of badger skins; 2) curtain of red rams' skins; 3) curtain of goats' hair; 4) inner curtain of finely-twined embroidered linen.

[37] N.A. "The Tabernacle of Ancient Israel." *Bible History Online.* Bible History Online, n.d. Web. 2012. http://www.bible-history.com/tabernacle/index.htm

Take the rest. Beloved empowers us with the set-aside times, and we should move forward only from there.

THE BRIDE'S TRUE LABELS; THE PATH TO PEACE

The solution to gaining strength for our job as ambassador relies on several elements, the most important being the decision to reject enmity and be obedient to Beloved. But, as we have seen, worship is a part of this as well. So is knowing we are loved by our Groom. We are motivated to move in victory when we recognize His majesty and His identity as *Dowd Shelomah*, the Beloved Peacemaker. But our Bridegroom knows we also are self-oriented, and to help us avoid the enmity trap, He shows us our names too, so we will choose to rest within the enclosure of His love. Let's discuss these bridal names:

WORDS FOR LOVE

Beloved gives you two names that translate as "love," and one that you share with Him. These were discussed in the first chapter. They are: 1) *Rayah*; marriage partner 2) *Ahabah*; passionate wife, and we add to this, 3) *Dowd*; God-love. These words make up your love vocabulary.

RAYAH

You have been searching for a name, and Beloved names you *Rayah*, translated as "Love," which means "wife," "partner," and "love." Beloved is your betrothed. There are no questions about this. You have sipped from the wedding cup to seal the decision. Let's add to this layer the next Love identifier.

AHABAH

"Love" is used to define you as Beloved's passionate wife. This is no casual relationship; it is purposeful. It means "to breathe after." I picture a doe or a hound dog sniffing the air. You are aware of Beloved whenever He is remotely there, and you pursue Him with every ounce of your being. You know He is superior to all others, and your relationship with Him supersedes any other agenda. Let's add another layer to your identity as "Love."

DOWD

Remember, in the last chapter we discussed how there are rare, fleeting moments, that your love is exactly like Beloved's love, and so twice He calls your love, "*Dowd*." This is His divine love, but it becomes your possession. Do you remember the location when you attain this? It is during your mountaintop visits to Lebanon. Do you remember what you are doing? You are partaking of Communion. Thus, when you commune fully with Him, you attain your highest potential. Through Communion, you experience spiritual unity with your Bridegroom.

LOVE, LOVE, LOVE...

With these three identifiers, you have the authority to change the world. As "Love" in all its forms, Beloved gives you His full authority, saying, *All things that the Father has are mine. Therefore I said that He will take of Mine, and declare it to you* (John 16:15). Your Beloved says, *These things I have spoken unto you, that in Me you may have peace. In the world you will have tribulation; but be of good cheer, I have overcome the world* (John 16:33). Your Beloved has given you His Name, authority, and most importantly His compassion for the world. He has done this because *The Lord is ... longsuffering toward us, not willing that any should perish, but that all should come to repentance* (2 Peter 3:9). So, the job of "ambassador" is the outcome of your title as "Love." Knowing this, is it any wonder why Satan tried to hide your identity from you? With this one title, used three ways, you are equipped. But you have other titles worth mentioning. Let's outline them here:

VINEDRESSER AND SHEPHERDESS

As Beloved's Bride, we have two jobs in the vignette because there is a modern-day parallel. As "vinedressers," we prepare the juice of Communion for those who will partake. As "shepherdesses," we disciple and evangelize, sharing the Word of faith. These, our appointed jobs, go hand-in-glove with our job as ambassador. We are to prioritize our time with Beloved, so we don't slip back into the works mentality, but our two jobs in the vignette continue to be our jobs today. So, although these jobs have become a ritual, they hold true spiritual significance that will be woven throughout the vignette.

Remember what these jobs reference: Vine dressing refers to communing with Beloved; Shepherding refers to our responsibility to evangelize. And "Love" references our marital status.

FAIREST AMONGST WOMEN

We also saw in Chapter One how the kind maiden says you are *fairest among women* (Song 1:8) She already knew you had the makings of a queen. It is as if she is setting you up to receive the many labels your Groom calls you. She calls you this because from the get-go you need to know without a doubt that Beloved accepts you despite any shortcomings.

What impresses your Husband-King is not an outward beauty, although you have this too, but the spiritual place of worship within the inner sanctuary of your heart. Why is Beloved not first demanding perfection before you can come to Him? Your Groom is not asking you to have a perfect heart because He alone is the perfection you seek. He is asking you to have a yielded heart, for He knows well how to perfect the heart of the yielded Bride. So, this is the requirement — that you are surrendered to His will, and His alone.

This goes hand-in-glove with your decision to obey Him and not give into enmity in any way it manifests. You avoid temptation by remaining fairest. How? You choose Beloved above all others, and any time temptation rears its ugly head, you choose to safeguard yourself in the sanctuary of worship.

LOVELY

The title "lovely" shows you are maturing. The King James renders this as "comely." It shows you are a glory carrier, being defined as "beautiful" and as being "at home."[38] Psalm 147:1 reads, *Praise the LORD! For* it is *good to sing praises to our God. For* it is *pleasant,* and *praise is beautiful.* Psalm 33:1 reads, *Rejoice in the LORD, O you righteous! For praise from the upright is beautiful.* This indicates you welcome the Spirit of God into your midst through worship, and your Beloved thinks you are beautiful as you do this. You are at home in your worship songs as you invite Him into your midst.

This is an ongoing process. Later in the vignette, Beloved Solomon will tell you, *Your cheeks are lovely* (Song 1:10a), when you smile at Him. He will say, *Your face is lovely* (Song 2:14b), when you rest in His embrace. He will assure you, *Your mouth is lovely* (Song 4:3), when you speak to Him your most intimate desires. When you marry your Groom, He will announce to His entourage that you, His Bride, are *Awesome as* an army *with victory banners* (Song 6:4b)! And yes, you will see the beryl-set, pierced hands of grace, spread wide, and sparkling with Heaven's glory, because your Husband-King is the Savior of the world (see Song 5:14).

CONCLUSION

It is time to lean into the divine embrace. This is how you attain victory, and this is how you are prepared, as a divine Bride, awaiting her Beloved Groom's embrace. Through worship, choosing obedience instead of enmity, and knowing His Names and yours, you are ready.

---

[38] Strong. OT #4998, #5000; used in SOS1:10; 2:14; 4:3; 6:4

As you delight in the Lord, there is a beautiful Spirit-to-spirit exchange. Grace falls upon your yearning soul like dew upon a morning glory, and Beloved embroiders His beautiful tapestry on the recesses of your heart as Beloved kisses your longing soul with the oil of gladness and newness of spirit.

Even in your brokenness, to your Groom you are *My Love* (Song 1:9b), you are *fairest among women* (Song 1:8b), and you are *dark but lovely* (Song 1:5b), being loved despite any imperfection, and being seen completed through your Bridegroom's eyes of grace. You also are a "vinedresser" and a "shepherd." This was no accident. These are your true identifiers. And with these job titles, you are shown to be Beloved's ambassador.

The next chapter will help you to lean upon Beloved even in the storms of life. But before we continue, let's identify with Beloved's labels for us—that of "Love," that of "fairest among women," "vinedresser," "shepherd," and "lovely"—by speaking confidently to Him in prayer. There's an old hymn that encourages us to trust and obey. Determine to do so. It is the way to wear your Groom's true identifiers well. No matter how well you know your Savior, determine to lean farther into Beloved's embrace.

Let's pray:

My Shepherd-King,

I release all who have spoken false labels over me. Instead, I accept Your true labels: "Love," in all its forms, I accept Your titles for me, and any You lead me to discover. I take my rightful place in the kingdom and as Your Bride, and I accept my responsibility to be Your ambassador.

Lead me to true "shepherds" and "kind maidens" of the Word who can help me in my discovery of You. I want to know Your characteristics, particularly those of "Beloved," divine love, and "Solomon," divine peace. You are majestic, and I ask You to reveal Yourself to me over time as the one true "Shepherd" who is superior to all others. I surrender my desires to You and to You alone. My Dowd Sheloma, my Beloved Peacemaker, my friend, and my Husband-King, for You are the One who knows me best.

Help me to serve You well. I will not yield to any other, and I will not give in to the temptation of enmity, for You alone are God. Hide me in the shelter of Your Tabernacle, and create within me a heart of worship, for within Your presence I will remain useful to you, my Husband-King.

Your Surrendered Bride,

Love

BRIDAL REFLECTION

1) In the vignette, who is Kedar? Describe his way of life, his religion, country of origin, and other facts about him. How does this absence of father and Kedar's bend toward enmity affect his life and yours?

2) Discuss the lives of Adam and Eve, Cain, Abraham and Sarah, Hagar, Isaac, and Ishmael. Why was it important for these characters to choose peace over enmity and faith over self-will? Which of these people succeeded?

3) What is your choice today? Do you choose love and peace or self-will and enmity? Write a brief one or two sentence prayer expressing your personal choice.

4) In the vignette, you are an ambassador of God's love and peace to your birthfather, Kedar. In the world today, are you the Bride of Christ still called to be Beloved's ambassador or has this calling subsided?

5) True or False: God has a destiny for all nations.

6) We all have "dark," false labels that have been imposed upon us. The way to overcome these is to reflect on Beloved's true labels for His Bride, that of "Love" (all three forms), "fairest amongst women," "vinedresser," "shepherd," and "lovely." Of these, share the label you relate to the most at this juncture of your journey. Share why this is so.

7) Describe the "inner curtain." What does this represent? How would you rate your inner curtain (of worship) at present: A) frail but pliable, B) lukewarm, C) on fire for God, D) other? Discuss this, and end by praying a blessing upon each person in your small group. If you are doing this study independently, pray a blessing upon yourself.

Chapter Three
The Oasis
*My beloved is to me a cluster of henna blooms
in the vineyards of En Gedi.*
~Song of Solomon 1:14

*"He who believes in Me... out of his heart
will flow rivers of living water."*
~John 7:38

Beloved is your *Dowd Shelomah*—your Beloved Peacemaker—regardless of circumstances. Your decision to tap into Beloved's presence can bring you victory even before you see circumstances line up with your faith confession. Beloved is the henna bouquet in the luscious vineyard; He is the Living Waters of En Gedi—an oasis in the midst of the desert. As you rest in Him, your peace can remain constant. Let's look at a modern-day example, and then we will explore scenes of the vignette.

My dear friend Betty had a rough childhood. Her family faced severe challenges due to a family member's illness, which, in turn, caused financial burdens and turmoil relating to caring for her loved one. However, Betty found an oasis of God's presence shielding her because of her mother's priorities. Her mother's devotion to God set the atmosphere for the home, and this taught Betty the oasis experience. If Betty didn't know where Mother was, she needed only go to the den, where she would find her reading the Bible.

Betty was sheltered in the oasis of God—a paradise in the midst of suffering. Her mother expressed this oasis experience to Betty in practical ways—through tea parties. Betty relates her memory with fond affection:

> When I was a little girl, Mother would invite me to tea parties in the sitting room parlor, which was "for guests only." I would dress in my mother's high heels and pearls and our tea party would begin. Mother would serve us real tea in her bone china teapot. We would sit at the antique coffee table, which was just my size. I enjoyed watching the spout as she poured our tea. With pinkies up, we would lift our cups and pretend together.

> Once, a neighbor scolded Mother, saying, "You need to get Betty some play teacups," to which Mother replied, "I must entertain my little girl." But I knew it was more than this. When Mother brought out her best china, it was her way of saying, "I love you extravagantly." To this day, I am appreciative of all things feminine, and I enjoy spoiling my clients. My inspiration for this is, of course, my own dear mother. In great measure, Mother's tea parties have defined who I have become.

Betty played with necklaces, dragged around pocketbooks, and practiced "pinkies up" before she was waist high. Now, as a professional merchant, Betty knows how to pamper women. She chose this career because she desires to make the same love deposit her mother made in her. And may I say—Betty is excellent at her profession.

Betty instinctively knew Mother's love could never be extinguished by trials. Betty was one-of-a-kind in Mother's eyes, and her actions said, "I love you," more than those three precious words. Mother played "tea party" with the intention of imparting love and peace into her daughter to sustain her through the trials, and Betty understood this.

What's more, Betty realized her mother's calm demeanor, despite tough circumstances, came solely from her reliance upon God. Betty knew the hardships her family faced, but she never focused on them. Why? Mother had created a safe place for Betty to come to in her mind, and she did just that. She had tea parties to focus on, so why should she worry about the rest? She didn't! Mother provided a refuge for Betty, and fond memories still do this for her today. This gave Betty the gift of childhood.

We can have an oasis, just like Betty did. In the midst of trauma, hardships, relational issues, illnesses, financial challenges, or disappointments of any kind—through all of these and more—the keeping presence of God can become for us a fruitful oasis. Allow Beloved's splendor to capture your focus, rather than permitting trauma to take center stage.

Focus! It's all about focus.

When our focus is upon Beloved, His strength gets us through trials. Far before we see victory in the natural, we acknowledge Beloved has come into the midst.

Rather than rehearsing the difficulties, our eyes remain focused upon Beloved Solomon—our *Dowd Sheloma*—the God of love and peace. His fixed love is assured in His Word, *Who shall separate us from the love of Christ? Shall tribulation, or distress, or persecution, or famine, or nakedness, or peril, or sword? ... Yet in all these things we are more than conquerors through him who loved us... [Nothing] shall be able to separate us from the love of God, which is in Christ Jesus our Lord* (Romans 8:35, 38, 39b).

Come into a sanctuary of God's love, where everything sweeps to the side. Fix your eyes upon Beloved Jesus and focus on His love. Allow Him to make an entrance into your spirit. The end result will be joy and peace. Let's look at one telling line of Scripture. In the vignette, you say, *My beloved is to me a cluster of henna* blooms *in the vineyards of En Gedi* (Song 1:14).

There's a sanctuary described in the above verse! En Gedi is an oasis surrounded by the dry, wind-swept land of the Dead Sea. Everything around this area is a barren wasteland, and yet, there stands En Gedi, with her vineyards and trees standing tall and fruitful amongst the desert sands and scorching heat. How is this possible? Underground springs rejuvenate the land, even cascading into waterfalls. Like Betty's mother tapped into the living springs of God's Word, and passed this onto Betty via peaceful tea parties where love abounded, we can do the same.

Let's look at the henna tree described in the above verse. This tree exudes sticky sap that is used to waterproof structures.[39] In Hebrew, "henna" means "pitch" that is used to tar or "cover over" something.[40] It can also mean a "ransom" given for payment.[41] Today, we refer to the henna as the cypress tree. The King James calls it the "camphire" tree.

Vernon McGee describes its beautiful flowers:

> The deep color of the bark, the light green of the foliage, and the softened mixture of white-yellow in the blossoms, present a combination as agreeable to the eye as the odor is to the scent. The flowers grow in dense clusters, the grateful fragrance of which is as much appreciated now as in the time of Solomon. The women take great pleasure in these clusters, hold them in their hand, carry them in their bosom, and keep them in their apartments to perfume the air.[42]

In the spiritual realm, Beloved covers over you with this fragrant and sappy henna, sealing you into His love. It is no coincidence that you hold in your hand a bundle of sticks! This could have been any flower, but it is a wooden-stemmed bouquet that you hold to your bosom. Your Lover romances you with an aromatic bouquet that says, "I love you with My life!" He gives Himself as this fragrant ransom; the demonstration of His sacrificial love is His work on Calvary.

Let's look at the vineyards of En Gedi. Beloved calls you to eat of the fruit of the vine—which

---

[39] Webster, Noah. *Webster's New Twentieth Century Dictionary of the English Language.* USA: Collins World, 1996. p. 261.
[40] Ibid.
[41] Strong's OT #3724, *kopher:* redemption-price. Root word OT #3722, *kaphar:* to cover.
[42] McGee, James V. *Thru the Bible Commentary Series, 1904-1988.* Nashville: Thomas Nelson Publishers, 1991. pg. 128.

calls to your remembrance His shed blood. *"I am the true vine, and My Father is the vinedresser… Abide in Me, and I in you. As the branch cannot bear fruit of itself, unless it abides in the vine, neither can you unless you abide in Me. I am the vine. You are the branches. He who abides in Me, and I in him, bears much fruit; for without Me you can do nothing"* (John 15:1a, 4a, 5a). He says this to you through the deserts of life and into eternity. The vineyard you eat from represents Beloved's role as Savior.

We see here an intentional oxymoron with the mention of henna clusters and fruit-bearing vineyards amid the fruitless desert sands that surround the En Gedi oasis. Just as Mother shielded Betty through tea parties, making for her a protected sanctuary to come to during the trials of life, Beloved shields you with His life's blood. Your Beloved Jesus demonstrates the oasis mindset perfectly.

An example of this is found in John 8:52-59. Here, Jesus walks through the midst of a raging crowd, and although a mob surrounds Him on all sides, they cannot touch Him. Why? His focus is on God the Father. He is out of reach of the haters through a miraculous protective act of His Father. Try as they may to destroy Him, He is untouchable because of this supernatural protection. It is the same with you, Love. Your Beloved surrounds you, and sometimes this protection manifests in a supernatural demonstration as He wills it to. Even when Beloved was crucified, Jesus was still out of enemy reach. Even when a believer is martyred, he is out of enemy reach because divine love envelops Him and them.

Do you remember what we were talking about in the last chapter? That's right. You were crying! You were remembering your "darkness" more than the love of God; therefore, emptiness had wrecked your emotions. But then, you learned from the kind maiden your Shepherd-King had come looking for you.

You began your search, focusing upon the footsteps of shepherds who had previously journeyed toward the Shepherd-King. Even though you scarcely knew Beloved, you recognized there was loveliness within you, so you followed the kind maiden's instructions to step out. As you searched for your Shepherd-King, you chose to let go of untrue labels by receiving a true relationship with Him. This included making the decision to allow Beloved to see your pain.

And then, you took action. You acknowledged your need for Beloved to be Lord of your life rather than relying on self-will. This paradigm shift affected not only you, but the entire world, including Saudi Arabia, Israel, and other nations. As you turned your eyes beyond the fields and looked toward Lebanon's mountain range, which is your ultimate destination, you stepped closer, journeying to the Sharon Valley to learn about and perhaps find your Shepherd-King. Did you know how to pray? No. You only knew to cry out! But Beloved interpreted your earnest cry as a prayer.

This takes us to the present situation. You don't need position, possessions, or power to have the oasis experience. You don't even need to have yourself all pulled together. It is better if you don't. Just cry out and allow Beloved Jesus to make an oasis of your current situation. Even if the circumstances in the natural don't change, you will find the henna of Beloved's love shielding you from life's blows.

Hold the Word of God to your bosom like a fragrant henna bouquet, and envision Beloved coming to you, His lovely Bride. Remember, Love, Beloved is able to work perfection into the heart of His surrendered Bride. But before He accomplishes this, He already accepts you as completed, because He has sacrificed His very life to redeem you. His strength is what you lean into, not your own achievements.

This next scene describes your first face-to-face encounter with Beloved. As you behold Him, it is as if eternity is in your Beloved's eyes, and He elevates you into the glorious oasis of divine love. He is as the henna bouquet of sweet, fragrant, enduring peace.

In Scene Three, it doesn't matter what challenges you face; for you have found your Beloved Peacemaker, and His gaze has captured your attention. While you have been adoring Him, He has surprised you by coming to you personally. When He does, His presence trumps every difficulty.

Where are you in Scene Three? Most likely you are in the field with the shepherds you've been learning from. This is the most plausible setting. Then again, you might be back home in the vineyards. Although the context is not explicitly revealed, what we do know is that the kind maidens are worshipping your unseen King with you.

Bride of Christ, it is likely you may be aware of Beloved's presence at this very moment. Press in, past the everyday routine, the mundane, and into the bosom of the One who perfects you. Linger in this presence. Beloved is here. He has made this very moment an opportunity for you to commune with Him face-to-face. Press into the arms of grace.

Why has Beloved appeared in Scene Three? You have invited Him, unawares, by your budding love and your worship. In doing so, you have found your place of respite despite any tempest. What you see on the horizon is not the difficulty; rather, it is the presence of your Beloved King.

Let's read the first of four overview scenes. These will teach you the oasis keys to abundant living. Step in, Bride, and experience them, knowing Beloved is with you:

*****

SONG OF SOLOMON 1:9-11
Scene Three: Meeting the Shepherd

SETTING: Undisclosed.
AT RISE: The MAIDENS weave gold coins, jewels, henna flowers,
                                  and silver studs into LOVE'S bridal headdress.

NARRATOR
Accompanying Love are the kind maidens who weave adornments into her bridal headdress. Each gold thread is jeweled, and then finished with a silver stud. The jeweled cornrows and the neck chains frame her face perfectly. The Bride's clothing is of fine linen and silk. On her neck, gold and silver chains hang. These adornments are gifts from her Groom. The Bride has accepted the Communion cup, and she waits for her Groom's appearance, spending her days preparing for her unseen Groom by listening to the shepherds' teachings. Her eyes glisten, for the words and songs she hears impact her spirit. As cleansing tears flow, she is becoming lovely in her spirit. She wonders if she is ready to meet her Groom.

KIND MAIDEN
Behold, here comes the King!
        (Enter, BELOVED, stage right, in a well-adorned chariot. LOVE gasps.)

BELOVED
⁹I have compared you, my love, to my filly among Pharaoh's chariots. ¹⁰Your cheeks are lovely with rows of jewels, your neck with chains *of gold.*

KIND MAIDEN
¹¹We will make you ornaments of gold with studs of silver.

NARRATOR
Beloved's splendor overtakes Love. She is radiant as she approaches the King's chariot.
        (LOVE falls to her knees. BELOVED lifts LOVE into His chariot. They depart quickly.)
Where are the Bride and Groom going? Beloved is taking His Bride to Father's banqueting house, where they will be wed. The romance of romances has begun. Love has found her identity in the

Shepherd-King.

*****

What is happening in this first overview scene? It was the Hebrew tradition for a bride to wait for her betrothed for about a year before the actual wedding took place. Weddings were arranged by the father, so some ladies never saw their groom's face until their wedding day. You have been this lady-in-waiting. Beloved gifts you with His sudden appearance, and you realize the time to depart to the wedding feast has come. This scene can be interpreted as the rapture of the Bride of Christ.

Based on the next overview scene, we discern that you are going to the banqueting table. What is significant about this? Through Communion, you can experience Beloved's presence in the here and now. Your rapture certainly is the culminating experience, but the Communion you partake of here gives you a foretaste of your ultimate wedding day feast.

OASIS KEY #ONE: ACCEPTANCE

We learn from this scene the first oasis key to abundant living. It is this: Acceptance.

Consider Beloved's first seven words, "I have compared you, my love." Beloved calls you "Love." It is likely you may still remember the past! The pain of your old life may be a persistent nagging memory you fight to lose sight of. Beloved makes sure you know from the very first instant your eyes meet that your name is "Love." The King James renders this "My love,"[43] *rayah*, marriage partner, so we have no doubt as to His identification with you as His Bride of choice. By this, He acknowledges your loveliness because you have accepted the wedding cup. This is implied and not directly stated. We know this because you and the maidens are making wedding preparations.

"Love," the very first identifier your Husband-King speaks, is the first key to the oasis way of life. While you are yet becoming one with Beloved, and before you have proven your passion for Him, He accepts you as His wife. Surely, this identifier, directly spoken, cancels the false labels of your past, and shows you His love is not performance-based. Beloved applies the henna sap of acceptance to the wounds of rejection, and with this He soothes your spirit, bringing you into the love oasis He has prepared for you at His Father's house.

In the Hebraic romance, betrothal, and resultant wedding, the groom and bride purified themselves by separately taking a ceremonial bath, called the *mikveh*. This bath symbolizes consecration one to another.[44] You have done this through your tears, although you are hardly aware of it. Your eyes are still wet when Beloved comes! As He purifies your spirit, your countenance becomes more beautiful over time. You remember the shepherds' teachings as cleansing tears flow. Perhaps daily, as you respond to the words of your Beloved, the shepherds open your understanding of Beloved's words, His gifts, and His character.

OASIS KEY # TWO: LORDSHIP

The second spiritual key is Lordship. As Beloved speaks your bridal name, "Love," He not only affirms your identity, He also calls forth your true potential. Beloved possesses your reins, and in return you have His authority. The impact of His identifying you as His wife is gradual. Initially, you say, *My beloved is mine, and I am his* (Song 2:16). As the relationship matures, you say, *I am my beloved's, and my beloved is mine* (Song 6:3). Finally, you say as you minister alongside Him, *I am my Beloved's and His desire is towards me* (Song 7:10). These are subtle but significant paradigm shifts as over time you align your thoughts to your Shepherd-King's lordship.

During each stage of spiritual maturity, Beloved's love for you remains constant. The more you accept His lordship, the more you open the door wide to the oasis way of life. The results are

---

[43] Strong. OT #7474 *rayah*
[44] Kay, Glenn. "Jewish Wedding Customs and the Bride of Messiah." *Congregation Netzar Torah Yeshua*. Glenn Kay, n.d. Web. 2012. http://www.messianicfellowship.50webs.com/wedding.html

Spirit gifts, freely given, of your Groom's choosing. How do you reach your highest potential? You accept Beloved's gifts represented by jewels, gold, and silver.

These bridal gifts from your Groom are called the *mattan*.[45] They represent the language of the Spirit. They grace your head and face and represent the anointing. Your Groom knows which gifts you are ready to receive and what is the perfect time to send them. Your destiny changes as you receive each one. You no longer cooperate with any other thoughts except godly ones; you reject thoughts foreign to the Spirit.

Your locks are as a veil,[46] which represents your Husband's covering.[47] You've submitted to Beloved's Lordship. You've accepted His gifts—silver and gold coins the maidens have woven onto this bridal headdress, the most ornate veil, and each bejeweled row is finished with a silver stud. Gold and silver coins also hang on the bridal headdress. Gold and silver chains have been draped on your neck. With the jeweled braids, the bridal veil, and the necklaces, Beloved gifts you with direction and purpose beyond your dreams.

You are of high value to Beloved, so He pays redemption's price to free His prospective Bride. We know this side of Calvary the silver foreshadows the cross. Each silver stud reminds us that we need forgiveness throughout our journey. There is not one silver stud—there are many. They are on every row of jeweled braids, and upon each of the veil adornments. The silver studs give you the reassurance that Beloved's forgiveness is always present.

The necklaces draped about your neck point you to a new direction. Why? You can turn your neck; thus, you can position yourself. You hold your head high because you are forgiven. Your thoughts are free, and your direction is godly.

This bridal headdress resembles a crown. The gold threads that fasten the jewels and coins speak of your heavenly estate. Malachi's prophecy records, *"They shall be Mine," says the LORD of hosts, "On the day, that I make them My jewels"* (Malachi 3:17). You are becoming His gloriously adorned Bride prepared for her Husband, and therein lies your beauty.

This crown upon your head reminds you that as you focus your thoughts on Beloved, He renews your mind. He loves you so much that this jeweled headdress encircles your entire head, extending from the crown of your forehead to beneath your chin and down over your shoulders. It is not just a head topper. This headdress the maidens construct is made from Beloved's gifts of jewels, gold, and silver.

Is it any wonder that in Revelation 4:10, the twenty-four elders are seen bowing and giving their heavenly crown to Beloved? Peter speaks of the crown that adorns your head as you humbly submit to your Groom's lordship, as he writes, *And when the Chief Shepherd appears, you will receive a crown of glory that does not fade away* (1 Peter 5:4). This is the crown you present, and any other crown of achievement you give to Him as well.

Your Beloved crowns you, His humble Bride, while He Himself first wears a crown of thorns before His Father adorns Him with a crown of glory. If Beloved is willing to submit to His Heavenly Father's will and pay the penalty of mankind's sin on Calvary's cross, then we can submit to our Groom's objectives. As we serve Him, there will be times that we may suffer, especially when we witness. Expect this. Do not turn away when Beloved calls you to a season and persecution ensues. In the book of Acts, the men and women suffered through great trials, but they overcame by focusing on their Lord's shed blood, and they held onto their testimonies at great cost. Their bodies may have pained them, but their spirits were untouchable—having been secured by the oasis of Beloved's love.

---

[45] Schauss, Hayim. "Ancient Jewish Marriage." *My Jewish Learning*. 70 Faces Media, n.d. Web. 2012. http://www.myjewishlearning.com/life/Relationships/Spouses_and_Partners/About_Marriage/ pg. 6.
[46] In the Revised Standard; "locks" translates as "veil"
[47] Wright, Fred H.

OASIS KEY #THREE: MIND RENEWAL

Renewal of the mind is the third oasis key. Paul writes, *And do not be conformed to this world; but be transformed by the renewing of your mind* (Romans 12:2a). He advises us to focus on the good we have through Beloved: *Whatever things are true… noble… just… pure… lovely… of good report; if there is any virtue, and if there is anything praiseworthy – meditate on these things* (Philippians 4:8-9 in part).

Mind renewal is vital, for as you enter into the oasis of God's love, it is likely that the same mockers are close at hand. What is different is that you are not focusing on them. These scorners will not dissuade you from your spiritual journey. You do not turn back. You are decisive about pressing into the oasis experience of Beloved and abiding there.

Why does the setting of this scene remain veiled? Perhaps it's because setting does not matter; purpose does. Where did you meet your King? You may remember as vividly as I do, but the question that matters is: Have we decided to never turn back? Have we purposed in our hearts to honor Jesus Christ our Beloved at all times and in all circumstances? You are written about in these pages, as am I, so the meeting place is not as important as the decision we've rendered to remain in love with our Savior. No matter what comes, our commitment to Him must be non-negotiable.

In this scene, what you are doing is readily identified. You are preparing to meet your Groom by learning about Him. Whether this takes place in the fields with the shepherds, which is the more likely scenario, or at home in the vineyards or someplace entirely different, is of no consequence. The maidens assist you in receiving the Spirit gifts. They spend time with you, preparing your head, for they know your Betrothed's arrival is soon approaching, so they make sure you have the right mindset. When you meet your Beloved, the geographical location becomes secondary to the spiritual transference that is going on. Beloved's face is all you see. It is a touch of eternity that is splendidly satisfying. Earth meets Heaven, and Heaven takes over.

For a long time, Beloved called to you. Because you were worrying, you unknowingly ignored Beloved's whispers and even His strong pleadings. Now, you have determined to set aside time to focus upon on the Shepherd-King and learn His Word. When you do so, you discover He has been there all along.

OASIS KEY #FOUR: FOCUSED TIME

This brings us to the fourth oasis key: focused time. Focused time is just that; it is time set aside exclusively for Beloved. This spiritual key is so important that Song of Solomon repeats it as a command three times. Let's meditate on these references:

- *I charge you, O daughters of Jerusalem, by the gazelles or by the does of the field, do not stir not up, nor awaken love, until it pleases.* (Song 2:7)
- *I charge you, O daughters of Jerusalem, by the gazelles or by the does of the field, do not stir not up, nor awaken love, until it pleases.* (Song 3:5)
- *I charge you, O daughters of Jerusalem, do not stir not up, nor awaken love, until it pleases.* (Song 8:4)

Who is the speaker? It is you. Three times in this short vignette, you remind the younger, less experienced believers you call "daughters" that focused time is imperative.

What is the duration of this focused time? You advise these spiritual daughters that as long as Beloved's presence is obvious during their tarrying time, it is wise to not break fellowship. "Don't awaken love," you advise. In other words, don't break out of fellowshipping with Beloved until it is pleasing to both parties to do so.

Unless we are intentional with our focused tarrying times, our Groom's messages that He wants to speak into our spirits are easy to miss. However, if we consistently give Him focused time, then we easily and sometimes imperceptibly enter the oasis of Beloved's divine love and peace—His *dowd* and *shelomah*. Notice the word "it" in these three passages. "It" can be rendered as "he" or as "she," and this is intentional. Fellowship with Beloved is for the duration you and your Groom mutually agree upon. If He releases us but we want to stay longer—He will never deny us. In fact, these, to me, are usually the sweetest, deepest fellowship times, and I implore you to go beyond the ordinary. Focused time is the connection that opens the voice of Beloved to us, and it is when our spiritual fruits develop, so spending time in worship is productive. The easiest way to accomplish this is to schedule tarrying times on a regular basis. An hour, as a starter, is a good workable tarry time.

When we make the commitment to secure focused time with Beloved, He is able to take us from glory to glory. Read His Word, pray, worship, and wait in His presence. I guarantee, distractions will come, but commit to giving Beloved first place despite any of these challenges. His presence will come as soft rain upon the thirsty ground of your spirit.

OASIS KEY #FIVE: OBEDIENCE

The fifth oasis key is obedience. In this scene, Beloved calls you a "filly." Is this a compliment? It is not. How do you know? You are a filly in Pharaoh's chariot. The King James renders "filly" as "a company of horses," which indicates several fillies in stampeding chariots. Uh oh! This looks like the self-will path to me, and we know that leads to enmity.

You are in the enemy Pharaoh's militia. That needs to change. And fast! Beloved tells you this so you will know it is imperative that you come under His authority. Paraphrased, Beloved is saying to you, "You are like an army of warring chariots in Pharaoh's army" (Song 1:9 paraphrased). Beloved likes your enthusiasm, but He is urging you to wait for His instructions. He is saying, "Wait for Me. I can use your strength, your passion, and your drive, but you must allow Me to turn you in the right direction!" Beloved does not belabor this point, so you recognize this as concern rather than condemnation. With this realization, you are more than willing for Beloved to rescue you.

I must admit there are times I've heard Beloved's direction and I've plunged headlong toward Pharaoh's camp. I didn't like the results. I'm sure, if you've done the same thing, you didn't either. Let's make the commitment to heed Beloved's instruction. We can harness fleshly tendencies by acknowledging Beloved truly does have the best answers. He has the solution, so we must be willing to receive His help.

What is not in Beloved's eyes even as He speaks correction? There is not one iota of condemnation. He loves you with a love beyond what you've ever imagined. He knows us completely—including every flaw—and He loves us despite our shortcomings. The awe-inspiring truth is, in His love we are completed. Permit Him to envelope you in the allure of romance.

Beloved's statement, *Your cheeks are lovely* (Song 1:10a) speaks value into your spirit. You are "Love" whose countenance is "lovely" despite any flaws. Notice the many jewels that appear on your cheeks. The King James denotes your cheeks as having *rows of jewels* (Song 1:10b KJV) that are hung upon *chains of gold* (Song 1:10b KJV). This describes your jeweled headdress meeting up with wide smile lines. The more Spirit-jewels you receive, the greater your smile becomes. It is a joy that remains regardless of circumstances. Both your smile lines and your tears of surrender are beautiful to your Groom, and these show the mind renewal that is going on.

Psalm 28:8 records how God's protection and favor come. David writes, *The LORD is their strength and He is the saving refuge of his anointed.* In Psalm 105:14-15, we read, *He permitted no one to do them wrong. Yes, he reproved kings for their sakes; saying, "Do not touch My anointed ones," and "Do My prophets no harm."* David is able to write this with fervor because he experienced Beloved's anointing and protection firsthand. David's enemy, King Saul, relentlessly pursued him, but without success because David hid in Beloved's love.

DAVID'S EN GEDI REFUGE

The refuge God provides David is located at En Gedi (see 1 Samuel 23:29, 24:1-22). This is the same refuge you come to. David and Saul come to terms at En Gedi, because Saul finally recognizes it is worthless to pursue an anointed man of God. Saul's attempts to ruin David results in the people favoring David more. When David is suffering persecution, his reaction is to seek Beloved's face even more. Beloved rewards him with an increase in the anointing. And so, the cycle continues. Every trial strengthens David even though there is pain in the experience. Expect the same, Love. Those who persecute you cannot ruin you. No person can ruin the anointed bride.

THE BRIDE'S EN GEDI REFUGE

One touch, as Beloved appears on the scene, turns despair and sorrow into rejoicing and strength for the redeemed of the Lord. Beloved covers His Bride with the henna sap of His presence. The painful experiences we face only serve to strengthen our resolve to seek Beloved with renewed purpose.

How close are you to seeing Beloved face-to-face at this very moment? Sometimes, we are a breath away from Him, and yet, unless we linger, we will never know this. Spend the time, fairest Bride, to allow Beloved to bejewel you with His anointings. Press in! Worship fully. Surrender all. And then, press a little farther. And then farther. Until Beloved's face is your total focus, continue… And then, tarry until you both have moved beyond satisfaction and into marital bliss.

Let's look at Scene Four. This overview scene contains the most revealing truth about Beloved's name. Envision the face of sacrificial love as you to dine with your Shepherd-King:

*****

SONG OF SOLOMON 1:12
Scene Four: Bridal Perfume

SETTING:	The Wedding Feast at FATHER'S house, accompanied by FAMILY. The round table is set with the most exquisite place settings. Raisin cakes, diced apples, fruits, breads, pitchers of milk, spices, and honey in the comb are set about in bowls. The dining room has a magenta and gold glow — a most unusual rainbow surrounding BELOVED and LOVE.
AT RISE:	FATHER and FAMILY are seated at the banqueting table.

(Enter FATHER, center stage. FATHER motions for the FAMILY to rise. Enter BELOVED and LOVE, stage right, dancing. The couple is arrayed in their wedding attire. BELOVED and LOVE encircle each other seven times while the FAMILY stands applauding. BELOVED seats LOVE beside Him. FATHER and the FAMILY sit, and the wedding feast begins.)

LOVE
12While the King *is* at his table, my spikenard sends forth its fragrance.
(BELOVED offers a raisin cake and an apple to LOVE. She partakes of these delicacies while leaning her head on BELOVED'S breast.)
*****

What is happening, Love? Even though this overview scene contains a single verse of Scripture, there is a deep truth hidden within. What is it? Herein is the language of romance — invitation unfeigned. Intimate, unbroken, equal, and loving fellowship shared by the Groom and His Bride at the Communion table is the sixth oasis key.

OASIS KEY #SIX: UNION THROUGH COMMUNION

You are united through Communion. This bears repeating: The Bride is unified through

Communion. Unless we've read farther into Song of Solomon, we don't even know what is on the banqueting table. Why? The emphasis is on the table itself. This is the underlying essential idea of this overview scene: The Communion table is our meeting place with Beloved.

THE ROUND COMMUNION TABLE

The Hebraic word used here identifies the shape of the table as "round." [48] Vernon McGee comments, "Very literally it is, 'While the king sitteth at his 'round table'… It is actually a round table where he either sits or reclines with his guests around the banquet table."[49]

There is no head at a round table! There is equality. You and Beloved are seated as one united couple. He does not dominate you, although you would accept this. Rather, Beloved honors you, as an equal marriage partner.

How can there possibly be this equality? Look at the activity at the table. You are communing with your King. And that is essential. As long as you commune at Beloved's round table, you prosper. So, although we indisputably are the weaker vessel, we become like our Lord when we are in communion with Him, respecting what the elements represent, which is the body and blood of our Savior.

ENCIRCLING LOVE

Whose table is this? The round table at which you are seated equally is Beloved's Communion table. The Communion table is defined as "that which surrounds or is round," "compass me about," or "enclose."[50] So we see the round table also represents Beloved's encircling love, and this is why He dines with you—to envelope you with His divine love.

LORD OF THE DANCE; COMMUNION AT THE TABLE OF REFUGE

Tradition states that you and your Groom would romance each other by performing an encircling dance, completed in seven rounds before communing at the round table.[51] Completion is represented here, but don't miss the clue that your dance with Beloved makes a circle just like the roundness of the Communion table your Groom then seats you at. So, in both the wedding dance and in the round table, we see the union that transpires when we commune with our Groom.

Sometimes we get lost in words. "Communion" sounds so official when we partake of the juice and the bread. But what does this word mean? Simply stated, it is "spiritual union."[52] True communion is shared at this round table where you feast as Bride. The Lord of the Dance encircles you, and in turn you encircle Beloved, and then you dine at His round table. Your conversation, as you partake of the bread, the wine, the apples, and the other delicacies, continues as you commune not only with your Groom, but also with the Father and family. Herein is your spiritual union. Whatever Beloved presents to you at the Communion table is all you need to be whole. This is the table of refuge.

THE BRIDE'S SPIKENARD

Let's explore your part as you sit at the round Communion table. What are you doing? You are releasing the fragrance of *spikenard* (Song 1:12). The ointment of spikenard was costly and used as a dowry. So, the symbolism here is again that of surrender and of your marriage. By giving your spikenard to Beloved, you are giving Him control of your future. It is His to direct! Your response to

---

[48] Strong. OT #4524, *mecab: Mecab* occurs 5 times, and refers to "that which surrounds or is round." pg. 162.
[49] McGee, J. Vernon. Pg. 25.
[50] Strong. OT #4524, *mecab*
[51] Rich, Tracey. "Marriage: a Typical Wedding Ceremony." *Judaism 101*. Prezi, n.d. Web. 2012. http://www.jewfaq.org/marriage.html Pg. 4
[52] *Encarta's English Dictionary. Dictionary.com.* Web. 2012. http://dictionary.reference.com/

this face-to-face encounter is to give the King of Kings your past, present, and future.

The spikenard plant contains oil in the head spike of the plant. The extraction process is laborious and, thus, costly, and it produces heavily aromatic oil that is so pungent it is often mixed with other oils. In Bible times, it was used as anointing oil.[53] The oil within the spike is called "nard." Spikenard means "trustworthy" and represents "persuasion" or "belief" and carries with it the idea of putting total "reliance" upon someone, not just mere belief.[54] Thus, the truth you are communicating to Beloved as you release this perfume is that you are putting your full reliance on what He has done for you through this Communion meal. You trust Him completely.

Mary of Bethany[55] is an example of this. She anointed Jesus with the oil of spikenard in preparation for His death. She willingly broke her alabaster dowry box she stored her costly spikenard in and poured this on Jesus' head and feet. This one act of surrender where she showed her loyalty to Jesus, even though His impending death loomed, impressed Him. Jesus said Mary's selfless devotion would be remembered throughout all generations. This was so significant; it is recorded in three of the four Gospels.

In Scene One, we see Beloved's kisses poured forth as the anointing oil of His presence. Now, you give your own oil of spikenard as you are enveloped in your Groom's majesty, and you participate in Communion with great desire. In future scenes, we will see Beloved's oil is frankincense and myrrh, the priestly and sacrificial gifts of the King of Kings, released as His giftings to the Bride.

Communion—it is a key to the oasis way of life. Remember this as we see the expanded version of this overview scene in Chapter Two of the vignette. Beloved chooses to show you this snippet first, so you will understand the fundamental truth that by sharing Communion, at the round banqueting table, you experience unity.

OASIS KEY #SEVEN: SPIRITUAL GROWTH

Next, let's look at the lovemaking that follows in Scenes Five and Six. This shows relationship building as a married couple. Notice the progression of intimacy. You come to Beloved time and again, choosing to spend time with Him. You kindle the spark of romance often, and He never turns you away. Thus, the final oasis key is progressive, continual, spiritual growth. Your relationship is vibrant, and you are a willing marriage partner. Beloved lets us glimpse in these overview scenes snippets of fundamental truths that will be expounded on later, just as He does in the round banqueting table scene.

Enter into relationship with your Husband-King, but remember, this is an allegorical representation of a spiritual union:

*****

SONG OF SOLOMON 1:13-14
Scene Five: The Groom's Embrace

SETTING: The wedding chamber represented by a curtain.
AT RISE: Backlighting outlines BELOVED and LOVE'S silhouettes
                                as they recline.

LOVE

[13]A bundle of myrrh *is* my Beloved unto me, that lies all night between my breasts. [14]My Beloved *is* to me as a cluster of henna *blooms* in the vineyards of En Gedi.

(Backlighting increases until the forms are obscured from view.)

---

53 "Spikenard." *Wikipedia: The Free Encyclopedia*. MediaWiki, n.d. Web. 2012. http://www.en.wikipedia.org/wiki/Spikenard
54 Strong. OT #5373, *nerd*; aromatic spikenard NT #3487, *nardos*; fragrant oil; NT#4101, *pistikos*; reliance
55 See Matthew 26:12; Mark 14:3; John 12:3

*****

SONG OF SOLOMON 1:15-16
Scene Six: At Home with Beloved

SETTING: BELOVED and LOVE's strong cedar home.
AT RISE: BELOVED and LOVE are seated upon a fresh couch of
                                             green meadow grasses and flowers.

BELOVED
(Tenderly strokes the side of LOVE'S face)
¹⁵Behold, you *are* fair, my love! Behold, you *are* fair! You *have* doves' eyes.

LOVE
(Points to the couch)
¹⁶Behold, You *are* handsome, my Beloved! Yes, pleasant! Also our bed *is* green.

BELOVED
(Points to the overhanging beams)
The beams of our house *are* cedar, *and* our rafters of fir.
(BELOVED and LOVE depart, slipping behind the veiled curtain. The couple's
silhouetted, backlit forms, are visible as they embrace.)

NARRATOR
The Bride and Groom are in no hurry. They fixate upon enjoying the evening together. They will
commune until morning. Their love is sure. The Bride is growing in her commitment to her Groom,
and she is becoming contented within the covenant of marital love.
*****

What is happening in these two love scenes? You and Beloved are enjoying the intimacy
exclusive of marriage partners. This process is unhurried, incredibly beautiful, and passion-driven.
Your romance has gotten better with time. Each time you commune, you are building a spiritual
"house;" a divine oasis; a strong union; an eternal embrace.

We could interpret these lovemaking scenes to be as few as the two outlined here or as many
as four. For instance, the romance at En Gedi could possibly be its own scene. The doves' eyes
mentioned could be interpreted as its own scene. I believe this is deliberate. That we cannot decisively
render the number of scenes brings emphasis to the focal point, which is ongoing relationship
building. There is intentionally more than one lovemaking scene because Beloved communes with
you not once, but as many times as you desire to enter into spiritual union with Him. This is the
wisdom found herein—with Beloved, you have never-ending satisfaction.

In Scene Five, you committed to lie all night in your Beloved's embrace as His fragrant oil of
myrrh and His henna bundle of flowers rest between your breasts. This teaches you to abide in the
oasis experience, as we also see here.

The concept is simple—by abiding in Beloved's presence when He comes during our tarry
times, we grow deeper in love with Him—but unless we actually carry through, spiritual growth will
be limited. Let's be the tarrying Bride. Once Beloved's presence comes, let's commit to remain in His
embrace!

THE EFFECT OF THE MYRRH BOUQUET
Myrrh was used as a burial spice. In Scene Five, as you hold the myrrh bouquet, Beloved is

showing you that He will conquer even death for you, and He fulfills this promise on Calvary's cross. Beloved is willing to suffer any hardship to redeem you. Who but the most loving King would commit to lay down His life for His Bride? Jesus Christ would, that's who.

Myrrh was also used as a spice of preparation. Esther held *oil of myrrh* (Esther 2:12) in her bosom when she was preparing to marry King Ahasuerus. This spice was used to purify her. So, when you hold the myrrh bouquet to your bosom, you, like Esther, are remembering the great sacrifice Beloved makes for you, and your remembrance produces a cleansing within your person.

Simultaneously, you identify yourself with Beloved's sacrificial love. You surrender by holding this myrrh bundle to your breasts, representative of the center of your being. What is being symbolized here is the Bride dying to self-will and yielding to purity. As self-will is dethroned, purity comes. You set aside your own agenda so you may commune with Beloved. Once again, the concept is simple, but applying this requires a decisive commitment.

THE BRIDE'S ORDINATION

These lovemaking scenes represent your ordination. Beloved is saying to you even today, *Ye have not chosen Me, but I have chosen you, and ordained*[56] *you, that ye should go and bring forth fruit,* and *that* your *fruit should remain: that whatsoever ye shall ask* of the *Father in my name, he may give it you* (John 15:16 KJV).

You are chosen.

Let those words sink in.

This bears repeating: You are chosen.

Say the words, Love, "I am chosen."

Who has chosen you? The King of the Universe has chosen and ordained you.

What is your job? As vinedresser and shepherd, you have been chosen to be His ambassador of Love, unifying souls, making Brides. As you abide in Him, spiritual fruit remains. Not of your own accord—but because you remain under the canopy of Beloved's love.

Truly, I can think of nothing more important than abiding within the Bridegroom's embrace. The result as we abide with Beloved is that we become comely—loveliness rises within us. What is more important than bearing spiritual fruit from this union? Nothing is. We both know this. So, let's prioritize spending time with our Beloved. Oh, we may get some squirrely-eyes and whispering yackers because we have set aside worship times, but this doesn't matter. The truth is, time with Beloved is the best activity ever. Choose to be a Mary of Bethany. Beloved honors this choice.

Lay everything else aside! Allow Beloved to rest all night betwixt your breasts. Permit Him to make you beautiful by the oils of His presence applied to your spirit, and release your fragrance of a surrendered heart to Him. The anointing you display is a gift from the King. Identify yourself with Beloved's sacrificial love and become royalty as you do so. There's glory in your bosom as you commune with the One who paid it all.

THE ROCK DOVE

In Scene Six, Beloved says *You* have *doves' eyes* (Song 1:15). This is a picture of the Spirit of God entering into your being so dramatically that you reflect His image within your own eyes. Therefore, when Beloved looks into your eyes, He sees His Spirit peering back at Him. You are this united.

Doves are singularly devoted, one to another, until death.[57] They coo and exchange loving glances constantly. They look into each other's eyes and, from there, outward to the world. This is how you and Beloved are in your relationship. Your communication is a free-flowing current of

---

[56] NKJV appointed; KJV ordained.
[57] "Mourning Doves." *Avian Web: Beauty of Birds*. Avian Web LLC, n.d. Web. 2012.
http://www.avianweb.com/mourningdoves.html

praise. Your gaze is ever upon Him. You have doves' eyes of focus—Beloved Jesus your Groom, being the lens through which you see the world.

The "dove" mentioned here is the "rock dove."[58] This bird abides in the clefts of the mountains. This dove represents the call to come up out of the drudgery of life and into the realm of the Spirit. This dove doesn't visit the mountain clefts—she lives there! She only flies from her mountaintop oasis to visit the valleys of necessity.

The rock dove is our modern-day homing pigeon.[59] She is able to find her way home from great distances. This dove was used to carry messages on the battlefield.[60] Through great trials, she returned home. Some rock doves won awards and medallions for their bravery and homing skills.[61] Likewise, the rock dove of Song of Solomon illustrates the necessity of focusing our eyes upon Beloved despite any trial.

Earlier, we saw silver as redemption, gold as heavenly thoughts, and sparkling jewels as glory—all descriptive of the Bride's crown, fashioned within your locks. We saw your countenance changing because of the Spirit gifts sent by your Groom. Your head, cheeks, and eyes, as Bride of Beloved, all reflected the beauty of your King. Scripture describes the rock dove as having silver and gold in her wings (see Psalm 68:13b). So, in like manner, the rock dove is jeweled with redemption's heavenly glory. The silver and gold glisten like jewels beneath its wings and upon its neck. This dove has a luminous purple, gold, green, and blue semi-circle on her neck, like a jeweled crown.

Is this coincidence? No. It's God having fun with His creation. It's a portrait of you as the jeweled Bride, prepared for your Husband-King. It is also a portrait of your Groom whose silver wings of redemption provide for you a heavenly refuge high above the battlefields of life. Come home, like the rock dove, and commune with Beloved. Then go again to minister. It is in this manner that your ministry will shape the world.

MOSES' FACE

Moses was a man who greatly reflected God's glory. During times of focused prayer his face shone so strongly that he covered his face with a veil. Otherwise, he'd frighten his onlookers (see Exodus 34:27-35). As Bride of Beloved, we can expect this same glory experience. Make the decision to remain saturated in Beloved's love. The result is that you will terrify the enemy.

FIR AND CEDAR: STRENGTH AND ENDURANCE

In Scene Six, two wood species represent your home's strength and endurance: these are fir and cedar. These woods are insect-and-rot-resistant woods that can last hundreds of years, so this represents eternity. In addition to their strength, cedar trees are full of sap, so the implication is that your home has a protective covering, like the camphor tree. Your relationship is based upon His handiwork of woods, and your home resides in the clefts. The cross, which erases, once and for all, every one of your shortcomings, is the symbol here.

Furthermore, a friendship has developed. Companionship is a strong element in relationship-building between you and your Groom. You and Beloved are in no hurry, and you spend time focusing on hearing each other's thoughts and caring. When we come to Beloved, let's shut out distractions, such as cell phones and televisions, so we can fully focus upon the King of Kings, our Bridegroom, and develop a cedar-strong friendship.

[58] Strong. OT #3123, *yownah*
[59] Hansell, Dr. Jean. "The Pigeon in History." *Pigeon Control Resource Centre*. Shopfront, n.d. Web. 2012. http://www.pigeoncoltrolresourcecentre.org/html/about-pigeons.html
[60] Levi, Wendell M. *The Pigeon*. Sumter, South Carolina: Levi Publishing Company, Inc., 1977.
[61] Ibid.

GREEN GRASS: VITALITY

Your bed is comprised of the fresh grass of the pasture. Why? There is life in your relationship with Beloved. You say, *our bed is green* (Song 1:16b). It is not old, musty, stale, brown hay stubble that you rest upon. Beloved's Word to you is revitalized every day. Even after your relationship has been firmly established, Beloved calls you into a continual romance of relationship building. This concluding line sums up this truth: If you and Beloved are gazing into each other's eyes while talking about the strength of your house, then you know you and Beloved will be romancing forever.

CONCLUSION

In four short overview scenes, we see many powerful truths. These entice us through the language of romance to commit to know our Beloved fully. For a lifetime, these truths will be remaking our beings as we hide in the oasis of Beloved's love.

Let's summarize the oasis keys:

The first is acceptance. Your identity is "Love" to Beloved. This key unlocks the door to all other truths. It represents your entrance into love through salvation. Beloved's boiling-hot, compassionate love is already there for you. Receive His acceptance as a gift of grace.

The second oasis key is lordship. Beloved calls you His own. You are bought with the life-giving blood of your Savior Jesus Christ. Lordship calls you into a progressive realization that you must allow Beloved to write your life's story and direct the course it takes.

The third oasis key is mind renewal. This renewal of the mind takes away painful memories so that you can enter into your new life with freedom. Your decision making is made certain as you learn to rule with your spirit and not from fleshly desires.

The fourth oasis key is focused time. You can focus on problems, or you can turn your gaze upon Beloved. He will tell you His perspective, but you only discover His will if you choose the oasis experience through focused time with Him.

The fifth oasis key is obedience. You acknowledge Beloved's direction rather than being tricked into working for the enemy's camp. You cannot side with both camps. Either you are exclusively the Lord's, or you are operating in disobedience. You obey Beloved rather than tradition or teaching. This is why anointed teachers are helpful, whereas religious dogma is not helpful.

The sixth oasis key is union through Communion. Beloved meets you at the round table. Within His encircling embrace you are equal because He completes you within His embrace. The important truth remains that this is only true within the Communion experience. The spikenard of anointing oil you exude from your skin shows you've surrendered to Beloved. Your fragrant dowry is a sign of your trust and reliance exclusively upon Him. His oil of myrrh shows the depth of His sacrificial love for you.

The final key is that of spiritual growth. Beloved's willingness to sacrifice His own life brings you into the vineyards of En Gedi, the oasis of streams in the midst of desert lands. You are willing to lie all night with your Beloved, allowing Him to transform you. Beloved purges your spirit by the oil of myrrh resting between your breasts. You hold the henna-stick bundle to your breast—a prophetic symbol of the cross. You are forever within Beloved's embrace, so much that your eyes are as "doves' eyes," reflecting His Spirit that resides within you. You become His representative. Your love becomes as strong and enduring as cedar, and the relationship you have is as fresh and renewing as a meadow of sweet grasses and fragrant lilies.

Each of these scenes gives us a key to the oasis experience. Is Beloved enticing us, through the language of romance, so that we will allow Him to catch us in His loving Spirit-embrace? Perhaps...

The next chapter is an expansion of the round Communion table experience. It is my prayer that you will leisurely partake of a Communion meal as you read. Find a cracker and grape juice, and prepare your heart to receive your Groom's best gift. His table is set, and He is ready to commune with you, His lovely Bride.

Let's bow and talk to our Husband-King.

My Husband-King,

 Thank You for saving me and for bringing me joy through Your oasis keys. As I continue my journey, help me exude the fragrant spikenard of desire. Make my eyes as turtledoves and our relationship as enduring as a cedar roof. Thank You for the unity I experience through Communion.

 I trust that as I partake of Communion in the next scene, You will be present in Spirit and You will extend to me Your bountiful grace, which represents Your gift to me through Calvary. Thank You for choosing me to be Your Bride. I love You.

Longingly,
Love

BRIDAL REFLECTION

1) Name the seven Oasis Keys of this chapter. Which do you most relate to?

2) Compare Song 2:7, 3:5, and 8:4. Which stage of development best describes your current relationship with Beloved?

3) King David found an oasis at En Gedi that made him unreachable by enemy attacks. He was sheltered in this refuge, so every attempt Saul made to injure him failed. Compare this to your bridal relationship with Jesus Christ.

4) Read Isaiah 54:17. Declare over your life that no weapon the enemy forms against you will prosper, because as the Bride of Christ you abide in the refuge of Beloved's divine love. Write the verse and decorate your paper.

5) Moses' face shone during times of worship. Can you, as Beloved's Bride, also expect to experience the glory, even if your face doesn't shine in the natural realm?

6) What shape is the Communion table? Discuss why this is so.

7) In the vignette, your skin exudes the fragrant oil of spikenard, expressing your desires to have a perfect marriage. Relate this to today. Share the desires you have to deepen your relationship with Beloved Jesus Christ.

Chapter Four
The Banqueting Table
He brought me to the banqueting house, and his banner over me was *love.*
~Song of Solomon 2:4

"This cup is the new covenant in My blood.
This do, as often as you drink it, *in remembrance of Me."*
~1 Corinthians 11:25b

The first time I took Communion and understood what I was doing was the evening I got saved. I had been proselytized by a Jewish family, so I knew God as Father. However, I had not yet met Jesus Christ.

A student at the university I was attending challenged me to read the Gospel of John. Having little in the form of a Christian upbringing, and having opposition from the agnostic relative, I had shelved the King James Bible my mother had given me as a teenager. I only knew God as Father; other than this, I had no faith foundation. However, the main reason I went to a university that was out of town was to explore my faith options. I wanted to make my own decisions regarding this matter, and I was ready.

"Father God," I said, "I do not want to offend You, but I need know who Jesus Christ is. Please show me truth. Who is He?" The Jewish family had taught me God was not a triune being, so I apologized to God as I opened my Bible to the New Testament. As my campus friend had instructed, I turned to the Gospel of John and began reading.

It did not take long for me to sense the conviction of the Holy Spirit. I was captivated by this passage where Jesus states, *If I do not the works of my Father, believe me not. But if I do, though ye believe not me, believe the works: that ye may know, and believe that the Father is in me, and I in him* (John 10:37-38 KJV).

The clinch-pin for me was the fact that the people did not argue whether Jesus did miracles. Instead, they disputed His authority to do such works. I concluded Jesus must have tapped into Father God's power, like Moses and other Old Testament characters, in order to perform such miracles.

I also realized Jesus was doing miracles on a regular basis—often enough to draw the attention of the Pharisees and religious zealots. That was a game changer for me. I concluded His miraculous power must far exceed the characters I had learned about from the Jewish family I hung out with. Therefore, Jesus' assertion that He was one with Father God made sense.

I did not want to read further until I asked Him to save me. But I did not know how, so I prayed, "Father God, how do I receive Your Son Jesus Christ as my Savior?"

In my spirit, I felt Father God say, *Partake of Communion.*

"But Father," I said, "I don't have the Communion elements. It's Saturday evening, and the church is closed, so there is no way for me to ask a pastor to administer them to me."

In my spirit, I felt another prompting, *Crackers and water will do.*

I searched around and found a pack of crackers in my backpack. One of them wasn't crushed, so I pulled it out, separating it from the crumbs. Then I went to the lavatory, took a Dixie cup from the sink, and poured water into it. I felt triumphant as I returned to my room.

Kneeling at my bedside, I partook of the cracker and a sip of water. I thanked Jesus Christ for His shed blood and His broken body. This was the first time I had ever talked to Him. Immediately I felt the tangible presence of Jesus Christ enveloping me. This took me by surprise. I had never felt the presence, ever, until then, nor did I know this was possible.

I continued to read my Bible through the night until early morning, consuming every word of the Gospel of John, reading and re-reading this sacred script. When I would get to the final chapters where Jesus was crucified, I'd weep enormous tears. The Communion embrace lasted until morning, where, as I awoke, the presence slowly faded.

Sunday attendance at the Episcopal cathedral was mandatory for all students, so I would attend church. I had taken Communion weekly throughout my freshman year. But this time, I wanted to attend. For the first time ever, as I listened to the readings of the pastor and the Scripture readers, the messages made sense.

I felt a strange warmth as I listened, which was unusual as it was cold in the cathedral. Its soaring ceilings with ornate columns and elaborate stained glass was impressive, but the heights made it chilly even during summer. I did not realize it then, but I do now; the Lord was already beginning to move upon me by the warmth of His presence.

When it was time to partake of Communion, I would have been satisfied with just taking it as a ritual as I was accustomed, but God had better plans. I thanked Jesus for saving me as I walked to the altar and partook of the bread and wine the priest administered. Once again, I experienced the tangible presence of Jesus Christ. His presence felt as if a warm electricity was coursing through my body. It was a strange sensation that I knew without a doubt was Jesus Christ revealing Himself to me.

I had planned on studying when I got back to my room, but instead I read and reread my Bible once more, mostly going through the Gospel of John, and exploring the other gospels, basking in the presence and marveling at Christ's life. As with the day prior, Jesus stayed with me all day and through the night, enveloping me in the warm, electric sensation I could not explain but did not want to pull away from.

I treasured the Bible my mother had given me—even gilding its pages as a do-it-yourself craft project—but now Jesus Christ was real to me. His Word took on new life, and most of what I read made sense. I wanted to memorize all of it.

On the Sunday of November 6, 1982, I became a born-again believer in the Lord Jesus Christ. November 6th is also my birthday, so I thought Father God did good to bring me into His glorious light on the same day of my physical birth.

I had no idea then that when I partook of my first two meaningful Communions, Father God had ushered me into the private wedding chamber experience of Song of Solomon, Scene One, and that the sensations I experienced were the tangible presence of my Beloved, embracing me with His peace, but this is exactly what had transpired. Just as the Bride is compelled to share how the kisses of her Beloved transform her, I also felt compelled to share my newfound faith with whomever would listen. "Jesus, I thought this was all about You," I said, "but now I see Communion is equally about sharing who You are with others. Teach me how to communicate the love I've found in You." Had you said "ambassador" to me, I would not have known how this applied, but ambassador I was.

Most of my family abjectly rejected me, and the "Jesus-freak" label surfaced once again. Only my mother, an uncle, and an aunt understood. Some of my college friends rejoiced with me, and for that I was glad. A preacher named Reverend Al Jenkins was the first person I told. He knew that when I went home, I would face persecution from the hostile family member who would strongly oppose my decision, so he gave me a crucifix.

"Hold onto this cross," Reverend Al said. "You belong to Jesus Christ now. Don't let any person persuade you to the contrary. Remember my words. You must remain strong."

I nodded and stuffed the oversized crucifix into my pocket. That crucifix stayed in every pocket, as attire. In fact, if my outfit didn't have a pocket, I'd choose something else to wear. I am not that fond of crucifixes—I prefer plain crosses—but the crucifix Reverend Al gave me symbolized my newfound faith in Christ's sacrifice. In fact, I still have it today, and it has resided above the doorway of every home my husband and I have ever rented or owned.

I felt Reverend Al had given me sound advice, and I was determined to remain faithful to Jesus Christ, knowing full well my personal decision to publicly declare Him would have unpleasant consequences. I shared with everyone—except for the agnostic relative.

As I expected, this relative eventually learned of my decision, and he took it upon himself to set me straight. On a visit to the family home, he shouted, "Do you believe in Jesus? Yes or no?" I held onto the crucifix in my pocket and shouted back, "I choose Jesus Christ as my Savior." Every time I acknowledged my faith, he pushed me farther into the chair he had me pinned in and choked me. I literally thought I was going to die right there, so I silently prayed for a rescue. The ruckus was so loud, two neighbors called, and I was able to escape to my room, locking the door. This gave another family member the opportunity to get involved, and the conflict ended.

After a few hours passed, the agnostic relative knocked on the door. His knock was soft, as was his voice. Dare I open it? Reluctantly, I opened it, praying it would not be "round two" of the incident, but knowing I would not cave regarding my belief in Jesus Christ. The relative said he was following advice to apologize, which was not his habit.

I answered, "I forgive you."

Immediately, a boldness came over me. I asked if he believed there was a god. When he could not deny the possibility, I said, "My God's Name is Jesus Christ. No matter what happens to me, I will never deny His Name. I belong to Jesus Christ now. He is and always will be my personal Savior."

The relative backed off and never again challenged my faith. He even gave me Christian gifts, and I have saved every one of them, treasuring the respect this showed regarding my decision. Unfortunately, this relative never chose to have faith in Jesus Christ as his personal Savior, and that makes me very sad. Salvation is a personal choice we make for ourselves, so I also respected his decision, even though I did not agree with it.

I am sharing this situation with you, not for you to feel sorry for me, but for you to know the depth of Jesus' love. He is no respecter of persons, so the love He permitted me to tangibly experience is the same love He has for you. His love is compelling. Only because my Beloved sealed me into His presence twice in two days' time, enveloping me with a love that surpassed anything I'd ever experienced, could I stand strong in my faith when persecution came. Since then, I have had many love-encounters with my Bridegroom, and I treasure each one.

You, Love, are of equal value to your Husband-King. Beloved. Loves. You. Let me say that again—Beloved loves YOU. Settle in on that unchanging truth.

The Scripture I first committed to memory was, *Fear not, for I have redeemed thee, I have called thee by thy name. Thou art mine* (Isaiah 43:1b KJV). There's an equivalent verse in Song of Solomon, *My Beloved is mine, and I am his* (Song 2:16). The entire Communion experience with the Bridegroom expresses the enveloping love He has for you, His Bride. This love is so deep that the analogy of a boiling pot scarcely describes it. Beloved's love is so majestic it is beyond what the natural expression can possibly define. And you, Bride of Christ, are the object of His love's expression.

As a matter of fact, my Beloved loves my agnostic relative just as much as He does me. And this stresses the reason we are His ambassadors—we can heal a wound by sharing Christ's love. Sometimes we don't see the fruit of this labor, since every person has a choice to accept or deny Christ, but there are many more times they will accept the Savior and His love than there are times they will deny Him, so share Him. Become a Jesus-freak. It's worth it.

As we partake of the bread and juice of Communion, we participate in Beloved's sacrificial love for the Bride. This is how He shows us He values us.

Like the Bible, Communion is living. It should be a fresh, intimate, cleansing experience that causes a renewal of our spirit each time we partake.

The suffering Jesus endured to unite us was a bridal price of great magnitude. Our Groom's hands, feet, and brow bled to give us life—because that's what divine love does—it gives. Remember: Jesus arose, but first He died.

Dr. A. R. Faucett writes, Communion is "a cup of wrath to Him, of mercy to us."[62] The price our Beloved paid to redeem us was this costly. Never forget that.

Communion. It's all about Jesus, as it should be—but notice the connection between His sacrifice and our obligation. Every drop of blood that ran down Calvary's cross, and from our Savior's side said, "I love you, world." Because Beloved has marked us, He is counting on us to fulfill The Great Commission.

As we explore this next scene, I invite you to prepare the Communion elements, and as you feel led, partake of them. Your private Communion experiences are as valid as your corporate Communion experiences, so have them. That's what I learned from the Dixie cup and cracker, versus the silver chalice and embossed wafer experiences. The heart attitude is what God values—not where or how we partake. Some may never agree with my viewpoint, and that's okay, but I've experienced Christ's tangible presence in both private and public Communion, so I urge you to have both.

What is happening in Scene Seven? This is your marriage celebration, and you are the star of the party! The Father rejoices with the Son. Your Groom says, "Rise, My Love," as He calls you to this elevated status as Bride of the Lebanon Mountain Range.

Listen… What do you hear?

Your spiritual family is cheering.

Look up… What do you see?

Waving in the breeze above the portico of the Father's house is a banner of love your Groom has fashioned, announcing His Bride has come home.

Step in, step up, and commune:

*****

SONG OF SOLOMON 2:1-7
Scene Seven: The Union of Communion

SETTING:	FATHER'S house. A magenta-and-gold banner announces the royal wedding reception at FATHER'S house, located in the mountaintop retreat of the Lebanon Mountain Range.
AT RISE:	Foreground: BELOVED and LOVE are dressed in their wedding attire, strolling the gardens that surround the mansion. FAMILY also walks the garden. Background: FAMILY feasts at the round table in FATHER's house.

NARRATOR

The royal couple wears their ornate wedding attire, with its jewels and treasures. Look at their white lily and Rose of Sharon lily garlands! As if to celebrate her humble beginnings, and her Groom's sacrificial love, they wear these lily garlands along with their fancy wedding attire. The Bride remembers the Sharon Valley, where she first learned about Beloved. White lilies grow in abundance. Beyond, the Rose of Sharon lily blooms in the craggy rock outcroppings at the base of the Lebanon mountain, as if beckoning the Bride to arise. Both these trumpet-shaped flowers sway in the breeze,

---

[62] Jamieson, Fausset & Brown. "Commentary on Song of Solomon 5." Blue Letter Bible. Sowing Circle. 19 Feb, 2000. Web. 13 Aug, 2014. http://www.blueletterbible.org/Comm/jfb/Sgs/Sgs/_005.cfm

releasing their fragrances. Look at the petals of both flowers—they are six-sided, just like Beloved's star. The Bride ascends with her Groom and walks in Father's garden estate located in the Lebanon Mountain Range.

BELOVED and LOVE
(Speaking together as one voice)
[1]I *am* the rose of Sharon, *and* the lily of the valleys.
(LOVE to BELOVED; adoring Him, lifts her lily garland to his nose.)

NARRATOR
Contrast the varieties of pure white fragrant lilies of the valley that bloom in abundance with the majesty of the rare and sweet purple and red Rose of Sharon lilies. The Bride and Groom wear these lily flower garlands as a reminder to return to the Sharon Valley to minister. They live in the mountain range, but they minister in the Sharon Valley.
(BELOVED faces LOVE. He holds out His hands slightly, tapping the tips of His fingers upon her own. LOVE places her fingers upon His palms. LOVE gazes fully upon her BELOVED.)
Look at Beloved's gentle yet strong hands. Beloved must have something special to say to His Bride. His scarred brow that first wore a crown of thorns and His pierced hands are now jeweled. His brow and hands glisten with reddish-golden beryl stones. Beloved's sacrificial love for His Bride is costly. Listen! The Groom compliments His Bride.

BELOVED
[2]Like a lily among thorns, so *is* My Love among the daughters.
(BELOVED and LOVE recline under a stately apple tree.)

NARRATOR
Love is overtaken, for she knows her beauty has been attained only by communing with Beloved, who has beautified her. How can the blushing Bride return her Lover's compliment?
(BELOVED touches LOVE'S forehead. LOVE turns her head upward.)
Beloved's gentle touch is a quest for knowledge. His Bride's thoughts matter to Him. Love sees the citrus tree, its fruits spread upon upright branches, its boughs almost touching the ground with an abundant bounty. She knows how she will return her Groom's praise.

LOVE
[3a]Like an apple tree among the trees of the woods, so *is* my Beloved among the sons.
(MAIDENS gather in front of LOVE.)
(LOVE addresses the MAIDENS)
[3b]I sat down in His shade with great delight, and His fruit *was* sweet to my taste.

NARRATOR
The apple—more likely a citron fruit—is juicy and comforting, just as Beloved's Spirit is to His Bride. Love reminisces about her wedding. She recalls the banner, waving above Father's house. Its colors and artistry remind her of their Communion experiences at Father's round banqueting table. She remembers the wedding party celebrating. Oh, what jubilee!

LOVE
(LOVE points to the waving banner; glances at BELOVED while addressing the MAIDENS)

⁴He brought me to the banqueting house, and His banner over me *was* love.

> (LOVE's voice trails off. She is captivated by her Groom's piercing yet loving glances. MAIDENS cheer; and then giggle.)

NARRATOR

The maidens know from the Bride's blushing face where her remembrance has gone to now. Love reminisces about the private wedding chamber and the banqueting table within. Only Beloved and Love know the intimacy of this inner sanctuary. The kisses of peace Beloved has bestowed upon His Bride have created an intimacy that goes beyond words.

> (Stage lights fade to purple; a see-through veil encloses LOVE and BELOVED)

LOVE

> (LOVE caresses BELOVED's scarred brow. Jewels sparkle where the thorns once pierced through. BELOVED shares a raisin cake and an apple. LOVE grasps hold of it and speaks.)

⁵Sustain me with cakes of raisins, refresh me with apples: for I *am* lovesick.

> (MAIDENS clasp hands together, smiling)

NARRATOR

Love speaks of the raisin cakes representative of the union of Communion and the satiating citron — representative of Beloved's Spirit. The Bride is love-stricken. It is through communing with her Beloved that she is able to receive His anointing oils of love.

LOVE

> (LOVE leans into BELOVED's embrace)

⁶His left hand *is* under my head, and His right hand embraces me.

> (LOVE motions for the MAIDENS)

NARRATOR

Listen closely, for the Bride is about to reveal the secret of the wedding chamber's embrace.

LOVE

> (In a hushed tone)

⁷I charge you, O daughters of Jerusalem, by the gazelles, and by the does of the field, do not stir up, nor awake love, until it pleases.

> (MAIDENS nod, then depart; LOVE and BELOVED remain, embracing behind the veil)
> (Stage lights dim)

NARRATOR

Love knows that when Beloved comes, it is best to remain in His embrace. She will abide in His presence for as long as He allows. Her finest words of advice to the maidens are to tarry there for as long as His Spirit overshadows them.

*****

What is happening in Scene Seven? This is your marriage celebration! You mention three places where you commune with your Groom: 1) the estate gardens, 2) Father's public banqueting table, and 3) Beloved's private Communion table located within the wedding chamber. Let's explore these.

THE ORDERING OF THE LOCATIONS

The garden stroll represents Beloved's discipleship. You, as well as Beloved, disciple believers. As you walk the gardens, you reminisce about the Sharon Valley where your romance began, and you vow to return to share your Groom's love.

Father's banqueting table represents Communion in the church setting. You experience renewal, and this causes jubilee as you taste the wine, feast on the foods, and watch the celebratory banner waving in the breeze. It is a party atmosphere.

Communion within Beloved's secluded wedding chamber represents the Holy of Holies. The blessed union you experience here draws you closer to your Husband-King, while simultaneously increasing your passion to share His love with the world.

In the vignette, these events are listed in reverse order of how they would have occurred. According to Jewish tradition, the Bride and Groom share private Communion first. But rather than recording your experiences in chronological order, you first share the garden stroll, followed by your experience dining at Father's table, and only then do you mention the private communion experience. Why is this so?

You are commissioned as Beloved's ambassador. Therefore, you are results-oriented as to the order of how you share. Because you are destined to reach others for Christ by discipling and evangelizing them, you share this first, even though the strength of your witness is dependent on the other two Communion experiences.

Another aspect we see here is that Communion is ongoing. It is not a one-time event. Communion should be a continual fellowship as it is portrayed here.

TRIUNE GOD REVEALED

It is worth noting that the Trinity is represented in Scene Seven. The Spirit brings the anointing, which is represented as the satiating, juicy "apple" you receive from your Groom; the Father hosts the banquet; and the Son feeds you the Communion elements[63] in a single juicy raisin cake wafer.

In all three of these settings, you stress to the maidens that tarrying is essential. You share that through abiding in Beloved's Communion embrace for extended periods of time, unity comes. You impart to your maidens that the Communion experience is vital and should supersede any other activity.

If we are to truly experience Scene Seven, we need to allow ourselves to be swept up into this divine romance, take time to rest in His divine love, and enjoy Beloved's communion embrace. There truly is no activity more important than this.

SPEAKERS; LITERARY STRUCTURE

There is a debate among scholars as to who is doing the speaking in the opening line of Scene Seven. It is my viewpoint that you and Beloved speak as one interconnected couple, having been intentionally paired. When we look at the literary structure, we will see that the words and phrases are paired,[64] being in the "construct state," which means the words are dependent one upon another. For instance, nouns are paired: "rose" with "Sharon;" "lily" with "valley," and so forth. Phrases also are paired: "rose of Sharon" with "lily of the valleys," "apple tree," with "trees of the wood," "my beloved" with "among the sons," and so forth. From this, we understand that the central theme is the unity of the Bride and Groom and that their unity brings unity to everything around them.

The first word that is paired[65] is not found in Scene Seven. Rather, it is found in Scene One.

---

[63] Song 2:5 KJV raisin-cakes in the NKJV — flagons in the KJV
[64] Zodihates, Dr. Spiros. *The Complete Word Study Old Testament.* Iowa Falls, IA: AMG Publishers, 1994. The words and phrases are in the construct state, which shows they are intentionally paired.
[65] Paired — in the construct state

The word "kisses" is paired with Beloved's "mouth" (Song 1:2a). Thus, the unity theme has already been established from the get-go, and that most intimately.

Looking back to Scene One, the Bride agrees to be wed when she sips from the Communion cup. This is her "yes!" regarding the covenantal relationship of marriage. Through Beloved's kisses, which He shares exclusively with His Bride, she experiences Him as her Beloved Solomon—*Dowd Shelomah*—Beloved Peacemaker.

Scene Seven emphasizes this unity theme. Consequently, it makes sense that the Bride and Groom speak as one unified couple and partake of Communion with a single element.

RAISIN CAKES OF COMMUNION

Let's look at the raisin cakes. These represent the wine and bread tightly compressed. In order to emphasize the unity theme, you receive Communion in a single mouthful. The body and blood of Jesus Christ are inseparable as the sacrifice necessary to redeem us as His Bride.

The root word for *cakes of raisins* (Song 2:5) means "fire."[66] Therefore, the raisin cakes also represent a spiritual cleansing. When we commune with Beloved, we partake of the purifying, divine fire of Beloved's sacrificial love.

THE MAIDENS

Let's look at the role of the maidens. You are deeply interconnected with your lady friends. They matter to you! Collectively they are referred to as *daughters of Jerusalem* (Song 2:2, 4, 7). The word "daughters," means "a builder of the family name"[67] and comes from a root word meaning "to build, establish, construct, or rebuild."[68] Expectedly, it is paired because the maidens also honor Beloved's name. They represent other Brides, for we are one body of believers—collectively the Bride of Christ. You also are a "daughter." This represents your willingness to build Jesus Christ's Name and has nothing to do with age or relationship—this is a spiritual parallel.

THE ANOINTING

Because you carry Beloved's Name and authority as your possession, you are fragranced with the oils of His love. The anointing oil from Beloved's Spirit has become your essential oil. How does this occur? You receive these fragrant oils as you recline in Beloved's bosom and stay there. The physical lovemaking implied in Scenes One, Five, and Six and again here in Scene Seven represent spiritual tarrying. By tarrying in the Communion embrace, we become empowered and unified.

Keep this in mind: There is no shortcut to this process. We are only effective in ministry when we have first tarried with Beloved.

We also see that you recline in Beloved's embrace in the garden. So, there is an aspect of Beloved's love that you can publicly share and other aspects that are private, where the only thing you can share is the kiss. Our public and private communion times are both vital.

THE GROOM'S BANNER

Above Beloved's Father's house, your Groom has fashioned a banner that waves in the breeze of the portico for all to see. Written on your Groom's banner is one word, Love (Song 2:4b). To fully appreciate this celebratory banner, let's look at the verbs used for "love" in this scene. Beloved says, *Like a lily among thorns, so is my love [rayah] among the daughters* (Song 2:2).[69] Remember, *rayah* describes your covenantal love as His wife or marriage partner. It is your title. However, *rayah* is not the word Beloved writes on the banner as we would expect.

---

[66] Strong. OT #784 *esh*.
[67] Strong. OT #1121 *ben*; son; OT #1123 *bat*; daughter
[68] Strong. OT #1120
[69] Strong's OT #7474, *Rayah*

Instead, Beloved writes the word, *ahabah*. This word translates as love for a lover. *Ahabah* is the natural love expressed as a passionate pursuit and is usually translated as "to breathe after," which describes your romantic pursuit of Beloved. This is the same term used when you say, *I am lovesick* (Song 2:5b). The best advice you give your maidens is that they remain lovesick.

So, why does Beloved write *ahabah* on the banner instead of *rayah*? He is, in essence, announcing that you have pursued loving Him until you have found Him. In today's vernacular, this banner might read, "She said yes!" Beloved gleefully announces your newfound love for Him, because you have finally agreed to His marriage proposal. There is nothing lukewarm about your commitment to your Bridegroom. Beloved writes *ahabah* because you are not just Bride of the mountain; you are a blushing, giddy, gleeful, passionate Bride whose greatest desire is to be lovesick for your Groom.

This contrasts with what He calls you when He comes in His chariot, which is *rayah*, or wife. So, the banner acknowledges your pursuit, whereas when He initially comes for you, He knows His presence will perfect you and bring out your passionate aspects and that you are maturing over time.

When you reach the banqueting house, you don't just know about your Groom and reluctantly agree to marry Him, you love Beloved with such passion that you want nothing less than to declare your love from the highest mountaintop and with such volume your voice could be heard in Sharon's Valley.

CONTRASTS IN LOVE

How does your love differ from Beloved's? Your Groom's love is the divine *dowd* of the covenant, having been established in the heavenlies before time began. His love is constant, eternal, and as dynamic and intense as a boiling pot. He is the very personification of this dynamic, effervescent love, and He loves you as much now as He ever will.

In contrast, you fell in love with your Beloved over time as you made a choice to pursue Him. Beloved announces with the banner that you are lovesick. Because His love—not yours—is the perfection that occurs, He is sure enough to pen it on the banner. As you remain in Him, you are completed, and your love becomes like His own.

THE GROOM'S HUMILITY

This "She said yes!" banner files high for all to see. You are taken aback! You have come to celebrate the King, and yet the banner your Husband-King flies announces your love for Him. Had He wanted to emphasize His importance, He would have written, "*Dowd* and *Rayah*;" these love-words translating as "Husband and Wife." But instead, He celebrates the divine unity the Bride has achieved with the Groom as He pens, "*Ahabah!*" meaning "She said yes!" The King of the Universe is secure enough in His identity to gleefully announce your newfound love. With passion driving you, Beloved knows you are ready to be wed.

FATHER'S BANQUETING HOUSE OF WINE

At Father's house, the word "banqueting" is coupled with the word "house." What does this tell us? "Banqueting" comes from a root word that means "effervesce, wine, or intoxication."[70] Thus, "the house of wine" is a more literal rendering of "banqueting house." "House" can refer to the physical structure or to the family unit.[71] This focuses us in on four aspects of Communion:

First, there's a party going on, and the people at this table are effervescent! They are filled with great joy! Second, the family of the Lord is the participants. Third, the people are intoxicated, not with liquor, but with divine joy. Fourth, this is as much about enjoying Father's presence as it is about

---

[70] Strong. OT #3196, *yayin*.
[71] Strong. OT #1004, *bayth*.

enjoying Beloved's and the Holy Spirit's. So, yet again, the Godhead is represented at the Communion table. Glory!

The house of wine is the backdrop of this scene. Although you and Beloved stroll the gardens, there is a never-ending party going on at Father's house, where you and Beloved are welcome to participate at any time.

LILY OF THE VALLEYS; ROSE OF SHARON

The field lily and the Rose of Sharon are beautiful metaphors used in Song of Solomon to picture the love between you and your Bridegroom. Both these are lilies. Let's discuss their significance:

Who is Beloved? He is the handsome but common pure white lilies of the Sharon Valley. He is equally the rare crimson-red Rose of Sharon. Beloved is the selfless, unifying, divine love of your relationship, and the beauty of the valleys comes from Him. And truly, He is the source of your newfound identity.

Who are you? In Beloved's celebration of you, He says you are *Like a lily among thorns* (Song 2:2a). It was not long ago that you thought of yourself as *dark but lovely* (Song 1:5). But now, He negates this "dark" description of your character by replacing it with the metaphor of the bright field lily. You stand for purity even when you are surrounded by prickly people—thorns in your flesh—nonetheless your beautiful composure remains undaunted now that the wine of Communion has cleansed you. Although Beloved is the source of all goodness within you, He praises you as this humble lily so you will recognize your own transformation.

The lilies also represent people. Both types of lilies—the Rose of Sharon and the lilies of the Valleys— are downward-facing, representing humility. This is the prerequisite for coming to Beloved—you must be, as He is, humble. Let's discuss each in further detail:

ROSE OF SHARON

The Rose of Sharon[72] grows amongst the limestone and dolomite cliff faces that are perilous to climb, so you discover this lily during your ascent. Its roots can grip even the shallowest crevice and prosper!

Not only do you and Beloved thrive even when faced with difficult people, represented here by the hostile desert atmosphere of the rocks where the Rose of Sharon grows, but you soften these individuals by sharing your unified love with them. Like the Rose of Sharon, you and Beloved bring divine love to them, which takes root and blooms in unshakable beauty. You are an evangelist. Love has compelled you to share your strengths there.

Once the roots of the Rose of Sharon lily gain a foothold in the rocky cliff faces, it softens the soil. The result is that the Rose of Sharon changes the landscape of the valley. In like manner, your unified love with Beloved changes the spiritual atmosphere. Bride of Beloved, unified love makes a difference even when hearts appear to be impenetrable. So, rest in this knowledge.

LILIES OF THE VALLEYS

Let's look at the lilies of the Sharon Valley. These bright white field lilies[73] are not a single type of lily but a variety. They represent the multitude of sanctified but ordinary valley people, but, when coupled with the Lord, they become extraordinary in beauty just as you have become. Through no effort of their own, but rather through belief in Beloved, they prosper.

The field lily is found not only in Sharon's Valley, but in many valleys throughout the region. Thus, the word "valleys" is plural to emphasize that Beloved's call is to people from every nation.

---

[72] Scientific name: Tulipa Sharonesis; Strong's OT #2261 *chabatstseleth*
[73] Scientific name: Convallaria Majalis; Strong's OT #7799 *showshannah*

Sharon's Valley represents one of the many valleys you and Beloved evangelize.

Much joy is represented here. The white field lily's root word means "bright," "cheerful," "mirth," "to rejoice" and to be "glad."[74] These flowers call us to rejoice! You have abundant joy beyond your imagination, and through Communion, you have become royalty. You are filled with Beloved's glory, and so you sparkle as the sun.

COMPARE AND CONTRAST

Contrast the blood-red color of the Rose of Sharon to the white field lily. Encircled within its petals is a yellow fringe. A purple stamen is in the very center. As this rare treasure waves in the breeze, it looks like a flame that is ablaze in the clefts in nearby Sharon's Valley. It is especially noticeable because of the backdrop of the common white field lilies.

This creates a picture for us of the consuming fire of God's presence which purifies His people through the blood of Jesus. The deep red stripes signify the furrows on Messiah's back. Its motion reminds us of His blood flowing freely from those furrows because of His love for us. We can appreciate this significance now, although this was probably a mystery to most who read Song of Solomon in ancient biblical times.

The rose lily, according to John Gill, is compounded from two words. One means, "to cover," and the other means "shadow," which, when coupled, is rendered as "the covering shadow."[75] This signifies the overshadowing presence of Beloved, and this fits well with the reference you give of the citron tree's overshadowing canopy when you compliment Beloved.

Both lilies—the rose lily and the field lily—have six-pointed petals that create a star shape as a representation of what the nation of Israel eventually chose as a symbol—a six-pointed star. Look at how this goes with the Communion scene. While you and Beloved are communing, your focus is equally on witnessing to the whole house of Israel. Both lilies also signify joyous resurrection, for they close and then bloom again with the morning light. Renewal of spirit has come to you and to Beloved's people.

You and Beloved are like the tender, sweet, fragrant, and rare rose lilies. These majestic beauties make quite a display as they dance and sway joyously, interspersed among the field grasses and white lilies at the base of the mountain. You and Beloved are also like these white lilies, being ordinary people, humble, and pure. Both lily types look like trumpets, proclaiming the goodness of the Savior. If a song of humility and praise could be pictured, this lily array would do.

SONS AND DAUGHTERS

In Scene Seven, you and Beloved have come to the solace of loves in the mountaintop retreat, but all the while you know you are destined to descend to the valleys to find the "sons" and "daughters" who likewise need rest within their troubled spirits. They, as you, need Beloved's kisses of peace. They need to become daughters and sons, having only toyed with the idea of salvation.

THE APPLE TREE

The tree under which you rest represents the overshadowing of Beloved's Holy Spirit. Your Groom says, *And I will pray the Father, and he shall give you another Comforter that he may abide with you forever* (John 14:16 KJV). You have the abiding, tangible presence of Beloved's Spirit within you at all times and in all places; even so, your desire for Him continues to mount. You are lovesick because you have tasted the goodness of the Lord (see Psalm 34:8).

The "apple" of this tree translates as the "citron;" which is our English word "citrus." So, it's probable that this is actually a tropical fruit such as an orange. In either instance, the comforting,

---

74 Strong. OT #7799 *showshannah*; root word, OT #7799, *suws*
75 Gill, John. *John Gill's Exposition of the Entire Bible.* 1743-1763.

overshadowing presence and refreshing sweetness of the Holy Spirit is what we are supposed to understand. You compliment your Lord by letting Him know how much His covering shadow means to you. You have been touched with the effervescence of enveloping love! You've tasted goodness from His lips. Therefore, spiritual union through Communion has become your greatest desire!

RESTORING ADAM AND EVE

Notice how the "apple" you are eating in this garden contrasts with the "apple" Adam and Eve ate in the Garden of Eden. What was lost through sin and compounded through enmity has been restored through the blood sacrifice of your Groom. Your Heavenly Father clothed Adam and Eve (see Genesis 3:21-23) with skins representative of Beloved Jesus Christ's broken body and shed blood. Isaiah 52:14 records that Beloved Jesus' crucified body did not even resemble a man because of the horror of it, but He willingly endured this to redeem us. Father God and Jesus thought we were worth the bridal price of death on Calvary's cross.

I once knew a so-called preacher who would not share Communion, nor would he preach about the blood of Jesus Christ. To him, it was irrelevant for today's modern people. Bride of Christ, don't let anyone ever convince you that Communion is irrelevant; it is pivotal! There's nothin' but the blood of Jesus, as the 'ol song goes, that can cleanse and restore His people.

As you receive Communion, acknowledge the high price your Groom paid to redeem His Bride. Here, we see it is pivotal to our Garden of Eden experience. The blood sacrifice of our Savior, represented each time we take Communion, is vital. And in this scene, we see it can be unhurried, as the Bride and Groom recline under the citron tree.

THE EMBRACE

Let's talk further about the message you share with the maidens regarding Beloved's embrace. They gather around as you recline under the apple tree with Beloved. They are eager for advice. You share two tips:

First, you mention your position. You say to them, *His left hand is under my head, and his right hand embraces me* (Song 2:6). What you are expressing is that there is security in this enveloping love. Your desire—and Beloved's—is to linger in this ardent embrace. His left hand supports your mind; all the while He supports your back with His right arm so that you can enjoy His presence. You know experientially that the embrace is when transformation takes place; the old nature flees; the new nature emerges in the encircling love of your Groom. The hand of Beloved is upon your head because He is aligning your thoughts with His.

Next, you speak to your maidens about the time commitment. "Do not disrupt the fellowship!" you caution. "When Beloved embraces you, stay in His arms until He decides that it's time to go." Thus, you instruct them to allow Beloved to finish the work that He starts. *I charge you, O ye daughters of Jerusalem, by the gazelles or by the does of the field, do not stir up, nor awake love until it please* (Song 2:7). H. A. Ironside points out that the phrase used here, "it please," uses a feminine verb, so this could be rendered, "He or she pleases."[76] We learn from this that Beloved is enjoying your embrace as much you are enjoying His. Both partners agree upon the duration of the encounter. The importance of uninterrupted communion, with tarrying included, is well illustrated here.

GAZELLES, YOUNG STAGS, AND DOES

Look at the *gazelles, young stags,* and *does* mentioned in Song of Solomon 2:7 and 9. As you instruct the maidens to stay in the Communion embrace, you make the same charge as your Beloved (see Song 2:6). What do these animals indicate? The "gazelle"[77] is a male, and the root word[78]

---

[76] Ironside, H. A. *Addresses on Song of Solomon*. 1933. Chapt. Two, Pg. 4. http://www.baptistbiblebelievers.com/
[77] Strong. OT #6643 ts^ebiy; roe in KJV
[78] Strong. OT #6638 tsabah

translates as "prominence," "splendor," and "glory." The "young stag" draws our attention to youthfulness and strength. The "doe"[79] is a female deer, and its root word indicates "strength."[80]

The "young stag" and "doe," are in the construct state, intentionally paired, but the "gazelle" is not paired.[81] From this, we see three characteristics. First, since "young" and "stag" are paired, this connects the concept of youthfulness to the stag, indicating Beloved's youthful or eternal qualities. Second, Beloved, as the "gazelle," has prominence, splendor, and glory, akin to this active gazelle, but He stands on His own. Third, the strength of the Bride is dependent upon her Groom. She needs to be dependent on her mate. Unless this fellowship between Groom and Bride remain undisturbed, it will not reach its desired conclusion. However, if we hedge ourselves in, away from distraction, and focus fully upon our Groom, He will do a work in us of matchless splendor.

The disciple John understood this Communion embrace better than any disciple. He was not ashamed to lean his head on Jesus' bosom during Communion. The longer John could lean into Beloved's bosom, the happier he was. John, who was once was known as "the son of thunder," became known as "the beloved disciple," all because he dared to tarry in a Communion embrace (see John 13:23). In contrast, perhaps this is the reason Judas Iscariot's fate was sealed. While the disciples celebrated Communion, Judas sought out the religious leaders, betraying Jesus with a kiss that brought death. This is the opposite of what Beloved's kiss of peace represents! While John dared to draw close, Judas dared to betray.

CONCLUSION

Let's conclude by imagining Beloved's celebratory banner. I pray we will see this beautiful banner in our spirit, even if we don't see it with our natural eyes. Imagine a banner with a soft magenta glow. Written on this banner, in the golden glory of Heaven's splendor, our Groom has penned, "She said yes!" or, "She loves Me!" as we might also pen it today. Because we have chosen to surrender our lives to the King of Kings, our Beloved has released us into the future He has intended for us to have all along. No matter how frail our love is compared to His, He completes us with the kisses of His peace within His divine embrace, and this work is accomplished even before we get to Father's banqueting house.

The banner declares to the whole world who and whose we are. We are the Bride of Christ, and we belong to our Beloved.

Love, what else is Beloved writing on your celebratory banner? Permit Him to whisper this into your heart. Journal the truth He may be speaking to you at this very moment... Partake of Communion, if you haven't already, and tarry in your personal Communion experience for as long as you and He desire…

Listen. Do you hear the cheers? Beloved's family is celebrating you! For you belong to a family of true believers.

Touch the arms of your strong Savior, whose nail pierced hands stretched wide to purchase your forgiveness.

Receive the fragrances of your Groom's anointing oil that He is depositing upon your skin. Your character is being softened by the oils of His love.

Lean into Beloved's eternal embrace. Settle right into His arm as He cradles your mind with His left hand, while speaking healthy thoughts into your being.

Smell the scent of your lily of the valleys and Rose of Sharon garland. Know you, an ordinary Bride, are extraordinary, sweet, and rare, to the One who kisses you.

Beloved. Loves. You.

---

[79] Strong. OT #354 *ayal*; KJV hind
[80] Strong. OT #352 *ayil*
[81] "young stag" and "doe" are in the construct state, intentionally paired.

That's right, Love. He loves YOU.

Let's continue our journey, but first, let's talk to our *Dowd Shelomah.* Remember to personalize these words as you desire. I invite you to snuggle close and go off script as you nestle into your Beloved's bosom.

Let's pray:

My Beloved Peacemaker,

Under Your banner of love, I celebrate You, as You also celebrate me. I acknowledge Your sacrifice upon Calvary's cross, here represented as Communion, and I accept Your marriage proposal represented by the raisin cakes.

Romance me, Lover of my soul, as I partake of Communion with You. Bring me to that timeless place, where Heaven meets Earth and I am able to receive Your divine kisses of peace.

Commission me to shepherd the broken and the lost lily people into Your arms of grace. Make me an ambassador of Your Gospel of peace.

Unified through Communion,
Love

BRIDAL REFLECTION

1) Share your salvation experience. If you have not yet gotten saved, would you like to do so today? If so, ask a saved friend, leader, or pastor to pray a salvation prayer with you.

2) True or False: The literary structure of Scene Seven, where phrases and/or words are paired, shows the unity of the Bride to her Groom Jesus Christ.

3) What does the raisin cake represent? Why is it one single element, while expressing the bread and wine of Communion?

4) Compare and contrast the Rose of Sharon with the lilies of the valleys.

5) Share a Communion experience that was special to you.

6) What is written on Beloved's banner that flies at Father's house? What does this mean? Reflect on this.

7) Have you said "yes!" to Beloved Jesus Christ's Communion invitation to be His Bride? If so, ask a friend, leader, or pastor to pray a prayer of commitment with you.

Chapter Five
Shadowboxing in Bether

Until the day breaks, and the shadows flee away, turn, my beloved,
and be like a gazelle or a young stag upon the mountains of Bether.
~Song of Solomon 2:17

For sin shall not have dominion over you,
for you are not under law, but under grace.
~Romans 6:14

David was CEO of a nationally recognized company. He had established a trusted leadership team, so he decided to take a month-long vacation. He announced his plans to the Board and made the necessary arrangements. Nonetheless, the day of his departure, he found himself pacing. Even though he had discussed each team member's responsibilities, he found himself rehearsing "what if" scenarios.

David said his goodbyes and started toward the elevator. He usually enjoyed the penthouse panoramic view, but this day he felt sick to his core. He stopped short and turned around.

"We've got this," Curtis said. "Go!"

The other leaders agreed.

David relented, shook each person's hand one last time, and stepped into the elevator.

Woosh! He held his stomach as he descended to the lobby.

As he exited the building, his driver, Jerome, greeted him, tipping his hat and opening the door. David sat in his Tesla.

"Home, sir?" Jerome said.

"Hum," David replied, his mind drifting, still questioning his decision. He usually conversed with Jerome, but he wasn't in the mood.

David watched the high-rise in the rearview mirror as Jerome pulled away from the curb. The building started to look like a toy. As the city streets broadened to four lanes, the luminous cement towers being replaced with decorative scrolled streetlamps amidst the residences, David realized he hadn't prayed about his decision to take a vacation. *A whole month?* he thought, pressing his abdomen again. *What was I thinking?*

David placed his hand on Jerome's shoulder. "First and Concord."

"But sir, we just came from…"

David was silent.

Jerome made a U-turn. "How fast can I…"

"Floor it."

"With pleasure," Jerome replied.

As soon as they reached the office complex, David scrambled to exit the Tesla. Jerome never got an opportunity to open David's door.

"I've been wanting to try out her power…" Jerome called out, stroking the dashboard, "She's a jewel!"

David bolted back into the elevator.

As the door to the executive penthouse opened, his team greeted him. They had never left the vicinity of the elevator because they predicted his return.

"Welcome back," Alan joked. "Did you enjoy your… let's see… twenty-three-minute vacation?"

David blushed.

"We placed bets as to how far you'd get," Julia said.

"Tell me, did you get past Fourth Street?" Stephen said, chuckling.

David pushed past Stephen.

"Hah! I get the cache!" Brian said, grabbing money from a dish. He fanned his face with the bills.

"You've trained us well," John said. "Let us prove that to you."

"Really! We've got this," Curtis added. "Go home and relax."

After some discussion, and after repeating the instructions David had already given his team, he stepped back into the elevator, and with six people pushing him, he didn't have a choice. Curtis and Brian stepped in with him, "to make sure you get into the Tesla."

Curtis addressed Jerome. "Make sure 'Mr. CEO' gets to his estate." Curtis snatched a bill from Brian's hand and passed it to Jerome. "Here's a tip to make sure."

"Hey, that's my fifty!" Brian complained.

"Thank you, sir," Jerome said, pocketing the bill.

David reclined into the leather seat. "Circle the building," he said.

"Should I drive slow, sir?"

"Yes. I want to remember what she looks like."

*****

David would vacation at home. That way he would be close to work—just in case. His estate had the finest amenities, so it was the perfect arrangement. He called home his "castle in the heights." David enjoyed watching the hustle and bustle of city life from his balcony, while enjoying the seclusion of his hilltop mansion.

David dedicated the first part of his vacation to working on his cars. He tightened a radiator hose on his Shelby while he hummed a familiar tune. As he reached for a wrench, he noticed his guitar resting in the corner.

It would be nice, he thought, *to compose a new song*. Notes to a melody started to form in his mind. *I should write those down,* he thought as he installed a supercharger in his Fiat. It was hard work, but he was happy to do it.

David tuned the engine and bled the brakes on his Cobra. He put down his wrench and hummed the lyrics that were forming in his mind...

Pray now! David heard in the recesses of his spirit.

"Later, God," he mumbled in protest. He continued his work.

Satan grinned, and shot a projectile...

David was unaware.

David washed the grease off his hands and retreated to his balcony. Although it seemed trivial, he longed to watch a sunset. With his work responsibilities, he rarely paused long enough to enjoy one. He entertained thoughts again of composing a song, but he suppressed the notion.

The melody gradually slipped away...

As sunset gave way to twilight, he watched the reds and blues paint the surrounding homes below in a deliciously dreamy color palette. He reached for his binoculars and watched the bats swooping at moths that gathered in front of a streetlight.

Lights flickered in the residences. They were like randomly appearing gems. David began to play a game as to which homes would light up next. He chuckled as some he guessed correctly while others he missed outright. Suddenly, he caught a glimpse of a woman rising from her bath. David gasped. *She's beautiful,* he thought, *but I should look away*. It was a war between flesh and spirit.

Satan fanned his arrow array. He released his bow.

The weapon stuck fast...

David found himself looking intently at the lady's form. He imagined the scent of her perfume, as he watched her towel-dry, dress, and lie down for bed. David continued to watch after her form was no longer visible, her silhouette having been impressed upon the recesses of his mind, the visual imagery taking shape in his imagination.

Satan shot another arrow…

David began to entertain thoughts. He tried to shake them off, but they kept coming. Soon, he found himself devising a secret scheme to sleep with the woman. Conflicting thoughts tore at his subconscious. *I should pray,* he thought. But instead, he entertained lustful desires.

Satan's grin widened. "I'm a self-made man," he said, shooting another projectile.

What harm will come out of a little sex? David reasoned. Before dawn, he had mastered a deceitful scheme. He knew just how he would proposition the woman without being discovered.

David had become an adulterer of the mind…

He phoned a buddy who disclosed the lady's identity. He now knew full well that the darling whom he lusted after was married—and her husband was a new hire, employed by his company. He knew all about the man—his salary, his work ethic, and even his hobbies. He knew he could order his phone buddy around, so he pulled him in on a scheme. Then he paid off this go-between to ensure his silence. At David's bidding, his buddy arranged an excuse for the lady to meet David at his estate the next evening. Surely, she would think it was work-related, since he had sent her husband on a business trip that very week.

This is going to be easier than I thought, he mused.

The trap was set—for David.

Satan folded his arms, propped his feet on a smoldering cinder, and watched his victim tumble further into transgression. Although unaware, David had become a marionette on a string, and Satan was the puppeteer.

David had never before entertained thoughts of having an affair, but now his mind was running helter-skelter. If only he had looked away, turned his chair, gone inside, composed a song… But David had not, and he did not want to stop now. The rational mind was cooking up some wicked schemes, and he was entertaining them with a passion. He had his dialogue polished and ready to try out. "Are you lonely when your husband leaves? Trust me to meet your needs. My, what a lovely dress! You have a beautiful smile…"

The knock at the door came. David opened the latch and smiled. It was Showtime! He would possess this woman! Sure enough, before the evening was over, he had enticed this prized beauty, and she had consented to a game of sex. Was it consensual, though? It was a seduction, in reality, but he convinced the lady she had agreed to the affair.

David had played the game of lust, and he had won the prize of sex.

*****

When David's vacation ended, he gladly returned to work. *Why did I ever leave?* he thought, guilt knocking on the door of his subconscious.

Satan hurled a ratchet between David and the lady. He didn't want them to repent or apologize, especially to God.

David pushed off any thoughts of the lady, and he buried himself in his work. He knew she'd be too embarrassed to tell anyone he had stolen her virtue, and he refused to speak to her. He watched, as humiliation fell upon her like a black cloak; daily she wore the garment of shame. He was satisfied and thought this was enough to buy her silence.

*****

As the days passed, one thought kept surfacing: *I desire truth within your spirit.* David suppressed it. He knew reckoning with his sin would be painful, and he didn't want to confess it. He was beginning to realize he wore the same garment of shame he had imposed upon the beautiful lady.

Weeks later, his buddy delivered the news.

"She's pregnant."

"Who's pregnant?"

"Davio, my boy, you're kidding me, right? You paid me to bring 'er to you, and I did. I'm still keeping your secret, but her belly's gonna tell on you soon enough. You might as well pack up your pencils and make room for the new CEO."

Would David come clean? He was too proud, so he schemed some more. He decided to bring the woman's husband home from his latest business trip. The woman, he rationalized, would entice her own husband to sleep with her because she would want to keep the secret more than he did. He called the employee home "to work on a small project."

David met the employee in the airport and handed him a roll of cash. "It's a gift," he alleged, "for the loyalty you have to the company. Take your wife to a posh restaurant! Treat her to a night on the town that she'll never forget." He sighed in relief. The conception date of the child needed to be close enough to the husband's visitation if this cover-up was going to work.

*****

David had hired this employee for his uprightness, but now that loyalty backfired. The employee checked into a nearby hotel, phoned his wife about the cash, and told her he needed to focus on his job assignment. He promised that when he came home, they would have a night on the town. To the roar of jets, David's employee finished the at-home assignment and left promptly to finish David's distant project.

The cover-up had gone bust! David thought he could resolve the issue by wit, but he had failed. He would not admit it yet, but his biggest sin was against God. He had shelved intimacy with his Creator. He didn't have the same inspiration he used to have for songwriting. He still played his old songs, but even those were starting to feel mechanical. Was his anointing slipping? He worried what would happen if this indiscretion surfaced. He knew he should turn to God, but he did not.

*****

Satan chuckled. He steadied his bow. "One, two, three. Murrr…"

Meanwhile, David was nursing hatred. That employee was causing him so much trouble! Why was he being so loyal? Couldn't he have just gone home and had sex with that woman? David wished the employee was gone. He'd have to get rid of him!

God cringed. "Come home, son. I'm still here. I still love you and the lady. Receive the wisdom that comes when you seek Me with your whole heart. Before there are worse consequences, come back to Me now!"

David dismissed the thoughts.

Satan laughed as he shot. "…derrrrr!"

*****

"Hey, buddy, I need you to do me a favor," David said to the go-between. "You think the last favor paid well? This will make that payoff look like chump change! I need you to arrange an accident."

"An... accident?"

"It needs to be on the jobsite. Make sure it looks convincing, or you won't get a dime."

*****

Dead.

David's faithful employee, Uriah, was dead.

The accomplice had successfully carried out David's murder plot. He was now free to take Bathsheba as his wife. The big secret was stifled. That is, it was stifled into David's subconscious, but he would not be free of the mental anguish until he came clean.

Meanwhile, David watched Bathsheba grieve the loss of her husband, Uriah, and the infant death of her firstborn son.

David finally wrote the song he was thinking about composing while on his vacation—Psalm 51 describes his heartfelt confession.

God swooped two repentant children into His arms—King David, the CEO-songwriter-poet, and Bathsheba, the beautiful lady. The Lord knew it would take a while, but He planned on working restoration into these broken vessels, for as long as they would allow. God began to spin the Potter's wheel, lovingly remolding two lives into beautiful vessels.

Satan retreated, sharpening his arrows, looking for his next opportunity.

*****

I'm pretty sure you recognized somewhere in your reading that the above "David" is "King David" of the Bible as we would see him in a modern-day setting. There are some liberties taken in the prose, so we are able to take a renewed look at his situation.

David's folly is something that can happen to us today. King David loved God, but when he got spiritually lazy, the enemy blindsided him with a powerful blow.

When spiritual leaders fall, God's message gets tainted.

Be watchful, Love, for how you shepherd the gift of Beloved's anointing is a matter of life or death to those in your sphere of influence. Be careful, Bride of Christ, to keep mud off your wedding dress.

David was anointed and gaining recognition of his public ministry when he transgressed. Why did he fall? He had not yielded one area of his life to the Master. David took his eyes off God long enough to get trapped by the enemy's ambush. He lost his first love—just for a moment—but that was the opportunity Satan was waiting for to launch his assault.

Was King David the enemy's focus? Part of Satan's plan was to cause David torment, but the real target was his kingdom. If David fell, the faith of nations could be shaken.

Thank God for the song David composed. God used his confession, recorded in Psalm 51, to reshape his and Bathsheba's lives, and this psalm gives us a model to follow as well.

Heartfelt sorrow is the ingredient the Lord needs to work redemption in our lives. The Psalmist David wrote, *The sacrifices of God* are *a broken spirit, a broken and a contrite heart — These, O God, You will not despise* (Psalm 51:17). How was he able to pen those words? He lived them; that's how. David experienced the separation that sin brings and God's compassion that repentance brings.

The most important point to remember about David's folly is that he had position, title, and a developing anointing when he fell. Sin entered David's clean heart while he was ascending. David's folly happened about one-third of the way into his reign.[82] As king of two nations—Judah and Israel—David's influence was far-reaching. His ministry was recognizable from across the miles. From the enemy's perspective, that was the perfect time to strike.

When we are making a spiritual ascent, it is the time to be the most cautious. This is a pattern we see repeated in Song of Solomon three times (see Song 2:10-17, 3:1-5, 5:1-6:9). If, in our eight-chapter vignette, the Lord warns us three times about the same theme, it is worth noting.

Many places in the Bible, the Lord reminds us to come away and be separate unto Him. For example, Paul writes, *But you* are *a chosen generation, a royal priesthood, a holy nation, His own special people, that you may proclaim the praises of Him who called you out of darkness into His marvelous light; who once* were *not a people but* are *now the people of God, who had not obtained mercy but now have obtained mercy* (1 Peter 2:9-11).

The bottom line is this—the human condition is bent toward sin even though God calls us to be in His holy image. This struggle between flesh and spirit has existed from the beginning of creation. But God's holy calling has also been upon us. We are chosen, and we have within our spiritual DNA the likeness of God.

Jesus faced His greatest temptation at the Garden of Gethsemane. He could have turned from

[82] "The Davidic Timeline." N.p., 2012. Web. http://www.kukis.org/Charts/davidictimeline.pdf

His assignment to pay the price of mankind's sin on Calvary's cross. Instead, He embraced Father's toughest assignment. Prayer made the difference. Because Jesus prayed it through in Gethsemane's garden, sweating great drops of blood, He was able to say "yes" to God's plan.

Notice this occurred when Jesus was at the peak of His public reign. Satan targeted Him then, figuring He would not stay strong. But we know God was not surprised, and He exalted Jesus because He withstood the trial. The very test that was meant to discredit Jesus became His triumphal moment.

Victory is ours, too, if we are wise. We can avoid temptation by being aware and by taking the time, at regularly scheduled intervals, to commune with our Lord Jesus Christ in unhurried, intimate fellowship.

How many television evangelists, actors, and CEOs need to fall before we realize they have targets on their backs by the enemy of their souls? Knowing this makes it easier to forgive them, but it also helps us to be cautious to press into the bosom of our Savior whenever we are reaching new heights of ministry, because it is then that we, too, are vulnerable to enemy attack.

Where were you in the last scene of the vignette, Love? You and Beloved were at the beginning of your public ministry. You shared Communion in the garden under the citron tree, at Father's house, and in the private chamber. Having been crowned Queen, you have the authority of your Husband-King to rule and to reign.

You have position, title, and a developing anointing, just like David did when he sinned.

It is time to walk carefully, Bride of Christ. People are watching you, so shepherd the anointing judiciously. They will observe your life in order to determine their beliefs about Beloved.

In these scenes, Beloved calls you to *come away* (Song 2:10b, 13b) As Bride of the mountains, your ascent will bring you into spiritual realms of glory you can experience nowhere else. The key to your ministry success is to purposefully yield to Beloved, for He knows how to equip His watchful Bride. The fuel of public ministry is never seen, for it develops most in the privacy of the Holy of Holies Beloved calls you into. In this secret chamber you are empowered.

Keep this in mind as well: God forgave King David, and He forgives you if you fall. Beloved is ever ready to forgive, so we never need to carry the bondage of guilt.

Come away, Warrior Bride. Step into your vignette:

*****

SONG OF SOLOMON 2:8-13
Scene Eight: Arise

SETTING: Sharon's Valley, with the orchard of Lebanon's Mountain Range, and Father's Mansion seen in the distance.

AT RISE: LOVE is seated with her MAIDENS under an apple tree.

NARRATOR
Some of the maidens who come to the Sharon Valley and listen to Love's teachings are the very ones who once ridiculed her. She is eager to teach them. On occasion, she cautions them to be watchful. Listen as Love shares a memory:

LOVE
⁸The voice of my Beloved! Behold, He comes leaping upon the mountains, skipping upon the hills. ⁹My Beloved is like a gazelle or a young stag. Behold, He stands behind our wall; He is looking through the windows, gazing through the lattice.

> (BELOVED enters, center stage. He stands behind LOVE and places His hands on her shoulders.)

74

LOVE

[10a]My beloved spoke, and said unto me:

BELOVED and LOVE

(Together as one voice)

[10b]Rise up, My love, My fair one, and come away. [11]For, lo, the winter is past, the rain is over *and* gone. [12a]The flowers appear on the earth;

BELOVED

[12b]The time of the singing has come, and the voice of the turtledove is heard in our land;
(LOVE touches BELOVED'S wrists, pulling His hands to her cheeks.)

LOVE

[13a]The fig tree puts forth her green figs, and the vines *with* the tender grapes give a *good* smell.

BELOVED

[13b]Rise up, My love, My fair one, and come away!
(LOVE grasps BELOVED's extended hand. BELOVED lifts her. They walk off stage, arm in arm.)

NARRATOR

As the wedded couple strolls into the sunset, Love makes no excuses for her departure. She must respond to the life-giving voice of her Beloved. She welcomes this exodus, for she knows the depth of her love is enhanced through Communion.

*****

What is happening in Scene Eight? This is the story of your public ministry and interspersed are the times of private communion. You draw people, much like you were once drawn by the kind maiden of Scene Two. You are still tending a flock, but now it is not sheep; it's people.

THE BRIDE'S ASCENT

As you teach, Beloved appears. You ascend the heights the moment your Groom calls you, making no excuse for your departure, for communion with Beloved is the source of your developing anointing. Unless you have these times, you will have no strength to teach the people.

The season is spring. This pictures your fresh start. Turtledoves comprise the "voice" of the hills, and flowers fill the valleys as a carpet. The fragrant fig trees and the grape vines bloom in abundance, budding with tender fruits upon their new shoots.

Beloved mentions the cleansing rains of the previous season. The rain of the Spirit has cleansed you as if it were a baptism. Like the ritual wedding bath that cleanses the Jewish bride,[83] your heart is washed for your Husband-King. He tells you the winter of your old life is *over* and *gone* (Song 2:11b) not to be found anywhere in the memory banks of your Beloved.

Notice the power of this phrase because it is doubly emphasized. Beloved says your past is *over* and *gone*. The alternate case indicates the word "*and*" has been added, so, literally, Beloved is saying that your old life is "Over! Gone!"

Picture the cross. As Beloved is crucified, He declares, *"It is finished"* (John 19:30)! When He does this, forgiveness arises. In the same manner, Beloved shows you that your old life has ended and your new life has begun.

It is important for us to maintain fellowship with Beloved through Communion if our

---

[83] Kay, Glenn.

wedding dress is to remain spotless. Of our own accord, we would make the same mistakes, affiliate with the same people, and participate in the same activities that weighed us down in the first place. Left to our own devices, we would end up in more of a mess than we had been in, so we need to know how to preserve this fresh start. Let's look at this.

THE GROOM'S VOICE

You say, *The voice of my beloved* (Song 2:8a)*!* Let's stop right there, because it's a nugget of gold. Beloved has a voice. This is the answer to your quest to remain clean. Prompt obedience to Beloved's voice is the key to avoiding Satan's schemes. Beloved is willing to warn His Bride, but we must be willing to exercise our spiritual ears.

We discern the voice of Beloved by reading our Bibles. This must be more than a casual read through; it must be our all-in-all. Become saturated in Beloved's written Word. Live, breathe, experience, and teach the Word of God.

Beloved also speaks through subtle promptings spoken directly into our spirit, through another believer, or, on rare occasions, He speaks through an angel or a vision. Be careful, though, because every communication must line up with the Bible. If it does not, then discard it. Experience will be your teacher. The Bible teaches us that *by reason of use* (Hebrews 5:14b) we will discern truth.

The words "voice" and "Beloved" are paired.[84] It is not just any voice we should heed; it is Beloved's wise voice we must follow. Three times in this one scene, Beloved instructs you by His "voice." These are: 1) *the voice of my beloved,* 2) *my beloved spoke,* and 3) *the voice of the turtledove* (Song 2:8a, 10a, 12b).

Twice, Beloved pleads with you in earnest to *come away* (Song 2:10b, 13b) and you do so. Notice the progression in this verse as Beloved draws you in measurable steps: You say, *Behold, he stands behind our wall; he is looking through the windows, gazing through the lattice* (Song 2:9). First, He stands behind the wall of the city. Next, He peers through the windows of your home. Finally, He comes into your prayer garden, covering part of His form with the weave of the lattice.

THE ALLURE OF ROMANCE

You tell your lady friends about Beloved's romancing you, that although His appearances are intriguing, He makes Himself discoverable. 1) He is not crouched behind the city wall; He is standing. 2) He is noticeable through the windows because as He looks at you, He reveals His eyes. 3) A garden lattice cannot possibly cover a figure completely, so He is allowing you to see Him in part. It is Beloved's intent to hide in plain sight. Nothing is forced; all is a discovery of your will. And, so, He hides in part, to entice you to search for Him. This is the allure of romance.

THE WALL VERSUS THE DOOR

You teach the ladies about the city wall (see Song 2:9, 3:2-3) This represents salvation. You have come into a protected place—the King's city. These walls have guards on them to keep out enemies, and yet they allow entrance to the Bridegroom because He owns the city. They, too, must make the decision to be saved in order to come under Beloved's protection.

This concept is repeated at the end of the vignette in Song 8:8-11 when the maidens describe a daughter, *if she is a wall* (Song 8:9a)—in other words, if she is saved—then she can have built upon her *a battlement of silver* (Song 8:9b). This indicates that the believer who comes away seeking holiness and spending time to abide in Beloved's presence is a candidate for a successful ministry. Silver represents redemption.

In contrast, if the daughter is a *door* (Song 8:9b) letting in the filth of the world, we are to *enclose her with boards of cedar* (Song 8:9b)—in other words, we are to lead her to the cross. Bride of

---

[84] construct state

76

Christ, choose to be the "wall," enclosed in your Bridegroom's love. This is the only way to have a successful public ministry.

THE GROOM'S GLANCES

When Beloved comes to your residence and is *looking through the windows* (Song 2:9b), the first impression we might get is that He is a peeping Tom, but this is not what is happening at all. Translated, His "looks" means that He "glances sharply."[85] This does not indicate an angry look — rather it indicates that He knows everything about you.[86] Thus, as you allow Him to look closer, His glances perfect any defect in you. Beloved is exchanging His strengths for your weaknesses. He allows you to notice what He sees in you — and that He loves who you are becoming as your romance continues.

Notice Beloved glances rather than stares. His glances are kind, even though they are piercing. Your Groom knows just how much interaction you can bear, so He does not push you beyond what imperfections you are ready to yield to Him. He sees your potential, and yet He accepts you, calling you "my love," and "my fair one" along your entire journey.

Let's look at Beloved's interaction as you press beyond the city wall, beyond the home visitation, and into your prayer garden retreat. For this last place is where your interaction with Beloved is most intimate.

THE PRAYER GARDEN; TWINKLING APPEARANCES

Beloved comes to your prayer garden, showing His form through the lattice. You say, He is *gazing through the lattice* (Song 2:9b). What does this indicate? The word, "gazing,"[87] means to "twinkle" or to reveal oneself.[88] Let's apply this. Have you ever watched a child fascinated by the twinkling of Christmas lights? That's where my mind goes when I read this description. Your King twinkles His glory, enticing you to watch for Him. When He reveals Himself — even though these encounters might be fleeting — you remember them.

The beauty of your King has a fascination to it. Beloved is willing to become as intimate as you allow Him to be. If you pursue Him, He delights to come even closer. Do you hear Him, Love? He is calling you to come beyond the lattice of your self-imposed enclosure to higher ground. But for this level of anointing, you must commit to private, intense, and undisturbed fellowship. It is there that He shares His most intimate secrets.

THE GAZELLE AND THE YOUNG STAG

What happens when you decide to pursue the deepest level of intimacy to come away with Beloved in private communion? A metaphorical description we read in the vignette is the dance of the gazelle as he courts his doe.

You say, *The voice of my beloved! Behold, he comes leaping upon the mountains, skipping upon the hills* (Song 2:8). The gazelle mentioned here conceptualizes prominence, splendor, and glory. We need only to check gazelle behavior to notice this.

This young stag makes quite a spectacle of himself during mating season. He stomps and leaps around his doe, snorting and flexing his shoulders. As if this behavior isn't enough, he leaps into the air and forcefully pounds the ground as he lands. In nature, this behavior is called "stotting." Why does the buck behave in this seemingly playful, yet warlike manner? One group of scientists describes this behavior as follows:

You'd think being able to run 40 mph (64 kph) would be fast enough to outrun any

---

[85] Strong. OT #7688, *shagach*
[86] Zodihates. The tense used here indicates "perfective action, viewed as a whole."
[87] KJV *sheweth*
[88] Strong. OT #6692, *tsuwts*

problem. But if you live… where one of your top predators is the cheetah… you're going to need a few more tricks in order to stay alive… Initially, biologists thought gazelles that stotted were altruistically warning the herd of an impending attack. While that still may be the case, another widely accepted theory is that they're also communicating with the predator… The gazelle is saying, "Look at me, cheetah, I'm so tough that I can afford to spend time jumping around because I'll still outrun you." The cheetah may assume that the gazelle is in good enough condition and that it's probably not worth its time.[89]

From this we learn our Beloved is a mighty Warrior, and He fights for us! He stots upon the mountaintop in order to frighten the enemy away. Lest any foe come near His ascending Bride, your Beloved is going to give him a mouthful of hooves. Does this make your ascent journey easier, knowing that Beloved is positioned as the warring Gazelle Stag, ready and able to defeat the enemy for you? Your Groom wants you to be lovesick for Him, and He will defend you as you ascend the heights and enclose yourself in private communion.

Remain lovesick, Bride. Your desire to worship Beloved is your most powerful weapon. You emphasize this to the maidens. Keep Beloved as your first love at all times and in all seasons. Allow this glorious stotting dance between you and Beloved to remain a reality to you.

There is another reason Beloved stots like a young gazelle—He is giddy. That's right. The reality that you desire Him causes your Groom to be giddy with joy. He is pleased that you accept His spiritual romance.

Let's look further at the behavior of the gazelle as he pursues a mate. In nature, the buck hangs back and waits to see the curiosity level of his prospective mate. If the doe pursues him,[90] then he mates with her. Otherwise, he moves on to find a more interested doe. This seems to be contradicting behavior. The gazelle remains steady, almost to the point of being shy, and refrains until she shows interest, but then he pursues and protects her with a warlike passion.

Your Beloved stands like a ten-point buck, displaying His strength, and He calls to you to come away with Him. He knows that if you do so His anointing will rest upon you heavily and He will be able to make you to be progressively more holy like Himself, but He waits to see what your choice will be. Your Beloved wants to impart His strength to you, but the condition is that you pursue Him.

Notice also that Beloved is portrayed as youthful—He is the *young stag* (Song 2:9b). So, He not only increases your anointing when you pursue Him, your youth is renewed. There is no devil from hell that can stop a pursuing Bride whose youthful Stag is a Warrior.

SPIRITUAL FRUITS

Beloved relates your spiritual life to maturing fruits—the green figs and tender grapes are in the process of maturing. Consequentially, they are vulnerable, but He protects them. Paul lists the spiritual fruits that Beloved develops in you: *love, joy, peace, longsuffering, kindness, goodness, faithfulness, gentleness, and self-control* (Galatians 5:22b). These beautify you as you shed the old rag of sin and don Beloved's righteousness.

COME AWAY

---

[89] Horton, Jennifer. "How Do Gazelles Use Body Language?" *How Stuff Works.* InfoSpace, LLC, n.d. Web. 2012. http://www.animals.howstuffworks.com/mammals/gazelle-body-language.html

[90] "Roe Deer." *Wikipedia, The Free Encyclopedia.* MediaWiki, n.d. Web. 2012. http://www.en.wikipedia.org/Roe_deer   You, Zhanggiang, and Jiang, Zhanggiang, Courtship and Mating Behaviors in Przewalski's Gazelle. https://www.europepmc.org/article/cba/502594

Let's look at the phrase *come away* (Song 2:10, 13). It translates as two inseparable words: [91] "Come"[92] is from *yalak*, meaning "to walk." This is an action word; indicating we are journeying rather than remaining stationary. "Away"[93] is the word, *halak*, which means to "behave while walking." The tense [94] indicates it is a command, rather than a suggestion. So, although Beloved waits and gives us choice, He is also saying that the only way we are going to be anointed is to set ourselves apart to commune with Him and receive His instruction.

Beloved is calling us to 1) walk with Him and 2) to permit Him to mold our character. When Beloved says, "Come," He is inviting you to draw away and journey with Him. He is saying, "Take a walk with Me." When Beloved says to come "away," He's saying, "Behave with Me." Your spiritual fruit is formed during these set-apart visitations as you yield to His loving inspection. As you allow Him to shape your behavior on these walks, you become more like Him.

Holiness is a process that is methodical in some aspects. It requires our repentance, time set apart unto Jesus, and obedience to Beloved's voice of wisdom as He instructs us. We need to guard this process. We can't expect to listen to a podcast while driving on a 70-mph highway and call it our set apart time with God. We need to be purposeful about our journey and schedule times that Beloved can have our exclusive attention where we commune together in undisturbed study of the Word, prayer, and worship.

Let's look at two examples:

- Enoch's[95] behavior was so upright that rather than dying a natural death, he was translated into God's presence. He accomplished this in a time where most people in his society were immoral.

- The patriarch Abraham set aside all worldly distractions, gave up his family clan (except for Lot), and travelled to a destination known only to his Maker. He could have said, "No thanks, Lord. I'd rather hang out in Ur with my kinfolk." But instead, he gave up his personal agenda in order to pursue God's objectives. The result, as we have studied previously, was that Abraham became the spiritual Father of Nations.

If Enoch and Abraham can accomplish this, so can we. Beloved calls us to walk with Him and to allow us to shape our behavior. Let's accept His invitation. He speaks these instructions during our tarry times.

Throughout Scenes Eight through Ten, Beloved repeats His request for you to arise and come away with Him. What do we learn from this repetition? There is no cap on your mountaintop experience. It continues and strengthens through abiding, moving you from one level of glory to the next.

In contrast, we can become so busy doing the Lord's work that we don't realize He has not approved of the work we are doing. Being too busy to have set-apart times to worship Beloved Jesus eventually results in us being under Satan's yoke.

THE TURTLEDOVE

At the start of Scene Eight, Beloved says to you, *"Rise up, my love, my fair one, and come away"* (Song 2:10b). At the scene's end, Beloved again says, *Rise up, my love, my fair one, and come away* (Song 2:13b)*!*

Tucked in-between is the mystery of the turtledove.

Beloved says, *And the voice of the turtledove is heard in our land* (Song 2:12). The turtledove's

---

[91] Zodihates. Waw Conjunctive, OT #104.

[92] Strong. OT #3212, *yalak;* walk

[93] Strong. OT #1980, *halak*, to walk, behave

[94] Zodihates. Qal Imperative tense, OT #94

[95] Genesis 5:24, *halak*, walked

behavior is summed up in one word: singularity. As we have learned from the Jewish wedding ceremony, the bride circles her groom seven times[96] to show she belongs to her husband and this is a lifelong covenant.

Turtledoves have a beautiful mating dance that involves circling one another while cooing a love song. This turtledove metaphorically depicts the intimacy found within the Holy of Holies. But, unless we come away, we will not experience this love-dance with our Lord.

Expectedly, the turtledove has a "voice," and this voice is heralded throughout the land. When you return from the mountaintops you speak His words to your audience who meets you in the valley.

Only after you've come aside do you have something to say! This is how you are able to teach the Word. You have a passion to share because you've received from your Beloved secrets within the Holy of Holies. Your relationship with Beloved is not just head knowledge; you have experienced firsthand His kisses of peace within the holy wedding chamber while you commune with Him.

The turtledove sums up the entire discourse of Scene Eight: Be singularly devoted to Beloved. Listen attentively to His voice and obey His promptings. Guard your heart from accepting any teaching other than what your Groom's Word supports.

THE ROCK DOVE OF SCENE NINE

A second bird appears in Scene Nine. This dove is, once again, the rock dove[97] that lives in the clefts. This dove reminds you to ascend higher than you can think to imagine and to abide there. This is the presence we must not disturb. How do you ascend to this level where the rock dove abides? The clue to your victorious transformation is unveiled in this next scene.

In Scene Nine, Beloved's presence is before you, and you are once again changed by His love. You see His form; you invite His perfecting glances; you obey His voice. And yet, there is even more…

You also have a voice, and Beloved is eager to hear you speak. Come away with your Beloved into His mountaintop sanctuary and speak:

*****

SONG OF SOLOMON 2:14-17
Scene Nine: Ascending

SETTING: Bether's steep mountain.

AT RISE: BELOVED ascends the steep cliff face with LOVE in tow, close behind Him.

NARRATOR

Beloved and Love climb the "stairs" of the mountains—the footholds and handholds to the solitary place where they commune privately. They are intent on hearing each other's voices. They ascend single file, with Love close behind her Beloved.

> (BELOVED reaches back and catches LOVE as she stumbles. He guides her to a level cleft, where they sit to rest.)

This journey is treacherous. Love is uncertain about her ability to ascend. Beloved reassures Love that He is attuned to her voice; He's not troubled when she shares a need. He asks her to call to Him whenever she desires.

BELOVED

[14]O My dove, in the clefts of the rock, in the secret *places* of the cliff, let Me see your face, let Me

---

[96] "Jewish Wedding." *Ahavat Israel*. Ahavat Israel, 2015. Web. http://www.ahavat-israel.com/torat/marriage.php.
[97] Strong. OT #3123, *yownah*, rock dove

hear your voice; for your voice *is* sweet, and your face *is* lovely.
>   (BELOVED extends His hand.)

LOVE

>   (Pleading)

¹⁵Catch us the foxes, the little foxes, that spoil the vines, for our vines *have* tender grapes. ¹⁶My Beloved *is* mine and I *am* his. He feeds *his flock* among the lilies.
>   (BELOVED and LOVE recline. LOVE snuggles into BELOVED's strong but
>   gentle embrace.)

NARRATOR

Love realizes that even the little things that would hinder her are important to Beloved. There is no little devil—no little fox—that she will allow to spoil her spiritual fruit! As Beloved and Love settle into an embrace, the sun's rays give way to twilight. Love watches the shadows dissipate. Likewise, the spiritual shadows—those troubling thoughts of the Bride—are being chased away by her Savior's enduring love.

LOVE

¹⁷Until the day breaks, and the shadows flee away, turn, my Beloved, and be like a gazelle or a young stag upon the mountains of Bether.

NARRATOR

Love unveils her deepest secrets. She looks at her shadow in the twilight. The afternoon sun had made it look long and twisted. Now that she is in Beloved's embrace, the tricks of the enemy are being exposed. She trusts Beloved to rid her of every lie. Her Groom is as splendid and majestic as the gazelle of the mountain. He is equally as the young stag—youthful and ambitious. He is willing to guard her pursuit of Him.
>   (LOVE sleepily leans into BELOVED's embrace, and she whispers a prayer,
>   inaudible to the audience. BELOVED rises and dances)

Love and Beloved are shadowboxing upon the mountains of Bether, although now it is a dream, for she has fallen into a deep slumber. Beloved keeps watch over His Bride through the night as well as through the night seasons of her life. The majestic Groom is stotting upon the mountains of Bether to protect His Bride.
>   (LOVE sleeps, while BELOVED dances and keeps watch.)

*****

What is happening in Scene Nine, Love? You are learning the art of spiritual ascent. There are secrets you'll discover if you dare to climb these treacherous heights! These cliff faces are riddled with dangers, so you are exposed, and yet, Beloved is right there.

It takes quick and total obedience to ascend with Him without falling. The enemy may not have noticed you when you were in Sharon Valley, but as you climb these steep cliff faces, you are fair game. But Beloved—His stotting dance protects you from danger.

DISCERNMENT

Bether (Song 2:71b) comes from a root word that means "division."⁹⁸ Because of the shadows in the crevices of the cliff faces, it takes quick and complete obedience to Beloved to discern which are handholds and which are shadows.

There is no room for compromise on Bether's mountain. In the light of Beloved's glory, the

---

⁹⁸ Strong. OT #1336, *Bether,* a craggy place in Palestine. OT #1334, *bather,* to chop up; divide.

true nature of things is revealed. Once, you were unaware, but now you see the shadows that were hidden from your view. Little indiscretions become apparent, and you want to make things right. Truth is becoming obvious; lies are being exposed. You and your Groom are shadowboxing upon the mountains of Bether.

THE BRIDE'S VOICE

Through this scene, your voice is more prominent than Beloved's. Why is this so? Beloved is willing to transform only what you are willing to yield. You say, *Catch us the foxes, the little foxes that spoil the vines for our vines* have *tender grapes* (Song 2:15). You are becoming spiritually fruitful, not from your own works, but by dialoguing with Beloved. Once again, the Romancer willingly waits. Although He knows you need His transforming love, He does not force this on you. Therefore, as you speak, He assists you. The process is simple: you yield, through speech, to your Romancer; He then sets things right.

LITTLE FOXES

Little foxes (Song 2:15b) are much easier to catch than sins that are well set in. The major sins have already been dealt with in Sharon Valley. Now, you will not allow even little indulgences of the flesh to creep into your spirit. Beloved is just too important to you for you to neglect spiritual maintenance as you once did. Your participation is necessary. You say, *Catch us* (Song 2:15a), not "You catch." You are involved in this holiness process.

Think of King David. He was the anointed songwriter-poet. His folly creeps into his life during a time of spiritual ascent. How did the enemy trick him? He didn't catch a little fox.

I am certain the Lord whispered to David, "Don't go onto the rooftop terrace tonight." Surely Beloved whispered, "Look away," as David coveted Bathsheba, but he ignored this inner voice. Because of this, he fell into a horrible trap.

Have you heard the Lord prompting you to do something in ministry, at your job, or in your family life that may seem insignificant? It might be Beloved's voice steering you around a potential little fox.

You are beautiful to Beloved, even if at this very moment you need to yield some little foxes, or even some wolves, or bears, to Beloved! He does not condemn you, even when He's on a fox hunt! Your voice is *sweet* (Song 2:14b) and your countenance is *lovely* (Song 2:14), even during a spiritual cleansing. As you look to Him, He does the cleansing.

THE BRIDE'S COUNTENANCE/VOICE

Beloved says to you, *Let me see your face* (Song 2:14a). The King James reads, *Let me see thy countenance*. Beloved wants to discern, from your facial expressions, your thoughts. In the brilliant light of Beloved's glory, nothing can be hidden; He already knows it all. When we are willing to allow Beloved to put His finger on a flaw, we can rest assured that He will provide the strength for us to make the correction.

Had King David allowed Beloved to hear his secret thoughts, "I'm struggling with lust, adultery, and hatred," it would have been painful, but it would have prevented his downfall. It would have been harder for him to commit adultery and murder an innocent man if he had allowed Beloved to inspect his thinking.

What furthered King David's actions and kept him trapped in deception was his silence. He walled off one area of his life and did not allow Beloved to inspect it. He did not speak his thoughts, as Beloved is showing you to do in Scene Nine. Psalm 51 shows that King David finally yielded to Beloved's loving inspection, and that's when God forgave him.

THE LOVESICK BRIDE

You have a voice. Speak your thoughts to Beloved and remain lovesick. This will save you from a myriad of sins. Twice in Song of Solomon, you say, *I am lovesick* (Song 2:5; 5:8). The first time you express this is at the round Communion table. The next time is when you have need of repentance. The word, "lovesick"[99] referenced in both passages, means "weak." There is strength in becoming weak. For when you are weak, Beloved becomes your strength.

Paul dialogued about being lovesick. He wrote, *And he [Beloved Jesus] said to me, "My grace is sufficient for you: for My strength is made perfect in weakness." Therefore most gladly, I will rather boast in my infirmities, that the power of Christ may rest upon me* (2 Corinthians 12:9). Paul was being buffeted by an enemy. He learned to win the battle by being transparent to the Lord. God didn't take his troubles away all at once; instead, He taught Paul dependency, just like He did with Abraham, and that is the more important lesson.

Paul was on the mountaintop with his Beloved during this dialogue, experiencing *inexpressible* (2 Corinthians 12:4) glorious dialogue. Paul couldn't even discern whether what he was experiencing was earthly or transitory. He only knew his decision to be lovesick was his greatest desire, and that's where the blessings flowed.

In Scene Nine, you decide to climb the mountain and come away with your Beloved Jesus, and you expose all of who you are—including your weaknesses—by dialoguing with Him. What attack is successful on the worshipping Bride who dialogues with her Groom so He can walk with her and show her the course to take? No attack is successful! The winning formula is to remain lovesick and to speak. It's not about works; rather, it's about transparency. That's why your voice is so important. Beloved knows all your secrets, so you might as well yield to His loving glances of unifying perfection.

Worship… it is the state of the ascending bride—solitary, abiding worship that says, "Examine me, Lord." This is your most effective weapon of warfare.

THE ROCK DOVE

Before we read Scene Ten, let's envision the rock dove of Scene Nine. She is a picture of forgiveness, redemption, and glory. With all the introspection and dialogue, it is important you get the picture Beloved is painting for you when He says you are His rock dove that hides *in the clefts of the rock* (Song 2:14).

Beneath your wings are silvery-grey feathers. Scripture records, "You will *be like the wings of a dove covered with silver, and her feathers with yellow gold*" (Psalm 68:13b). Why is there silver and gold beneath those outstretched wings? You soar upon the silver of redemption that is built into the fabric of your being. You are also graced with the sparkling gold dust of Heaven. Beloved promises you that you will soar on the wings of His redemption and glory as you dialogue with Him.

SCENE TEN

Now let's look at the final scene of this section. Even in slumber you are winning the battle. In fact, the deepest transformation happens while you are in this dream-like state.

Step into the vignette. Your Beloved awaits:

*****

SONG OF SOLOMON 3:1-5
Scene Ten: The City Dream

SETTING:	LOVE'S home, and the surrounding villages.
AT RISE:	Stage Left: LOVE is on her bed, dreaming.

---

[99] Strong. OT #2470, *chalah*

Stage Right: Mimes perform the dream sequence as
LOVE reminisces.
Lighting:
Stage Left: soft yellow and blue.
Stage Right: Harsh crimson and indigo.

NARRATOR

Listen, friends. Love remembers a troublesome dream. What could it mean?

LOVE
(LOVE sits up on her bed, weeping! MAIDENS rush to her side.)
[1]By night on my bed I sought the One I love: I sought Him, but I did not find Him. "[2a]I will rise now," *I said*, "and go about the city; in the streets and the squares I will seek the One I love."
(Standing, speaking emphatically)
[2b]I sought Him, but I did not find Him.
(Pacing)
[3]The watchmen who go about the city found me. *I said*, "Have you seen the One I love?" Scarcely had I passed by them, when I found the One I love. I held Him, and would not let Him go, until I had brought Him to the house of my mother, and into the chamber of her who conceived me.
(LOVE embraces herself as if BELOVED is with her.)
[5]I charge you, O ye daughters of Jerusalem, by the gazelles or by the does of the field, do not stir up, nor awaken love, until it pleases.

*****

Hello, Love. Are you awake? I see you've had a troubling dream, so let's discuss this. Dreams act as a purifying screen. If something is bothering us, we might dream about it. Sometimes, though, it is more than just a processing of events. Dreams can be messages from Beloved. This is one of those times. Beloved gifts you with a divinely inspired dream. This is because He wants you to yield even your subconscious to His loving examination.

THE CITY STREETS

The dream begins with a search scene. You look everywhere for your Beloved. You look, saying, *"I will rise now... and go about the city in the streets and in the squares"* (Song 3:2). Beloved is not there! Panic sets in. You search further, but you still do not find Him. "Beloved! Where are You?" You call for Him repeatedly.

You have forgotten where to look for Him. Notice you are on the lowest level of intimacy. No longer are you on the mountaintop with your Lord, rather you are in the city. This is disturbing to you because, in reality, you've chosen the heights where the rock dove lives. Beloved communes with you deeply, so in the dream, when you lose this intimacy you resolve to abide in the clefts without question. You want to be like the rock dove.

What is worse is that you are on the streets, exposed to every thug who intends to harm you. The city squares, which in the King James is translated, *broad ways* (Song 3:2 KJV), is not where you want to be. Beloved has said, *"Enter by the narrow gate; for wide is the gate, and broad is the way that leads to destruction, and there are many who go in by it. Because narrow is the gate, and difficult is the way, which leads to life, and there are few who find it"* (Matthew 7:13-14).

You want nothing to do with the broad ways and the destruction that results in following this path. Beloved is found on the narrow path of truth. He says, *"I am the way, the truth, and the life. No one comes to the Father except through Me"* (John 14:6). Beloved Jesus Christ is the only One who satisfies!

The word picture that the city streets and squares indicate is a hustle-bustle of activity, and the night life that accompanies it is in opposition to the peace you find in your Groom. This dream is

Beloved's way of emphasizing to you the contrasting choices you can make.

THE BRIDE'S CHOICE

You can choose. Do you want to live a fanatical, free-for-all lifestyle or a disciplined life, which includes solitude with your Beloved? Do you want the city streets party scene? Or do you want the life of ascent, where you come away with Beloved for times of private communion? The second scenario takes commitment, but you realize it is worth it. Your choice to follow Beloved is best, even though it is difficult to ascend the cliffs.

In this dream sequence, a phrase that is repeated four times tells what you, as Beloved's Bride, have chosen. It is the phrase, *the one I love* (Song 3:1b, 2b, 3b, 4b). You have made the choice to love only Beloved. He exclusively is the Bridegroom you have chosen. You want nothing to do with worldly impurities. To you, Beloved is choice. Perhaps this phrase is repeated four times because the number four represents "creation and things that are made."[100] In all the world, you have chosen Beloved. He has worked this into your heart and created it anew.

THE STRANGE WATCHMEN

In your dream, rather than finding Beloved, you are met by strange *watchmen* (Song 3:3a). You do not immediately discern that these watchmen are not true believers. You only figure out these watchmen have evil intentions when they withhold Beloved's location from you.

In Scene Two, the maidens were eager to lead you to Beloved. They tell you about Sharon Valley and the shepherds who can teach you.

In contrast, these evil watchmen who are on the walls, watching who comes and goes, certainly know Beloved's location, but they won't share it with you. In your dream language, these watchmen are a warning about relationships. You need to spend time with fellow believers, not pretenders. Discernment is key.

THE GROOM'S QUICK RESCUE

Notice that Beloved rescues you quickly. Beloved is communicating to you that, even if you stray and then repent, He comes to your rescue quickly. He knows you want to be with Him. Beloved makes sure this is in the dream because He knows we are flesh. He desires to rescue His Bride, and He does not withhold a rescue just because we've sinned.

You say, *Scarcely had I passed by them, when I found him* (Song 3:4a). Beloved does not permit you to suffer separation for long, even in this dream. He is there for you quickly.

THE BRIDE'S MOTHER'S HOME

Next comes a strange sounding passage, but it is beautiful when we learn the significance. You take Beloved to your mother's house (see Song 3:4b), and all the way into her bedroom. Why is this so? There are three reasons:

First, your home signifies your identity, and your mother's bedroom where you were conceived represents the most intimate place of the family tie. You recognize Beloved is Lord of your entire life, present, past, and future. Therefore, to bring Him to the place where your life had its beginning makes total sense. You want Him to be Lord of the beginnings and the endings and everything in-between of your life. By bringing Beloved to your mother's bedroom, you are saying, "Beloved, I give You full access to who I am. I surrender. There is no part of me that I withhold from You."

Second, by bringing Beloved to the most intimate place you know of—your mother's bedroom—you acknowledge the intimate nature of your relationship. In so doing, you recognize

---

[100] Brewer, Troy. *Numbers that Preach.* Aventine Press. Chula Vista, CA. 2016. Pg. 53.

Beloved is your Spouse. This is a bridal covenant, and you are acknowledging its unbreakable bond.

Finally, *mother* (Song 3:4b) in your dream language, represents the Holy Spirit. "Mother" is the one who nourishes. She carries you in her womb, and she raises you. Notice this dream language is symbolic, for your real mother was not a nurturer at all and she was partially responsible for the dysfunctional family in which you grow up. But, here in the dream, you have the perfect mother. The Holy Spirit nourishes you far better than a mother could.

This dream language in no way is indicating the Holy Spirit is a female; it is simply a metaphor that helps you understand His nurturing aspect.

ESTABLISHING PRIORITIES

When you awake, you share with the maidens that they must get their priorities straight. May I suggest that we write on our daily planners, "Meeting with the King"? If our devotion time is our top priority, it's a wise decision to schedule it. There is no activity more important, and yet, it is often the first to slide off the agenda, only to be remembered when we're struggling with a little fox that could have easily been avoided if we had prioritized our set-apart times with our Beloved.

CONCLUSION

When you awake from this dream, you are convinced that your love for Beloved is solid because the dream's message of potential loss of intimacy repulses you. You do not even remotely desire your former life. Until you had this dream, you did not know this.

What this dream does for you is to solidify your priorities. As you do so, you have a firm foundation upon which to build your marriage. Intimacy with Beloved is the life you have chosen, and even your subconscious thoughts show this as your value system.

The next chapter describes your Bridegroom's quick return. Are you ready for your soon-coming King? Let's explore this, but before we do so, let's seal our decision to make Beloved King of every aspect of our being, whether awake or asleep.

Let's pray:

My Warrior King,

I desire truth within my innermost being. Cleanse my heart, hear my voice, and help me to respond to Your life-giving voice. Teach me to live the life of ascent. I trust You to protect me from the enemy's attacks. As I fix my gaze upon You, give me wisdom and discernment.

I trust in You alone, for You are my Warring Savior and I give You first place in my heart. There is nothing I will withhold from You. Rather, I invite Your piercing yet loving glances to examine me often, for I know Your love will purify me. Take me to Your side. Sweep me into Your chariot to ride. For only in You will I abide.

Abiding in You,
Love

BRIDAL REFLECTION

1) In the modern-day example of King David, we saw he had position, title, and a developing anointing when he transgressed. You, as Bride, have these same characteristics. What must you do to shepherd the anointing carefully?

2) King David repented and wrote Psalm 51. Read this Psalm and pray its principles for your own life. How can you be watchful for enemy traps?

3) Why is it important to conquer the "little foxes" in your bridal experience?

4) Read Song of Solomon 2:11 NKJV. What does the phrase, "over *and* gone" emphasize about your old life versus your new life as Bride of Beloved?

5) In Song of Solomon 2:9, Beloved comes to you, "gazing" through the garden lattice. The word, "gazing," means "twinkling," and this indicates He is revealing His glory to you, enticing you to come beyond the known and into a deeper relationship with Him. Describe a time you felt He was doing this in today's times. How did your communion with Him strengthen as He revealed Himself to you?

6) Do you have a prayer garden retreat, whether it is in a garden or in a room, closet, chair, or other location? How does having a specific place to pray strengthen your relationship with Beloved Jesus?

7) What did you think of the idea of writing on our day timers, "Meeting with the King," as a way to remind ourselves Beloved Jesus Christ is the most important person we will meet with all day?

Chapter Six
The Chariot Rider

Go forth, O daughters of Zion, and see King Solomon
with the crown with which his mother crowned him on the
day of his wedding, the day of the gladness of his heart.
~Song of Solomon 3:11

And He has on His robe and on His thigh a name written,
KING OF KINGS, AND LORD OF LORDS.
~Revelation 19:16

The Jewish bride of ancient biblical times is a lady in waiting. Only the groom's father knows the time when he will dispatch his son to marry his bride. She has agreed to the betrothal, so when she is whisked away, "kidnapped," so to speak, by her groom, the family celebrates.

The betrothed could come at any moment, and when He appears, bridal preparation stops. Either she has made herself ready or she is left behind. Zola Levitt writes about this Hebraic wedding tradition, "All the Jewish brides were 'stolen.' The Jews had a special understanding of a woman's heart. What a thrill for her, to be 'abducted' and carried off into the night, not by a stranger but by one who loved her."[101]

This sounds romantic, but sometimes a bride would not have met her prospective groom. Would the prospect of being swept into a chariot and wafted away with a man you had not met be appealing? Would you go with this gentleman? I thought so! I wouldn't go either!

Our Western customs are much different from what is portrayed in Song of Solomon, so let's take a step back in time and explore the biblical setting for this chariot ride. We will learn what the groom does so his bride is ready to depart with him and how she knows his love is sincere. This will help us understand the chariot ride Scene Eleven portrays.

We usually begin our chapters with the vignette, but so that we can get everything out of the next scene, let's set the backdrop via discussion. Let's pretend…

FAMILY INVOLVEMENT

You are a lady of marrying age and you are ready to choose a husband. How does a Hebrew gentleman of early biblical times interact with you? Does he invite you to a school dance? Does he message you on MeWe or Parler? Does he date you at all? He does none of these things. In ancient biblical times, Hebraic marriages were prearranged. The parents of each family talk to you about your groom, most likely for years. Even if you don't know your prospective groom, your parents know a lot about him and his family, and they share this with you. The groom's father negotiates the terms with your father. You do not have to measure up the way we are used to doing in today's dating scenario. In fact, you do not date at all.

THE PROPOSAL CUP

Your part is minimal but vital, nonetheless. After this long-distance review, you and your spouse usually meet with the family, and the groom offers you a cup of wine as a symbol of his marriage proposal. If your answer is "yes," you accept the cup.[102] If it is "no," you refuse to sip this

---

[101] Levitt, Zola. *A Christian Love Story*. Dallas, TX: Great Impressions Printing, 1978. http://www.levitt.com
[102] Showers, Dr Renald. "Jewish Marriage Customs." *Bible Study Manuals*. Bible Study Manuals, 2012. Web.

wine.

Today's parallel, as we have previously discussed, is the Communion cup, so every time you partake of Communion, you not only are remembering Calvary, you are renewing your wedding vows to your Beloved Groom, Jesus Christ. These vows He signed in His own blood on Calvary's cross are precious to you. Who but the most committed groom would sign the wedding proposal in His own life's blood? Beloved Jesus Christ would—that's who.

PREPARATION

As a Bride-to-be, you participate in two ceremonies: 1) the betrothal called the *erusin* and 2) the wedding called the *nissuin*.[103] One or two years separate these two events, and both are taken very seriously.

THE BETROTHAL—THE ERUSIN

During the betrothal, or *erusin*, you and your groom-to-be enter into *kiddushin*, which is a waiting period indicating a couple's decision to prepare for their marriage. *Kiddushin* means "sanctification," or "set apart."[104] You do much introspection so your marriage will be lasting once it comes. Oftentimes the *kiddushin* is a long-distance relationship. You and your fiancé prepare separately for the ensuing wedding and the marriage to follow. Your communication is through messages sent to each other through friends. You do not meet in private. Consequentially, there are no messy boyfriend breakups, no flirtations, and no sex.

Pay close attention, Love, because you are in this betrothal phase of your marriage to Beloved right now. Your job is to ready yourself for the soon return of your Bridegroom-King. You are to set yourself apart as a Jewish bride would do. Be watchful so that when your Beloved appears and is ready to whisk you into His chariot, you are a sanctified, spotless Bride. Prepare for your departure, not by what you can accomplish, but by trusting Beloved to work His cleansing within your heart.

THE MARRIAGE CONTRACT—THE KETUBAH

The betrothal ceremony is witnessed by family.[105] This might happen face-to-face or long-distance. As a pledge that Beloved will keep His agreement to marry you, He gives or sends to you a *ketubah*, which is a formal written marriage contract. Your *ketubah* is your most precious possession, because it details in writing the way your groom agrees to take care of you. Your parents and your groom's parents also read your fiancé's written contract. This contract must be approved by both sets of parents and meet their high standards.

Today, most Jews display their *ketubah* in a prominent place in their home. The calligraphy, graphics, and frame are ornate, which shows the couple honors the godly marriage it represents. But, the *ketubah* is not simply text artwork, it is a legally binding document.

Do you have a *ketubah* that you can hold onto today? In fact, you do. Lift your Bible into the air; this is your *ketubah*. Treasure and read your *ketubah*. It is filled with Beloved's promises, and every word has been or will be fulfilled. This legally binding document speaks of the covenant of love Beloved has promised to you, His cherished Bride. It is Beloved's love letter, and it outlines the promises He had made to take care of you, the Bride of Christ.

Furthermore, Father God agrees with every word His Son has written in this *ketubah*. Therefore, just like the Jewish bride had knowledge of her unseen fiancé by reading her *ketubah*, so you have knowledge of your Beloved by reading your Bible. Even though you may not have seen

---

http://www.biblestudymanuals.net/jewish_marriage_customs.html
[103] Di Gilio, Rev. Barbara. "A Fresh Look at the Jewish Wedding." *Mayim Hayim Study*. Mayim Hayim Ministries Teaching Tools, 1998. Web. http://www.mayimhayim.org/JewishWedding.html
[104] Glenn, Kay.
[105] Schauss, Hayim.

Him face-to-face, you know all about Him and you have this love letter as well as what your parents have told you about Him.

How do you prepare for your wedding? You read your ketubah — the Bible — and you get to know your Fiancé well by agreeing with His written Word. Your soon-coming King has shown you His character through His Word, which is your *ketubah*.

In ancient biblical times you and your groom would be referred to as "wife" and "husband," even during the betrothal stage, because this marriage contract is legally binding. This indicates that before the wedding ceremony takes place, the pledge is already secured. It would not be right in the eyes of a Hebrew in biblical times to back out of this *ketubah*. The groom would have to acquire a formal divorce to annul this engagement.[106] Beloved considers you to be His wife right now for this same reason — because His Word is likewise binding. Thus, even before you are wed, Beloved references you as "Love," meaning "Wife."

THE VEIL

During the betrothal stage — the *erusin* — you wear a veil.[107] You are happy about this because this headpiece indicates your fiancé has chosen you. The marriage will occur some time off, but it is certain to happen. This head covering signals to other eligible bachelors that you belonged exclusively to your fiancé. Today's equivalent is an engagement ring.

HOME BUILDING

It is customary for the father of the groom to give his son an inheritance on the family estate. Your fiancé spends the entire time of the betrothal period building a home for you. Sometimes the son builds an addition onto his father's home, or it could involve building an entirely separate structure. Father and son decide this, and then the son makes the preparatory arrangements. This is one reason there is this waiting period.

I'm sure you recognize the comparison. Beloved is busy readying a home for you on His Father's estate in Heaven right now, for He says in your *ketubah*, "*In my Father's house are many mansions; if it were not so, I would have told you. I go to prepare a place for you. And if I go and prepare a place for you, I will come again, and receive you to Myself; that where I am,* there *you may be also*" (John 14:2-3). Messianic Jews understood this dialogue better than we, perhaps because they knew betrothals involved this temporary separation of the bride and groom.

LADY IN WAITING

As an Israelite bride, you are preparing your wedding gown. Your bridesmaids help you so that you are gorgeously adorned for your groom when he comes. Since you do not know the exact time of your fiancé's arrival, you are on the ready at all times. Your bridesmaids will travel with you, so they prepare also. How does this apply to your marriage to Beloved as the Bride of Christ? Just imagine all the girl talk! Let's listen in to your bridesmaid's conversation:

"Your Beloved is generous, like His Father!"

"Did you know Beloved is building you a multi-room mansion?"

"Your merciful King pardoned someone who committed a horrible crime."

"Oh, your Beloved is so peaceful! I love to be in His presence."

"Read your *ketubah* to us, Love. We want to hear Beloved's promises to you!"

"Yes, please do. We enjoy hearing your Husband-King's promises."

These, and many more, are the conversations your bridesmaids have with you as they reflect on your soon-coming King, for your long-distance romance has begun.

---

[106] Glenn, Kay.
[107] Showers, Dr. Renald

And, in fact, it already has…

We see that this separation does the opposite of what we would expect if we viewed this scenario from Western culture standards. Rather than this set-apart time causing you to distance yourself from your prospective groom, it strengthens your bond. From your *ketubah*, you learn of your Fiancé's character as you study every word, and you relish the loving promises your Fiancé has made to you, even committing your *ketubah* to memory, speaking your Groom's words as if they are honey on your tongue.

Beloved speaks a parable about this waiting period that's recorded in Matthew 25:1-3, where He equates His Brides to ten young virgins who have entered the betrothal period. Although all ten are supposed to be preparing for their groom, only five do so. Regrettably, the lazy virgins get left behind while the groom whisks away the five who are ready. Be like the five wise virgins who have welcomed Beloved by studying and agreeing with His Word. But do more than a head-study; allow the Word of God to be the love letter that you cherish, because He wants a passionate bride who loves Him.

Imagine Beloved's character. Read His love letters — His *ketubah* — your Bible. Treasure everything you learn about your Groom, and in this entire discovery, yearn earnestly for His surprise arrival.

How close are we to Beloved's return? We can only guess.

What we do know for certain is that we are in the season of His return, so I say to you in earnest — prepare! Stay on the ready! Don't entangle yourself with the cares of this world and the evils therein. Remain in love with your Beloved and stay committed to Him. He will come for us faster than we can blink. He longs to commune with us face-to-face, so prepare.

Continually stay in a state of readiness. We are able to do this! How? We can commune with our Beloved through the spirit-to-Spirit connection, even though He is not quite visible yet, except perhaps through the twinkling glances of His eyes, which appear behind the garden lattice while we are deep in prayer.

What is the wedding dress made of that you are sewing? Beloved says it is a garment of prayer, *The fragrance of your garments* is *like the fragrance of Lebanon* (Song 4:11b). Praise your Groom's holy Name and converse with Him through prayer. This makes you a fashionable Bride. Because you have been saved, your wedding dress is pure, having been washed white by the blood of your Savior. Keep your dress spotless by refusing the enemy's temptations. Don't turn back to the ways of the world. Repent if you have done so.

THE GROOM'S GIFTS — THE MATTAN

A Hebraic groom of biblical ancient times gives gifts to his fiancée, called the *mattan*.[108] Beloved gives gifts[109] to you even now through His Spirit impartations. Your Groom's gifts to you are His kisses of peace. These come upon you as you rest in His Spirit. Can you see Him? Not usually, but He is, even so, very much present.

THE BRIDAL PRICE — THE MOHAR

Your father would receive a "bridal price," from your groom called the *mohar*.[110] The groom would have to pay this bridal price in full before the bride's father would grant her hand in marriage.[111] Zola Levitt writes, "The young man had no delusion that he was getting something for nothing. He would pay dearly to marry the girl of his choice."[112]

---

[108] Risk, Bill.

[109] 2 Corinthians 1:20-22, 12:1, 4, Luke 24:49, John 14:25-27, 20:21-22, Acts 1:4-8, 2:4, 17-19, 38-39, 4:31-33

[110] Glenn, Kay.

[111] Levitt, Zola.

[112] Ibid.

I am sure you immediately think of the high price we spoke of that Beloved has paid for you. Your redemption has been bought with the Son of God's blood as He died on Calvary and then arose. Beloved Jesus describes the *mohar* in John chapter 3, noting that He and His Father have already decided you are worth this high price. This *mohar,* indeed, is a costly gift to both Father and Son.

THE RAPTURE

In ancient biblical times, the groom comes for his bride at an appointed day known only by his father.[113] He usually comes in the evening and whisks his bride away, with the wedding processional in tow. The groomsmen would either carry the bride on a canopied loveseat or it would be similar to what is described in the vignette, which is a horse-drawn chariot.

Beloved will surprise you, Love. Only Father God knows His Son's secret arrival time (see Mark 13:12). He will come with an entourage of His gentlemen friends. They will shout praises as Beloved blows the *shofar*.[114] This will be the most memorable ride of your life as He whisks you to Heaven.

THE WEDDING—THE NISSUIN

Now that we've explored the betrothal stage—the *erusin*, let's explore the wedding—called the *nissuin*. This term, *nissuin*, means "elevated,"[115] "taken by him,"[116] "to carry"[117] or "home-taking."[118] The groom whisks his bride away to his father's house, and when you arrive your engagement ends. What happens next?

SEVEN DAYS OF HUPPAH/PRIVATE COMMUNION

For seven days prior to the formal wedding ceremony, the bride and groom are enclosed in the bridal chamber. Friends bring meals, but aside from these brief interactions, the couple is in seclusion. This is called "The Seven Days of *Huppah*."[119]

What is the significance of this term? *Huppah* means "to cover" or "bridal chamber."[120]

What happens within the chamber? The couple converses and shares private Communion meals. They spend time getting to know each other without interruptions. Eventually, their first physical encounter happens within the privacy of the bridal chamber. The bride and groom consummate their marriage when they are mutually ready.

FATHER'S SEVEN BLESSINGS/PUBLIC COMMUNION

After The Seven Days of *Huppah,* the groom announces to the awaiting groomsmen that the marriage has been consummated. The formal wedding that follows is simply an acknowledgment of the union that has already taken place within the bridal chamber. This is the most sanctified view of marriage. After this, seven blessings are read over the couple and the groom's father hosts a Communion celebration, which usually lasts seven more days.

Oddly enough—to our thinking, but not to the Jew in ancient biblical times—the romance within the wedding chamber comes first, before the marriage celebration.[121] At that moment of marital bliss, as the couple consummates their union, they are considered "married." Since a strong bond has already developed during the *erusin,* or waiting period, they are ready for this. Thus, their

---

[113] Risk, Bill
[114] *shofar*; ram's horn trumpet.
[115] Strong. OT #3947 *laqach;* married
[116] Risk, Bill
[117] Glenn, Kay
[118] Di Gilio, Barbara, Rev..
[119] Showers, Dr. Renald.
[120] Glenn, Kay.
[121] Levitt, Zola.

full privileges as husband and wife are then recognized and the public marriage feast begins.

SPIRITUAL PARALLEL

The above parallels what will happen to you when Beloved brings you to Father's house in Heaven. There is, however, one exception: the sexual union is an allegorical representation of the spiritual realm. On your wedding day, as the Bride of Christ, He will bring you into the Holy of Holies which Christ opened for us through His death on the cross and as the veil tore.[122] In this holy place, you will receive Beloved's spiritual kisses of peace in full measure, face-to-face.

Let's look at the order of events again, applying this to you and Beloved:

Sequentially, you and your Groom romance through a long-distance relationship, with the *ketubah* contract—which is your Bible—securing your future marriage. You prepare for your wedding day by learning about Beloved through these written messages. While you are preparing, Beloved is preparing to receive you, building your home in Heaven. He says, *"I go to prepare a place for you"* (John 14:2b). The bridal price with which He has purchased you has been accomplished through Calvary's cross. Beloved says to you, *"Greater love has no man than this, than to lay down one's life for his friends"* (John 15:13). Furthermore, Beloved says, *"And I, if I am lifted up from the earth, will draw all peoples to Myself." This He said, signifying by what death he would die* (John 12:32-33).

Beloved bestows on you the down-payment of His Spirit. *"You did not choose Me, but I chose you and appointed you that you should go and bear fruit, and that your fruit should remain, that whatever you ask the Father in My name, He may give you"* (John 15:16). These spiritual 'fruits" are the *mattan*—Beloved's Spirit gifts deposited into your spirit, even though your formal wedding is yet to come. You have His authority even now. And evidence of this gifting is the divine love you carry within your spirit, *"These things I command you, that you love one another"* (John 15:17).

After this, you are swept into the chariot and brought to Father's house where you and Beloved meet in the Holy of Holies—the private wedding chamber. Within this holy place, and being fully in Beloved's presence, face-to-face with the One you love—is the full and limitless supply of Beloved's Spirit-impartation. Even now, you can glimpse into this wedding chamber, for your *ketubah* records, *Then, behold, the veil of the temple was torn in two from top to bottom; and the earth quaked, and the rocks were split, and the graves were opened; and many bodies of the saints who had fallen asleep were raised; and coming out of the graves after His resurrection, they went into the city and appeared to many.* (Matthew 27:51-53). As the Holy of Holies of the earthly Temple opened, an explosion of power from Beloved's Spirit also caused graves to open and life to come into these departed believers, while an earthquake rumbled the ground and rearranged the scenery, because of Beloved's life-giving force.

The torn veil could only have happened as an act of God. Josephus records that in King Herod's day, the thirty-cubit veil was increased to forty cubits in height, a sixty-foot equivalency.[123] According to Jewish tradition, the veil was four inches thick.[124] So the tearing of the veil was beyond what even an earthquake could do. It was an act of God. Jesus Christ's atonement for our sins opened the veil to us, His Bride.

Think what this means for you today as Beloved's wife. You are equipped even now with His life-giving power, and you will be completely empowered at your homegoing to Heaven. Can you imagine how fantastic this heavenly celebration will be? It is what Beloved reminisces about in Luke 22:15-20, when He eats the Passover with His disciples for the final time on Earth, saying, *"With fervent desire I have desired to eat this Passover with you before I suffer; for I say to you, I will no longer eat of it until it is fulfilled in the kingdom of God"* (Luke 22:15-16).

In Heaven, you will finally join family at the marriage feast that He and Father are preparing.

---

[122] Luke 23:45; Matthew 27:51; Hebrews 9:11-12
[123] "What was the significance of the Temple veil being torn in two when Jesus died? Got Questions.org. https://www.gotquestions.org/temple-veil-torn.html
[124] Ibid.

With fervent desire, Beloved wants to celebrate this feast with you. The price of His blood has been paid, you have sipped from the wedding cup of Communion in His blood, and when He whisks you into His chariot, you will commune in the Holy of Holies and then with Father at the public Communion feast. Glory!

HOLY OF HOLIES

Rabbi Akiba understood the allegorical language as representative of your spiritual union within the Holy of Holies. As believers, we have met the Groom Jesus Christ. From Scene One we ascertain we've entered the *huppah*. Truly, as we do this, we attain an elevated state of being, having been made whole by Beloved's kisses of peace as we behold our Groom face-to-face.

What happens inside this wedding chamber is a purer form of love than we usually think about because it's not performance-based. Beloved doesn't have to choose you; He already has. His heart boils for you with the pure, effervescent divine love, called *dowd*. John 3:16 shows that His choosing is sure, for He has journaled this in His marriage contract, your *ketubah*, the Bible.

He has weighed the cost, and He has paid the ransom price, even though this required His death and subsequent resurrection. He has voluntarily paid this bridal price.

You are totally accepted, fully loved, and eternally secure.

This, dear Bride, is the kiss of peace He offers to you, the bride He has been dreaming about and hoping you will say "yes" to His marriage proposal. This. Is. True. Love. His love is pure, and His love is sure.

TODAY'S BRIDE

Love, who are you right now? You are this lady in waiting. You have entered into a long-distance romance with the King of Kings. There is a measure of completeness that will only be experienced in Heaven, within the Holy of Holies—Heaven's *huppah*. Even so, rest assured that Beloved's divine love—*His dowd*—is already a reality for you right now.

Today, as you reach to Him in prayer, the Holy of Holies becomes available to you, particularly through Communion.

The veil has been torn; He has parted it as an invitation for you to enter the holiest place. Here in part, and there in full measure (see 1 Corinthians 13:12-13), Beloved invites you to know the Savior's kisses of peace.

Truly, He is your *Dowd Sheloma*, your Beloved Peacemaker.

Let's look at the choosing part of this. Your Beloved's answer is always, "Yes, Love, let's go higher. Let's go deeper. Let's get to know each other more intimately." I know my answer is not always so certain. Sometimes I tap the brakes on this holy romance. Rest assured that if you struggle with the same issue, Beloved is still there and His Word is sure. Simply stated, divorce is not in His vocabulary. The only one who can end this relationship is us. Unless we totally turn from Him, He will wait for us to be ready.

Now that we're equipped to experience Scene Eleven, let's enter in. What is happening? Beloved has come to you in His chariot, dressed in royal attire, and wearing His ceremonial crown. The preparatory period has ended. You become the star of this royal procession as Beloved brings you home. He has been waiting to show you the mansion He custom created for you. And now, the time of His appearing has finally come. It is time to wed Him.

Are you prepared for Beloved's appearing? You are, Bride of Christ! You are overcome with emotion as you hold out your hand to your joyful Bridegroom-King...

Oh, I think I see a twinkle on your radiant face, as you enter the arms of grace, and as you ride high into the split midnight sky! Beloved King Solomon has returned just as He promised. He is wearing the fragrances of sacrificial love.

Step into the chariot, royal queen. Your Chariot-Rider awaits:

*****

SONG OF SOLOMON 3:6-11
Scene Eleven: The Chariot Rider

SETTING:	Center Stage, Foreground: LOVE's home. Upon LOVE's nightstand sits a lit oil lamp and an oil vessel.
	Stage Left, Foreground: The village homes. It is night. Maidens are sleeping within their homes. The sky is aglow with a blood-red moon.
AT RISE:	LOVE and her MAIDENS are embroidering her wedding dress. One MAIDEN has fallen asleep.

NARRATOR

Love has been expecting Beloved's arrival for some time now. Only Father knows the exact date that He will send His Son. Not even Beloved knows, until the very moment His Father gives the signal, the time when Beloved is to bring His Bride home. Consequentially, Love and her bridesmaids have remained in a state of readiness. Even when Love sleeps, she keeps her lamp filled, for she is dreaming of the day her chariot rider will whisk her away.

(Stage right: Smoke rolls in as BELOVED in His horse-drawn chariot and WARRIORS enter on stallions. They shout, announcing BELOVED'S arrival, while BELOVED blows the *shofar* three times. LOVE and her MAIDENS run outside. One sleepy MAIDEN is left behind. BELOVED sweeps LOVE into His chariot and the MAIDENS join the wedding party. The entourage disappears, stage left.)

SLEEPY MAIDEN

(Awakes. Walks outside. Sees the entourage departing. Puts hand to chin, puzzled. Lifts chin and waves face, as if smelling the lingering aroma.)

⁶Who *is* this coming out of the wilderness like pillars of smoke, perfumed with myrrh and frankincense, with all the merchant's fragrant powders?

VILLAGE MAIDEN ONE

(Enters; points to stage left)

⁷Behold, it *is* Solomon's couch; *with* sixty valiant men around it, of the valiant of Israel. ⁸They all hold swords, *being* expert in war. Every man *has* his sword upon his thigh because of fear in the night.

VILLAGE MAIDEN TWO

⁹Of the wood of Lebanon, Solomon the King. ¹⁰made himself a palanquin: he made the pillars *of* silver, its support *of* gold, its seat *of* purple, its interior paved *with* love, by the daughters of Jerusalem.

THE THREE MAIDENS

(Speaking in tandem, as other MAIDENS gather)

¹¹Go forth, O daughters of Zion, and see King Solomon with the crown with which His mother crowned Him on the day of His wedding, the day of the gladness of His heart.

*****

I have a question for you, Love. You've been reading your Groom's love letter and making preparations for this face-to-face encounter of Scene Eleven. I'm sure you have a lot to say to Beloved, so why are your maidens the only ones who speak?

What's that? This departure happens quickly? That's right, it does. Paul describes your ascension as occurring *in a moment, in the twinkling of an eye, at the last trumpet* (1 Corinthians 15:52a). This portrait of the rapture happens so fast you are not even there long enough to speak to those who are left behind. As if to emphasize this, the scene is a secondhand recitation only, for you and Beloved have already vanished.

Look at the grandeur of Beloved's entrance. Suddenly, wham! The sky splits open, and the Lord of Glory charges in on His chariot, and with Him is an armed militia of sixty expert warriors. Beloved's men are toting swords. They are at the ready, holding the handles of their weapons because *fear in the night* (Song 3:8b) has gripped believers. Beloved has the authority and military power to secure your victory. He catches you into His chariot, and you ride high into the heavenly realm and are translated onto the streets of gold that are aglow with sparkling glory dust.

Oh, by the way, gentlemen readers, I need some help with the sound effects here: "bat-a-tat, pow, shireeee…" Beloved and His armed warriors return to enforce His reign here on earth. His warriors slash and batter our enemies to shreds!

And, yes, Love, you take pot shots at Satan, too, because Beloved has made you a victorious Bride. If I remember Revelation's dialogue correctly, we all mount horses once we are raptured and wed, and we fight the final battle right alongside our Beloved. With the full authority of our Husband-King, we enforce the kingdom of Heaven's reign here on Earth.

THE GROOM'S HEAVENLY LIMOUSINE

While writing this book, I shared some of these revelations with a ladies' Bible study group that was meeting in my home. When we got to the chariot ride, I wondered how I could communicate Beloved's grand entrance in a way the ladies would never forget.

I sent an email: "For our next meeting, please wear a pretty dress or gown, and come hungry." The night of the Bible Study, the ladies boarded a limousine, and we laughed all the way to the restaurant. I explained that this exquisite ride was meant to be for them a modern-day representation of the chariot ride. I don't think any of us will ever forget that evening.

What do we understand by our Groom coming to get the Bride of Christ in a chariot—our modern-day limousine? Beloved spares no expense to satisfy His beautiful queen. Your Chariot Rider is coming for you in majesty, and He places supreme value on His Bride. As soon as Father gives the okay, Beloved will come on the wings of the wind. He will burst forth into full view wearing His royal robes, driving His chariot, accompanied by His angelic host. And just think, He does this for you! You are the Bride He loves. His entrance is a glorious display to honor you! Beloved is starry-eyed in love with you!

THE BRIDE AND GROOM'S CROWNING

Let's look at the crowning: Beloved Solomon receives a crown from His *mother* (Song 3:9). In the Hebraic tradition, there was an exchange of crowns. These crowns were given to the bride and groom by their parents. The giver, Solomon's "mother," represents the Holy Spirit. As I mentioned before, this does not in any way indicate that the Holy Spirit is female. He is not. This is allegorical, as are many other things in Song of Solomon.

The Hebrew word used for "mother" is *Em*,[125] which indicates any parental figure, be it a grandmother, a mother, or any other nurturing family member. The term is used in a broad sense to represent "the family bond."[126] The Holy Spirit makes the Word real to us, edifies us, and, in this way, bonds us to Beloved. Thus, this description of Beloved receiving the crown from His mother is consistent with the Holy Spirit's function within the Godhead.

You receive a crown from the Holy Spirit also. According to Hebraic tradition, the father and

---

[125] Strong. OT #517, *em*
[126] Ibid

mother of the bride would have been part of the wedding party who traveled with the groom. Therefore, notice that your Heavenly Father and the Holy Spirit are there with you as you step into Beloved's chariot. The Holy Spirit crowns you, and this brings much *gladness* (Song 3:11) to the Godhead, and, in particular, to Beloved. They crown you with a lily headpiece. In Hebraic tradition, this lily garland represents renewal and joy. They might have so many lilies adorning this headpiece that it drapes onto your neck. You already wear the bridal crown Beloved has given you, which is very ornate, and made of coins, jewels, and silver. This crown encircles your entire face, and draped on your neck are many chains your Beloved has sent you. This lily crown drapes atop this ornate headdress.

Today, this tradition of giving the lily crown is still carried out, but it differs from ancient biblical days. The wedding couple places a lily garland crown on their mother, particularly if it is her last child who is being wed, in respect of the years the mother has spent rearing children. This tradition honors the mother's office as the nurturer, and it symbolizes joy, for the couple has successfully completed their betrothal time of separation and introspection. The lily flowers indicate a new day has come and that the bride's mother has done her job respectably.

We see the nurturing aspect of the Holy Spirit in the previous scene's dream sequence where you choose to bring Beloved to the wedding chamber of your *mother* (Song 3:4b). This is symbolic of you sharing all you are with Beloved without reservation, as you would to a mothering figure. You open your entire life to Beloved's loving examination. Your mother's chamber represents the nurturing aspect vital to your healthy relationships. Remember, in Scene Two your earthly mother rejected you outright, yet in the dream you have the perfect mother because this is symbolic of the Holy Spirit.

This wedding day is of the entire Bride of Christ. The King James renders *the day of His wedding* as *the day of His espousals* (Song 3:11b KJV). Notice there is more than one Bride, because "espousals" is plural. The emphasis throughout Song of Solomon has been the personal relationship you and Beloved have, so the point is made with this single reference to the collective body of believers, and then the dialogue reverts to you and Beloved.

Let's look at the chariot you step into.

SILVER CROSSBEAMS

The floor and sides are made from *the wood of Lebanon* (Song 3:9). Look closely because there is something beautiful portrayed here: Beloved Jesus hung on a wooden cross. The lower crossbeams of the chariot are wooden so you will remember this. Furthermore, the phrase, "of Lebanon," indicates the prayers Beloved has spoken to His Father so you would be completely forgiven and cleansed. It is on Calvary's cross that Beloved secured you as His Bride. Forgiveness was extended to you through the cross. What we see in this scene is an encoding of your Beloved as Intercessor, having the crossbeams of suffering represented as the underpinning support structure of the chariot itself.

Built into the chariot are *pillars of silver* (Song 3:10a). Without the wooden crossbeams and these supporting silver pillars, the chariot would collapse. Silver symbolizes redemption. Recognize the significance here. Beloved knows you need this support structure. Redemption houses you in this chariot like a roll cage in a racecar. Without redemption, you'd be crushed! Yet, the very strength of the chariot is based on this holy roll cage! Your sins are forgiven—past, present, and future—and Beloved's chariot is structured around redemption's wooden crossbeams that are covered with silver.

GOLD DUST FLOOR SUPPORTS

The floor of the chariot is made of gold. *He made pillars of silver, its supports of gold.* (Song 3:10a). Silver, along with gold, is what supports you as you step inside the chariot. Why? Your destination is to walk on Heaven's streets of gold, so Beloved has borrowed some of Heaven's pathway to gild the base of His chariot. Imagine this, Love—your feet will rest in the gold dust of

Heaven before you ever arrive at your destination. Glory!

The word used here means "shimmering oil of gold."[127] Thus, we can see that your feet will rest in the anointing oil of Heaven as you board the chariot. Beloved anoints your feet with holy oil and gold dust in respect for the days you walked dusty roads witnessing to a neighbor or bringing a loaf of bread to a needy person or speaking a comforting word to a struggling sinner. To men forgotten by others, you have traveled in love. Does your witness matter? Here, we see it does, and Beloved rewards you for doing so.

TAPESTRY CHARIOT LOVESEAT

The *seat* (Song 3:10)[128] of the chariot is purple. This seat is translated as a "couch."[129] This is the loveseat you and Beloved sit on. It is also called a *palanquin* (Song 3:9), which literally means "separation chair,"[130] or a *chariot* (Song 3:9 KJV), representing you are set apart with Beloved, holy unto Him. The purple color symbolizes royalty. We see an example of this in Proverbs 31:21 where the lady is clothed in silk and purple. You wear such luxuries because you are a spiritually prepared woman. No longer do you neglect your spiritual life as you initially did in Scene Two. Rather, tending to your spiritual needs has become your priority. Beloved says, "*Watch*" (Matthew 25:13a). And you do.

Look at the tapestry on the loveseat. The word, *paved* (Song 3:10b), translates as "to embroider as if with bright stones." [131] Thus, the seat is embroidered with thread that resembles sparkling jewels. I am sure even now you recall some of those heavenly encounters that will make up the artwork of this embroidery cloth. I can hear Beloved as you gallop away, saying, "Recall the time, My Love?" as He touches an embroidered remembrance.

Who has embroidered the seat? You have, sweet Queen, in tandem with the daughters of Jerusalem. Beloved built the chariot and wove the stitches, but you and *the daughters of Jerusalem* (Song 9:10b) have adorned the King's seat by your remembrances He has stitched there. You and your maidens—even the youngest believers; "daughters," no less—have fashioned this needlework loveseat in the spiritual realm. The "daughters of Jerusalem" are the Bride of Christ, collectively. The kind maidens who prepare you to meet your King are these daughters of Jerusalem. Any true believer in Jesus is a daughter of Jerusalem, including yourself. The embroidery of bright stones represents the glorious journey. Your life story is stitched one thread at a time into this bright tapestry of royal jewels by your praises, and just think, this is only a portrait of your beginning as Bride of Christ!

How have you fashioned this beautiful tapestry? As you think about Beloved, this tapestry is woven in the Heavenly realm. It is hidden from your view at the present moment; however, when Beloved returns, He will show you the love letter you sent to Him. Each beautiful thought of yours He has stitched into this loveseat. Look at the location of the tapestry. In the midst of Beloved's chariot, your love letter is displayed, dear Queen. Beloved has seated you on your very own tapestry of love, which He has placed central in His chariot.

We might think the word *love* in Song of Solomon 3:10 would translate as *ahab* which would indicate natural affection, but it is *ahabah*, which indicates godly, passionate love. Why is this so? It is my opinion that Beloved is indicating He has accepted your love letter and He has transformed it. Beloved has covered the seat of the chariot with your love expressions to honor you. He does not care that your love expressions fall short of His heavenly love; rather, He is delighted that you have made the effort to draw close. Through His perfecting action, it is as if Beloved is saying, "My Bride, I've received and displayed your love letters. I am passionate about you, and I've perfected your love

---

127 Strong. OT #2091; *zahab*; shimmering; oil; clear sky; gold
128 "covering" in KJV
129 Strong. OT #4817; *merkab*; covering; seat; saddle; chariot.
130 Strong. OT #668 *appirywon*; palanquin or chariot
131 Strong. OT #7528, *ratsaph*; to embroider as if with bright stones.

letters with My Heavenly *Ahabah*."

Beloved is like your Editor-in-Chief. He makes sure your manuscript is perfected by His divine love. Your love does not have to be perfect to please your King. Here, we see you simply give love to Him. He knows how to perfect your love expressions and make them heavenly. Your love letters may look elementary to you, but sprinkled with His divine love, they become masterpieces.

Notice the similarities Beloved's chariot has with the Ark of the Covenant described in Exodus 25:10-22. The Ark is made of shittim wood, overlaid with pure gold, and carried by the priestly army. A golden crown surrounds the ark. Within the Ark is the love letter of God, His Word. The mercy seat of God's love, located in the center of the Ark, is overshadowed by warrior cherubs who protect the holiness therein. In this mercy seat, God meets and communes with His people.

SMOKE RISING

Like pillars of smoke (Song 3:6b)[132] is also representative of the prayers of Beloved which rise to Heaven's throne where Father resides. This smoky pillar is representative of Beloved's presence, just like the smoky pillar of God's presence that directed Moses throughout his exodus. "Smoke" means "vapor."[133] Its root word means "anger."[134] What does this indicate? Beloved Solomon is the Warrior-King, whose prayers ascend heavenward, perfecting ours. He fights the battle for us, so we are able to step into His chariot victoriously. Beloved is the King of Kings. He has authority, reigns with victory, and rules with vengeance upon the wicked serpent and his cohorts.

In Revelation 8:4, we see the prayers of the saints rising as incense. Beloved receives and perfects our prayers. In the vignette, *smoke, perfumed with myrrh and frankincense, with all the merchant's fragrant powders* (Song 3:6b) are activated. The vapors your Groom is perfumed with are the fragrances of suffering and kingship. Beloved is fragranced with the priestly myrrh, and the fragrance of His crucifixion is the frankincense; He returns as the Warrior-King who is fragranced with Heaven's glory—for all the powders of the merchant adorn Him. This represents the riches of Heaven.

Let me say again, Beloved receives your prayers. He is the Warrior-King, who secures the victory for the Bride He cherishes. His prayers perfect yours, and He Himself intercedes to Father God on your behalf. What follows is the victory battle. Father heeds the united prayers of the Son and His Bride. The Holy Spirit acts as the bonding agent, making sure your prayers reach Heaven.

Dr. Bruce M. Metzger writes, "Is it too fanciful to suppose, as some have suggested, that everything in heaven halts so that the prayers of the saints may be heard?"[135] Think of that, Love. Beloved and all of Heaven hears our prayers. We are not forgotten; we are heard.

CONCLUSION

Let's review: As Beloved's Bride you have prepared for His coming. Now, He sweeps you away in this glorious chariot. It is sprinkled with glory stones, and your feet rest in shimmering gold dust oil. Its support structure—the roll cage—are the silver pillars of redemption. The bottom support structure is of wood—Calvary's wooden crossbeam of forgiveness, adorned with silver. Heaven's gold covers and makes up the support structure of the floor. The seat upon which you and Beloved sit is upholstered in the embroidered tapestry of your very own love letters, which He gladly accepts, and then perfects by His passionate and heavenly love. Glory!

There are four aspects to remember regarding your preparation for this wedding:

First, four times (Song 2:7, 3:5, 5:8, 8:4) you are advised to not break fellowship with Beloved but, instead, to remain lovesick. Beloved says, *Do not stir up, nor awaken love, till it please* (Song 2:7b).

---

[132] Song 3:6. Strong's OT#6051; *anan*; smoke, vapor.

[133] Ibid

[134] Strong. OT #6225; *ashan*; anger. Root word for OT#6051; *anan*; smoke; vapor.

[135] Metzger, Bruce Manning. *Breaking the Code: Understanding the Book of Revelation.*1993. Nashville: Abington Press. Pg. 62.

This is the most important aspect of your preparation. There are no shortcuts. Focused time with Beloved gives you the ability to enter the Holy of Holies. When we relate our sacrifice of time to Beloved's sacrifice on Calvary's cross as the payment price for our wedded bliss, things come into perspective. Beloved has already made the ultimate sacrifice; He is simply asking us to acknowledge Him. You are told to *go forth* (Song 3:11a) and to fully look at Him. In other words, you are to behold your Bridegroom as King Solomon. To behold Beloved is to worship Him! Behold Him as your King of Glory. Behold Him as your *Shelomah*—your Prince of Peace. Not only will worship help you maintain fellowship with your Beloved, it is your most powerful weapon against enemy attack.

Second, you have a *ketubah*—Beloved's written marriage covenant. Daily, your Bible is available. Read this *ketubah* regularly and purposefully. Not only are you reading your covenant when you pick up your Bible, you are reading the book Beloved authored. He is the Word of God. John says, *In the beginning was the Word, and the Word was with God, and the Word was God* (John 1:1b). It is your Beloved Jesus who *became flesh and dwelt among us* (John 1:14b). He is the Living Word.

Third, acknowledge the role of the Holy Spirit as nurturer. The Holy Spirit is willing to assist you as you press into the bosom of Beloved. The Holy Spirit brings all things to your remembrance, and He teaches you all things (see John 14:26). He teaches you how to walk and behave with Beloved. So, press into and acknowledge His role as you draw close. Press further than you think is possible, because the Holy Spirit makes the impossible attainable.

Finally, when Beloved's presence does come, rather than being satisfied with the experience, stay in this elevated state of worship. Don't step out of this relationship! Move with the heartbeat of Beloved in your tarrying times. This is how your relationship matures. Because Beloved has sent His Holy Spirit to you, there is no distance. Heaven's glory is a prayer away. Beloved has left us the Comforter, who is active and present within us to enliven our worship. Each time you come to Beloved, the Holy Spirit is there, and He usually makes His presence known. Know this also: The Holy Spirit is Beloved's Spirit.

In the next scene, we will behold Beloved King Solomon with the praises from our lips in the Holy of Holies. We will experience Beloved's holiness most intimately within the *huppah* in Scene Twelve. Prepare to encounter Jesus! Who is this Intercessor who makes us alive with heavenly love? Who is He who wears the smoke of ascending prayers mingled with the prayers of His Bride? The King of Glory, the Lord Jesus, is the One who is mighty in battle. Beloved Solomon—*Dowd-Shelomah*—is this King of Glory, and because of His divine love for you, He rides.

I invite you to lift a fragrant prayer to your magnificent Chariot Rider. Allow Him to mingle His kingly fragrances of myrrh and frankincense with your fragrant spikenard oil of desire. Enter into prayer, blessed Queen.

My Chariot Rider,

I joyfully anticipate the day of Your return, and I look forward to the chariot ride I'll experience at the rapture. Thank You, my Groom, for being my King of Glory and for securing my victory through Your sacrificial love. Thank You for being ever present. Most of all, thank You that as I sit on the mercy seat that is centrally located in Your chariot, my natural love is transformed into Your passionate and godly love.

Thank You that my fleshly nature will change further as I read about the sacred marriage bed in Your mountaintop oasis. My Beloved, because Your Holy Spirit is with me, I anticipate the glory of Your marriage bed that will be revealed to me. I know You have crowned me as queen, but I willingly lay my crown at Your feet. To You be all honor, glory, and praise! You, my sweet Lord Jesus, for truly You are my Dowd-Shelomah.

Elevated,
Love

BRIDAL REFLECTION

1) Describe how the differences between the Jewish marriage of ancient biblical times contrast

with today's bridal customs.

2) Your Bible equates today to your *ketubah* of the Jewish wedding. What is a *ketubah*? Share your favorite verse in your Bible that your Groom writes to you.

3) How does the high bridal price—the *mohar*—of Beloved, who was willing to go to Calvary to redeem you as His Bride, make you feel about the depth of love your Groom has for you?

4) Your love story is embroidered on the "tapestry seat" of Beloved's chariot. Who embroiders this seat? Share your testimony and aspects of your relationship with Beloved Jesus Christ that are most important to you.

5) What do the crossbeams of the chariot represent? Why are they made of silver? Why is the floor of the chariot covered with gold dust? Where does this gold dust originate?

6) What did Rabbi Akiba believe about Song of Solomon in relation to the Holy of Holies? What happens in the *huppah,* and how does this spiritually represent the Holy of Holies? How many days do the bride and groom spend in the *huppah*?

7) Describe how Beloved's chariot is like a limousine ride. How does this assure you He has your best interests at heart? Celebrate reading this chapter by making a fancy dinner or going out to eat. Invite friends!

Chapter Seven
Behind the Veil

A garden enclosed is my sister, my spouse.
~Song of Solomon 4:12a

Now in the place where He was crucified there was a garden, and in the garden
a new tomb in which no one had yet been laid. So there they laid Jesus.
~John 19:41-42a

Randi Fenoli, or another Kleinfield Consultant, assists the bride. We all watch, transfixed by the television broadcast, *Say Yes to the Dress*. At first, it is all about the dress. Should it be a mermaid style? Perhaps it should be a full ballgown. What embellishments should it have? The list is endless.

The scene changes as the bride considers a selection and Randy completes the look with a veil. All of a sudden, the atmosphere changes. The bride cries, as does her mother, and everyone in the bridal party pulls out tissues, even any burly men in the entourage.

Randy smiles his best as he pops the question, "Are you saying yes to the dress?" The bride agrees. Everyone hugs, and the bride nearly floats on air as she exits the boutique.

The crowning of the veil puts the bride over the top, in love with silk and lace, pearls and feathers, and the assortment of shiny things adorning her dress. She is firm in her decision, and she absolutely adores her dress.

What is it about this veil that changes the atmosphere? Perhaps when the bride is graced with a veil, her focus changes from the dress to the decision.

The veil reminds her she is making a lifelong decision to the groom. She is getting married. She is about to be a Mrs. Her thoughts are no longer on the dress—her focus is upon the one she loves.

In Scene Twelve of the vignette, you don this veil as you take a bridal stroll through the Lebanon mountain range, for the whole mountain scene experience represents your veiling as the Bride of Christ and, particularly, at the enclosed garden, for His presence comes upon you in increasing measure.

As you and your Husband-King take a bridal stroll, you come under the covering veil of Beloved's presence. This stroll represents donning the veil of Beloved's glorious splendor. The Garden of Eden and its shame are completely erased as you come into Beloved's secluded garden located at Mt. Hermon. Here, you and He experience the height of intimacy. Mt. Hermon's garden marks the culmination of your spiritual union. Spices flow, spring-fed living water effervesces, and your marriage reaches full fruitfulness. You experience divine love at its best as your Groom gifts you with multiple kisses of divine love and peace, represented by spices, a spring, and various other Spirit giftings.

Note in the dialogue that as you ascend the Lebanon mountain range on this quest to find the enclosed garden, there first is a dialogue about Mt. Gilead, Mt. Myrrh, and Frankincense Hill. If it were not for the healing Beloved offers you represented by Mt. Gilead, the priestly role your Groom takes represented by Mt. Myrrh, and the suffering servant your Groom takes upon Himself, represented by Frankincense Hill, there would be no bridal stroll. Nor would you have experienced the ultimate veiling of Beloved's presence in the garden of Mt. Hermon. Because of these three locations, this scene takes on a reverent meaning for the Christian.

From Mt. Gilead's healing waters to Mt. Hermon's secluded prayer garden, explore the intimacy that is found exclusively in Beloved Solomon—the Beloved Peacemaker, Jesus Christ.

It is my prayer that as you stroll each of these locations of the Lebanon mountain range and, particularly as you come behind the veil of the Holy of Holies in the secluded garden at Mt. Hermon, you will consider this a bridal kiss. Receive each spiritual kiss your Groom wants to impart, for with each kiss you set into motion Christ's Lordship. These are the giftings of the Bride.

Ascend, Bride of Christ. Your Husband-King's sacrificial love has made this scene possible:

*****

SONG OF SOLOMON 4:1-5:1
Scene Twelve: The Bridal Stroll Behind the Veil

SETTING:	The Mountains of Ascent in the Lebanon mountain range.
	Screen Projections: Each mountain BELOVED and LOVE visit is represented by a screen projection.
	Center Stage: Backlit veil of soft linen; Rose of Sharon lilies, white lilies, and herbs are scattered about.
	Stage Lights: Soft indigo and yellow
AT RISE:	BELOVED and LOVE wear their white lily and rose of Sharon lily garlands. LOVE leans into BELOVED's gentle embrace.

NARRATOR
Beloved and Love have begun their spiritual journey through the mountain range of Lebanon. Each location they visit represents a different aspect of their relationship. The final location is the secluded garden at Mt. Hermon, where Beloved takes Love behind the veil of the Holy of Holies.
Love begins her journey at Mt. Gilead. This mountain represents the Groom's commitment to complete His Bride and to heal her from all brokenness. He desires to heal her of every pain, no matter how deep-set it is or how long it has existed. How can Beloved exchange healing for the Bride's pain? What intimacy lies within this mountain stroll? Let's listen in to find our answers:

BELOVED
[1]Behold, you *are* fair, My love! Behold, you *are* fair! You *have* doves' eyes behind your veil. Your hair *is* like a flock of goats, going down from Mount Gilead.
> (BELOVED rests His fingers under LOVE'S chin. LOVE smiles.)

[2]Your teeth *are* like a flock of shorn *sheep*, which have come up from the washing, every one of which bears twins, and none *is* barren among them.
> (BELOVED places a finger upon LOVE'S lips.)

[3]Your lips are like a strand of scarlet, and your mouth *is* lovely.
> (BELOVED brushes His fingers up LOVE's cheek and head.)

[4]Your temples behind your veil *are* like a piece of a pomegranate.
> (BELOVED lifts one chain on LOVE'S neck.)

[5]Your neck *is* like the tower of David, built for an armory, on which hang a thousand bucklers, all shields of mighty men.
> (BELOVED draws LOVE into an embrace.)

[6]Your two breasts *are* like two fawns, twins of a gazelle, which feed among the lilies.
> (BELOVED and LOVE face each other, holding hands.)
> (Screen Projection: The mountain of myrrh [the Garden of Gethsemane] followed by the hill of frankincense [Calvary].)

(Stage Lights: Red)

NARRATOR

Love recollects the mountain of myrrh, representative of the Garden of Gethsemane, and the Hill of Frankincense, reminiscent of Calvary's Hill. In these two locations, Beloved's greatest sacrifice was given and His most important prayers were lifted up for His Bride. She is nourished now, but if not for His sacrificial gift of love, she would have been lost forever. The Bride references Mt. Bether. It is here that she received her salvation. Beloved rescued her from the shadowy lies, divisions, and schemes that plagued her life. Love has learned to lean upon her Beloved, and she is grateful for her transformed life because of Beloved's sacrificial love for her.

LOVE

(Bows before BELOVED, weeping)
⁶Until the day breaks, and the shadows flee away, I will go my way to the mountain of myrrh, and to the hill of frankincense.

BELOVED

(Kneels before LOVE; lifts her chin, palms outward-facing.)
⁷You *are* all fair, My love, and *there is* no spot in you.
(LOVE, still kneeling, kisses BELOVED'S outstretched hands.)

NARRATOR

Having purified Love by His grace, Beloved speaks of His Bride's beauty. Love has conquered Mt. Bether. How does Beloved know this? Love's acknowledgment of the mountain of myrrh and the hill of frankincense testifies that she has received her Groom's sacrificial love.
(BELOVED lifts LOVE; they walk together.)
(Screen Projection: Mt. Lebanon's snowy peaks.)
(Stage Lights: White and sky blue)

BELOVED

(Embracing LOVE; pointing upward)
⁸Come with Me from Lebanon, *My* spouse, with Me from Lebanon. Look from the top of Amana, from the top of Senir, and Hermon, from the lion's dens, from the mountains of the leopards.
(LOVE follows BELOVED.)

NARRATOR

Love has decided to ascend the high mountains with her Groom. She desires to venture forth, and so hand in hand, she strolls with her Beloved through Lebanon's mountain range.
(Screen Projection: Mt. Amana's heights.)
(Stage Lights: Purple)
(BELOVED and LOVE kneel together, praying. LOVE nods.)
Love's nod is vital. Without prayer agreement at Mt. Amana, Love would be saved but not fruitful. There is so much she is able to do because she has learned to pray in Beloved's authority and to call upon His name. Beloved's thoughts have become her own thoughts, and she yearns to know Him even more.
(Screen Projection: Mt. Senir's steep cliffs.)
(Stage Lights: Black and white Strobe Lights)
(BELOVED and LOVE look toward the valley people, hands to brow, watchful.)
Love watches the lions and leopards in their dens below, learning spiritual warfare from her

Intercessor-King. They climb, as one united couple, strategizing a victory plan for the valley people below.

>(BELOVED takes LOVE'S hand; they walk farther.)
>(Screen Projection: Mt. Hermon's high, snow-covered peaks and the prayer garden hidden within)
>(Stage Lighting: Golden glow)

Where are Beloved and Love now? They are communing in the highest mountain, Mt. Hermon. As they come into the secluded prayer garden, with its streams of living waters fed by the spring of Lebanon, they will be united in Spirit. This prayer garden represents the Holy of Holies, the blessed wedding chamber.

BELOVED

>(BELOVED embracing LOVE)

⁹You have ravished My heart, My sister, *My* spouse; you have ravished My heart with one *look* of your eyes, with one link of your necklace. ¹⁰How fair is your love, My sister, *My* spouse! How much better than wine is your love, and the scent of your perfumes than all spices!

NARRATOR

What kind of love does Beloved's Bride display in the garden at Mt. Hermon? It is God-love, my friend. The Bride has finally attained Beloved's *dowd* — His divine love — in full measure.

BELOVED

>(Touches LOVE's lips with His fingers)

¹¹Your lips, O *My* spouse, drip *as* the honeycomb: honey and milk *are* under your tongue; and the fragrance of your garments *is* like the fragrance of Lebanon.

>(BELOVED and LOVE dance, exiting behind the veil. They continue dancing, and their silhouettes remain visible.)
>(Screen Projection: Holy of Holies.)
>(Backlighting behind the veil increases until the forms are obscured)
>(Stage Overhead: Glitter snowflakes cascade above the veil)

NARRATOR

High in Mt. Hermon, tucked away from all distractions, Beloved and Love have become one united couple.

BELOVED

>(Voice only)

¹²A garden enclosed *is* My sister, *My* spouse; a spring shut up, a fountain sealed. ¹³Your plants *are* an orchard of pomegranates, with pleasant fruits, fragrant henna, with spikenard, ¹⁴spikenard and saffron; calamus and cinnamon, with all trees of frankincense, myrrh and aloes, with all the chief spices — ¹⁵A fountain of gardens, a well of living waters, and streams from Lebanon.

LOVE

>(Voice only)

¹⁶Awake, O north *wind*; and come, O south! Blow upon my garden, *that* its spices may flow out. Let my Beloved come to His garden, and eat its pleasant fruits.

NARRATOR

Love receives the compliments of her Husband-King. She acknowledges that she acquires the beauty of holiness as she rests in His embrace. She requests the dew of anointing spices from her Beloved.

BELOVED

(Voice only)

^{5:1a}I have come into My garden, My sister, *My* spouse: I have gathered My myrrh with My spice; I have eaten My honeycomb with My honey; I have drunk My wine with My milk.

(Scene projection: The Valley of Sharon.)
(Stage Lights: Green.)
(LOVE comes out from behind the veil.)

LOVE

^{5:1b}Eat, O friends! Drink, yes, drink deeply, O beloved ones!

NARRATOR

Love reminisces to her maidens about the garden experience. She is satisfied, and having been filled to overflow with anointing oils, she is prepared to minister. Beloved's kisses of peace have become to her a reality.

(Spotlight on LOVE.)
(LOVE stretches her hands upward.)
(Glitter gently cascades from above, covering LOVE.)

*****

What is happening in this scene? Beloved has come into your midst. His kisses of peace complete you as you walk with Him through the mountain range. The veil of His presence intensifies until you are completely secluded within the Holy of Holies at Mt. Hermon. There, you wear the veil in full measure as you and your Groom are united.

In Scene Eight, we discussed how you come away with Beloved and walk with Him. This bridal stroll is an expanded version of the concept of "coming away." Remember that in Hebrew to "come away" translates as two inseparable words, "*yalak,*" which means "to walk," and "*halak,*" which means "to behave." So, as you come away for this bridal stroll, you are coming for the express purpose of uniting with your Husband-King and learning His desires. In this secluded setting, as you set yourself apart, you and Beloved become united.

Beloved gifts you with aspects of His character at each location. Each spiritual gift you receive brings you peace, and you become a refined image of your Husband-King. Notice also that the veil of His presence is progressive, as is the holiness you experience. Remember, Love, you can come broken—in fact, He wants you to. His love is what perfects you. Desire for Him to draw you, and He will. You never had to earn your salvation, nor do you have to earn the veil of His presence. As was salvation, the veiled experience is a gift from your Groom. Receive each gift as a kiss from your willing Groom.

Notice that in Scene Twelve Beloved is the primary speaker. Usually it has been you, but in this scene, Beloved does all the talking until you emerge from behind the veil. He takes you into seclusion by noticing your curls behind your veiled face, and from there, He finally brings you into the secluded garden of Mt Hermon and into the Holy of Holies wedding experience.

This scene traverses the entire Lebanon Mountain Range, beginning at Mt. Gilead and concluding at Mt Hermon's enclosed garden. You receive gifts, that you can think of as being His kisses of peace, at each location:

MOUNT GILEAD (Song 4:1-5) The Gift of Healing

You begin your journey atop Mt. Gilead. The gift Beloved imparts to you is healing. This location sets the tone for your journey. Beloved has come to complete you. You are broken, and He has come to make you whole as you come behind the veil. This is the first gift Beloved imparts to you as a promise. It includes every area — physical, emotional, mental, and spiritual. As you tarry behind the veil, this promise activates.

In Beloved's opening line, He says, *You* have *doves' eyes behind your veil* (Song 4:1b). The King James translates this as, *within thy locks* (Song 4:1b KJV). Several other translations render the word "locks" as "veil."[136] What Beloved is communicating here, whether we look at this as being the bridal veil or as the hair of our head, is that both of these spiritually represent Beloved's veil of covering that He gave you during your betrothal. It is at Mount Gilead that this is first spoken because He wants to stress that you can be healed of all hurts whether they are physical, mental, emotional, or spiritual.

Remember, Love, a veil in biblical times was like the engagement ring of today. The veil announced that you belong to Beloved. The covering veil is a safe place to be. It shows that Beloved has redeemed you. Even in your brokenness, He has covered you. And so, what does He see when He looks at your beautiful eyes that are visible behind the veil? Your eyes reflect that Beloved's Spirit resides within you and that you desire Him. Your character is as the turtledove of solidarity. You gladly wear the veil, for you desire to be Beloved's. This veil becomes your most treasured possession, representing Beloved's kisses within this holy sanctuary and His resolute love for you as His cherished Bride and your budding love for Him.

Can you see why the enemy tried to keep you from ascending? As you yield to Beloved's grace, He perfects you. It never has been about performance. Beloved knows how to make His Bride perfect. By an impartation of His holy *dowd,* He makes us new. Let me stress again, we cannot accomplish this of our own accord, but we can receive this as His gift.

Your hair is made up of flowing black curls that cascade over your shoulders. These are most strikingly gorgeous and healthy. It reminds your Husband-King of the *flock of goats, going down from Mount Gilead* (Song 4:1b). This represents that Beloved's unconditional love is healing to the body, soul, and spirit. He is the soothing balm of Mt. Gilead.

In Proverbs 27:23 we read, *Be diligent to know the state of your flocks,* and *attend to your herds.* This passage continues, showing the value of livestock, including the goats mentioned here. Goats were used as collateral to obtain lands and also to supply milk and meat to the family. Therefore, the wise man tended to his flock, knowing that their healthiness mattered. Sick goats don't sell well in the marketplace! The analogy Beloved is making is that our spiritual health matters to Him. As we focus upon Him, He is able to bring us into good health. Beloved has chosen to gaze upon you, and you, likewise, have chosen to gaze upon Him.

Beloved says, *Your teeth* are *like a flock of shorn* sheep, *which have come up from the washing, every one of which bears twins, and none is barren among them* (Song 4:2). Let's discern two character traits He is showing us here. In the King James, this passage reads, *even shorn.* Think of the results of an uneven tooth. Even one misshapen tooth can cause the entire jaw to misalign. Other teeth will begin to shift and move until the whole mouth functions less than optimally, to the point that some teeth may rot from the root.

Your teeth are lined up straight! Why? Your speech is wholly and perfectly aligned with Beloved's Spirit of Truth. Beloved acknowledges your wide toothy smile. This is His way of saying that you don't miss one opportunity to speak well of Him.

Your teeth are washed and they bear twins. In other words, your speech is pure and it inspires people to praise Him with you. Think of this as a Colgate-fresh smile in the spiritual realm. You have *come up from the washing* (Song 4:2a), representing baptism, and you are cleansed from past sins.

One of my dogs is excellent at rolling in every dirty spot of the yard every time I bathe her. She rolls off the objectionable clean smell with dirt, sticks, and grass. The washed sheep in this passage have done the opposite; they have come up from the washing after having been evenly shorn,

---

136 NIV, RSV, CJB.

and they stay clean. Beloved is showing you the opposite of my muddy dog that I deal with at bath time. Relish in this spiritual cleansing you have received from Beloved. Choose to stay clean and to not return to the mudpuddle of sin.

Beloved says, *Your lips* are *like a strand of scarlet, and your mouth is lovely* (Song 4:3). The King James renders this as, *thy speech is comely* (Song 4:3 KJV). What Beloved is communicating here is that you are the loveliest when you are praising Him! What is the strand of scarlet within your lips? It is the Savior's story of sacrificial love, evident from Genesis to Revelation, which you speak about and you tell your own redemptive story as well. Are your lips kissing Beloved? In the spiritual realm, I am sure they are! Your beauty increases as you kiss the Lord of Glory with your praises and your worship! This is reminiscent of Scene One. You are, in return, kissed with unspeakable peace and your Groom's glory descends.

Beloved declares, *Behold, you* are *fair, my love! Behold, you* are *fair!* (Song 4:1a) Beloved must really want you to know this, because there is repetition here, and says this again in verse 7. Beloved has given you His Name—the Name above all names—and He erases sin from you, His Bride. In verse 7, He says, *You* are *all fair, my love* (Song 4:7). He shows you there is not one dirty spot on or within you. He has cleansed you completely. You are "all fair." You are not muddy at all. Sin has no hold on you, the Bride whom Beloved has cleansed with His divine, healing love.

Beloved says, *Your temples behind your veil* are *like a piece of pomegranate* (Song 4:3b). Temples represent your thoughts—and they are pure. Why? You remain behind the veil of covenantal love even when you are not physically there. You belong to Beloved and you think, speak, act, and behave as if Beloved is watching—and the reality is, He always is watching, even when we are unaware. Your thoughts are as nourishing as a pomegranate, which is a natural aphrodisiac. Your focus is upon Beloved regardless of your circumstances.

You have gained confidence in your identity. Beloved says, *Your neck is like the tower of David* (Song 4:4a). You hold your head high, for upon your neck are gifts of jewelry—the silver and gold of redemption and glory. These necklaces mark you as a lady who is treasured by her spouse. These are your Husband's spiritual gifts, His *mattan*. In contrast to Scene Two, where you had a crumbling watchtower that had been invaded by predators and prickly people, in this scene your watchtower resembles a tower that David would have built in his kingdom. There is not just one chain on your neck; He has gifted you with many necklaces. The armory of strength has come to you. You are alert, watchful, and diligent, and, therefore, He entrusts you with many spiritual giftings.

Your neck is strong like an armory that holds *bucklers* (Song 4:4b). You do not wear a single buckler; you wear *a thousand bucklers, all shields of* [David's] *mighty men* (Song 4:4b). These bucklers are as shields, and they represent your faith statements. They equip you to defeat the enemy's lies. These are important weapons in your armory. These shields are like a charm bracelet that remind you of important times in your life. These shields remind you of the reliance you have in the Word of God.

You have perhaps accumulated these during times of trial. These shields hang over your heart, protecting your spirit. Paul writes, *above all, take the shield of faith, with which you will be able to quench all the fiery darts of the wicked one* (Ephesians 6:16). According to Paul's statement, you need only one faith shield to quench every single fiery dart of Satan, but in this scene a thousand truth bucklers hang as an impenetrable faith shield about you. You are as powerful as David's mighty warriors. Glory!

Your breasts are like young twin gazelle fawns that are romping upon the fertile meadows of Sharon, with its white lilies—representative of purity, humility, and truth. Beloved is communicating here that you are carefree. You rest and romp in the Sharon Valley's field grasses and lily flowers like playful roes. Why are there two? You are doubly secured within the knowledge of Beloved's divine love. There is not a worry that can stay when you yield it to Beloved's piercing, yet loving glances.

How have you come into this most holy place where Beloved compliments you in this joyous stream of unending praise? Although your dialogue is sparse, this you do say as you move beyond the shadowy lies of Mt. Bether, *I will go my way to the mountain of myrrh, and to the hill of frankincense*

(Song 4:6b) By visiting these two locations, you receive the salvation Beloved offers.

MOUNT BETHER (Song 4:6) The Gift of Salvation

This scene serves as a continuation of Scene Eight where Beloved attained your victory in Mt. Bether, dissipating shadowy distortions by the light of His glory. Beloved fought for you there as you yielded to His loving examination. The gift Beloved imparts to you is soul salvation.

The vignette is a prophetic foretelling of Beloved Jesus' suffering, death, burial, and resurrection. We see this because He imparts the myrrh and the frankincense, symbols of His priestly and sacrificial roles.

Compare the dialogue of Scenes Eight and Twelve. In Scene Eight, you said, *Until the day breaks, and the shadows flee away, turn, my beloved* (Song 2:17). In Scene Twelve, you also say, *Until the day break and the shadows flee away, I will go my way to the mountain of myrrh and the hill of frankincense* (Song 4:6). So, this is an obvious remembrance of the battle Beloved fought for you and won with the light of His glory at Mt. Bether, and this is representative of Beloved's priestly and sacrificial roles of Gethsemane and Calvary.

In Scene Twelve, you have conquered Bether's division by acknowledging the significance of the mountain of myrrh and the hill of frankincense. You've conquered Mt. Bether because you made the commitment to guard your spiritual life, coming to Beloved often so He could dispel the shadowy lies with the light of His truth. Now, every time a shadowy lie comes to distort or divide, you retain the victory by submitting the thought to Beloved. You discern the truth based on His character as the suffering Savior. This reliance on Him is the foundation from which all other blessings come. This, your salvation experience, becomes the catalyst to receive daily blessings, being cleansed by His love. Let's look further at the myrrh and frankincense.

THE MOUNTAIN OF MYRRH/THE HILL OF FRANKINCENSE (Song 4:6)
The Gifts of Beloved's Priestly and Suffering Savior Roles

The mountain of myrrh prophetically represents our High Priest's suffering in the Garden of Gethsemane. Our High Priest shed sweat as drops of blood long before He was crucified on the cross of Calvary. Did this mental, physical, and spiritual anguish cause Him to turn away from us? No. Beloved chose to redeem us at Gethsemane's garden despite the high cost.

The hill of frankincense prophetically represents Beloved's sacrificial redemption upon the hill of Calvary. Beloved became the atoning sacrifice for all mankind. Sin's price was reckoned through Beloved's crucified body. Frankincense was used to sprinkle on the sacrifices as a cleansing fragrance.

The sap within myrrh and frankincense bushes produces anointing fragrances. How are these treasures unlocked? The bushes are harvested by piercing and then slashing the trunks, which then ooze precious sap over the course of time. The harvester then collects the sappy tears of the sticky substance. This process makes both resins expensive — myrrh being more precious than gold.

This is a visual representation of the suffering of Messiah. The tears of myrrh remind us of Beloved's willingness to suffer. He was pierced and slashed, and He oozed His life-substance in like fashion as these two myrrh and frankincense bushes are pierced and slashed, consequentially oozing their life substance.

Myrrh and frankincense were used in biblical times in priestly rituals (see Exodus 30:23-38). The difference in the two is that myrrh was mixed with olive oil to make holy anointing oil for the priests, and frankincense was made into a holy perfume for the priests to sprinkle on the sacrifices or to burn as incense. Thus, the myrrh is representative of Beloved's priesthood, whereas the frankincense is representative of His suffering. Therefore, Mt. Myrrh represents Gethsemane, whereas Frankincense Hill represents Calvary.

Myrrh and frankincense were also used as burial spices. The most notable use of myrrh is at the burial of Jesus (see John 19:37-42). The two friends, Joseph of Arimathea and Nicodemus, prepared a hundred pounds of myrrh to anoint the body of our Beloved Messiah as He temporarily lay dead in the tomb.

The Hebraic word for "frankincense" is *lᵉbownah*,[137] its root word meaning "whiteness" or "smoke." The peak of Lebanon's mountain is topped with white snow and mist. Thus, we see frankincense is representative of Beloved's ascending prayers and ours. Frankincense was called the "oil of Lebanon,"[138] and the highest value was set on frankincense that was silver in color. Silver is representative of redemption, so the frankincense is representative of the redemptive prayers of Beloved.

The root word for "myrrh"[139] means "bitter" or "distilling drops." It is spoken of in all four Gospels,[140] and is detailed in Luke 22:44. Our Beloved sweat drops of bloody tears because of the bitter anguish of His heart. He chose to redeem us, fully aware of redemption's cost, speaking at last, *"O My Father if this cup cannot pass away from Me, unless I drink it, Your will be done"* (Matthew 26:42). It is in the Garden of Gethsemane that Beloved Jesus wrestled for our salvation; He accepted Father's will and died in our place. He loved us that much! Father God knew all along that Beloved's Bride was worth the high price of His Son's bloody tears at Gethsemane, to be followed by the flow of blood from Calvary's cross.

The Garden of Gethsemane is located at the Mount of Olives amongst olive trees.[141] What is the significance of this? Beloved's sweaty tears mixed with the aroma of pressed olives on the garden's floor represents the priestly anointing oil of myrrh. The true High Priest is Beloved Jesus! He is the One who is fragranced with the oil of suffering.

THE BRIDE AS PRIESTESS

In Esther, the "oil of myrrh" and "sweet odors" (Esther 2:12) — perhaps frankincense being among these — were used to purify a bride. This purification process went on for twelve months. This correlates with the espousal period of most Hebraic marriages. Six months were set aside for the purification of myrrh and six months by the aroma of spices.

We know from the overview scenes that a bundle of myrrh rests in your bosom and within the marriage bed. Myrrh is among the anointing oils, fragrances, and spices that a wedded couple enjoys. What's the significance? You have entered into the priestly position with Beloved through your marriage. The oil of myrrh is your holy, purifying, priestly anointing oil. You are what is recorded in 1 Peter, *But you* are *a chosen generation, a royal priesthood, a holy nation, His own special people, that you may proclaim the praises of Him who called you out of darkness into His marvelous light; who once* were *not a people, but* are *now the people of God, who had not obtained mercy but now have obtained mercy* (1 Peter 2:9-10).

By acknowledging the myrrh, you have decided to identify with Beloved's suffering. We know the conclusion of this. We read in Philippians, *For to you it has been granted on behalf of Christ, not only to believe in Him, but also to suffer for His sake* (Philippians 1:29). You have decided that Beloved is worth persecution, or suffering, or any other path that brings Him glory.

THE GROOM'S HUMILITY

Why is the hill of frankincense not a mountain, as are the other locations? Surely, the sacrificial love of Beloved should be touted from the highest mountaintop! Because Beloved represents Jesus Christ, humility is represented here. Therefore, in Scene Twelve the hill of frankincense — Calvary's

---

137 Strong. OT #3828; frankincense; *lᵉbownah*; root word OT #3836, *laban*; white or smoke
138 "Frankincense." *Wikipedia: The Free Encyclopedia*. MediaWiki, n.d. Web. 2012. http://www.en.wikipedia.org/wiki/Frankincense
139 Strong. OT #4753, myrrh, *mor*; root word OT #4843, *marar*; distilling into drops, or bitter
140 Matthew 26:36; Mark 14:32; Luke 22:39; John 18:1
141 Matthew 26:30; Mark 14:26; Luke22:39

Hill — is depicted as a little hill. Beloved is your Humble Intercessor represented by this location.

THE TORN VEIL

At Gethsemane's Garden, where Jesus Christ chooses to redeem us, and at Calvary's Hill, where He gives His life as the love-payment for our sins, He makes the way for us. As He does so, the veil of the Temple of the Holy of Holies that separated the people from God is torn from the top to the bottom. This happens at the precise moment that Jesus shouts, *"It is finished"* (John 19:30). By giving His life, the veil of the Holy of Holies opens to us. Therefore, we can now enter into our bridal experience.

Jesus' sacrificial love pierces hearts, changing the atmosphere completely. He veils His Bride in the spiritual realm at the darkest moment in history. We needed this pardon for sin, and He made sure we could have it. There are gifts behind the veil of the Holy of Holies that our Groom secures for us that we cannot do for ourselves. He gives His life so ours can be full. Therefore, Love, receive the veil of your Groom's presence and boldly enter into the holy place behind the veil. It is His will that you do so.

MOUNT LEBANON (Song 4:8) The Mountain Experience

Let's continue our stroll. First, let's discuss the significance of Mt. Lebanon. This represents the activity that happens to us as Bride, regardless of the location, as Lebanon is a mountain range with multiple locations. What is common? Prayer is. The gift of prayer runs through the whole scene.

In Lebanon, you learn aspects of prayer. Beloved repeats the statement, *Come with me from Lebanon,* my *spouse* (Song 4:8). This repetition shows that prayer is an essential building block needed for other spiritual blessings to flow. There are various kinds of prayer, represented by the various locations within Lebanon's mountain range. Even in your salvation at Mt. Bether, you cry out to Beloved, which is a form of prayer.

As you journey upon the mountaintops of prayer, your Bridegroom kisses you with peace to assure you that He cares about the things that are of value to you. He teaches you that as you speak thoughts that match up with His desires, you have authority. You adjust your thinking whenever necessary until it aligns with the realm of eternal wisdom.

In Mt. Lebanon, you speak to Beloved with your mouth, and you believe with your heart this confession. *Leb*, in Hebrew, means "heart," and can refer to the physical or the spiritual heart of a person. Thus, in the spiritual realm, your heart is joined with Beloved's heart; your spoken desires becoming an ascending prayer of glorious proportion. The pure white snowdrifts of the mountain remind you of your purity and your yielded heart. Paul echoes this concept as he writes in Romans, *that if you confess with your mouth the Lord Jesus and believe in your heart that God has raised Him from the dead, you will be saved. For with the heart one believes unto righteousness, and with the mouth confession is made unto salvation.* (Romans 10:9-10). With the heart, we render an active belief through faith.

MOUNT AMANA (Song 4:8) The Gift of Prayer Agreement

Next, you stand atop Mt. Amana and Beloved gifts you with prayer agreement. Your heart and Beloved's dream the same dream, speak the same desire, and work the same work because you have learned to flow with the heartbeat of His Spirit. We might dub this "Agreement Mountain"! Here, opportunities open to you that you could not ever imagine. You see beyond obstacles in this high abode. United, your love becomes as your Husband-King's, because your heart is in complete agreement with His. You possess the *dowd* of your Beloved as from the pinnacle, your Beloved says, *Look from the top of Amana* (Song 4:8).

Mt. Amana[142] gets its name from the word, *amen*. *Strong's Concordance* reads, "The *amen* was an

---

[142] Strong. OT #548, *amana*; OT #549, Mt. *Amana*. Root word for both: OT #543; *amen*

affirmation of the covenant…It functions as an assertion of a person's agreement with the intent of a speech just delivered." *Amen* can mean a covenant, allowance, or portion.[143] You are in covenantal agreement with your Lord. You not only hear Beloved's speech; you take to heart His words as truth. You agree with all the intricacies that make Beloved's words of higher purpose than your own.

In short, you are granted spiritual sight to agree with the purposes of your King. In Mt. Amana, you ask in Jesus' Name. Beloved says, *"Until now you have asked nothing in My name. Ask, and you will receive, that your joy may be full"* (John 16:24b). *Dake's Annotated Reference Bible* study notes describe this covenantal agreement as "the Christian's power of attorney."[144]

MOUNT SENIR/MOUNT HERMON (Song 4:8) The Gifts of Spiritual Warfare/ Unity

From Mt. Amana, Beloved takes you to an unusual location. The Twins—Mount Senir and Mount Hermon—which are one in the same mountain. He gifts you with spiritual warfare and unity as a package deal. The name, "Mt. Senir," reminds you that with every spiritual ascent, you must be on guard for enemy attack and prepared for spiritual warfare. The name, "Mt. Hermon," reminds you that the reward for spiritual ascent is the anointing dew of your Beloved. Therefore, both names are used, even though they are the same location.

The Scripture was written so that ownership of the mountain was made clear for all generations. Moses' warriors defeated their enemies in the valley beneath this mountain. Some of the enemies were fierce giants. The war rages on, even into today. To the Israelites, the region was called Mt. Hermon, but to the enemies living in the valley it was called Mt. Senir. Thus, Beloved records the name as both Mt. Senir and Mt. Hermon, because, by whichever name this location is called, God owns the mountain!

Beloved teaches us the victory keys: spiritual warfare and spiritual unity operate at the same time. Both must be in operation simultaneously in order for us to conquer. Remember King David's pain when he committed adultery during a time of ascent and during the height of his leadership of two nations? This is the value we learn here by noting spiritual warfare fits hand in glove with spiritual ascent. We must be on guard any time we are ascending, as is described here.

The definition of "Senir" is "pointed,"[145] so we know you have reached the highest point of your journey. "Look from the top," Beloved beckons us. This is the spiritual key: We are to rise above enemy onslaught. We can conquer any foe when our focus is solely on Beloved. We can remain stable in our emotions when we take this approach. The call to come to Mt. Senir is a call to arise as a spiritual warrior. It's impossible for us to solve our problems from the valley! Only when we ascend, does Beloved gift us with viable solutions.

From Mt. Senir, Beloved shows you how to recognize the enemies' strategies before they can be carried out. Lions' and leopards' dens are beneath you, so there is not the constant onslaught of distractions and destructions. You are aware of the enemy that prowls. "Ah!" you may say, "God's plan is so simple; why didn't I know the solution before?" Only from the peak of Senir's cliff faces can we see the path of truth with clarity.

Atop Mt. Senir, victory is assured. The roar of the Lion of Judah silences the enemy's wimpy lion. The swift, decisive, life-giving action of the Leopard stops the advances of Satan's little leopards of death and destruction.

MT. HERMON

Next, you climb even farther, to Mt. Hermon. How high up are you? Mt. Hermon has the

---

[143] Strong. OT #548 fixed, allowance, portion
[144] Dake, Finis Jennings. *Dake's Annotated Reference Bible: The Holy Bible, KJV.* Laurenceville, GA: Dake Publishing, Inc., 2012. Pg. 199.
[145] Strong. OT #8149.

highest recorded peak of the Lebanon mountain range at 8,232 feet above sea level.[146] Consequentially, Mt. Hermon is covered in snow, regardless of the season. It is known as "gray-haired mountain"[147] or "mountain of snow."[148] The best descriptive name for Mt. Hermon is "the eyes of the nation,"[149] because the mountain's height gives the Israelite guards the best lookout possible.

Upon Mt. Hermon, you are covered with the heavenly dew of anointing oil. The root word for "Hermon" means "devoted."[150] Psalm 133 describes the anointing oil that flowed from Mt. Hermon and down Aaron's beard. Our unity is as mature as Aaron's, who was in the priestly office. We are anointed ministers with national impact. Another name for Mt Hermon is Mt. Zion (Sion), which always references the children of God. These are the people of God's inheritance, who will go to Heaven.

In the heights of Lebanon's mountain range, you and Beloved travel together. He guides you to Mt. Amana where you speak the *amen*—the prayer of agreement. From Mt. Senir, you attain victory over evil schemes. Simultaneously, from Mt. Hermon, Beloved's oil flows over you from head to toe like the liquid, golden anointing oil of Psalm 133 and you emulate the boiling-hot passionate *dowd* of Beloved's persona.

Could this prayer walk get any better? Yes, Love. For you are called to traverse the enclosed mountain hidden within Mt. Hermon. In the garden, your veil will be completed.

THE ENCLOSED GARDEN (Song 4:9-5:1) The Gift of Spiritual Unity

What is the spiritual kiss we, as Bride, experience within the garden enclosure high upon Mt. Hermon? It is *dowd.* Beloved ecstatically says, *You have ravished my heart, my sister,* my *spouse; you have ravished my heart with one look of your eyes, with one link of your necklace. How fair is your love* [dowd], *my sister,* my *spouse! How much better than wine is your love* [dowd], *and the scent of your perfume than all spices* (Song 4:9)! Both words for "love" in this passage both translate as the plural form of *dowd.* Within the veil of covering, secluded within the prayer garden, within in Mt Hermon's heights, your love becomes nothing less than Beloved's own holy, glorious *dowd!* Glory!

Without being united with Beloved you could not achieve this godly love. And yet, in Mt. Hermon your love becomes an expression of His heavenly *dowd.* This gives your Lover as much effervescent joy as the best wine could!

Notice the activity—you are reciting to Beloved the promises written on the shields hanging from your necklace. This brings Beloved great joy when we recite the Word of God with a passionate heart of belief.

You are a willing marriage partner. You are committed. You remember, *A bundle of myrrh is my well-beloved unto me; he shall lie all night betwixt my breasts* (Song 1:13 KJV). You value resting and remaining with Beloved in unbroken fellowship. Only to teach and to help others do you depart from your secure mountaintop retreat. Your glorious covering of curls billow in the wind of the high mountains as a song of joy resounds from your mouth. Your Beloved responds, *Behold, you are fair, my love! Behold, you are fair! You have dove's eyes within your veil* (Song 4:1). Notice the repetition. Whenever we see this, we know Beloved wants to emphasize His point, and here, He wants us to know we are made new in Him. Unblemished. Because of His divine kiss…

THE BRIDE IS SISTER-SPOUSE

Beloved's kisses of peace have come upon you in Mt. Hermon's prayer garden. Beloved says,

---

[146] https://www.en.wikipedia.org/wiki/Mount_Lebanon
[147] "Mt. Hermon." *Wikipedia: The Free Encyclopedia.* MediaWiki, n.d. Web. 2012. http://www.en.wikipedia.org/wiki/Mount_Hermon
[148] "Mt. Hermon." *Lion Tracks Q & A.* Lion Tracks, n.d. Web. 2015. http://www.bibleistrue.com/qna/pqna44.html
[149] Ibid
[150] Strong. OT #2768 *Chemown;* "abrupt;" "Mt. Hermon;" root word OT #2763 *Chormah;* devoted, Mt. Hermon.

How much better than wine is your love (Song 4:10b). The satisfying taste of wine—Beloved's life-giving blood—is portrayed within these kisses. The holy anointing ointment of myrrh and the smoke of frankincense are likewise pictured within each kiss. As a result of retreating to the enclosure, you bear the fruit of righteousness. Sanctification occurs because Beloved has become your only priority. Although you are called to minister to those in the Sharon Valley, not even ministry will divert you from these times of seclusion with Beloved. He is that important to you. You covet the anointing of His covering veil.

Beloved describes you as *my sister, my spouse* (Song 4:9) but remember that the second "my" has been added for clarity purposes only. Therefore, it could read, "my sister-spouse." I can just imagine Father and Beloved discussing how they would express the closeness of this spousal bond. "Write 'sister'" Father may have said. "How about 'spouse?'" the Son may have suggested. And in the end, the closest they could record was, "sister-spouse," knowing that even this term would only approximate the inexpressible beauty of the marriage bond.

THE CLEANSING FOUNTAIN

The root word for "bride"[151] in Hebrew indicates a completion of an action. You are complete in your Groom. *A garden enclosed is my sister, my spouse* (Song 4:12) describes you perfectly. You are the enclosed one, completed in your Husband's love. Do you remember the *mikevah*, or ritual immersion, that you went through during your courtship stage? This you did in preparation for your Spouse. Within the garden where you commune with Beloved, the waters of the Holy Spirit continue to flow as a never-ending baptismal pool of cleansing! This is amazing—in the Garden you never get filthy! Why? In Beloved's presence there is fullness of joy, peace, love, grace, and cleansing. The springs of the garden are like the healing pool of Gilead, yet they are even better because they bubble continually.

WHOSE GARDEN IS THIS?

It is worth noting whose enclosure this garden belongs to. Do you remember the chariot ride? Your tapestry love letter is embroidered on the mercy seat located in the center of the chariot. Likewise, Beloved has fashioned the garden, but the garden belongs to you, so you need to grant Him access. Beloved has given you the seeds and a fountain of living water to tend your garden with. Nonetheless, it is your choice to sow the seeds and to permit the living waters of the Holy Spirit to flow, which will cause your spiritual garden to grow. Beloved is a perfect gentleman. He is tender and gentle, so He waits, entering by invitation only. This is your "Eden." He has given you charge over it.

THE SWEETNESS OF THE BRIDAL KISS

As you call to Beloved, He awakens the garden of spices, the anointing dew of prayer, the streams of living waters, and the breeze of the Holy Spirit. Your dress becomes a fragrant fine linen garment of anointing that is as beautiful to behold as it is to smell, for Your perfumes are your Husband-King's anointing spices.

Your Bridegroom says, *Your lips, O my spouse, drip as the honeycomb: honey and milk are under your tongue; and the fragrance of your garments is like the fragrance of Lebanon* (Song 4:11). The anointing is described here as milk and honey. It is choice nourishment that Beloved has given you. Remember Scene One, where the Bride describes her experience behind the veil as the Groom's kiss? This is why we can think of each location as our Groom's kiss.

Let's look at the honey from the comb. Your lips are praising Beloved as the best honey—the very sweetest, for the best honey is enclosed. When honey is mature, worker bees seal it into the

---

[151] Strong. OT #3618, *kallah*; bride. Root word Strong. OT #3615; complete; the end of a process or action

comb. The result is that this sealed honey is protected from contaminants; therefore, it has the sweetest flavor.[152] This honey is as you are—mature, sweet, and pure—all because you have chosen to meet Beloved within your prayer garden retreat. So, this is not only a kiss, it is a sweet kiss. It is not only a sweet kiss; it is the sweetest kiss available.

This kiss is reciprocated. It is not only the Bride or Groom's kiss; it is a mutual kiss.

THE BRIDE IS AN ENCLOSED GARDEN

You are *a garden enclosed* (Song 4:12a). This garden is fertile ground because you are walled off from everything else. You are *a spring shut up, a fountain sealed* (Song 4:12b). Life bubbles refreshingly within your spirit as you tap into the Spirit! Everything that happens in this scene is within the Holy of Holies.

Perhaps you are being called to go into a place of ministry. Wait for empowerment. Enclose yourself within the prayer garden. Tarry. Only then will you be able to minister efficiently. Come often into the prayer garden enclosure so that you will remain fresh. You can accomplish nothing on your own. It is only by abiding within the veil of covering that you will receive power.

I say again—wait. Empowerment is worth the wait.

SPICES WITHIN THE BRIDE'S GARDEN

Look at the spices! There is an array of spices that you and Beloved feast on. Notice they are paired as the Communion scene was. An orchard of pomegranates is paired with pleasant fruits; fragrant henna is paired with spikenard. Spikenard is also paired with saffron. Calamus is paired with cinnamon, and the trees of frankincense are many. Myrrh is paired with aloes, and there is an abundance of other unnamed chief spices.

These spices are expensive; there are none ordinary. A brief explanation is as follows: Pomegranates speak of the purified mind. Fragrant henna speaks of a covering, like pitch or tar, as a shield for you. Spikenard is processed as anointing oil. Saffron is a flower pistil used to flavor rice, and because each flower has only four pistil stems, its harvest is laborious, thus making it more costly per ounce than gold. Sweet calamus, sweet cinnamon, and myrrh, along with other spices and olive oil, were mixed into an apothecary to consecrate priests (see Exodus 30:23-31). Thus, the spiritual significance of these three spices is that you are consecrated as a minister set apart as a royal priest unto the Lord Jesus Christ. Frankincense was used as a perfume to place upon offerings of fire.[153] It represents your willingness to identify with Beloved's sacrifice. Beloved gives Himself as a burnt offering to redeem His Bride. In turn, you give yourself as a living sacrifice (see Romans 12:1), completely dedicated to Him. Frankincense and aloes were the spices used to anoint Jesus' body at His burial (see John 19:39). The frankincense was for fragrance and the aloe for suppleness. Through these, you acknowledge His sacrificial love.

ABIDING, SPEAKING

In your garden enclosure, you invite Beloved to reign in all seasons of life. You conclude your garden experience by saying, *Awake, O north wind, and come, O south. Blow upon my garden, that its spices may flow out. Let my beloved come into his garden, and eat his pleasant fruits* (Song 4:16). Until now, we have only heard your voice when you mentioned Mt. Bether. Beloved has been the speaker. But now, you acknowledge Beloved's Lordship. How so? The mystery is encoded in the winds. Let's explore.

---

[152] Judith Long of Long Family Farm shared the information on honey bees.
[153] Exodus 30:23, Leviticus 2:1-2, 2:15-16.

ALL-SEASON BRIDE

The north winds usher in winter. It doesn't matter to you if spiritually, you have pleasant or wintery weather. What matters is that you remain faithful to Beloved. The warm wind of the south ushers in spring. This is reminiscent of your rebirth. The winter of your old life is over and gone! You are more alive with Beloved in your surrendered lifestyle than you ever were when you followed your own desires.

You welcome your Beloved's lordship, regardless of its comforts or difficulties. You are no fair-weather friend! As you invite the winds to blow upon your garden, you are choosing to follow the direction of the Spirit, whether this will cause suffering or joy. Because you cherish your Beloved King Solomon, you will praise Him in all seasons.

Never forget this: Empowerment precedes ministry. And for this, we must wait for the Groom's veiled kiss. Unless there's a calling away into the Holy of Holies, there will be sameness. Only when you come first to the high mountains of the Lebanon Mountain range can you be assured that your ministry is dynamic. Jesus Himself set the example. After His baptism, He went into seclusion. Only then did He step into public ministry. If Beloved Jesus—who is perfect in every way—needed time to be anointed by His Father, then you need time to be anointed by your Husband-King.

Out of the refreshing empowerment of the secluded garden, Beloved then shares an invitation, *Eat, O friends! drink, yes, drink deeply, O beloved ones* (Song 5:1b)! Beloved's final dialogue line of this scene expresses His passion for us to spend time in the garden retreat. He then invites you to share your veiled experience with others. Will we accept His invitation to evangelize and disciple others? This is the responsibility of the veiled Bride.

CONCLUSION

It all begins in Bether as a tenacious ascent. The Hart of the mountains sweeps you into a glorious romance! Beloved calls your name, and He dances upon the mountains of Bether. When you fall, Beloved catches you. In order to ascend the heights of Mt. Lebanon, Mt. Amana, Mt. Senir, and Mt. Hermon, the Mt. Bether experience is necessary. This, your salvation experience, precedes them all. And then, you begin your ascent into the Lebanon mountain range, and, ultimately, to the enclosed garden of Mt. Hermon representing the bridal chamber.

Your veiled experience is progressive. With each location, your veil becomes more prominent as the presence visits you. As you come into the final location, this garden is dreamy with the Lord's presence and thick, His choosing of you being obvious, and your unity reaching its culmination.

What's next in your journey? Beloved wants to teach you through a dream. This next scene will help you to determine how to remain faithful no matter the trial. Before we explore, let's pray, and remember to go off script. Beloved Jesus honors your own whispers of love:

My Dowd Shelomah,

Thank You for Lebanon's mountain range with its various locations and experiences. I love You! I desire to go with You often to Your mountaintop sanctuary. Cleanse and anoint me as I enter my secluded garden with its springs of living waters and spices that You endow it with.

Thank You for equipping me to be an effective minister of the Gospel. Thank You for being my Prayer Partner at Mt. Lebanon; my Agreement at Mt. Amana; my Warrior at Mt. Senir; and my Unity at Mt. Hermon. Awaken me as I travel the mountains often. Empower me to receive every one of Your kisses of peace as I come behind the veil in the enclosed prayer garden.

Oh, my Beloved, lest I climb Mt. Bether to wrestle with a sin, abide with me as the Hart of Peace. I lean upon You, knowing that Your grace will cleanse me from all divisive ways. Thank You for being my suffering High Priest of Gethsemane and the Savior of Calvary, as represented by the mountain of myrrh and the little hill of frankincense.

Your Bowing Queen,
Love

BRIDAL REFLECTION

1) Describe a wedding that you witnessed. How does the bridal veil of today's marriages relate to the bridal veil of the vignette? Does knowing Beloved desires an eternal marriage covenant with you, His Bride, bring you security in the strength of His love and the depth of His commitment?

2) The Lebanon Mountain Range equates to Prayer Mountain. You, as Bride, visit the seven locations therein: 1) Mt. Gilead; 2) Mt. Bether; 3) Mt. Myrrh; 4) Frankincense Hill; 5) Mt. Hermon; 6) Mt. Amana; 7) Mt. Senir/Mt Hermon. What is your favorite location?

3) Have you ever experienced a healing or miracle as Mt. Bether alludes to what was and still is available to us as Beloved's Bride? If so, share your healing/miracle testimony. Read Hebrews 13:8 from several translations of the Bible. What do you conclude?

4) Describe Mt. Amana. Why is it important to be in agreement with Beloved's Word in order to be in agreement with Him?

5) In Song 4:7, Beloved says you are "all fair," therefore beautiful to Him in spirit. Have you received His forgiveness for past, present, and future sins? How does this strengthen your relationship with Beloved Jesus Christ?

6) Describe the enclosed garden found in Mt. Hermon. What does this location equate to in the spiritual realm? (Hint: Rabbi Akiba drew the same conclusion)

7) How has your view of Beloved Solomon in the vignette, who allegorically equates to Jesus Christ, changed so far during this study? Share the ways you have experienced spiritual growth.

Chapter Eight
Night Visitors

*I sleep, but my heart is awake: it is the voice of my beloved! He knocks,
saying, 'Open for me, my sister, my love, my dove, my perfect one: for my head
is covered with dew, my locks with the drops of the night.'*
~Song of Solomon 5:2

*And being in an agony, He prayed more earnestly. Then His sweat
Became like great drops of blood falling down to the ground.*
~Luke 22:44

Ted Williams' story broke with a flurry of media attention. On January 3, 2011, Ted was panhandling at 71st Street and Hudson in Columbus, Ohio. Videographer Doral Chenowith, who knew about Ted's former career as a radio announcer, offered him a twenty-dollar bill with the condition that he would first speak in his "radio voice" while Doral recorded a video.

The video of Ted speaking in his booming bass "radio voice" became an overnight sensation, immediately receiving more than 20,000 hits, earning Ted the nickname, "The Man with the Golden Voice." As Ted recalled the incident, he said money was his motivation. "I wanted that twenty dollars," Ted said, "To a street person, twenty dollars is like a million would be to you."

Next came the transformation of Ted's outer appearance. He received a shower, a fresh shave, a new wardrobe, a trendy hairstyle, and a dental makeover. Interviews from major TV and radio stations rolled in, and job offers came fast and furious. On January 5th, a mere two days after the video went viral, Ted received invitations to perform the lead-over voice for *The Today Show* and to be interviewed on *The Early Show*. He looked great on the outside with his trendy new jackets and stylish haircut, but inwardly he was vulnerable.

A tear trickled down his cheek in one of the interviews. This revealed Ted's inner condition—he was breaking on the inside. When questioned about his fragile emotions, Ted responded honestly, "I sure could use a drink right now!" Almost as quickly as physical help was emerging, Ted was sinking into a pit of despair. He had gotten saved only a week prior to the video shoot, and he said to another interviewer, "I had prayed God would use my voice, but I really didn't think my answer would come right away." Ted needed support.

The viral video brought him into the spotlight, but it did not solve these preexisting conditions, nor the emotional issues they developed from. Ted Williams' former life had been sorted. He had plunged headlong into cocaine and alcohol use to dull the emotional pain he felt in his daily life. To pay for the narcotics and liquor, he resorted to stealing and other activities that would net a quick dollar. He did not know how to live clean or sober. Anger was his primary issue.

When the reality of Ted's need for an inner transformation did surface, which should not have surprised anyone, the media was on Ted like a hound dog on a raccoon. They published a series of unflattering articles—Ted had fought with his sister at a hotel parking lot. Ted fought again with family. After a two-week residency at Origins Recovery Center, a rehab center arranged by Dr. Phil McGraw, Ted had abruptly left after a mere twelve-day stay. Doral never came against Ted, but the media was completely at odds with him.

Here Ted was, a homeless man, still not knowing how to conquer his past issues, now feeling betrayed by the media as well. Thus, the old nemeses that had provided pseudo comfort to Ted—cocaine use and drinking—became temptations once again, and he gave into them. Ted was on a fast-paced downward spiral that was worse than what had caused his homelessness in the first place.

Because the media was so eager to report Ted's failings, he felt gut-punched by the very people who had just praised him. When Ted's personal issues surfaced, sponsors rescinded their offers, compounding Ted's feelings of worthlessness.

Over time, Ted realized he had the ultimate responsibility as to whether he would be healed or remain an addict. In February, he tried sobriety again, checking into a sober house. By March 2011, Ted was ready to take the next step, and he checked into a rehab. He worked with counselors to resolve the anger issues and he put aside cocaine and alcohol use altogether. May 14, 2012, marked Ted's one-year anniversary of being clean and sober. He recognized free will was as much a gift from God as was his unique "radio voice."

Ted's soul transformation did not happen overnight like the viral video. It is ongoing — a fact Ted readily admits. He recognizes he needs God's graces daily in order to keep him grounded. He said on a television interview, "It was mustard-seed faith that made a difference." As he spoke this, he lifted a vial of mustard seeds he now wears around his neck. "Before I had my mother's faith or my church's faith, but now I have my own faith. It takes a personal relationship with Jesus to make a difference."

Over the past ten years, Ted has continued to work to reverse the course of his life. He now gives back not only by performing on radio stations such as WWGH and with sponsors such as Kraft and Pepsi, but also by volunteering at a homeless shelter where he teaches his friends that reformation is possible when we trust God to come alongside us.

Ted has co-authored a book with Bret Witter, entitled, *A Golden Voice: How Faith, Hard Work, and Humility Brought Me from the Streets to Salvation*. He plans on hosting a reality television show managed by Scott Anthony, called, *Second Chances*.

Ted shared that even after ten years of working on his issues he occasionally struggles with forgiving, and his finances are usually "upside-down." But it is obvious that God has determined to complete the work He began in His son. As Ted yields, the blessings pour in. What Ted has learned is that lordship must be coupled with salvation. Jesus is not merely a blessing-dispenser; He is the Anointed One to whom every knee must bow.

How does Ted's transformation apply to the vignette? Our decision-making, like Ted's, starts with salvation, *For the wages of sin is death, but the gift of God is eternal life in Christ Jesus our Lord* (Romans 6:23). That's a great start, but lordship is also required if we want to live the blessed life. We are responsible for making choices. These will affect the quality of our life. We, as Ted did, must choose daily the path we are on, and do this for the remainder of our lives.

Prospering spiritually is not a one-and-done decision. Ted's fall can happen to any of us. Ted had the idyllic life — he was a radio announcer on a prestigious show. But, with Jesus Christ missing from this equation, sin and hopeless feelings crept in at the same time he was ascending in his career. We discussed the solution in Scene Two where we, as Bride, yield our struggles to Beloved at Mt. Bether.

In Scene Thirteen, and in the previous scene, you were communing in the enclosed garden of Mt. Hermon, experiencing spiritual heights you had never known. Does this spiritual intimacy continue? It does, so keep that in mind.

But first, you lose hope, just like Ted did…

In this scene, you believe Beloved has departed, perhaps forever, and you reason your personal failures are the cause. Evil watchmen posing to be ministry folk beat you, tossing your veil into the dust, trampling on this, your most cherished possession, which is representative of your marriage covenant.

You find your lady friends and say, *I charge you, O daughters of Jerusalem, if you find my beloved, that you tell him I am lovesick* (Song 5:8)*!* Did you catch that? There's an "if" in the dialogue you speak to your most trusted friends. You say, "if…" You don't say, "when…" The "if" statement shows you are feeling the same despair and hopelessness Ted felt.

Notice this is an ordinary arrow in Satan's cache. That is why this issue is addressed in Song of Solomon. Beloved wants you to be confident in your relationship and His eternal love for you, and this dream—although unpleasant—is His way of showing you the solution.

As you read Scene Thirteen, be on the lookout for the four character-traits about the Bride that remain true no matter what stage of development we are in, whether we are newly saved or a seasoned Bride. We must cling to the fragrance our Groom deposits on the Bride's fingertips. This cologne is essential in bridal transformation.

Love, you might feel like a failure, but you are not. Your breakthrough will come, just like Ted Williams' did, if you continue to press through. Ted's breakthrough came via prearranged circumstances only God could ordain, and God finished what He started in Ted. How did this happen? First, he got saved. Salvation is always the foundational stone to our relationship. Next, Ted in essence learned the four character-traits we are about to learn about in Scene Thirteen. Ted learned the steadfast love Beloved has for him. We need to know this, too, and take a break from "if" mentality. Lastly, there is a continual call to evangelize and disciple, and some of these come at inconvenient times.

I have to be honest—I've had moments of doubt where I was touting the "if" mentality and the "if" statements won. The "if" of despair crept into my heart so severely that I believed every one of the enemy's lies. Does this drill sound familiar to you? The enemy's voice sounds like this: "Why would my Beloved call me to—write, sing, parent, paint, act, run a business—if I am incapable of accomplishing this?" Your breakthrough will come through, so don't give up! Remember, Beloved's love is not performance-based. Ted simply needed to yield, and when he did, he discovered who he is as a Bride. Furthermore, just like I have a responsibility to disciple, so does Ted, and he is doing well at that. We don't have to be at a certain status to have this ministry calling. We all have it, and there is no escaping this.

This next scene begins with you as Bride saying, *I sleep, but my heart is awake* (Song 5:2a). Thus, you are sleeping; but your spirit remains open to Beloved's communication. In the first dream of Scene Ten, you as Bride learned this—that even in sleep we must yield, and even our subconscious must be yielded. In this first dream, we learned to choose the narrow path that leads to eternal life.

The added factors in this dream scene are the four character-statements Beloved imparts. Tuck these into your spiritual armor bag so you can silence the enemy the next time he tries to sow despair. Equally important are the fragrance Beloved is wearing and the knocking.

Enter into Scene Thirteen, Love:

*****

SONG OF SOLOMON 5:2-5:9
Scene Thirteen—Night Visitors

SETTING:	Stage Right: The door to LOVE'S home is wide open. LOVE is dressed in her nightclothes, sobbing on her bed. Stage Left: Streamers of linen dangle from the ceiling, moving slightly from the air.
AT RISE:	Stage Right: LOVE covers her face, sobbing. The MAIDENS comfort her as she recalls a terrible dream. Stage Left: MIMES wearing white painted faces, white gloves, and black leotards, dance through the streamers, miming LOVE'S dream recitation. LIGHTING: Stage Right; soft pale-yellow moonbeam spotlight. Stage Left: Indigo blue and purple spotlights.

(Loud knocking; modest knocking; faint knocking; knocking stops)

NARRATOR

Love is recounting a dream to her maidens. The clue Beloved gives her is hidden in the sound of His arrival, the scent of His cologne, and how His "My"-statements contradict her "if"-statements of doubt.

(Knocking resumes...)

Knock, knock! Who's there?

And why is Someone knocking in the dead of night? If it is Beloved, why are His knockings so urgent? Could it be He can determine timing and spiritual factors Love cannot?

Will Love attune herself to the Groom's knockings? These are signaling her to go with Him to minister. Whether His calling is at a convenient time or perceived as a disruption, Beloved knows best. Let's listen in as Love describes the dream to her maidens...

(Knocking gradually fades)

LOVE

[2]I sleep, but my heart is awake: *it is* the voice of my Beloved! He knocks, *saying*, "Open for Me, My sister, My love, My dove, My perfect one: for My head is covered with dew, My locks with the drops of the night.

(The MAIDENS comfort LOVE; she continues her recitation.)

[3]I have taken off my robe; how can I put it on *again*? I have washed my feet; how can I defile them?

NARRATOR

Why did Love not respond to Beloved? Her excuse is that she was already bathed and settled for a night's rest. But then, she smelled the oils of His cologne...

LOVE

(Rising; hand on belly)

[4]My Beloved put in His hand by the latch *of the door*, and my heart yearned for Him.

(Shows the MAIDENS her fingers)

[5]I arose up to open for my Beloved; and my hands dripped *with* myrrh, my fingers with liquid myrrh, on the handles of the lock.

(Opens the door)

[6]I opened for my Beloved; but my Beloved had turned away, *and* was gone; my heart leaped up when He spoke: I sought Him, but I could not find Him; I called Him, but he gave me no answer.

(LOVE recoils, frightened. The MAIDENS lean in.)

[7]The watchmen who went about the city found me. They struck me, they wounded me; the keepers of the walls took my veil away from me.

NARRATOR

In the dream, everything the queen holds dear has been stripped away. It appears she is no longer Beloved's wife because the evil watchmen have snatched her veil, trampled it, and stolen it away, whilst injuring her in the ruckus. The veil that represents her marriage is... gone? Or is it? What is oozing from the latchet of Love's locked door?

(LOVE, still sobbing, rises. She touches the door. Myrrh oozes from the lock.)

(Spotlight on myrrh)

As Love touches the latchet hole, real oil of myrrh drips onto her fingers! Did Beloved really visit her during the night, or was this a dream? Love is remorseful! Is it too late to answer Beloved's call?

(LOVE drops to her knees, opens her palms, and shows the MAIDENS her myrrh-laden fingers.)

LOVE

[8]I charge you, O daughters of Jerusalem, if you find my Beloved, that you tell Him, I *am* lovesick!

NARRATOR

Love must find Beloved! One maiden asks her a pragmatic question, knowing introspection will guide her to His current location.

MAIDEN ONE

[9]What *is* your Beloved more than *another* beloved, O fairest among women? What *is* your Beloved more than *another* beloved, that you so charge us?

NARRATOR

Love holds her myrrh-drenched fingers to her nose as she ponders how she will answer. The myrrh reminds her the King's greatest attribute is self-sacrificing love.
(LOVE rises, hand to chin)
How can Love describe Beloved? All the words of a lifetime would not adequately portray how wonderful He is. She fears she has lost Him forever!
(Spotlight on veil lying in a chair; LOVE picks it up. The MAIDENS bow respectfully.)
As the sun begins to rise, Love presses her tear-streaked face into her veil. She realizes it was just a dream after all, for she still has her veil. And yet, Beloved must have visited her in the night by this dream because He left her the gift of myrrh. This dream was His way of saying, "Even in the inconvenient times, you must watch for My return." Love now knows she must awaken to the voice of her Beloved at all times and in all seasons, even if it is the midnight hour.
(LOVE kisses the veil, hugging it eagerly)
Love kisses her veil and reminisces about her wedding day and the kisses of peace Beloved bestowed upon her while she was enclosed within the Holy of Holies. This sacred chamber of Scene One is the pivotal event to which all other experiences are compared. It is in the wedding chamber that the Bride experienced her Beloved's divine love, His *dowd*, as her own possession. Now, Love's fingertips again drip with His myrrh. She will dress and address her maidens.

*****

What is happening in this dream? Decisions loom, and the night is full of visitors. There are evil "watchmen" disguised as guards, but in actuality, they are invaders waiting to destroy the Bride. Will you escape their blows? It seems you are back at the beginning, wrestling on the mountain of Bether.

You keep hearing this incessant knocking! You try to sleep, but you cannot.

A fragrance permeates the room. Oil that drips from the inner hole of the door to your home catches your attention. You rise and touch the lock. Myrrh drips onto your fingertips. Your hands are coated with the same cologne Beloved wears! You recognize it was Beloved who came for you! You open the lock and find He is no longer there.

Just like Scene Two, where you saw the Shepherd's footprint and staff prints amongst the sand, you realize you have again neglected Beloved's request for fellowship. You weep. Will you find your Love once again? You search outside. The evil invaders reach for you! You wrestle with them and they strike you, throwing you to the ground. They steal your veil!

"Beloved! Where are You?" you cry. But you think your cry is futile. Doubt plagues you.

THE "IF" STATEMENT

When the maidens visit, you share the dream and touch the myrrh-laden door latch. You say,

If you find my beloved, …you tell him I am lovesick (Song 5:8b)! This is the "if" statement that wreaks havoc in your emotions. You reason that Beloved is gone forever. Have you digressed so far that His grace cannot rescue you? The answer is emphatically, "No!" Beloved's love is constant. That is why He has graced the door with the myrrh. If you had gone too far into sin, you would not be wondering if you had.

You bury your face in your hands. As you do so, the fragrance of myrrh wafts to your nose, reminding you of Beloved's everlasting love. You wonder if Beloved left His cologne on the door handle so you would know where to find Him. It is a clue. Beloved is using your dream language as a discovery tool to help you to discern His character and yours.

Beloved is also emphasizing by the myrrh residue how important your partnership with Him is. You have a ministry role to fulfill. But you must submit to His timing and His Lordship. Because of this, He states four characteristics of you as Bride that are always true. We find these in Song 5:2b. These bridal titles chase away the "if" statement of doubt. We will discuss these at length, but first, let's learn about the setting and how Beloved overcomes even the darkest night. There are five reasons Beloved comes late at night. Let's look at them:

INCONVENIENCE

First, night represents inconvenience. We must be willing to respond to Him with only a moment's notice. Beloved's timing cannot be too late or too early. He sees the total picture; we only see it when we are communing in the Garden of Mt. Hermon. We must trust Him for guidance and so He can help us avoid hidden pitfalls.

TROUBLE

Second, night represents a season of trouble. Beloved guards us when we are attuned to His voice. But often, we are asleep. In this dream you are asleep and awake, so this shows partial commitment. Remember, when Abraham was called, he learned God required total obedience. Beloved is calling us to be spiritually awake at all times. The enemy lurks, plotting the inconvenient moments and studying the vulnerability of the Bride. If Beloved wakens us, He may be doing so in order to prepare us to preempt the enemy's attack.

REMAIN ALERT

Third, we see this concept of remaining alert when we compare Beloved's Gethsemane prayer to what is happening in this scene. Jesus asks the disciples to stay awake while He prays, yet they kept falling asleep (see Mark 14:37-41). Had they prayed when Beloved beckoned them to do so, they could have prepared for the troubling days ahead (see Matthew 26:31-56, Mark 14:27-50). This is our job too. At all times, even when we are sleeping, we must be spiritually attuned. Beloved was taken from the garden of Gethsemane at night. This scene serves as a prophetic foretelling of this event. He remained alert so He was ready, whereas His disciples slept.

BELOVED'S LORDSHIP

Fourth, dreams represent our subconscious, so just as in the first dream of Scene Ten, where we recognized we must yield our subconscious thoughts, this is still true in this dream of Scene Thirteen. Every portion of our being—flesh, soul, and spirit—must be yielded to Beloved's inspection. The body is vulnerable to temptation and emotions lie, but our spirit can be attuned to Beloved's loving voice. He guides us rightly. He is Lord, and we must respect that at all times. The enemy picks a fight when we are most vulnerable. The solution is to remain under Beloved's lordship at all times.

THE BRIDE AS AMBASSADOR

The final concept, expectedly, is that of evangelism. Could it be that someone, like Ted

Williams, has come to a point of decision, and Beloved is calling us to sacrifice our own comfort in order to beautify the life of a friend? Beloved knows the urgency with which this wounded soul needs a response. Just as Beloved calls the Bride to draw away into the mountaintop retreat at certain times, Beloved also calls her to minister in the valleys at specific times. As I write this, I am rearranging my schedule to take a lady friend I have been ministering to for over a year to a church near her home. No amount of inconvenience could stop me from doing this; I am delighted she is showing readiness.

We love the times Beloved calls us to retreat and be filled at Mt. Hermon's secluded garden, but are we equally excited when Beloved calls us to the streets to minister to a homeless man like Ted Williams who was addicted to cocaine? The friends who helped him had persevered, even when Ted didn't think he needed their guidance.

Let's face it—ministry is messy. But the Ted Williamses of the world are just as valuable as we are, and if we honestly look back, we must acknowledge our story is messy too. Perhaps what we needed to overcome was different than what Ted overcame, but we had a need Beloved met through someone who answered Beloved's call to minister. We, too, are called to be the Bride who partners in soul transformation.

THE GROOM'S KNOCKING

Remember the shadow game we struggled with at Mt. Bether? Truth came when Beloved's anointing shone on the shadowy lies. Beloved says, *"I have come as a light into the world, that whoever believes in Me should not abide in darkness"* (John 12:46). Beloved turned our season of shadowy distortions into glorious light.

As His representative, we can help a friend who is in a night season conquer their Mt. Bether. This is what the media missed when they came against Ted. We are there to help rather than to criticize. That's what people of light are called to do. Some, like Dr. Phil McGraw, offered real help.

Our spiritual vineyard was once as neglected as Ted's. But then, someone pointed us in a specific direction where we could find our identity in the King. These are "maidens" in the vignette. Furthermore, "shepherds" taught us. They even pastured our "kids" as they grounded us in the truth of God's Word. Were these times always convenient? No, but their hands dripped with the same myrrh that Beloved has graced your fingertips with, and so, they came, and our answer also must be to answer the call.

When we visit the enclosed garden, it is not only for personal gain—it is equally an equipping for this ministry calling. Beloved calls us to minister from the overflow of anointing that He blesses us with during our garden visits. In Scene Thirteen, you are so in love with Beloved that even while you sleep, you are attuned to His Spirit. This is the reason you hear the persistent knocking.

Beloved's calling on the Bride will not lift. Even when He departs, He leaves the cologne as a clue so we can reunite and resume our calling to minister alongside Him.

PROPHETIC FORETELLING

Let's look at how prophecy fits into this night visitation.

Remember, one element the night season represents is trouble looming. Evil is lurking. Its shadowy presence is hidden in the night. It is like a coward, afraid of the light of truth that can expose it.

This night scene reminds us Beloved Jesus wrestled in the courts during the night. Why? Had the leaders tried this trickery during the daytime, the crowds would have resisted. Beloved was spat upon, mocked, beaten, whipped, and crucified—and each of these events happened at night. Even as the cock crowed, signifying the dawning of a new day, Beloved suffered willingly so we could have freedom from oppression and life instead of death, which was the rightful penalty of sins.

The Dake's Bible points out that according to the Talmud, criminal proceedings could not legally be conducted during the night.[154] It was an anomaly that Jesus' persecutors came during the night. In the vignette, Beloved's brow is drenched with drops of dew of the night; this is a prophetic foretelling of the events above where He secured life for us by giving His own.

THE GROOM'S NIGHT SONG

Beloved has covenantal love for every believer, especially for the lost, and His love spans all seasons. Psalm 42:8a says, *The LORD will command His lovingkindness in the daytime, and in the night His song* shall *be with me.* When we call out to Beloved, especially in our night seasons, He runs to our rescue. Beloved does not leave us stranded and helpless; He has an urgency to minister. And so must we.

Imagine what music should accompany this vignette scene. Is it a dirge? Is it melancholy? Perhaps it is a violin twining… Permit yourself to go off script here. What is the Lord revealing to you about this melody?

THE BRIDE'S VEIL

Your veil represent solidarity. You are fastened to Beloved by His kisses under this covering veil, representative of the wedding chamber of the Holy of Holies. During the betrothal period, you don the veil, and Beloved's glory hems you in. He wants you to remember that it is only from behind this veil that He equips you. Beloved's locks represent that He alone is your life source. Your veil, or locks, are only life-giving if you abide in Him. This is why He pleads with you. You are exclusively Beloved's. Recognize this, Love.

THE BRIDE'S DOOR LATCHET

In biblical times, homes had a hole instead of a doorknob. The door lock was located on the inside beneath this hole. Beloved leaves the oil of myrrh on the hole of the door, which drips onto the inner lock and onto your fingertips. His hands drip with myrrh in this scene, emphasizing your Husband's priestly role, and yours. The anointing oil Beloved has graced your fingers with is your Groom's invitation to participate in this world-reaching ministry.

Beloved does not open the door. It is locked, and He respects that. We learn here that He does not force His will on us. He has great love not only for us but also for others. He implores us to answer His plea to minister alongside Him, but the choice is ours. This is reminiscent of Revelation 3:20, where Beloved knocks on the door of the believer's heart, desiring to sup with her and make her an overcomer and a Bride, but respecting her choices. Only she can open the door, for her gentleman Bridegroom will not force entry.

THE GROOM'S MYRRH-DRENCHED HANDS, CROWN, AND CURLS

In order to understand how majestic our Groom is, let's look at the anointing oil of our Groom and how and where this appears. The fragrant oil of myrrh not only drips from our Savior's hands—it also drips from His brow and cascades down each one of His dark black curls.

THE GROOM AS HIGH PRIEST

Beloved is the anointed High Priest and Messiah in this dream scene. Had He mentioned that His head was dripping with frankincense, we would have focused on His role as the Suffering Servant. But we focus on His priestly role because of the myrrh reference, even though we know frankincense is present. Envision Beloved's myrrh-drenched curls, and look upon His brow, envisioning also His dew-kissed crown. This will help us to choose what

---

[154] *Dake's Annotated Reference Bible*; p. 203, footnote K.

is best—to minister alongside our High Priest.

THE GROOM'S DEW

Let's look further at Beloved's myrrh-drenched brow. The New King James renders the phrase, *"For my head is covered with dew"* (Song 5:2a). The King James renders it, *for my head is filled with dew* (Song 5:2 KJV). This gives us insight as to what is going on here. Beloved's anointing is more pronounced than what we see in Psalm 133 where the anointing comes upon Aaron. Not only does this dew come upon Beloved, His curls are drenched from the inner flow emanating from within His person. Could this be so? Can each curl be filled with dew, within and without? Yes. Further study of this passage shows the curls are ductal, so each curl has an inner channel that holds the anointing oil.

Let's define the word, "dew." The dew on Beloved's brow comes from a root word that means a "covering," "to strew over" as one would do to protect tender vegetation, or an "overshadowing."[155] This is what Beloved does; He covers and protects you. Beloved secured this for you on Mt. Hermon. Otherwise, you would be vulnerable to enemy attack. He is showing you that remaining united is important.

WIFE, HUSBAND, LIFE

Your fingers drip with myrrh because He needs you to know you are called but also to know that ministry is costly. Your curls, or locks, represent the veil of covering as Beloved's wife; however, Beloved's myrrh-drenched locks have an additional meaning.

Not only is Beloved your Husband, He is the source of life. The root word for "locks" means, "to spring forth," "to bud," or "to sprout."[156] Thus, Beloved's locks represent resurrection life. This is a foretelling of His resurrection and ascension.

THE GROOM'S HEALING FLOW

Myrrh drips from His curls to represent healing. The word "drops"[157] comes from a root word that means "to pulverize" or "to temper." What we see here is that the drops on Beloved's locks represent something that is broken. Beloved has "pulverized;" every obstacle is removed by His broken body, which He has willingly laid down for mankind's redemption.

FORGIVENESS FROM THE GROOM

It was in the Garden of Gethsemane, where Beloved chose obedience to Father's will and Beloved's myrrh-drenched curls spoke forgiveness. As an act of His will, He chose to accept Father's ministry calling, even though it cost Him His life.

Was this inconvenient? You bet it was! But the sweaty blood that oozed from His skin at that prayer garden spoke of His commitment to suffer. Beloved loves you, and myrrh is the fragrance that shows His love best.

He could have said, "No!" because He had free will just like we do. But His answer was emphatically, "Yes, Daddy, I will go and redeem My Bride. I love her and will willingly die for her so that her redemption story can be written." His Bride needed forgiveness, so our High Priest chose the tough "yes," despite its consequences.

THE LOVE APOTHACARY OF THE GROOM

Frankincense and myrrh were mixed into the anointing oil to fragrance the burnt offering sacrifices. The oil would burn while the fragrance remained in the air. Beloved was totally spent on

---

[155] Strong. OT #2919 *tal*; Root word OT #2926 *talal*
[156] Strong. OT # 6779, *tsamach*.
[157] Strong. OT #7447, *raciyc*; ruin, dew drop, breach. From OT #7450, *raca*; to temper. See Matthew 5:22 for Jesus' warning about anger. It could result in serious consequences.

127

Calvary's cross. His body died there. This is what Frankincense Hill represents. Beloved conquered death, but first, He became this burnt offering to redeem us.

Thus, the myrrh that drips from His brow represents this act of sacrificial love that He knows He will do next. The myrrh and frankincense were used not only as the priestly oil of anointing and of sacrifices but also as embalming oil. Thus, Beloved's fragrance is a prophetic foretelling of the death, burial, and resurrection of the Lord Jesus Christ.

PIERCING/SLASHING OF THE GROOM

Do you remember how both the myrrh and frankincense are processed? It is through piercing and slashing into the bushes that these precious ointments flow. A cruel, multi-strapped whip, which was embedded with projectiles that would slash and cut the flesh of the victim, was used on Beloved before He hung from the cross. Each piercing of His hands, brow, feet, and side, as well as each stripe upon His body, said, "I love you, Bride!" He knew that the only way to release the anointing oil of myrrh into the spiritual realm as He positioned Himself as High Priest was to be willing to be this spent offering for you and for me. So, although He emphasizes the myrrh so we as Bride know our position to minister alongside Him, the High Priest and Suffering Servant were a package deal. He could not serve as High Priest without also being the Suffering Servant.

THE BRIDE'S ROLE

Now that we have an appreciation of Beloved's character, it is time to look at what He says about our position as His Bride. Who are we? Beloved alone has made us worthy by four character-traits He mentions. Beloved does not criticize you as His Bride in the opening lines or anywhere in the scene. In fact, He pleads with you based on your godly character. You say, "*It is* the voice of my beloved! He knocks, *saying,* Open for me, my sister, my love, my dove, my perfect one" (Song 5:2). Let's examine His statement:

WHY FOUR?

Remember Pastor Troy Brewer's thoughts on this? He states the number four represents worldly systems versus godly systems. He writes in his book *Numbers That Preach,* "Four is the number God stamps on things that represent His work in creation in the positive. In the negative it represents worldliness and worldly systems."[158] We can conclude Beloved is showing us the godliness and newness we possess as His Bride.

No matter what lie Satan tries to whisper, you are godly and you are the new creation Paul speaks of in 2 Corinthians 5:17, *Therefore, if anyone is in Christ, he is a new creation; old things have passed away; behold, all things have become new.*

MY SISTER

Beloved first shows you the closeness of your relationship. You are as dear to Him as a "sister" for He is your Kinsman-Redeemer. You are of equal family status. Had He said, "my daughter," this would have indicated a lesser status. But Beloved shows you that He loves you as closely as a sister and, thus, as an equal.

MY LOVE

Beloved's second statement is a continuation of the first. He says, "my love." He wants you to recognize you have become so close that you are more than a sister could be because you are His wife. Beloved called you "sister-spouse" in the marriage bed scene. Here, Beloved shows you that your very name means "spouse."

---

[158] Brewer, Troy. *Numbers that Preach.* Pg. 55.

The word used here for your name, "Love," is *rayah*,[159] and it means "marriage partner" or "wife." Therefore, your Beloved Husband is fully trusting you to participate equally in every aspect of ministry. Each time He speaks your name, this reminds you of your position as His wife. You consequently have your Beloved's authority.

MY DOVE

Beloved's third statement reminds you His Holy Spirit resides within your own spirit. You are a reflection of the Lord of glory, and people are attracted to the Spirit they see working within you. Beloved's ideas are your ideas; His love is your love. You are in tune with Beloved's Spirit. He sees you from the perspective of completion, and He knows you will return because He Himself is working His holiness within your spirit.

The "dove" represented here is the "rock dove" that abides in the heights. This is the dove that has silver wings and a gold and purple crown at the nape of her neck. This indicates your Beloved has graced your journey with the silver of redemption and He has crowned your head and neck with spiritual giftings from Heaven.

Beloved's statement reminds you that even on your worst days your Husband-King will see you through. It also is a reminder of His Lordship. You are not your own person. Paul records your identity, *Or do you not know that your body is the temple of the Holy Spirit,* who is *in you, whom you have from God, and you are not your own? For you were bought with a price; therefore glorify God in your body, and in your spirit, which are God's* (1 Corinthians 6:19-20).

MY PERFECT ONE

Beloved calls you *my perfect one* (Song 5:2b). The King James renders this, *my undefiled* (Song 5:2b KJV). This fourth statement reminds you that no matter how much you have messed up you are completely forgiven. Beloved has purchased your new life.

You are not defined by your mistakes; instead, Beloved defines you by your potential. You are spotless! Your past sins are forgiven, and your present and future sins are too. Why? To Beloved, forgiveness is an ongoing status and is attained through repentance.

We don't need to hold on to past failures. Beloved doesn't, so neither should we. John writes, *If we confess our sins, he is faithful and just to forgive us our sins, and to cleanse us from all unrighteousness* (1 John 1:9).

Remember Scene Three, where the maidens weave gold and silver and jewels into our hair. The silver is a sign of redemption. It is built into who we are as Bride. He loves us at all times and in all seasons. He loves us when our spirit is healthy, but He also loves us when our spirit is faltering. His love is constant, and it's not performance based. As we receive Him, He works His perfection within us.

Think of the principle expressed in this fourth plea. Beloved is continually preparing us for a future we do not see. He does see everything that lies ahead; there are no surprises for Him, so He can help us to avoid every pitfall. But, even when we do stumble, our majestic Groom knows that, still loves us, and picks us up. As soon as we reach for Him, we are cleansed and our ministry is restored.

BELOVED'S LOCATION

Where is Beloved? He is either at the mountaintop oasis blessing other Brides, or He is in Sharon's Valley harvesting souls. The myrrh-drenched curls identifying Beloved as the Anointed One who is ready to minister show you it is the latter. He has not rejected His Bride; however, He must fulfill His calling with or without our participation.

---

[159] Strong. OT #7474, *rayah*

THE BRIDE'S COAT

Now, we come to the error. It is my blunder too. In the vignette, we, as the Bride, have been unwilling to put on our coat, and we have been unwilling to dirty our washed feet to rise for our Groom. This is temporary, because we do answer the door, but not quickly enough because Beloved has an urgency to harvest spiritual fruit the moment it is ripening. So, although He wants us to share in His soul-saving ministry, His priority is in getting the job done at the precise season, before it's too late.

When Beloved comes to us, do we sleep rather than answering His call? Do we prioritize communing with the King, guarding those times we have scheduled to fellowship with Him? If we will see Beloved for Who He is—as royalty—then we will prioritize our Daily Planners accordingly. I've got to be honest. I've done this. I am guilty! Especially when He comes unexpectedly, I don't always answer quickly. I admit, I sometimes choose convenience rather than an urgent ministry need.

Compound this with the fact that Satan cloaks himself in urgent, seemingly important issues that are really distractions we need to avoid. It takes discernment to know when this is the calling of Beloved and when it is not.

THE EXCUSE

You make an excuse, saying, *I have taken off my robe; how shall I put it on* again (Song 5:3a)? The solution to this is to never take the ministry clothing off! When the Bride is envisioned in Mt. Hermon's garden retreat, does she have her robe off? The answer appears to be "yes," since it's the marriage bed scene, but the answer is "no."

Let's see why the excuse to shed the robe doesn't hold water:

The word, "robe" or, "coat" in the King James, [160] comes from a root word that means, "to cover." It is more aptly rendered as an "undergarment," for it refers to the garment worn closest to the skin. Beloved gives you this beautiful inner robe as your covering, so, when you say, *I have taken off my robe* (Song 5:3a), it is applicable to saying, "I've set aside my anointing." We are called to keep the anointing at all times.

Look at what Beloved says, *How fair is your love, my sister,* my *spouse… and the fragrance of your garments* is *like the fragrance of Lebanon* (Song 4:10a, 11b). This set-aside time where the Bride ravishes Beloved with one look of her eyes, and where her love becomes as Beloved's holy love—His *dowd*—is where our ministry coat becomes sparkling with Heaven's glory.

We are to stay in a perpetual state of prayer and to permit His anointing to remain upon us even in our sleep. We are never, ever to leave Beloved's side. But, Love, we all do, and it is in these times that He rescues us. This is the reason for the dream—that you will know He still loves you, and you are still called to minister by His side.

FORMULA FOR VICTORIOUS LIVING

This brings us back to the first line of Scene Thirteen, where you say, *I sleep but my heart is awake* (Song 5:2a). From this one line, we know you will gain victory over sin because you desire Him—although imperfectly—and so He can perfect you. You are the anointed, glorious, spotless, robed ministry partner your Husband-King desires.

In Revelation, John shares what our robes look like, *And the armies in heaven, clothed in fine linen, white and clean, followed Him on white horses* (Revelation 19:14).

How do we effectively clothe ourselves with the love of God? At our set aside tarrying times, and at any time Beloved calls us, we must choose to give Him our full attention. Tarrying must be purposeful and focused. It is best not to break fellowship for even a moment. Take the phone off the

---

[160] Strong. OT #3801; *kᵉthoneth*; coat. Root word. OT #3802, *katheth*; clothe; the shoulder cover. From OT #3803; *kathar*; enclose, crown, compass. The coat was a knee length tunic.

hook, shut the door to your prayer room or garden, and give Beloved the attention He deserves. Then, He will be able to effectively clothe you with ministry robes. This is the winning formula that brings victorious living.

THE BRIDE'S FEET

Our next excuse is that we don't feel like getting our feet dirty. You say, *I have washed my feet; how can I defile them?* (Song 5:3b) Ministry is messy. We need to accept this.

When we recognize Beloved's willingness to meet us at our point of need, it becomes easier for us to do the same for others. Beloved searched for us when we, His Bride, were *dark, but lovely* (Song 1:5). The daughters of Jerusalem also met us there and tended to our many needs.

RECENTERING OF THE BRIDE

How do we minister and not resent the messiness of the process? The key here is to go into the world, anointed. Otherwise, we are either impatient or vulnerable to the enticements the world may present.

The re-equipping of the Bride is not accomplished by us proving our worth; rather, by acknowledging Beloved's worth as we, through focused worship times, re-center our thoughts. This is how we become whole.

This is why taking periodic spiritual retreats are effective tools in shepherding the anointing that Beloved imparts to us. This may include taking time to read Beloved's Word, resting in His love, receiving Communion. This, Bride of Christ, should be the norm, and we also should daily meet with Him for refreshing periods of prayer and Bible reading, along with meeting at our church at least weekly. This may seem like a lot, but if we want to stay out of Satan's grasp and be filled instead with Beloved's anointing, it is advice worth heeding.

CONCLUSION

So that you'll enjoy the praise of your Redeemer-King in this next scene, know ahead of time that you are wearing your jeweled veil as you complete this sweet discourse. There is no earning back of Beloved's grace because He has never taken it from you! He loves you, His Queen, always, at all times, and even during your night seasons.

Worship your Husband-King. Your High Priest's hands, crown, and curls drip with the anointing oil of myrrh. This oil drips for you, equipping you, for you are Beloved's forgiven, redeemed, and cleansed Bride now and forever.

Decisions… I know you've decided, as have I, to give Beloved my wholehearted devotion, especially in the inopportune moments. Let's pray:

My High Priest,

I repent of the times I've been casual with our relationship and the ministry callings You have on my life. As Your anointed Bride whose fingertips drip with the priestly oil of myrrh, send me to minister to the "Ted Williamses" of the world during their seasons of need. Help me to answer Your pleadings without delay, for there are seasons of fruitfulness in others I must respond to as soon as these individuals are ready to be harvested.

I receive my titles that chase away the "if" statements of doubt. I am Sister, Love, Dove, and Perfected One. I will keep my gaze upon You, my Groom, for I am set apart, being undefiled because I rest under the canopy of Your redemptive glory. Thank You for adorning me with my bridal veil and royal robe, which represent solidarity, my spiritual authority as Your wife, and Your lordship over me.

You, my anointed High Priest, whose hands, brow, and curls drip with myrrh, are the One I adore, and I praise You with my whole heart. To You, I give my exclusive allegiance and love.

Enclosed,
Love

BRIDAL REFLECTION

1) Did you relate to Ted Williams' salvation story? How can you help the "Teds" in your sphere of influence maintain a relationship with Beloved Jesus Christ?

2) Describe Beloved's myrrh-drenched, ductal, oil-infused, raven-black curls. What do each of these mean as they relate to Beloved's character?

3) Beloved wears the oil of myrrh, as well as the oil of frankincense. Why does He only deposit the oil of myrrh on the latch of the door? What role is He trying to emphasize—High Priest or Suffering Savior? How does this relate to your calling to minister alongside Him?

4) Are you willing to get your feet "dirty" in order to respond to Beloved's ministry calling? What are ways you can minister and not resent the messy task this presents?

5) Have you had a "night visitation" where Beloved called you to witness at an inopportune time? Did you respond quickly enough? How does knowing Beloved leaves the myrrh help you to know you are still called?

6) Why must your robe remain on and you never take it off? What does the robe represent?

7) If Beloved were visible, what would you say to Him first? Write a prayer to Him, envisioning Him as your Bridegroom who loves you in all seasons.

Chapter Nine
My Beloved

What is your beloved more than another beloved,
O fairest among women?
~Song of Solomon 5:9a

"Who do men say that I, the Son of Man, am?"
~Matthew 16:13b

"My Beloved Jesus is _____." Can you finish the sentence? I am sure by now you can! In fact, you probably need a paragraph or several pages, rather than a space. Our relationship with Beloved is living, so each time we think about our Groom, our answer may be different as we notice various aspects of His personality. Our Groom will be many things to us, but two character descriptions are fundamental: Beloved Jesus, allegorically Beloved Solomon, *Dowd Sheloma*, is the God of divine love and peace and is that personified.

In the previous chapter, we discussed the Groom's character traits, His gift of myrrh, and His role as High Priest and our fourfold character description that is true of us as Bride, even when we are going through times where our commitment to Him has wavered. Beloved still calls us "My Sister," "My Love," "My Dove," and "My Perfect One," and He covers us with His love, waiting for us to return, gifting us with myrrh-drenched fingertips so we know He still loves us and calls us to minister by His side.

Not only did we discuss our Groom's role, we envisioned Him as the anointed High Priest, filled to overflowing with sweet-smelling myrrh, whose crown, hands, and ductal curls ooze the myrrh of forgiveness, emanating from within each strand of His jet-black curls.

Now I ask you to ponder the question: Who is Jesus to you at this very moment? Please, Love, anchor your heart in truth by writing a reply. There is no right answer, so jot down the attribute Beloved is whispering into your spirit right now. "My Beloved Jesus is _____." Your praise is the key to bridal restoration. Beloved accepts your response, and He adores your words of adoration.

In Scene Thirteen, you describe attributes of your Beloved that lead you to give Him first place at all times and in all circumstances. No longer will you do so only when it is convenient. You declare at the close, I am *my beloved's and my beloved is mine* (Song 6:3a). This is a wise paradigm shift because you recognize He must lead His Bride.

Where is Beloved? He has gone down to the garden valleys *to gather lilies* (Song 6:2b), you say to the maidens. The lily people are those ready for salvation or discipleship, so Beloved has come to rescue each of them as their needs dictate. These are the "Ted Williamses" of the day.

The Bridegroom calls out to His creation. A heart for souls becomes your identity as you realize evangelism and discipleship is your *Dowd Shelomah's* dearest love-expression. At Mt. Hermon, you climbed the highest mountain and entered into the secluded garden of spices. You tasted of Beloved's goodness and touched your Groom's crimson-pierced, gem-set hands. You participated in the healing flow of living waters that effervesced with joy. This is the preparation you needed to minister alongside Beloved in the Sharon Valley.

When you find the myrrh upon the latch of your door, you conclude Beloved has gone to minister in the Valley once again because He has deposited the priestly anointing upon the door latch. This is where you will find Him, and your myrrh-drenched fingertips indicate He has called you to minister alongside Him. Bride of Christ, the redeeming love Beloved has for each of us keeps us from staying in guilt where the enemy would like to trap us. It is time to return to your fondest memories of the Bridegroom-King, and by describing Him to your lady friends, you will become whole again and will be ready to depart on your ministry trip. Praise Him!

"My Beloved Jesus is…" Your responses of intimate recollections comprise this next scene:

*****

SONG OF SOLOMON 5:10-6:3
Scene Fourteen: My Beloved Is…

SETTING:	Stage Left: LOVE'S home.
	Stage Right: LOVE's village. Rising sun; far right.
	Stage Lights: Star lights turn off one at a time. Spotlights of red, yellow, and blue gradually increase, representing sunrise.
AT RISE:	LOVE is deep in thought, sitting on her bed, dressed in royal attire, except for her veil. This, she holds in her hands. She looks out the window. The village MAIDENS and a YOUNG MAIDEN are gathering outside her home.

NARRATOR

Who is Beloved? How is He different than any other? The maidens have gathered outside Love's home, eagerly awaiting their Queen's appearance and her response to this question.

(Lighting changes to deep purple and red)

Look! The sun crests the horizon of the dark sky. Beams of deep purple and red decorate the firmament. It is fitting that Beloved has chosen to adorn the dawn with the colors of royalty.

(LOVE rises; goes to the window; dabs her eyes.)

Love looks at her veil. Dare she put this headdress on? Yes, she must acknowledge that Beloved's love for her is constant, despite her human frailties.

(LOVE puts on her veil, opens the door, and steps outside. The MAIDENS stand reverentially. LOVE motions for them to sit; they comply.)

The maidens honor their Queen. She is not perfect yet, but her heart is, and Beloved calls her His "perfect one" because He sees her outside of the restraints of time, and His perfecting love. Because Love pursues Him, to the maidens she is "fairest amongst women." She wears the glory of her Husband-King as clothing to her spirit. Her tear-drenched face is now aglow with remembrances. Let's listen in:

LOVE

[10]My Beloved *is* white and ruddy, Chief among ten thousand. [11]His head *is like* the finest gold; His locks *are* wavy, *and* black as the raven. [12]His eyes *are* like doves by the rivers of waters, washed with milk, *and* fitly set.

(Cups cheeks with hands)

[13]His cheeks *are* like a bed of spices, banks of scented herbs. His lips *are* lilies, dripping liquid myrrh.

(Kisses fingers; touches fingers to lips)

NARRATOR

Love kisses the fragrant myrrh that Beloved deposited upon her fingertips. It represents the gift of forgiveness her Groom has extended to her by His priestly love.

LOVE
(Stretches hands out; holds palms upward)
¹⁴His hands *are* rods of gold set with the beryl. His body *is* carved ivory inlaid *with* sapphires.
(Touches thighs; folds hands in a prayer gesture; looks up)
¹⁵His legs *are* pillars of marble, set on bases of fine gold. His countenance *is* like Lebanon, excellent as the cedars.
(Touches one finger to mouth)
¹⁶His mouth *is* most sweet: yes, He *is* altogether lovely.
(Looks directly at the MAIDENS; points her finger upwards)
¹⁷This *is* my Beloved, and this *is* my Friend, O daughters of Jerusalem!
(Extends hand to MAIDENS)

YOUNG MAIDEN
(Stands, playfully takes LOVE'S hand)
⁶:¹Where has your Beloved gone, O fairest among women? Where has your Beloved turned aside that we may seek Him with you?

NARRATOR
It is the innocence of this young maiden's question that will help Love conquer her fears. He once enticed her to follow Him by peering with inquisitive glances through the lattice of her garden enclosure. Again, Beloved is testing her willingness to respond. Will she play this game of "hide-and-seek"? This young damsel that addresses the Queen certainly hopes so!
(The MAIDENS join the YOUNG MAIDEN, chattering their desire to find BELOVED with her. They touch LOVE'S myrrh-drenched fingers and point to the sunrise, asking if they can all go with her.)

LOVE
²My Beloved has gone to His garden, to the beds of spices, to feed *His flock* in the gardens, and to gather lilies.
(Bows reverently to her unseen BELOVED)

NARRATOR
Love knows where she will find her Beloved, for she realizes the gift of myrrh also speaks of the importance of ministry, even when it is inopportune. Truly, it is the dawning of a new day for this bowing Queen. Beloved has descended to the valleys, to pasture with His lily people — those preparing their hearts to meet Him — and there He will be, shepherding and perfecting them, gathering them into His sheepfold.

LOVE
(Rises)
I *am* my Beloved's and my Beloved *is* mine: He feeds *his flock* among the lilies.
(LOVE walks while the YOUNG MAIDEN skips. They all run, stage right, holding hands, exit, being exuberant, playful, and joyful)

NARRATOR
As the first rays of sun kiss the mountaintops and cascade into the city streets, chasing the shadows away, Love and her maidens join hands, singing, as together they search for Beloved. Strength through humility graces the Queen as she leads her entourage. They are headed to the fertile plains of the Sharon Valley where the Bride is certain she will find her King. She finds solace by imagining

Beloved's welcoming arms and His kisses of everlasting peace.

*****

What is happening in Scene Fourteen? The dialogue you have with your maidens is most insightful. Meditate on the truths that you share with the maidens about Beloved's character.

Contrast these scenes:

- In Scene Seven, the charge you gave your maidens is to be lovesick at all times.
- In Scene Thirteen, you say, *If you find my beloved… tell him I am lovesick* (Song 5:8b).
- In Scene Fourteen, you say *I am my beloved's and my beloved is mine* (Song 6:3a).

The contrast between Scenes Thirteen and Fourteen indicate you've had a mindset renewal. Praise defeats doubts. The enemy would have you say, "Because you said, 'if,' you've gone too far and Beloved won't take you back." That's a lie! Don't believe it!

Beloved doesn't need to take you back, because He never left you. He deposited His cologne of myrrh on the doorknob so you would know His love remains constant and He still desires you to be with Him, ministering. Your High Priest reminds you, by this gift of myrrh, that forgiveness is ongoing.

Praise is the key to awakening to Beloved's constant love for you.

And so, Scene Fourteen outlines your praise, as you recall each character trait of your true love. As you awaken from your spiritual slumber, you join Him in the harvest fields, knowing He wants you by His side.

Let's look at these fields:

THE HARVEST FIELDS

Your Beloved Harvester is responding to the tender cries of the lilies of the valley. These lily people represent souls humble enough to call out to Beloved. They are in need of a witness, as you once were. In Scene Two, the kind maiden helped you embark on your spiritual pilgrimage, and, in tears, you followed the footsteps of the Shepherd to the Sharon Valley. It was there you learned from kind shepherds. To Beloved, the cry of the lily people equates to a love call, and He feels compelled to come alongside these wounded souls as He once did for you.

From Genesis to Revelation there has always been a harvesting of souls. So, for Beloved to expect His Bride to be a harvester is no surprise. For example:

- In Genesis, when the human race was starting over after the flood, God tells Noah, *"While the earth remains, seedtime and harvest…shall not cease"* (Genesis 8:22). The Lord indicates a spiritual harvest as much as He is speaking of fruitful terra firma. The ark symbolizes a safety boat that ensures the continuance of a people who will serve God wholeheartedly.
- In Matthew, Beloved Jesus says, *"The harvest truly is plentiful, but the laborers are few. Therefore pray the Lord of the harvest to send out laborers into His harvest"* (Matthew 9:37-38).
- In Revelation, the battles and conquests conclude in Beloved's marriage supper invitation for His Brides, which are harvested souls, *Then he said to me, "Write: 'Blessed are those who are called to the marriage supper of the Lamb'"* (Revelation 19:9)!

THE LOVESICK BRIDE

Notice in this present scene, your lovesick state compels you to speak to the maidens as if you are face-to-face with Beloved as you recall each memory. This shows you that you remain head-over-heels in love with your Groom. Although you erred in not immediately answering His pleas and you were complacent, you are still in love with Him. You accept Beloved's description of you as Sister, Love, Dove, and Perfect One.

136

As you describe Beloved, you allude to His positions both as Son of Man and Son of God. You conclude your discourse by mentioning the sweetness of Beloved's kisses of peace and the friendship you possess with Him.

QUESTION ONE: HOW IS BELOVED SUPERIOR TO OTHER BELOVEDS?

At the close of Scene Thirteen, the maidens ask you, *What is your beloved more than* another *beloved* (Song 5:9)*?* They want you to compare, and in this scene, compare you do. To you, He is more majestic than anyone! It takes all of Scene Fourteen, which is comprised of sixteen verses, for you to answer one question.

KENOSIS

With every character trait you mention, you recognize Beloved's heavenly, followed by His earthly, attributes. There's a reason for this. It has to do with *kenosis*. Remember, in theology, *kenosis* would purport that Father God exalted Jesus Christ because He was willing to be humbled. This trait distinguishes Him best.

By definition, *kenosis* means "to empty oneself."[161] Beloved knows He is the "Son of God," which references His heavenly character traits. However, in the Gospels, He also often identifies Himself as the "Son of Man," which references His humanity, because He is humble. Had He not been so, He would not have come to the earth; He would have remained aloof and lofted in Heaven.

Your King set aside His divine nature in order to redeem mankind, putting off the convenient and kingly in order to rescue His Bride. Dr. H. L. Wilmington writes, "Who can comprehend such unbelievable condescension? It is as if a mighty and magnificent earthly king would determine to lay aside for a while his fantastic storehouse of wealth and, leaving behind an adoring and amazed court, take upon himself the body of a lowly ant. 'The Son of Man' was… our Lord's favorite name for himself while on earth."[162]

The Apostle Paul concurs, penning, *And being found in appearance as a man, He humbled Himself, and became obedient to the point of death, even the death of the cross. Therefore God also has highly exalted Him, and given Him the name which is above every name, that at the name of Jesus every knee should bow, of those in heaven, and of those on earth, and of those under the earth, and that every tongue should confess that Jesus Christ is Lord, to the glory of God the Father* (Philippians 2:8-11).

Is it any guess why Beloved calls us as His Bride to empty ourselves of our own self-will in order to attain right standing and answer the call to minister? Our Groom is asking us to do exactly what He has done. We must be willing to be inconvenienced and humbled, so we can minister with the absence of pride, enmity, or self-will. The end result, as we will see, is our exaltation.

As the Bride of Christ, you are a royal Queen. Because of this, people find hope as you set a godly example for them, but in order to serve rightly, you must be relatable, and this requires you to be humble like your Groom.

Every person has this ministry calling of the Groom; He is no respecter of persons, and there is as much of a calling on an ordinary person as there is on someone who is a professional pastor, speaker, Bible teacher, or the like. The Bride is called. Each of us is the called Bride.

THE GROOM'S WHITE COMPLEXION

You begin your discourse by saying, *My beloved* is *white and ruddy, Chief among ten thousand*

---

[161] Strong. OT #2758, *kenoo*
[162] Wilmington, Dr. H. L. *Wilmington's Guide to the Bible*. 1984. Tyndale House. Carol Stream, Illinois. Pg. 484.

(Song 5:10). The only place in the Old Testament where this particular word for "white" is used is in this single passage of Song of Solomon. It is used no other place in the Old Testament. Other words translate as "white," but in a different way, so let's look at this unique word used in the vignette. In the Hebrew, this translates as *tsicheh,* and it means "to glow."[163]

Thus, you are presenting Him as the glorious Lord of Heaven. Our Beloved Savior glows! You first emphasize to your maidens that when you gaze upon Beloved, you see glory! This distinguishing trait is found exclusively through Him. He is the only One who has this characteristic. Only as we hide ourselves in Him can we glow with heavenly brightness.

The word "white" also indicates cleanness. Thus, in this exceptional passage you indicate Beloved is totally pure. He is unblemished. Therefore, He is able to glorify and cleanse His Bride.

This two-fold character trait has an advantage. In order to qualify to defeat sins, Beloved needs to have no blemishes whatsoever; otherwise, He would not qualify to erase our transgressions. The penalty of sin is death, and the perfect God-Man named Beloved Jesus Christ is the only One who qualifies to pay sin's price. Romans 6:23 reads, *For the wages of sin is death, but the gift of God is eternal life in Christ Jesus our Lord.* Paul records, *But God demonstrates His own love toward us, in that while we were still sinners, Christ died for us* (Romans 5:8). Jesus' sinless, spotless state qualifies Him to do so.

The New Testament equivalent for "white" is *leukos,*[164] which means "aglow" or "light." Unlike this unique passage in Song of Solomon, the New Testament term is used regularly. It is found in all four Gospels, and it is used most frequently in Revelation. Of the twenty-six references, twenty-five of these portray *leukos* as descriptive of Beloved's resurrection glory.

Here are two New Testament examples:

- Matthew 17:1-2, *Now after six days, Jesus took Peter, James, and John his brother, led them up on a high mountain by themselves, and He was transfigured before them. His face shone like the sun, and his clothes became as white as the light.*
- Revelation 1:14, *His head and hair* were *white like wool, as white as snow, and his eyes like a flame of fire.*

Other descriptions in Revelation go into even more detail about your glowing Savior's appearance. For example, John describes Beloved as having an angelic-looking face that shines as the sun and wearing a halo that is as colorful as a rainbow (Revelation 10:1).

The one reference left in the New Testament, translated as "white," is about the Bride. We will discuss this at the close of this chapter. We, as Bride, are also "white" when we are in Him, so keep this truth close to your heart.

THE GROOM'S RUDDY COMPLEXION

Your Groom, the Son of God, is aglow with Heaven's glory, but in your dream of Scene Thirteen, He places His hand through the hole of the door with myrrh-drenched fingers, demonstrating He loves you unconditionally. Thus, it is fitting that you next speak of Beloved's *ruddy* (Song 5:10b)[165] complexion indicating His position as Son of Man.

Beloved's ruddy appearance means He's a down-to-earth sort of guy. He is as reachable as the pastor who comes to church wearing jeans with a business jacket. Do you remember the dark sunburn you had at the beginning of your journey? Beloved is a worker too! His ruddy appearance indicates He relates to us, but there is one activity He refuses to participate in, and that is sin. If He had sinned even once this would have disqualified Him to be our Redeemer.

Beloved was capable of sinning, but He chose not to. Paul records Beloved's earthly attributes

---

[163] Strong. OT #6703; *tsicheh;* to glow.
[164] Word family: *Strong's* NT #3022, *leukos;* light, white. NT #3021; *leukaino;* to whiten; make white.
[165] Strong. OT #132; *admoniy;* reddish, ruddy

this way, *For we do not have a High Priest who cannot sympathize with our weaknesses, but was in all* points *tempted as* we are, yet *without sin* (Hebrews 4:15). Based on this verse, where is the sin of a repentant person? When we repent, all sins — even purposeful sins — are wiped away, and cleansing becomes ours, because Beloved perfectly qualified to pay the penalty of death for sin.

The use of the word ruddy also identifies Beloved as an outdoorsman. He is the humble Shepherd who seeks to guide souls rather than sheep. He actively participates in soul salvation. He is involved, not unreachable and lofted on a cloud. He is here, as Emmanuel — the "with" of God — participating in soul salvation.

Let's look at another "ruddy" fellow mentioned in the Bible: David. The prophet Samuel anointed David, a lowly shepherd, who also was described as a "ruddy" young man (see 1 Samuel 16:7-13). Everyone relates to David as a nice fellow, but they don't recognize his ministry potential. Even his father, Jesse, almost overlooks David because he seems so ordinary. Samuel, however, likes that David is a worker who relates to even the tiniest lamb. In Samuel's understanding, David's humility is what qualifies him to be the King of Israel.

When you describe Beloved as "ruddy," you are not negating His kingly qualities, but rather emphasizing He is relatable. Beloved does not perch upon a King's pedestal and expect us to find Him; He searches for us, taking the role of a Shepherd, watching for the repentant heart and immediately responding to the sinner's cry, getting "dirty" in the job of soul hunting but never dirtying Himself with the blemish of sin.

THE GROOM IS CHIEF AMONG TEN THOUSAND

You say Beloved is *Chief among ten thousand* (Song 5:10b). This statement is akin to today's phrase, "You're one in a million." Beloved is choice! You are awestruck at His magnificence. In order to be the chief person among ten thousand, Beloved must be the King of Kings, and He is, being more worthy than any other. There is no Name higher than the Lord Jesus Christ our Beloved.

Paul records in Ephesians that God *seated Him at His right hand in the heavenly* places, *far above all principality and power and might and dominion, and every name that is named, not only in this age but also in that which is to come. And He put all* things *under His feet, and gave Him* to be *head over all things to the church, which is His body, the fullness of Him who fills all in all. And you He* made alive, *who were dead in trespasses and sins* (Ephesians 1:20b-2:1).

Paul also records, *Nor is there salvation in any other, for there is no other name under heaven given among men by which we must be saved* (Acts 4:12).

Thus, we conclude that although Beloved is "ruddy," and involved in men's affairs, He is King and exalted above any other. Beloved is not just exalted; He is the most exalted one. He is "Chief." Beloved perfectly embodies the titles Son of Man, as well as Son of God. As Son of Man, He is the "ruddy" one, who is fully a man. As Son of God, He is "Chief among ten thousand," the exalted one who is fully God.

THE GROOM'S CURLS OF FINE-GOLD, RAVEN-BLACK, WAVY LOCKS

You say, *His head* is like *the finest gold, His locks* are *wavy*, and *black as a raven* (Song 5:11). With these metaphors, you describe Beloved's mindset.

Beloved's head is anointed, for He wears a sprinkling of Heaven's "finest gold." He has heavenly wisdom that surpasses all others — represented by the gold. Your High Priest's head sports gold-laced, myrrh-drenched locks. Furthermore, there is not only gold in Beloved's locks — it is *the finest gold* (Song 5:11b) which indicates it is the best available.

This word used for "gold" [166] means "pure gold" or "refined gold," indicating its purity level is best. Beloved wears refined gold as it would appear if it were heated in a blazing fire. Just as the

---

[166] Strong. OT #6337; *paz*; from OT #6338, pure, or refined gold

word "white" defines Beloved's luminous anointing and purity, the gold of His locks conveys the same uniqueness of meaning. He is purer than pure. There is repetition here because you want your maidens to get the message. Beloved's value is beyond any earthly treasure! He is the best of the best, and then, even more so. He is a treasure who surpasses all others.

Imagine Beloved's head and beard, His flowing curls, dusted with the gold of Heaven's glorious light, also shining black and almost appearing purple like raven's feathers. When you say His locks are as *black as a raven* (Song 5:11b), you are indicating Beloved's hair is healthy, for His black curls shine. You are also showing that He is royalty, for His curls shine purple. But there is more.

You portray Beloved's locks as *wavy* (Song 5:11b), which the King James renders as *bushy* (Song 5:11b KJV) With this description, you are not just saying that Beloved has a lot of hair — there's prophetic significance encoded in this description.

By definition, Beloved's "wavy"[167] locks are "pendulous," literally "ductile"[168] curls that wave in abundance. So, as we previously discussed, there is a duct — which is a hollow channel — within each curl, where the living well of oil flows out, that has been built into Beloved's anatomy. There is not a mere dollop of oil that has been poured upon Beloved as a symbol of His Kingly and Priestly roles — it flows from within Him. The anointing oil does not just come upon Him, He is the source of its flow.

The Gesenius Lexicon[169] traces the root word for "locks" as meaning "lofty" and "exalted" "pendulous palm branches." The oil well within Beloved's locks signifies Beloved is the Anointed One of Palm Sunday. On the first Palm Sunday, people waved palm branches, exalting Beloved as King of Kings and Lord of Lords.

But He was equally the suffering Messiah; therefore, He accepts His mission to hang on Calvary's cross, His life's blood pouring from His anointed brow and overflowing upon His anointed, oil-filled locks. This is *kenosis* to the max. Who but the most loving King would accept this fate when He is the very source of the anointing, which emanates from His own person?

THE GROOM'S EYES AS DOVE'S EYES

Now, you come face-to-face and eyeball-to-eyeball as you imagine Beloved. You focus right in on Beloved's eyes, saying, *His eyes* are *like doves by the rivers of waters, washed with milk,* and *fitly set* (Song 5:12a). Let's look at each of these:

You remember the Holy Spirit Dove reflecting within His eyes. The dove mentioned here is the rock dove. Remember, this dove is a word picture of ascent, glory, and redemption. You are also remembering your mountaintop experiences in Mt. Hermon, where your eyes also reflected the Spirit Dove of glory. So, you are letting the maidens know He is at home in the heights of Heaven's glory.

RIVERS OF LIVING WATERS EMANATING FROM THE GROOM

Furthermore, you describe the rivers and springs of living waters that originate in the heights of Lebanon's mountain range and flow into the valleys below. You describe Beloved as having dove's eyes positioned beside these *rivers of waters* (Song 5:12b). Notice these are not puddles — they are free-flowing rivers teeming with life resultant from prayer. From Mt. Bether's secluded prayer garden of Scene Nine, we know these originate from a spring, having been described as *a fountain of gardens, a well of living waters, and streams from Lebanon* (Song 4:15b).

Your remembrance brings us back to the importance of tarrying in prayer, which is vital in maintaining a healthy relationship. As you permit Beloved's purifying, piercing glances, you are able to step right into the river of living waters. Tarrying is such a serene activity that we are not always

---

[167] Strong. OT #8534 *taltal'*; bushy. From *Strong's* OT #8524 *taltal*; exalted, lofty

[168] Blue Letter Bible. International Bible Encyclopedia. KJV Search Results for "bushy." http://www.blueletterbible.org/search/cfm?criteria=bushy&+=KJV#s=-primary-0-17

[169] Ibid.

aware of the strength and anointing that flow to us from there. But they do. So, have them. Beloved does, and He prepares blessings to flow to His Bride from these waters.

THE GROOM'S EYES; WASHED WITH MILK; FITLY SET

You describe Beloved's eyes as *washed with milk* and *fitly set* (Song 5:12b). Beloved nourishes your spirit as "milk" nourishes a baby, and as His eyes are "fitly set" because His teachings are balanced. There is nothing askew about them.

As you enter into the secluded prayer garden, you can drink fundamental teachings of "milk," as well as drinking the deep truths; and in either pursuit, you can bask with Him just to enjoy His presence. Beloved comforts you in either pursuit! He knows you need to visit both the pastures and the high mountains, and He is ready to meet your desire.

THE GROOM'S CHEEKS AND LIPS

You say, *His cheeks* are *like a bed of spices, banks of scented herbs. His lips* are *lilies, dripping liquid myrrh* (Song 5:13). This is a portrait of your marriage bed experience within the enclosed garden upon Lebanon's mountains. Do you remember what the bed of spices contains? It includes the holy anointing oil used to consecrate the priests. Although there are other spices mentioned in your marriage bed experience, you specifically mention the "myrrh," pointing to Beloved's priestly role. Here, you highlight the myrrh, but you also reference the *banks of scented herbs* (Song 5:13b). Let's explore three aspects of this description:

First, as aforementioned, Beloved is the High Priest who consecrates you to minister alongside Him. The apothecary mixture of calamus, cinnamon, cassia, and the myrrh make up the anointing oil (see Exodus 30:23-30). So, you acknowledge you and Beloved both have priestly roles. He anoints you to share the Gospel message. Therefore, it is imperative that you find Him and minister alongside Him. You are a minister.

Second, the apothecary mixture of myrrh represents Beloved's death, burial, and resurrection because these were used as burial spices, so you speak prophetically of Messiah to come. Nicodemus anoints Beloved Jesus with *a mixture of myrrh and aloes, about a hundred pounds* (John 19:39b) when His body lay in the tomb before He arose from the grave. Beloved paid the full price of death for your salvation.

Third, you remember how Beloved has come to you personally, leaving the residue of His heavenly, yet earthly perfume upon the handles of your locked door. This speaks of forgiveness that has already been extended to you, not once, but as many times as you need it. Put simply—Beloved does not know how to hold a grudge—He wants you to receive His love, forgiveness, and the freedom that comes as you make Him Lord of your life. You are forgiven.

How do you show Beloved as bringing you the myrrh? The holy anointing oil is like a bed of spices upon His cheeks that smile at you approvingly. The myrrh is upon Beloved's lips as *lilies, dripping liquid myrrh* (Song 5:13), your Bridegroom's sweet myrrh touching your lips, because He is gentle and He gives forgiveness. Beloved's lips kiss you with *dowd*; these lips are like lilies of His peace. His lips are the rare but sweetly fragranced Rose of Sharon. His cheeks are as these sweet flowers, the humble field lilies and the Rose of Sharon lilies whose perpetual beauty adorns Sharon Valley and Mt. Lebanon's base.

The description of Beloved's "cheeks" is the best characterization of Beloved's *kenosis*. Let's look at two examples from both testaments in Beloved's own words:

- In Isaiah 50:6, Beloved says, *I gave My back to those who struck* Me, *and My cheeks to those who plucked out the beard: I did not hide My face from shame and spitting.*
- In Matthew 5:38, Beloved says, *"You have heard that it was said, 'An eye for an eye and a tooth for a tooth.' But I tell you not to resist an evil person. But whoever slaps you on your right cheek, turn the other to him also."*

Can you imagine the scene? Beloved's beard had channels of the priestly and kingly anointing oils flowing from it, and the source of the anointing was within Him, and yet in order to redeem mankind He permitted desecration of His person. At any moment, Beloved could have prevented this horrifying scene at Calvary continuing, and yet, because of His love for even His accusers and abusers, Beloved stepped through death's door. Even though He was the King of Kings, the Lord of Glory, and the Great High Priest, He allowed these haters to slap both cheeks and then to pluck His beard from His tender face! How close were these enemies to the lips that desired to impart divine peace?

The root word for *cheeks* (Song 5:13a)[170] literally means "to be soft," as the cheek and jawbone area is soft on a face. This focuses on Beloved's human side. Let's not pass by this description without meditating on it. Beloved paid the highest price to redeem mankind. A slap on the cheek is painful and humiliating. In your marriage bed experience of the enclosed garden, Beloved's cheeks impart the kiss and He speaks kind words to you. These are the same cheeks that the haters smite here. He could have stopped them, but He chose not to. Humility through suffering, in order to bring resurrection life, describes Beloved. This is *kenosis* at its best.

THE GROOM'S HANDS OF GOLD RINGS

Now, you focus on Beloved's gorgeous hands. You say, *His hands* are *as rods of gold set with the beryl* (Song 5:14a). Let's examine these aspects.

The "gold" on Beloved's hands originates from Heaven, and shimmers beautifully. From its definition, the word "gold" can be rendered as "something gold-colored as oil."[171] Thus, Beloved's hands represent His promise to anoint you with the shimmering oil from Heaven. The oil you receive is the priestly myrrh of forgiveness.

When we look at this same passage in the King James, we read, *His hands* are as *gold rings set with the beryl* (Song 5:14a KJV). I like the emphasis the King James gives, that these are not straight rods—rather, they are rings.

A ring is the symbol for eternity. Eternity has no ending, nor does the shape of the ring. Beloved's hands, therefore, symbolize the eternity found when we enter into a relationship with Him. His hands, like gold rings, represents His encircling love—His divine *dowd*—that has no ending, and with this love, He embraces His Bride. Both hands are shimmering with this gold, so we are doubly encircled with His eternal love.

In Scene Seven, Beloved shared Communion with you as you reclined in the apple orchard below Father's house, embracing you with both of His hands. Envision this embrace as an eternally surrounding presence that will never, ever end. Beloved's golden hands embracing you form the symbol of His marriage vow. As well, each of His ten fingers is like a ring—so we can see He is eternity to the max. His love is that rich!

Why all the repetitiveness in the symbolism here? I liken the above to my three-year-old daughter's description of the love she felt for Mommy and Daddy. She would say, "I love you as much as two skies," and then she would throw her hands in the air. We knew what she meant—she had had no way to quantitatively describe the love she felt for us. We got it! Here, you are describing the depth of Beloved's eternal *dowd* love, and there is no description that fits—so you describe your Groom's embracing hands, and you mention every finger, each one being like an eternal love embrace that never ends. Had you desired, you could have mentioned His toes, for His feet were pierced through and shimmering in gold in the spiritual realm.

There's another aspect of a ring that is important to notice. In ancient biblical times a dignitary would stamp in wax his seal of approval by use of the signet ring. Based on Beloved's gem-set hands,

---

[170] Strong. OT #3895; *l^echiy*

[171] Strong. OT #2091; *zahab*; to shimmer, gold, figuratively: yellow oil, a clear sky

as wife of Beloved, you have the authority to enforce Heaven's reign here on Earth, for He has given you His signet ring of authority.

With this final notation, our vignette once again prophesizes the Savior in amazing detail, for there is more about His hands. They are gold-laced, as rings, and they are gem-set, but how? Let's explore.

THE GROOM'S GEM-SET HANDS

Gems are set into holes. As the Bride, you describe Beloved's hands as having holes because nails once pierced them. So here in the vignette, far before Beloved pays Calvary's price to redeem His Bride, Song of Solomon records this event. These hands pierced at Calvary are now set with gemstones. Thus, Beloved's victory over death, Hell, and the grave is foretold in the vignette. Father God sets into the palms of His risen Son precious gems, as a signet of His authority. When Beloved humbles Himself as the Son of Man, Father God exalts Him as the Son of God. This is again a picture of *kenosis*.

After Jesus' resurrection, when He appears to His disciples, Thomas sees the holes (see John 20:19-29), but he only sees voids that are not yet gem-filled because Jesus has not yet ascended. When Beloved takes His residency in Heaven, God sets them with the beryl.

What you describe to the maidens is more than what Thomas sees, for you see His glorified hands set with the beryl-stone gems. This is how we will see Him too. These glorified hands that Beloved willingly stretches out upon a cross are the hands that now encircle you. As Bride of Christ, we can choose to live our whole life from within this eternal embrace. In fact, Beloved desires for you to do this—He wants you to do this—for He is the personification of eternal love.

The word "gem" translates as the Hebrew word, *tarshiysh*.[172] In ancient biblical times, the port of Tarshish in the Mediterranean was a center of merchant activities, which included gem imports. This indicates Beloved is rich beyond measure. It's not just an ordinary gem set into the Son's wounds; it is the richest gem.

Scholars debate what the beryl stone translates to in today's language. Some say it must be the golden topaz; others say it is a reddish stone, either a ruby or a red diamond, representative of Jesus' shed blood. But consider this—you are describing Beloved's heavenly quality—so perhaps this gemstone is unidentifiable because the beryl stone is a heavenly stone that has no earthly equivalent. If Father God set into His Son's hands the beryl stones, why would He use any of our stones when He could choose a gemstone from the treasuries of Heaven? Even the gemstones of Tarshish would fall short when compared to Heaven's stones. The heavenly authority this gemstone represents centers around Beloved's sacrificial love, and *kenosis* is the emphasis and the Suffering Savior now being glorified to the highest position.

THE GROOM'S TORSO; OVERLAID WITH IVORY AND SAPPHIRES

Next, you describe Beloved's *body* (Song 5:14b)[173] representative of His inner man. The King James renders "body" as "torso" or "belly." This, the center of Beloved's physical body, is defined as "the seat of generation." Beloved's belly is as *carved ivory inlaid* with *sapphires* (Song 5:14b).

Beloved's inner man is as strong as ivory and purer than white ivory. He also is sparkling in glory just like this bright ivory is overlaid with sparkling *sapphires* (Song 5:14b). These "sapphires"[174] are not the sapphire of today; rather, they are the diamond or something better than this. Again, it has, most likely, a heavenly stone as its origin. Beloved is superior to all others, and His ivory torso set with heavenly diamonds shows His Spirit is better than best.

---

[172] Strong. OT #8658; *tarshiysh*; OT#8659, *Tarshiysh*; The Mediterranean port of Tarshish.
[173] Strong. OT #4578, *meeh*.
[174] Strong. OT #5601; *cappiyr*; a gem used for scratching other gems; thus, the diamond.

The diamond is the gem of standard to which all other gemstones are compared, and all others pale in comparison. At the center of your Groom's being, He is sparkling with Heaven's diamond, indicating He is perfection times infinity that is richer than the finest diamond.

THE GROOM'S MARBLE LEGS; CEDAR COUNTENANCE

You say, *His legs* are *pillars of marble, set on bases of fine gold. His countenance* is *like Lebanon, excellent as the cedars* (Song 5:15). This indicates that not only does Beloved pray with excellence, His standards are unchangeable.

The prophet Malachi records, *"For I am the LORD, I do not change"* (Malachi 3:6). Thus, the marble pillar is a perfect description of Beloved's strong, stable stance. When He moves, the joints of His legs are as fine gold—strong and heavenly, and His standards of purity and truth do not change. Because your Groom consistently walks predictably on the straight and narrow, perfect path, you can trust Him to direct the course of your life. This, you relay to the maidens.

Beloved's *countenance* is *like Lebanon, excellent as the cedars* (Song 5:15b). You focus your maidens on the importance of maintaining a consistent prayer life. But there's more to this. It's the quality of prayer that you exemplify here. His prayers are "excellent as the cedars." Cedar wood is resistant to rot, and insects will not eat it. It can be weathered for a long time and exhibits little to no wear. Thus, it is the perfect building material. So, Beloved is the perfect One we can build our lives upon. Cedar is the choice wood used to build the Temple, and, as such, you recognize Beloved not only as Builder, He is the foundation of the church.

Because Beloved's stature is built upon this solid foundation of prayer, He is impenetrable by the enemy. Paul writes, *The effective, fervent prayer of a righteous man avails much* (James 5:16b). When your prayers are propelled forward by Beloved's prayers, all things are possible! He desires for your prayers to be as effectual as His own, and this is possible as we pray in His Name, according to His desires.

THE BRIDEGROOM'S KISS OF PEACE AND FRIENDSHIP

You save the best description for the culmination. At long last, you describe Beloved's kisses of peace. You say, *His mouth* is *most sweet, yes, he is altogether lovely* (Song 5:16a). You have come full circle to the memory that you told the maidens about in Scene One. The kisses of Beloved's peace in the wedding chamber anchor all other remembrances. This is your favorite memory, for in order to receive your Groom's kisses of peace, you must come behind the veil of the Holy of Holies in your remembrances. Only here are you completed within your *Dowd Shelomah's* embrace. You are finally ready to recite this cherished memory once again.

You say Beloved is not only lovely; He is *altogether lovely* (Song 5:16b). You say Beloved is not only sweet, He is the *most sweet* (Song 5:16a). Honey in the honeycomb is the sweetest, and this is how your Beloved's love is to you. His love is the absolute best! Beloved is the sweetest of all persons, and His kisses of peace are perfection personified. Beloved has the most excellent character, and no other person compares to your *Dowd Shelomah*.

You conclude this scene by saying to the maidens, *This* is *my Beloved, and this* is *my friend, O daughters of Jerusalem* (Song 5:16)! Your closing thought is like the cherry on top of the sundae. Who did you marry? You married your friend, who kisses you. He is not a controlling spouse—He is like a friend who is also your Husband and King. The term used here for "friend" is *reya*,[175] which is the masculine equivalent for *rayah*.[176] It is interesting to note that both of these terms meaning "marriage partner" can also mean "friend."

When my husband and I sent out our wedding invitations, our card read, "This day I will

---

[175] Strong. OT #7453; *reya.*
[176] Strong. OT #7474; *rayah*

144

marry my friend; the one I laugh with, live for, dream with, love." We still look on this as a summarization of our vows. It is obvious here that Beloved has the same sentiment toward you. You are the Bride He is friends with, and with you He lives, dreams, and loves.

Think of all the heavenly characteristics you've just described, interspersed equally with the earthly characteristics you confidently declare, and you conclude with this wedding chamber embrace where Beloved becomes your friend. This is mind-boggling! Your Holy Beloved is reachable, and the best description you can think of to sum up your relationship with Him is "friend." Glory! Who is Beloved Jesus to you, Love? He is the One who speaks these words to you, His Bride, *"Greater love has no man than this, than to lay down one's life for his friends"* (John 15:13). And He has done that perfectly because of His action on Calvary's cross, as the culminating deed of *kenosis*.

THE RESTORED BRIDE

Where is the Son of Man found? He is working the harvest fields, searching for "lilies" — those people ready for a harvest and for those who have spiritual fruits that are ripe for harvest.

By praising your Husband's character, you have centered your thoughts aright. You stand tall, knowing your Husband-Friend is the One who will kiss you with peace when you find Him. In your thoughts, He has become to you *Dowd Shelomah* once again.

You desire to return to your Lover's side, and you realize He has never left you spiritually and He never will. He has departed physically, but your marriage is still intact. The myrrh He has deposited on your door latchet that dripped onto your fingertips is the clue as to where you must find Him.

QUESTION TWO: WHERE IS BELOVED?

The young maiden question revolved around Beloved's character in comparison to other people. The kind maiden's question is, *Where has your Beloved gone, O fairest among women… that we may seek him with you?* (Song 6:1). You answer, *My beloved has gone to his garden, to the beds of spices, to feed his flock in the gardens, and to gather lilies* (Song 6:2).

You realize Beloved is discoverable after all because, since your humble Groom is a Sheepherder of Souls, He will be in the Sharon Valley teaching His Brides. You now know your myrrh-drenched fingertips represent your invitation to minister alongside your Groom once you get there. You will teach right by His side.

However, let's look at a mystery. You say, *My beloved has gone to his garden, to the beds of spices* (Song 6:2a), but you also say He has gone *to feed* his flock *in the gardens, and to gather lilies* (Song 6:2b). This leaves the reader hanging. Has Beloved gone to the prayer garden retreat of Mt. Hermon or to Sharon's Valley? It is both, but spiritually so. Let me explain.

In Scene Two, you learned from the shepherds, and your mindset became comely as you studied alongside the shepherds who had not compromised in their study of the Word. Finally, you were so irresistible to Beloved that He met you in person. He described you as an unruly *filly among Pharaoh's chariots* (Song 1:9b), and acting as a warrior army, but nonetheless, He met you because you were teachable at that moment of spiritual growth.

What you are describing in Scene Fourteen is a spiritual concept. In this current scene, you go to minister alongside your Husband-King in Sharon's Valley. But what matters more than location is the transference that happens there; your Husband-King makes a "garden" of the current situation any individual is faced with. Think of our brother-in-Christ Ted Williams. He met Jesus when he was still hooked on cocaine and alcohol and living an ungodly lifestyle. But Beloved met him right there as soon as Ted began pasturing with his Lord. Ted's spiritual condition is what Beloved was meeting. Ted's "garden" probably looked like a field of dandelion weeds, just as mine did when I first met Beloved. But Jesus met us right where we were, and He glorified us every time we came to Him. Beloved recognizes that each time we come to the "valley" this is an act of tarrying, and as we do so, we are teachable.

Even though Beloved meets us in the valleys, in the spiritual realm, He makes our "valley" a "garden" that is richer, more heavenly, and filled with the sweetest lilies and all sorts of spiritual "spices." So, even though we might physically be in the "valley," the very act of pasturing makes it become a garden. This is the meaning of the passage. The spiritual truth we are supposed to see is that when we meet Beloved, He turns wherever we are into a rich garden.

As this becomes a garden, Beloved comes to us as we plow the rows. He looks for dug up dirt. The phrase, *beds of spices* (Song 6:2b) indicates the spices are planted in tilled rows of heaped and furrowed dirt.[177] When we humble ourselves, as the lily flower indicates for us to do, we are a prime target for Beloved's presence and partnership. So, the "valley" indicates spiritual teachability, whereas the "garden" indicates spiritual fruit can potentially form, and the "beds of spices" show how we become spiritually fragrant and mature. In the spirit realm, this shows the spiritual progression of the Bride.

Thus, Beloved may initially come to the Valley, but He makes sure He stays while the one He loves becomes as a plowed garden, fruitful, and abiding in Him. Beloved wants you to be this sort of minister—one who stays and completes the job of evangelizing, discipling, and honing, until the ones you minister to are tarrying Brides.

I AM MY BELOVED'S AND MY BELOVED IS MINE

We all go through desert times where the Lord seems distant. In our dry times, we must come back to the basics and build ourselves up by meditating on the fundamental teachings of the Word. We can pasture in the valleys, tarry in remembrances, or rest in His garden retreat and rest in His embrace of love and peace.

We can confidently declare the last statement of this scene, *I am my beloved's and my beloved is mine. He feeds* his flock *among the lilies* (Song 6:3b). With this final statement your priorities are set right! You have pulled away from spiritual slumber and are fully awake, responsive, and ready to observe the lordship of Beloved.

You once said, "My beloved is mine and I *am* his" (Song 2:16a) as you tarried in Bether's heights. Everyone begins their relationship with this perspective. But in this scene, you say, *I am my beloved's and my beloved is mine* (Song 6:3a). Rather than your will being in play, you have emptied yourself of self-desire so much that you say, *He feeds* his flock *among the lilies* (Song 6:3b). Here we see you as Bride also displaying *kenosis*. Glory!

How can we not surrender to Beloved's Lordship and minister alongside Him? For our Groom has won us not by force, but by love! The *dowd* of Beloved—His boiling-pot of liquid love—has captivated our hearts! We must come to the realization that Beloved is a Harvester at the core of His being. This also explains why Beloved is in a hurry to respond. He wants to protect His budding Brides. And because Beloved shepherds lily people, so must we.

How can we share Beloved's love with others effectively? Truly, Love, this is not hard We can all do it. We tell our stories of how He won our hearts, and we share the Word He has made real to us. People will respond to our sincerity. This is how we can effectively evangelize and disciple souls.

SOULS WHITE FOR HARVEST

You began your discourse about your Groom by saying, *My beloved* is *white* (Song 5:10a). We learned that exclusively in this passage, the Hebrew word used for "white" is *tsicheh*, and it means "to glow."[178] We also learned the New Testament Greek equivalent, *leukos*,[179] which is used twenty-six

---

[177] Gesenius' Hebrew-Chaldee Lexicon, OT #H6170, bed, *aruwgah* Blue Letter Bible.
[178] Strong. OT #6703; *tsicheh*; to glow.
[179] Word family: *Strong's* NT #3022, *leukos*; light, white. NT #3021; *leukaino*; to whiten; make white.

times, and of the twenty-six references, twenty-five of these portray *leukos* as descriptive of Beloved's resurrection glory.

Let's now discuss the one remaining reference. It is found in John 4:35b. The disciple records Beloved as saying, *"Behold I say to you, lift up your eyes, and look at the fields, for they are already white for harvest"* (John 4:35b)! What is the take-away? The people we are called to witness to are sparkling inside with Beloved's glory!

Don't worry if someone looks messed up; instead, look for a sparkle… If someone is responding to Beloved's spirit, we should be able to discern this. If we see even the slightest spark of interest, then we are supposed to witness. There are "gems" who are responding to Beloved's glory who at the moment resemble a lump of coal. But, if we are ready to put a polish on these gems-in-the-rough, they will sparkle!

Ted Williams had just a slight sparkle in his eyes when Doral Chenowith made the video of him speaking in his radio voice. Doral went to Ted because he could discern Ted's sparkle! Ted desired Jesus—and Doral took the time to notice. Even now, he is helping his friend. This has made a difference, and Ted's shine becomes brighter every day. Are you willing to make a difference?

Who is the "Ted Williams" you are assigned to at this moment? Respond promptly! Beloved will empower you to harvest this budding soul. He alone knows the timing, and you can bank on the timing occasionally being at an inconvenient time.

CONCLUSION

You have become whole by describing your Beloved, but there is more… In the next scene, Beloved describes you. This brings even more restoration. But before we read on, let's bask in who your Groom is. Look over the character traits of your Groom and choose a favorite. Allow yourself to come face-to-face with Him and connect, spirit-to-Spirit, in unhurried fellowship. There is no activity more important than resting in the embrace of your Savior, for you, Bride of Christ, are chosen by your Bridegroom-King. He is so confident in His decision; He even calls you "friend."

When you're ready, let's pray:

My Glorious Peacemaker,
You are indescribably magnificent, for Your character is divine and earthly at the same time. I acknowledge You are equally the Son of Man and the Son of God. Thank You for every one of Your character traits. As I reflect on each one, bring me into Your glorious presence.
Thank You that You exemplify divine love through kenosis. Help me to humble myself, too, so I can harvest souls alongside You. Because You pursue souls, I gladly choose to answer Your ministry call to harvest and disciple souls. Give me humility of spirit so that I can reach every willing soul. Your eternal love and Your humility will be my guide.

Your Harvesting Bride,
Love

BRIDAL REFLECTION

1) Fill in the blank: My Beloved Jesus is _____.

2) Are you still "lovesick" for your Groom Jesus Christ? Describe your relationship with Him. Give Him praise for being in your life.

3) Describe Beloved's earthly and His heavenly characteristics that you most admire.

4) Define the term, *kenosis*. How does this relate to Beloved Jesus Christ?

5) Has Beloved Jesus Christ ever sinned? Read Hebrews 4:15 to check your answer. How does being sinless relate to Beloved's ability to redeem you, His Bride?

6) Describe Beloved's eyes, cheeks, hands, and His divine kiss of peace.

7) Do you feel you can describe your relationship with Beloved as a friendship? Explain.

Chapter Ten
My Love

O my love, you are as beautiful as Tirzah, lovely as Jerusalem,
awesome as an army with banners! Turn your eyes away
from me, for they have overcome me.
~Song of Solomon 6:4-5a

Then I, John, saw the holy city, New Jerusalem,
coming down out of heaven from God,
prepared as a bride adorned for her husband.
~Revelation 21:2

I will never forget, when at the university I attended, Valentine's Day brought with it a special treat. A carrier would deliver a dozen red roses to a number of dorm-mates. Each time, I'd set my textbooks aside and enter the hallway, eager to hear the inevitable cry of whomever the lucky gal would be. Oh, I knew other squeals would follow, as a stampede of girls would charge the dorm room to see her bouquet and congratulate her. I wouldn't be one of them, but the least I could do was to come into the hallway and applaud her.

For three years straight, I'd seen this happen, so when I saw another dozen wafting down the hallway, I prepared to congratulate a classmate. I was surprised to learn the gal was me! I squealed so loud Martians probably heard me. I did not think my boyfriend Phil would send roses. Surely, he could not, as he was working his way through the university, and was on a shoe-string budget. But, to my delight, he did.

We were attending separate universities—I in Tennessee, and my beloved in Florida. As the red roses floated down the hallway, and continued past every door to mine, which was second from last, I felt flushed the closer he got. As the carrier stopped at my dorm room, I thought I would faint right on top of him.

More than the gesture of my beloved sending me pretty roses, this bouquet carried with it a promise of love. Phil loved me. Right there on the card, I read those words. To follow was a phone confirmation, which in those days was a shared dorm floor phone booth.

He loved me…

He said the words.

And he confirmed the sentiment with roses.

Do you know how difficult it is to take notes with a vase of red roses sitting on your desk? I managed. The first day I carried them to every class. Then I parked my roses in the Forestry Hall—not to be touched by anyone—since that building was my getaway place to study and to hang out. I'm not sure I learned anything that week from my professors, but I did learn about love.

I was distracted by love…

What I learned on Valentine's Day, February 14, 1986, had nothing to do with my major in forestry. My soon-to-be-husband's red-rose-expression captured my attention, and I leaned into true love. Had he popped the question, "Will you marry me?" over the phone, I would have answered, "Yes!"

Even though we pretended nothing had changed, we were both smitten. Although this was a long-distance romance, I knew my beloved would eventually marry me. To him, I was a keeper. No longer would the thought even cross my mind that he'd find someone more desirable than me. The roses my Valentine sent to me were akin to a wedding ring. It didn't take long for him to slide the engagement ring on my finger.

Saint Valentine, who lived in Rome during the early years of Christianity, also valued love. In his day, there were strict laws imposed by Emperor Claudius II, which forbade Roman soldiers to marry. In resistance to this ordinance, Saint Valentine began to secretly marry these soldiers in Christian ceremonies, and as a result of his defiance of Claudius II, the king sentenced Saint Valentine to death on February 14, 270 AD.

The final act Saint Valentine accomplished was to heal a blind girl. Even though he knew he would be executed for this and the secret marriages, he stood firm, valuing love. The importance he placed on love—especially romantic love—remains to this day. We celebrate Valentine's Day, not only in the USA, but all over the world.[180]

Love…

What is this thing we call love that captures our attention so much that Saint Valentine chose death over life to promote it? What is it about love that caused Beloved to choose death on a cross to demonstrate His enduring love for us, His Bride? Paul writes, *But God demonstrates His own love toward us, in that while we were still sinners, Christ died for us* (Romans 5:8). In Beloved's own words He says, *"Greater love has no one than this, than to lay down one's life for his friends"* (John 15:13).

Let's face it. Mankind is a love magnet. Love is a primal need. This is why men send red roses and buy sparkling diamonds. This is why the written love note, or the handcrafted trinket, or the novelty gift elicits strong emotions. Men, as well as their chosen brides, need to find an expression for love.

Love goes deeper than romance. We need to know we are loved, not only by a husband, but also by a child, brother, father, or mother. But our deepest desire is to know we are loved by our Creator. Father God made sure we got the message by sending His only begotten Son, Jesus Christ, to demonstrate that He loves us—and that not by roses but through Calvary's cross. Jesus became mankind's Valentine, and then some. Our Bridegroom is Beloved Solomon—our *Dowd Shelomah*—the God of divine love and peace personified.

In Chapter Eight of the vignette, you declare to Beloved, *Set me as a seal upon your heart, as a seal upon your arm; for love* [ahabah] *is as strong as death, jealousy as cruel as the grave; its flames are flames of fire, a most vehement flame. Many waters cannot quench love* [ahabah], *nor can the floods drown it. If a man would give for love* [ahabah] *all the wealth of his house, it would be utterly despised* (Song 8:6-7).

We would think the word usage in the above passage would be *dowd*—divine God-love—but it is not. The word used here is *ahabah,*[181] and as such, it is a notch lower than *dowd*. It can sometimes indicate God-love, but it usually references lovers' passionate desire one for another. I point this out because if romantic *ahabah* love is this powerful, think of how much more powerful Beloved's divine *dowd* love is for you. Glory!

We place such value on natural, romantic love, that we've set aside a holiday to celebrate it. We are willing to sacrifice wealth, activities, and, as shown here in the vignette, even life itself, to attain romantic love.

How much better is Beloved's divine love for you, His Bride? Paul writes about this. He says, *For I am persuaded that neither death nor life, nor angels nor principalities nor powers, nor things present nor things to come, nor height nor depth, nor any other created thing, shall be able to separate us from the love of God which is in Christ Jesus our Lord* (Romans 8:38-39).

Jesus Christ is our Valentine.

In Scene Fifteen, your Valentine speaks, Love. As you read your Beloved's compliments, savor

---

[180] ____. Roses Only; The Early History of Valentine's Day. https://www.rosesonly.com.au/what-is-valentines-day
[181] Strong. OT #160 *ahabah,* natural human love or sexual desire, or divine love

the praises He has penned just for you. Receive each compliment as if it is a rose from the red rose bouquet. But they are more than an expression of natural love, they express your Groom's divine, everlasting love.

Permit yourself to feel the grandeur of love's expression, from the Groom who is coming again. And when He does, He will sweep you into His wedding chariot. Personalize this scene, Love, for you are the recipient of this red rose bouquet of compliments.

Your Valentine speaks.

"My Love is…" comprises this next scene.

Bow to your Husband-King, for His love for you grows deeper within your spirit every time you reflect on His praises. From this overflow, you are being equipped to evangelize nations.

Enter in, Valentine of Christ:

*****

SONG OF SOLOMON 6:4-13
Scene Fifteen: My Love is…

SETTING:	The Sharon Valley. Dew covers the fertile grasses which are dotted with Rose of Sharon and white lily flowers. VALLEY PEOPLE stand with BELOVED, listening to His discourse.
	Lighting: Purple and gold; representing sunlight
AT RISE:	LOVE and her MAIDENS crest the hill to the Sharon Valley, center stage.

NARRATOR

Love has begun her journey back to the Sharon Valley. She desires Beloved's kiss. Nothing else will satisfy her except for face-to-face intimacy with her Groom. Love's perspective has changed; she prioritizes their relationship. Instead of putting her own needs first, she declares, "I am my beloved's, and my beloved is mine: he feeds *his flock* among the lilies." Look! Here comes Beloved! Let's listen:

(LOVE falls prostrate before BELOVED. He reaches toward her, beckoning her to rise.)

BELOVED

(Addresses LOVE)

⁴O My Love, you *are* as beautiful as Tirzah, lovely as Jerusalem, awesome as *an army* with banners.

(LOVE gazes at BELOVED longingly; He turns his head slightly)

⁵ᵃTurn your eyes away from me, for they have overcome me.

(BELOVED embraces LOVE and strokes her hair.)

⁵ᵇYour hair *is* like a flock of goats going down from Gilead.

(LOVE smiles, giddy with love, blushing)

NARRATOR

How can Love, a mere lady, touch the heart of a perfect King? It is through a true heart of worship that her eyes have overcome Him. This is why He mentions His Bride's adoring eyes, which are a reflection of His Spirit within her, and the washed sheep of Gilead, which represent her healthy and pure thoughts toward Him.

BELOVED

(BELOVED touches LOVE'S smile lines; LOVE'S smile broadens)

⁶Your teeth *are* like a flock of sheep which have come up from the washing; every one bears twins,

and none is barren among them.

NARRATOR

Beloved knows Love's every thought. He assures her she is accepted. Love knows this, too, for she smiles so wide her Groom points out her joyful countenance.
>(LOVE bows, kissing BELOVED's toes. Stooping, BELOVED gently lifts LOVE'S gaze to behold His own.)

BELOVED

[7]Like a piece of a pomegranate *are* your temples behind your veil.
>(BELOVED and LOVE stand, and embrace)

NARRATOR

The veil shows the Groom and Bride value their marriage covenant. Although Love is imperfect in many ways; her heart is submitted to Beloved's lordship and, therefore, she has won His favor.

BELOVED

>(Looking into LOVE'S eyes; holding both of her hands.)

[8] There are sixty queens, and eighty concubines, and virgins without number. [9a] My dove, my perfect one, is the only one…
>(Gazes into LOVE'S eyes; embraces her; almost kissing her)

NARRATOR

Why does Beloved's speech trail off? He is captivated by the Bride's blushing cheeks and focused gaze. Love knows she belongs to her Husband-King forever. She never wants to leave His side ever again! When Beloved calls her, she will be determined to answer quickly! Beloved boldly proclaims His Bride is of great value to Him. Listen! He now addresses the valley people.

BELOVED

>(Addressing the VALLEY PEOPLE and MAIDENS)

…[9b]the only one of her mother; the favorite of the one who bore her.
>(BELOVED motions to the MAIDENS)

MAIDENS

>(The MAIDENS address the VALLEY PEOPLE, continuing where BELOVED left off)

The daughters saw her, and called her blessed, the queens and the concubines, and they praised her. [10]Who is she that looks forth as the morning, fair as the moon, clear as the sun, awesome as an army with banners?
>(BELOVED and LOVE walk amongst the people, greeting each one with a handshake or a side hug)

NARRATOR

Who is this woman called Love? She is Beloved's ministry partner, wife, and His very best friend. True love compels them to make plans to visit other valleys.
>(BELOVED brushes LOVE'S cheek.)

Why does a tear trickle from the Bride's eye? Love had wanted her earthly mother's approval, but she never received it; and yet, she now knows that to Beloved she is like a choice daughter of the Holy Spirit; cherished and greatly valued. This expunges the pain of family rejection. Who else could love her like Beloved does?

(BELOVED and LOVE exit, stage right, arm in arm.)
(Lighting: Golden-green glow.)
(LOVE reappears, stage left; the MAIDENS gather around her.)
The maidens are eager to hear about Love's travels. What did she experience while she was on a ministry trip with Beloved? This will be the first of many to come. Let's listen in.

LOVE

[11]I went down into the garden of nuts to see the verdure of the valley, and to see whether the vine had budded, *and* the pomegranates had bloomed. [12]Before I was even aware, my soul had made me *as* the chariots of my noble people.

NARRATOR

Love speaks of the noble people of Ammi-nadib. She knows she is faithful, like them, and she is yoked to Beloved as a horse to his chariot-rider.
(LOVE exits; stage right; hand to ear, as if listening to Beloved's distant voice)
(Center stage; stage right; stage left; VALLEY PEOPLE searching)

VALLEY PERSON ONE

[13a]Return, return, O Shulamite; return, return, that we may look upon you!

LOVE

[13b]What will you see in the Shulamite —

VALLEY PERSON ONE

[13c]As it were, the dance of the two camps?

NARRATOR

Love is like a company of two armies. For she is on the earth but attuned to the angelic army of her Husband-King. She is robust in spirit and committed to Beloved in all of her ways. She has departed to be where He is. She will remain close to Him, never leaving His Spirit's embrace and keeping within earshot of His voice of wisdom. She is His partner in ministry.

*****

What's happening in this scene? As you approach your Groom, you realize not only does He love you, He notices your love for Him has matured so you have won His favor. You can see it in His eyes! Beloved has been captivated by your glances of love. By worshipping, you have become to your Groom a sight most beautiful to behold.

As we explore each of Beloved's compliments, pay particular attention to the people and places, animals, fruits, and other such things Beloved uses to metaphorically define your character.

THE BRIDE AS TIRZAH

With Beloved's first compliment, He compares you to the woman named Tirzah. He says, *O my love, you* are *as beautiful as Tirzah, lovely as Jerusalem, awesome as* an army *with banners* (Song 6:4)!

This first compliment begs the question, who was Tirzah?

Tirzah was a daughter of Zelophehad.[182] She was born during Moses' exodus out of Egypt. Because Zelophehad had no sons, only daughters, this presented a dilemma. Tirzah and her sisters wondered what would happen to their father's family name. When they reached the Promised Land, would they inherit Zelophehad's portion of land? Or would they lose their inheritance? They did not

---

[182] Numbers 26:33, 27:1-11, 36:11; Joshua 17:3

know the answer because it was customary for men to inherit the lands. Tirzah decided that as soon as they reached the Promised Land, she would ask Moses to give them their father's inheritance.[183]

As Moses prayed, God spoke favorably regarding the daughters' dilemma. Accordingly, Moses passed the inheritance Zelophehad would have received to his daughters. God not only instructed Moses to grace Tirzah and her sisters with an inheritance, but He also told Moses to make this the governing rule. If a man had no sons, the inheritance was to go to his daughters, and if he had no daughters, the inheritance was to go to his brothers or close kinsmen.

There is no doubt about God's opinion. Gender did not cause Him to erase Zelophehad's family name. They remained among their people with the full rights as any other Israelite citizen. Eventually, Zelophehad's daughters married into the family lines of Manasseh, but even then, they honored and remembered their father Zelophehad's name.

Let's look at the meaning of "Tirzah." This name comes from a root word that means "favorable."[184] Favor graced Tirzah and her sisters, and they received identity through their ancestry, when their father's name, Zelophehad, was honored.

The daughter Tirzah, being the spokesperson for her sisters, gained even more favor. There's a territory named after her which is recorded to be "the seat of the kingdom"[185] in its day. Therefore, we see that not only did God preserve the family name, but He also empowered Tirzah to rule a territory, and she did so with excellence.

How does this apply to you as the Bride? Because you honor Beloved's name, He speaks favor over you just as Moses spoke favor over Tirzah. You are not forgotten. In fact, He is so enthralled with you that you rule with Kingdom authority! Once, you were rejected by your parental bloodline; but now, you are prized as Beloved's own inheritance.

Not only have you won Beloved's favor, you have the authority to reign with the seat of kingdom's power as Tirzah once reigned in her territory. What is this kingdom you reign in? All Beloved is in charge of—both in Heaven and on earth—is yours. The Lord's Prayer, *Your kingdom come. Your will be done on earth as* it is *in heaven* (Matthew 6:10), is a reality to you.

If you are of Beloved's family line, then why does He say you are the choice of your mother (see Song 6:9b)? She clearly rejected you (see Song 1:6). The word used here is *Em,*[186] and as we discussed earlier, it means "the bond of the family." Remember, the Holy Spirit is this bonding agent. He is not female, but Scripture sometimes references the Holy Spirit in this fashion to show He is a nurturer. So, in an allegorical rather than a literal sense, the Holy Spirit is similar to a mother. Here, the Holy Spirit has nurtured you, and it is He who has bonded you to your Beloved. The Holy Spirit has come alongside you, making Beloved real to your heart.

With Beloved's first compliment, this fact is clear—Beloved never has shared your family's opinion of you. Their approval or disapproval is not an issue to your Bridegroom. You belong to Beloved. Period. His Spirit lives within you, and He has graced you with an earthly and a spiritual inheritance. He knew your destiny long before you did, and although the pain you felt from being expelled from your family hurt you to your core, Beloved has taken you as His very own inheritance. He encourages you to embrace your godly heritage in Him. All that Heaven holds you now have access to through your Savior. He has made you "the seat of authority" from whom His words flow.

This means Beloved is counting on you to evangelize people. Will you reach others who are rejected as you once were? Furthermore, will you reach out to those who hurt you as the opportunity presents itself? Ouch! In order to have the boldness and the love necessary to accomplish this task, your hands must drip with the same myrrh that dripped from Beloved's fingers. His myrrh-drenched hands symbolize forgiveness, priesthood, and *kenosis*. As you share Beloved's love with those who

---

183 Numbers 27:1-4
184 Strong. OT #8656; *tirtsah*; delightsomeness; from OT #7521; *ratsah*; favourable
185 *Blue Letter Bible.* Word search on *tirzah.* Gesenisus's Lexicon.
186 Strong. OT #517; *Em*

have lost their destiny to the weight of sin, they also will realize they are Beloved's treasured possession.

Why does Beloved entrust you with this mission? Tirzah also means "pleasantness." The love you share with Beloved makes your speech pleasant. Therefore, your inner transformation makes you attractive to others. They will seek you out because they will see Beloved's Spirit within you. As they do, you'll know the timing is right. Beloved's words will be on your lips because they are deep within your heart. You have centered your spirit in Beloved. You reflect on His love. You share His identity. You speak His words…

In this one word, "Tirzah," Beloved reveals your favored status, your inheritance as the seat of authority, and your pleasant speech. These are the hidden truths of this verse. Once you have grasped this, these truths will stay with you as jewels of wisdom from above. Not only are you not forgotten, but you will not forget these truths.

THE BRIDE IS BEAUTIFUL; LOVELY

Let's look at the rest of Beloved's compliment in this passage. Beloved says you are *beautiful*, and *lovely* (6:4b).[187] These words are essentially the same. Other synonyms for these include "fairest," "suitable," and "pleasant." The maidens call you "fairest" often, as does Beloved.

So, what's the point? Psychologists say it takes a lot of compliments to negate a negative comment. Beloved wants to make sure you get the point by using repetition. He makes sure you receive an abundance of praises from His very own lips. He believes in you! His acceptance brings you back to the beginning of your discovery when He spoke favorably to your wounded heart. He makes sure you still know, through the maidens' words and through His very own words, that you are *as beautiful as Tirzah, lovely as Jerusalem* (Song 6:4b). I am certain He speaks other choice words of praise.

He also restores your inheritance, saying you belong in Jerusalem. You are lovely there, so between this and His reference to Tirzah, He makes sure you belong. Spiritually, He is assuring you that you belong to the family of believers. Christians weren't on the scene yet, so He could not have penned "lovely as a Christian," but the message is there.

THE BRIDE IS AWESOME; TERRIBLE

You also are *awesome* (Song 6:4b). The King James rendered this as *terrible* (Song 6:4b KJV). The definition is, "frightening."[188] What is pleasant about this description? It doesn't seem to fit any positive connotation for Beloved to say His Bride is frightening. However, when we realize who we are frightening, it makes perfect sense. The enemy—Satan—is so terrified of you and me, that he flees every time we shoot a love-glance toward Beloved Jesus Christ!

Notice that Beloved says your "eyes" overcome Him. Because you have learned to praise Him, your glances work fear into the heart of the enemy. Tirzah was "the seat of authority" in her day. You have Beloved's authority today, and the enemy knows this is true. Your "dove's eyes," that reflect the Holy Spirit within you, overcome Beloved and He is drawn to you, while at the same time these glances frighten Satan and this little imp flees from you.

THE BRIDE OF JERUSALEM; ARMY WITH BANNERS

You are *lovely as Jerusalem, awesome as* an army *with banners* (Song 6:4b). What does this mean? As "Jerusalem," you are the favored city. As "an army with banners," you are hailed as Queen, with the favor not only of your Husband-King, but also of His people, some of whom make up your army. Both terms point again to the fact that you have authority. God's people who live in Jerusalem

---

[187] Strong. OT #3303; *yapheh*; OT #5000; naveh
[188] Strong. OT #366; *ayom*, frightful, terrible

possess an army of soldiers who fight under the banner of their King. You are Beloved's representative, so you rule, too, in the spiritual realm.

Remember what is written on the banner that Beloved flies in Heaven? It is a single, yet powerful word, "Love." This is an unusual army banner to fly, but, oh, how fitting it is! This banner indicates that as Beloved's chosen Bride, you have His approval, favor, and authority to reign. However, you win battles not out of conquest but by bringing love to captive hearts who are longing to find their identity in the King of Glory.

The people you bring into God's kingdom are the oppressed, wounded, hurting souls whose banner is shame and rejection. Because you once felt these emotions, you identify with their outcast feelings. You know rightly how to bring them under the banner of Beloved's love.

THE BRIDE'S OVERCOMING GLANCES

Beloved says, *Turn your eyes away from me, for they have overcome me* (Song 6:5a). Beloved's praises mimic the marriage bed scene, where He was captivated by your love and where for the first time you were able to twice return *dowd*-love to Him. The ensuing compliments are of the same tone, with some repetition of phrases.

Beloved begins His compliments by noting the reflection of His Holy Spirit in your eyes. He allows you to know He is *overcome* (Song 6:5b) by your worshipful spirit. Here, the word "overcome" means "to be captured."[189] Think of the significance—Beloved is Lord of all—but He allows Himself to be captured by our praises! Why? He values our exaltation of Him.

How do we enter into worship? We climb Lebanon's mountain range: the place of purity, prayer, and praise. We enter Amana's *amen* agreement. We climb Senir's peaks and war in the Spirit until there is nothing left to be concerned with. What remains after this Amana experience is the marriage bed experience of Mt. Hermon where we enter into true worship and into the consuming *dowd* of our Beloved's holiness within the covenant of marriage. This progression of worship is not only what makes our victory possible, it is how we capture Beloved's heart. He wants us to give Him focused, unbroken attention. The result is time in the Throne room, the Holy of Holies, where we come face-to-face with our Bridegroom.

Do you have a challenge today? The solution is not found by rehearsing the problem; rather, the victory comes by praising Beloved and acknowledging His lordship over you. I love what my friend Steve Bailey said when I asked him to describe who Beloved is. He responded, "He is the quiet in any storm." When Beloved is in the midst, how can difficulties stay? They can't! Praise chases troubles away!

THE BRIDE'S HAIR; VEIL

Beloved says, *Your hair* is *like a flock of goats going down from Gilead* (Song 6:5b). Your hair is the physical veil worn as a symbol of your marriage covenant. In several Bible versions, the words "hair" and "veil" are interchangeable, both meaning the same. So, your hair represents solidarity just like your veil does.

Your hair also represents purity. Is your hair dirty, as your veil was in the previous dream sequence? No! It has been washed, and so have you. You are clean. Beloved doesn't hold grudges, so He makes sure you know you are pure. You will be strongest when, in any point of weakness, you yield to Beloved's loving inspection. Repentance enables us to turn from self-will to dependence.

What do we do when we have struggles? As much as we want to remain completely pure, we fall short. There are no exceptions. Paul writes, *for all have sinned and fall short of the glory of God* (Romans 3:23). What do we do? Paul also writes, *being justified freely by His [God's] grace through the redemption that is in Christ Jesus* (Romans 3:24). In Song of Solomon, we see Beloved empowering us to

---

[189] Strong. OT #7292; *rahab*; to capture, be importune, or strengthen.

start again, write a new chapter, become a new person. In this scene, we see that we are made new. Paul also writes, *For He [God] made* Him *who knew no sin* to be *sin for us, that we might become the righteousness of God in Him* (Romans 5:21).

Our washed hair shows our marriage covenant is secured by our perfect Groom. When our thoughts are on Him, they become purified. This is also why Paul advises us to fix our eyes on Jesus, the Author and Finisher of our faith (see Hebrews 12:1-3). Just keep gazing, Love, and you will be the spotless Bride your Bridegroom knows is your destiny.

THE BRIDE OF GILEAD

Let's look further at the word, "Gilead." In the book of Jeremiah 8:22, we learn that Gilead was known for its balm that was used for cleansing and healing wounds. Your wounds have been cleansed and healed, having been washed and ointment applied, but there is more.

In this scene, you have come up from the healing waters of Gilead, which would have been the Jordan River of today. Thus, you have been immersed in the baptismal waters of Jordan's healing streams. The act of being immersed in Gilead's waters symbolizes the death of self-will and rising anew in Christ Jesus. You have set aside your own will and yielded to Beloved's will.

In the New Testament, John the Baptist chose the Jordan River to baptize believers as a sign of death to the old nature and a birthing of the new nature. Thus, we see Beloved Jesus Christ prophetically revealed yet again in Song of Solomon. Remember, self-will produces enmity, whereas dependence produces faith. When we have great faith, we see healings and miracles. They just come.

Beloved loves us despite our weaknesses. Each time we worship, weaknesses lose their hold on us. Sometimes Beloved will whisper a change that is needful, but it's always done in love. He never accuses us, or corrects in anger.

Most of the changes that happen as we immerse ourselves in the healing waters of Beloved's love happen while we are unaware of the transformation that is taking place. Beloved is that gentle. While we rest in Him, our Groom washes us with the cleansing waters of Gilead. Problems slip away, and we arise renewed. And as aforementioned, physical healings also come.

This is the reason we must closely guard our tarrying times and come often to these streams of living water. It is important to schedule tarrying times so that this becomes a purposeful and regular cleansing activity.

THE BRIDE'S WIDE-EYED, PERFECT SMILE

Beloved says, *Your teeth* are *like a flock of sheep which have come up from the washing; every one bears twins, and none is barren among them* (Song 6:6). Why does Beloved reference teeth? It is because as your joy is being restored so you are smiling again! Healthy words are flowing from your lips, and you do not miss one opportunity to praise Beloved. These praises bring remembrances to you of the intimacy you experience in Lebanon's mountaintop retreat.

Compare Scene Twelve with Scene Fifteen. In Scene Twelve, Beloved says, *Your teeth* are *like a flock of shorn* sheep *which have come up from the washing, every one of which bears twins, and none is barren among them. Your lips* are *like a strand of scarlet, and your mouth is lovely* (Song 4:2-3a). Scene Fifteen is very similar.

The point Beloved is repeating here, is that you are fully His, just as you were in the previous scene, which culminated in Mt. Hermon's secluded prayer garden. He is showing you that you can still be intimately in love with Him. Beloved does not withdraw His love because we make mistakes. His love is constant, even when ours is not.

THE GROOM'S GIFT OF POMEGRANATES

We can guard our thought life, which is evidenced by the words that flow from our lips. Are they negative or positive thoughts? Paul instructs us to think on whatever things are: true, noble, just, pure, lovely, of good report, virtuous, and praiseworthy (see Philippians 4:8). What we think on is what we will do (Philippians 4:9). So, we must order our thoughts on right things. But the loveliest thoughts to think are about Beloved Himself. As we think on Him, we become like Him. Therefore, the vignette seamlessly moves from the praises of our lips to the pomegranate representative of wisdom from above.

Notice that the pomegranate theme is repeated also from Scene Twelve (compare Song 4:3b with 6:7). In Scene Twelve, Beloved says, *Your temples behind your veil* are *like a piece of pomegranate* (Song 4:3b). Here, in Scene Fifteen, He says, *Like a piece of a pomegranate* are *your temples behind your veil* (Song 6:7). Again, repetition is used to anchor the truth. In Scene Fifteen, and elsewhere, the words "veil" and "locks" are used interchangeably for the same concept—pure thoughts. The King James even renders "veil" as "locks" in this passage.

A pomegranate is an aphrodisiac. You are in a state of solidarity with your Husband-King, your thoughts constantly drifting to Him. You are united as Bride, the veil or locks representing the marriage covenant.

Pomegranates also represent wise, nourishing, wholesome thoughts. The thoughts you think reflect kingdom living. This is pleasing to your Groom. Wisdom is what you seek. James writes, *If any of you lack wisdom, let him ask of God, who gives to all liberally and without reproach* (James 1:5a). If we want spiritual wisdom, all we need to do is ask. There are no dumb questions—if we don't know how we should think on a matter, Beloved is willing to teach us. In Scene Fifteen, you have done just that. Rather than trusting in your own ways, you have submitted to Beloved's leadership. This results in Beloved's compliment about your temples resembling pomegranates of wisdom.

But it is more than ordering our thoughts aright, what matters to our Beloved is our decision to order our thoughts on Him. This is what makes a difference. In this scene, you've eaten the aphrodisiac of love and you are lovesick to the max. This perpetual lovesick state, where all you want to do is to gaze at your Beloved and spend time thinking about Him, is what perfects you. When we order our day where Beloved is first, we of default become wiser in our decision making.

THE BRIDE'S PERFECTION

Beloved says, *There are sixty queens, and eighty concubines, and virgins without number…* (Song 6:8). This passage refers to peoples. Dignitaries would be the "queens." Those who have religious duties out of obligation would be the "concubines." "Virgins without number" would refer to believers in general. There are many in the valley, but your King favors you among them all. Why? The next compliment expounds on this. It has to do with your purity, so let's continue reading the passage.

Beloved, along with the maidens, continue, saying, *…My dove, my perfect one, is the only one of her mother, the favorite of the one who bore her. The daughters saw her, and called her blessed, the queens and the concubines, and they praised her* (Song 6:9). Beloved's Holy Spirit has come alongside you and become your Teacher. He favors you. You are clean; undefiled by worldliness and anything that has been imposed on you or how sin has defiled you. You are not impure—you have been washed by Beloved's Holy Spirit. You are complete, whole, forgiven, perfected. He once again is making certain you know He accepts you. You are not defined by your past where you were considered an outcast among your family and friends. You are not defined by your present either. Because you have a yielded heart, He favors you. You have a single mindset. You desire to do whatever His will is. He makes sure you know that, although you might have felt you would never achieve anything of value, the very choice you have made to value Him makes you His choice Bride.

Think of a girl with beautiful ribbons in her hair and a frilly dress, sitting in a room full of guests. Where do all the eyes go? Everyone looks at that little girl. Her innocence captures their attention. You, Bride of Christ, are like that sweet little girl. You are carefree, silly-in-love, and brand new. You are like an only daughter, treasured by her mother.

Beloved is captivated by your innocent trust. He is overtaken by your eyes of faith. He is glad that you believe He has all the answers. And, blessed Bride, He does.

THE MAIDENS' COMPLIMENTS

The maiden says, *Who is she who looks forth as the morning, fair as the moon, clear as the sun, awesome as* an army *with banners?* (Song 6:10). Where Beloved left off, they continue. They have some choice compliments that describe four aspects of your character. Let's discuss these.

THE BRIDE AS THE MORNING

First, the maidens say, *Who is she who looks forth as the morning* (Song 6:10a)? Do you know what they are indicating? They are speaking of your commitment. You truly are Beloved's, and He truly does come to you. Morning rises like clockwork; it comes consistently. You can count on its arrival. Your commitment to Beloved is like this clock. You are not sporadic in your commitment — you are consistent. This pleases Beloved, and the maidens remind you of this.

Is it any wonder that you have Beloved's approval? He knows you have conquered complacency. You come consistently and regularly to Him as you read His Word and worship Him through your songs and thoughts of praise. What began as obedience continues as zealous joy, for Beloved has become the treasure of your longing heart.

THE BRIDE AS THE MOON

Second, the maidens describe you as *fair as the moon* (Song 6:10b). What they are describing here is your interdependence. A moon does not have its own light source. Neither do you rely on your own strength. The Spirit of Beloved empowers you; that's why you are fair.

Your beauty is a reflection of the Spirit of God inside your spirit. Truth shines from within you, softly and gently, just as the moon glows softly on a starry night. People depend on the insight you have, and they receive comfort from your words of peace. How do you have such beautiful words? You echo Beloved's sentiments.

THE BRIDE AS THE SUN

Third, the maidens compliment your purity. You are *clear as the sun* (Song 6:10b). If the sun were a jewel, where would its pureness rate? It would be off the charts! You are that jewel to God. Beloved has purified you, with fires greater than the blazing sun, and you stand guiltless before Him. You enlighten everything around you with the wisdom of your Beloved! Shadows flee, confusion lifts, and people are nourished. You are able do this because you are tapped into the energy source who is Beloved. The Son of God is your "sun."

THE BRIDE'S ARMY BANNERS

Fourth, the maidens describe that you are *awesome as* an army *with banners* (Song 6:10b). They are letting you know what Beloved previously spoke to you by referencing Tirzah. He is revealing your divine authority. This is your inheritance as His Bride.

The greatest weapon in your arsenal is your words of praise. Beloved has given you His authority to draw upon. His banner of love for you flies high for all to see. Even the enemy sees Beloved's love-banner that waves over the Bride, and it frightens him. People follow you. Beloved backs you with a heavenly regime. You are on Earth, but Beloved's army backs your works here. So, whatever is available to you in the heavenly realm is available to you here too.

THE BRIDE'S MISSIONARY JOURNEY

Next, you go with Beloved to the valley. This portion is abbreviated, probably to demonstrate that this is your natural course of life now. Consequentially, nothing is written to detail this out; but as you reappear on the stage of the vignette, we are aware that your travels with Beloved are something you cherished because the maidens ask you about them. The maidens want to know where you went and what Beloved showed you.

You respond, *I went down to the garden of nuts to see the verdure of the valley, to see whether the vine had budded,* and *the pomegranates had bloomed* (Song 6:11). What is being communicated here? Beloved has shown you how to know when someone is ready to commit to Him. You look for the light of God inside of people.

Remember, from John 4:35b, we know He tells you to look for those who are *white* — those who have a spark of glory in their eyes. These you know are ready to harvest. You look for this little spark of glory within their spirits. It is all you need to kindle the Spirit flame within them. But you don't stop there. You disciple them. You nurture spiritual fruits at all their levels of productivity. You want a lush green garden littered with blossoms and fruits of the Spirit within the people you minister to. This is the discipleship process, which is as important as evangelism.

You have come to the Sharon Valley because it is here that you will find many ready souls. Do your words ignite them? To those who have the spark of God, your pleasant speech will be fertilizer for their spirits.

Once, you were searching for Beloved. Now, it's your turn to cultivate the spiritual beauty of others because you've found Him. Will you be a faithful witness? If you are to be effective, then you will be an observer of spiritual fruits, valuing each individual for the person that he or she is and spurring them forward. Rather than learning rhetoric, you learn to observe people's needs. Then you edify each individual.

THE NOBLE PEOPLE OF AMMI-NADIB

You share with the maidens that you are linked with Beloved as a horse to its chariot-rider. You say, *Before I was even aware, my soul made me as the chariots of my noble people* (Song 6:12). The King James reads, *Or ever I was aware, my soul made me* like *the chariots of Ammi-nadib* (Song 6:12 KJV).

Who are the noble people of Ammi-nadib? The priest Ammi-nadib willingly bore the Ark of the Covenant.[190] His name means, "people of liberality."[191] Therefore, this is a much better description of you than the freely charging stallion of Scene Three where Beloved described you as His *filly among Pharaoh's chariots* (Song 2:9b). You are no longer a wild horse; rather, you are a bridled horse. You have strength and purpose because Beloved's words direct you. He is your chariot rider, and you are His pure and powerful filly.

You are a covenant keeper. You are Beloved's and He is yours. Furthermore, the strength and solidarity you have gained has been so gradual you scarcely have been aware of this transforming process. While you have been serving Beloved, and from the overflow of the Holy Spirit's anointing you have been serving others, Beloved has been shoring you up and perfecting you unaware.

THE MAIDENS' PLEA

The maidens beckon you, *Return, return, O Shulamite; return, return, that we may look upon you* (Song 6:13)! Four times they say "return." You respond, *What would you see in the Shulamite?* Predictably, they respond, *As it were the dance of two armies* (Song 6:13b). The people recognize that your beauty is a reflection of Beloved, whom you adore. You are no longer your own person.

Four times, as in four Gospels, the valley people plead, *Return!* They want to look at you. Why? They see that your earthly army and Beloved's heavenly army is united. As you pray, Heaven and Earth join, and the kingdom of Heaven becomes available to the people. Healings and the spirit gifts mentioned in 1 Corinthians 12-14 flow freely.

---

190 See 11 Chronicles 15:11, 14-15
191 Strong. OT #5991 *Ammimadib*

You, Bride of Christ, are a gateway to the heavenlies. The people you serve know that when you come, so does the *dowd* of Beloved. Whether you are sharing the ABCs of salvation or you are teaching advanced truths, you do so in love. Simply stated, God-love wins, and the people desire you to share more, for yours is a holy dance with the King of Kings. Beloved is your dance partner, and they desire to be as unified as you. When the Dancer twirls His cherished Bride, the audience of believers is likewise blessed.

CONCLUSION

Who are you, Love? What you stated last in the dialogue of the previous scene was a simple statement, but it is true. In Scene Fourteen you said, *I am my Beloved's and my Beloved is mine; he feeds his flock among the lilies* (Song 6:3). Three character-traits you mention is that you belong to Beloved, He adores you, and He trusts you to meet the spiritual needs of His people. This is your ministry in action.

You obey, feeding humble souls who are responding to Beloved's words. For those who are "white" with glory and ready for harvest, you go, obedient to your Husband-King. You remain on the ready, waiting to share Beloved's love with the people.

Most would walk right by a hungry soul, but not you! Because Beloved's love is boiling-hot inside of you, you care about discipling people. The *dowd* of God within you is active, and it cannot remain within itself. By its very nature, it is an active love force that must be shared.

Who does Beloved say you are? You are a beautiful, pure, empowered, awesome, balanced, healed, baptized, and glorious reflection of your King, and these are just a few of your Groom's choice praises. You, Bride of Christ, are blessed to be united with the King of Glory, and so are the people.

In Scene Sixteen, we will discern what the people say about you. But first, let's pray to the Lord of the Dance. Remember, Love, to go off script as you desire:

My Perfect Valentine,
Fan into flame the spark of glory You've placed within my spirit. Make this glory flame to rise as a consuming fire, so that all that remains of me is Your Spirit within my own spirit. Help me to be completely united with You. Make me a reflection Your divine love and peace.

As I praise You, reside in me as Ammi-Nadib who carried Your covenant. With You as Commander of the heavenly army, and I as your earthly ambassador, I will be Your vessel to bring to Earth what is commonplace in Heaven.

Give me a heart for people. Let me discern even the slightest spark of Your glory within the eyes of those You are sending me to. Love them through me, and help me to shepherd and disciple them. Empower me to witness in Your authority, and Your glory. Give me wisdom, anointing, and rest.

Above all, help me to treasure You as the love of my life, and the breath within my soul. For You, my true Valentine, are the reason I live. I exist here and into Heaven to honor You.
Your Valentine,
Love

BRIDAL REFLECTION

1) Describe a Valentine gift you have received or sent. How does this relate to the power of love?

2) Discuss Saint Valentine and his commitment to honor love. How does Beloved Jesus' love surpass these expressions?

3) Who is Tirzah? Where is she mentioned in Song of Solomon? What correlation does Tirzah's life have regarding your spiritual inheritance as the Bride of Christ?

4) When Beloved Jesus says you are "awesome" (KJV "terrible"), who are you frightening by your spiritual authority as the Bride of Christ?

5) Why does Beloved say your eyes are like doves? How is it they have overcome your Groom?

6) How do you know when someone is ready to receive a witness? (Hint: "white.")

7) Write a prayer to your Beloved Valentine.

Chapter Eleven
A Search for Lilies

Come, my beloved, let us go forth to the field; let us lodge in the villages.
Let us get up early to the vineyards; let us see if the vine has budded, whether
the grape blossoms are open, and the pomegranates are in bloom.
There will I give you my love.
~Song of Solomon 7:11-12

"You did not choose Me, but I chose you, and appointed you
that you should go and bear fruit, and that your fruit should remain,
that whatever you ask the Father in My name, He may give you."
~John 15:16

If you were going on a trip, what would you pack? Let's see, would a good pair of shoes be on your list? What's that? Shoes would top your list? They'd top mine too!

Shoes need to fit the activity and they need to be in good repair. Recently, I put on my gardening shoes. I was unaware of the tiny hole in the toe. But I sure did know it when my socks got wet! Brr! I might as well have gone barefoot. When I ride trails, I wear my cowgirl boots. Those boots aren't just for looks; they have a job to do! If I wear sneakers, I get sore ankles. Only my riding boots will do. When I walk trails, I wear my hiking boots. I need the traction these boots provide so I can negotiate slick trails. All of my shoes have a purpose, and I'm glad they do their jobs.

A decent pair of shoes is as important to my goings-on as my Bible is to my spiritual journey. My Bible has a hole straight through the cover, but I will never replace it. We've traveled some miles together, my Bible and I, and I treasure my Beloved Bridegroom Jesus Christ who wrote the words. He has become my Best Friend. Those gardening shoes? Eventually I will get a new pair, but for now a little shoe glue will keep the sole together and my feet dry.

Gals, what does your professional shoe closet look like? What's that? You have a collection? Me? Oh, yes, I have an assortment too. When I bought my pink tapestry kitten heels, I had nothing to wear with them. Not a single blouse, skirt, or sweater. But I liked them so much I built an entire outfit around them. We all like ribbons and bows, tapestry on our toes, as well as a little sparkle.

Guys, I'm guessing you don't have a collection—perhaps owning one or two pairs—but let me meddle a little—I'll bet each pair cost a pretty penny. Oh yes, I agree—they are worth the price. They need to be stylish, practical, and durable, so they can't be cheap. Some pairs may even need to perform double duty. My son wears a steel toe, so he looks professional but is also kept safe in the warehouse. They are pricy too.

Let's talk about the value of shoes in ancient biblical times. They had similar importance as they do now. Rabbi Jacob Chintz records shoes as being "a symbol of dignified dress."[192] The Israelites had dress shoes that were as much of a status symbol as they are for us today. Chintz explains shoes were worn by the high and middle-class persons, while the commoner walked barefoot. To go without shoes, unless it was for the purpose of worshipping God, meant that you were of a lower economic status.

In the vignette, your Beloved Groom has given you a commission—to reach the people of the valleys for Him—and He has graced your feet with dignity and style. Thus, even your shoes become

---

[192] Rabbi Jacob Chintz, "The Role of Shoes in the Bible." *Jewish Bible Quarterly.* Vol. 35, No. 1, 2007.

part of your testimony. They must be eye-catching because people comment on them right away. Your shoes' sparkle goes all the way to the joints of your thighs! This sparkle, in the spiritual realm, represents your glorious and anointed journey. Beloved has clothed you with as much dignity and grace as the virtuous woman, with her silk and purple outfits.

Step out in style, Love, and into your vignette, knowing that every place He sends you to go is commissioned by your Husband-King. Shine bright, and fill every dark place with Beloved's light. Those you desire to reach are counting on you to exchange their ashes of grief for beauty from the Lord, darkness for light, despair for hope, and barrenness for fruitfulness, so shine bright, Bride of Christ.

Sparkle for Jesus Christ.

You are adorned with the finest shoes, and you are a beauty to behold, not only because you are Queen, but because you are a glory carrier. Beloved's love and peace permeate you from your veil to your shoes, and your friends want you to minister to them.

Enter into the scene, glorious Bride:

*****

SONG OF SOLOMON 7:1-13
Scene Sixteen: A Search for Lilies

SETTING: Foreground: The Sharon Valley
                                                   Background: Lebanon's mountain range, surrounding valleys, and vineyards.

AT RISE: LOVE walks amidst the VALLEY PEOPLE.

NARRATOR
In the Sharon Valley, Love teaches the people. She walks as a Queen, dignified and kind, and glorious within her spirit, and she is outwardly beautiful to behold.

VALLEY PERSON ONE
[1]How beautiful are your feet in sandals, O prince's daughter! [2]The curves of your thighs *are* like jewels, the work of the hands of a skillful workman.
      (LOVE curtseys, looking at her shoes.)

VALLEY PERSON TWO
[3]Your navel *is* a round goblet; It lacks no blended beverage. Your waist *is* a heap of wheat set about with lilies.
      (LOVE places her hand on her belly.)

VALLEY PERSON THREE
[4]Your two breasts *are* like two fawns, twins of a gazelle.
      (LOVE nods.)

VALLEY PERSON TWO
[5]Your neck *is* like an ivory tower, your eyes *like* the pools in Heshbon, by the gates of Bath Rabbim. Your nose *is* like the tower of Lebanon which looks toward Damascus.
      (LOVE looks up, praising BELOVED whom she imagines.)

VALLEY PERSON ONE
[6a]Your head *crowns* you like *Mount* Carmel, and the hair of your head *is* like purple.

(LOVE strokes her hair, pulling it to the front.)

VALLEY PERSON THREE

6bA king is held captive by *your* tresses.
(BELOVED enters, stage right. He takes LOVE by the hand. They walk together.)

BELOVED

7How fair and how pleasant you are, O Love, for delights! This stature of yours is like a palm tree, and your breasts *like* its clusters.

LOVE

(LOVE waves her hands, like palm branches, reminiscing of Palm Sunday)
8aI said, "I will go up to the palm tree, I will take hold of its branches."

BELOVED

8bLet now your breasts be like clusters of the vine, the fragrance of your breath like apples, 9aand the roof of your mouth like the best wine.
(LOVE touches her fingers to her lips.)

LOVE

9b*The wine* goes *down* smoothly for my Beloved…

BELOVED and LOVE

(Speaking as one voice; touching each other's lips with their fingertips.)
9b.…Moving gently the lips of sleepers.

NARRATOR

A spiritual awakening for the people is what Beloved and Love desire! The Spirit which moves upon their lips also moves upon the lips of the valley people, causing their utterances of praise to be above their natural ability. Heaven meets earth as each believers' lips are kissed with the sweet peace of the Groom. Beloved and Love's romance has caused this spiritual resonance.

LOVE

(Addressing the people)
10I *am* my Beloved's and His desire *is* toward me.
(Looking toward the valleys in the distance)
11Come, my Beloved, let us go forth to the field; let us lodge in the villages. 12Let us get up early to the vineyards; let us see if the vine has budded, *whether* the grape blossoms are open, *and* the pomegranates are in bloom.
(Kisses fingers; waves them toward the people)
There will I give you my love.
(LOVE blows a kiss to her BELOVED.)

NARRATOR

The people are each named "Love" to the Queen. Each of these saved souls is her delight. She knows the very best gift she can offer Beloved is a transformed soul. She wants to give Him as many "Loves" as possible.
(LOVE offers BELOVED a mandrake fruit; He receives it.)

LOVE

[13]The mandrakes give off a fragrance, and at our gates *are* pleasant *fruits*, all manner, new and old, which I have laid up for You, my Beloved.

       (BELOVED and LOVE stroll, hand-in-hand, gazing at each)

NARRATOR

The couple's romance continues, and so does their ministry. Each step the Queen takes is graced with her Husband's glory, for the kisses of His peace have permeated her from head to toe. If her gift to Beloved is souls, why does she offer Him the mandrake? In so doing, she notes that discipling believers is as equally important as soul winning.

       (BELOVED and LOVE wave to the VALLEY PEOPLE)

       (Spotlight on LOVE's shoes; center stage)

Beloved and Love are on a journey to win souls. They will return to disciple those in the Sharon Valley. As the sunlight streams into the beautiful valley, Love's shoes begin to sparkle. She is stepping out in ministry, and she is gloriously adorned by her Husband-King.

*****

       Hello, Love. Are your shoes still sparkling? I'm sure they are! Although you cannot usually see this glory with your natural eye, your spiritual life is radiant, and every time you step out to minister and with Beloved, your life takes on a new dimension and you sparkle a bit more.

       Scene Sixteen is divided into two sections: First, the valley people describe you as the beautiful Queen who carries Beloved's authority. Next, you and Beloved dialogue about your continuing romance and your plans to help the people reach their greatest potential. We will discuss both.

THE PEOPLE'S DISCOURSE
THE BRIDE'S SHOES

       Your shoes are an important part of your spiritual armor; you have *shod your feet with the preparation of the gospel of peace* (Ephesians 6:15b). You are conquering territory for Beloved. Therefore, everywhere you visit, Beloved's kingdom increases, while Satan's kingdom diminishes.

       Not only do you wear shoes—which alone speak of your dignified respected position among the people—but they are gorgeous! So, go forth in confidence, luminous Bride, with the Gospel of peace, and with the love of your Savior, knowing that He clothes you with the very best attire at His disposal.

       Listed here are some examples of how the Lord blesses as we witness. Try to guess the biblical pattern common to each, as you read these:

- ESTHER: In Esther 10:3, she paves the way for her people to live bondage-free by witnessing to King Ahasuerus. Her uncle Mordecai becomes second in command of Shushan, next only to the king. With Mordecai in charge, God's values are relayed to the whole community, whether Jew or Gentile.
- RAHAB: In Joshua 2 and repeated in Matthew 1:5, we read Rahab's story. She hides Joshua's spies, and her family receives salvation. Then, she bears Boaz,[193] an ancestor of the Messiah.
- RUTH: In Ruth 4:13-17, and repeated in Matthew 1:5, Ruth refuses to depart from her godly mother-in-law Naomi during a famine. This results in her marriage to the godly ruler Boaz, and she gives birth to a new generation of believers to whom the Messiah is to be born.
- THE ISRAELITE CHILDREN: In Daniel 3:20-30, Shadrach, Meshach, and Abednego trust God to deliver them, even though they are thrust into a fiery pit. But they tell King Nebuchadnezzar they will be loyal to God even if they die. The king, witnessing their miraculous deliverance, writes laws dictating that his kingdom is to honor the God of these

---

[193] Joshua 2; Matthew 1:5 Boaz is Booz

three courageous young men.

- DANIEL: In Daniel 6:26-28, we read about the lions' den. When Daniel is thrown into it, he is miraculously saved. Not one lion bites Daniel. As a result, King Darius becomes a believer and writes laws instructing his people to honor Daniel's God.
- PAUL: At Paul's conversion in Acts 9:1-22, he is struck with a blinding light, falls to the ground, and Jesus speaks. This causes Paul (then called Saul) to re-think his agenda. No longer will he persecute Christians; instead, he joins their ranks and becomes the most noted evangelist of all time, being obedient to preach wherever Beloved sends him, despite personal consequences.

Did you guess the take-away for the above examples? Let's look at two results: 1) First, the person witnessing affects more than the ones whom they initially evangelize. We should anticipate these same results. When we step out in the anointing, Beloved Jesus is able to carry the anointing further, and, like falling dominoes, our obedience to His call causes not just a single event, but a chain of events. 2) Second, notice that, although Beloved's empowerment is obvious in every example noted, sometimes it was a trepid situation where it appears as if He is not on the scene and didn't care. But when the person obeys Beloved, witnessing despite personal consequences, the miraculous results, indicating that our unseen Beloved has been on the scene all along.

What can we learn from this? When Beloved gives us our marching orders, we need to move forth courageously in faith, knowing the results will be wide-reaching. Also, we must witness regardless of personal consequences. The men and women in the above example, and those listed in Hebrew's Hall of Faith (see Hebrews 11,12), and so many others, suffered great persecutions. But they never quit. Because they loved Beloved, they kept witnessing, stepping toward the finish line, even being willing to die for their faith in order to champion Beloved's Gospel message. We must do likewise.

Let's look at our Lord's witness. Beloved Jesus travels for three years, witnessing and discipling the twelve apostles. Then He walks, with cross in hand and pressed upon His striped back, His blood streaming onto Jerusalem's streets. He does what no man could do because He is filled to the brim with love for the people. His eleven disciples continue His missionary journey. And now, His witness continues through us.

We have spiritual authority everywhere God has us set our feet to travel. Beloved has ordained us to go to the neighbor next door or to our co-worker in the adjoining cubicle, as much as He has ordained us to go to the ends of the world. He says to us, *"All authority has been given to Me in heaven and on earth. Go therefore, and make disciples of all nations, baptizing them in the name of the Father and of the Son and of the Holy Spirit, teaching them to observe all things that I have commanded you; and, lo, I am with you always, even to the end of the age* (Matthew 28:18b-20a). Beloved is with us in this quest. He says so in this verse.

With this commissioning, how can we not respond? From the overflow of anointing, we are equipped. Our Groom has provided more than enough anointing so that even our thighs sparkle with jewels of Heaven. Beloved has set glory within you, His cherished Bride, and He stays with you as you minister. He has ordained you to do so. This commissioning of the Bride is repeated in all four Gospels.[194] Is there a price? You betcha there is, but the price is worth it because Beloved has called us into this battlefield for souls.

Let's not be ashamed to witness. As Bride, our feet are shod with the most exquisite shoes. They are more gorgeous than my pink tapestry kitten pumps. Beloved graces our feet with royal attire such that the people mention them first. Those who come to the Sharon Valley are

---

[194] Matthew 28:18b-20a the disciples commissioned; Mark 16:15b-18 the disciples commissioned; Luke 24:46b-49 the men on the Emmaus Road commissioned; John 21 Peter re-commissioned

demonstrating their readiness.

Remember Beloved's words, *Behold, I say to you, lift up your eyes, and look at the fields, for they are already white for harvest* (John 4:35b)*!* The people He sends you to may look rough around the edges, but a spark of luminous light is within them. When we see that miniscule glory-spark in their eyes, we know their spirits are ready to receive and we must step forth with a bold but loving witness as He commands us to do.

Let's not judge who Beloved sends us to by their rough appearance. When the maidens first witnessed to us, we too looked rough on the outside. When the shepherds taught us, our life was still a big mess. When Beloved met us on our Bether climb, we looked very unkempt. But we were willing to lean on Him and share our secrets. This is when real change happened. This Bether experience resulted in our salvation, and our marriage to Him followed.

Even when the maidens wove the silver and gold wedding threads into our hair, we still needed perfecting. The gold let us know Heaven was part of our journey, but the silver let us know redemption would be needful and available at every juncture. So, let's ignore the outward appearance of those we are sent to. Think of people as Brides who are in differing stages of their glorious transformation and needing discipleship so they can sparkle more and more over time.

THE BRIDE'S GAIT

You have a beautiful gait. Your jeweled thighs represent an effective witness, a filled-to-the-brim anointing, and your position is Queen. The people notice the curves of your thighs right away. They say, *The curves of your thighs* are *like jewels, the work of the hands of a skillful workman* (Song 7:1b). Who is this skillful workman? It is Jesus, your Beloved. He releases into your gait His regal glory. You are on a predictable path and your witness is ordained of God. In ancient biblical times, covenants were sometimes made by touching the thigh. Subsequently, this description of your thighs means you are in covenantal partnership with your Beloved.

Beloved sets up what may seem like coincidences, but, in reality, they are God-ordained circumstances. Your Skillful Workman locates you to certain places at certain times so you can carry out His glorious purposes. He cuts the path for you and brings you into position to speak to those He knows who are ready for your words. Often this is inconvenient, but He knows you will heed His calling. God loves the lily people of the Sharon Valley that much, and so do you.

Let's look a little closer at the word *skillful* (Song 7:1b), which in the King James translates as *cunning.* (Song 7:1b KJV)[195] There's a secret hidden in this definition that the Lord wants us to discover. This Hebrew word translates as *aman*, and it comes from the same word family as *amen*. It points to our agreement with His will. *Aman* means "expert." Therefore, we can conclude that Beloved is an expert at equipping us to accomplish His ministry purposes.

Recall that at Mt. Amana in the Lebanon Mountain Range, you climbed with your Beloved, and He approved of you by speaking His "amen" over your life. Therefore, as we witness, we can envision our Beloved saying, "Amen!" to the messages of love we are sharing. That is such a great discovery, it needs repeating—while we as Bride are witnessing, Beloved is shouting, "Amen!" Hallelujah!

THE BRIDE'S MIDSECTION

Your midsection represents a glory-filled spirit. The people say, *Your navel* is *a rounded goblet; it lacks no blended beverage* (Song 7:2a). Your abdomen or waist, they describe as *a heap of wheat set about with lilies* (Song 7:2b). Your midsection is as a wineglass, or a *goblet* (Song 7:2b), and it looks like a pile of flour has been heaped onto it. Let's decipher these metaphors:

Think of your belly as a reservoir filled to the tippy-top and flowing over with the best wine

---

[195] Strong. OT #542, *aman.*

from your Beloved. Where does your mind go with this description? This goblet of wine is the Communion of the Bride, but it is not just a ritual, it has become who we are.

Furthermore, this is a word picture of a wineglass that lacks nothing. The New King James renders the passage as, *It lacks no blended beverage* (Song 7:2b), and the King James renders this as it, *wanteth not liquor* (Song 7:2b KJV). What is being shown here is completeness. The Bride has no need of any other beverage—not even of strong liquor—to cause her to effervesce with joy. Her wine glass is filled by Beloved Himself, and it represents His sacrificial blood atonement, shed to make this bridal covenant a reality.

You have Beloved in the center of your belly, representative of being Spirit-filled. Thus, when the people look at you, they know you have sipped from the Communion table with your Lord and in covenantal relationship with your Savior, needing no other beloved but Him.

What else is with the wineglass? Predictably, the bread of Communion is in your belly also, and the wheat is piled high, which pictures that He is more than enough. John records Jesus as saying, *For the bread of God is He who comes down from heaven and gives life to the world"* (John 6:33). Beloved's living bread is complete nourishment for your spirit. His words are as your words because you've melded your spirit with His and you agree with Beloved's message.

Your belly is *set about with lilies* (Song 7:2). I love what this represents. These are the people, the lily representing humble people who are searching to know Beloved. The lily reminds you of the perpetual beauty you have acquired within your person, for the Rose of Sharon lily, which blooms in autumn, gives way to the lilies of the valley that adorn Sharon's Valley in the spring, and this renewal He has worked within you. Now, you are working this renewal within those around you. Your belly is surrounded by lilies. Why? People come to you. Whether their spiritual season is fall, winter, spring, or summer, they know you will help them covenant with the King of Kings.

THE NOURISHED BRIDE

The lily people describe your breasts. They say, *Your two breasts* are *like two fawns, twins of a gazelle* (Song 7:3b). I believe it would be beneficial for me to share a scene that just played out in the wooded area of my backyard. From the forest, a mature doe cautiously stepped into a grassy area. She was looking hither and yon, qualifying every step with a timid glance. Next, two younger does, who were taking their traveling instructions from this lead doe, stepped into the grassy area also, timidly, but with a bit more pep in their steps.

What happened next? As if to set even the chipmunks at ease, two young roes stumbled up behind these three. These two young gents butted heads, romping, playing tag around the trees, and munching on everything available, having the most gleeful time as they played in the clearing. They were bumble-bucks, carefree and living life to the max! I couldn't help but laugh out loud as I watched these two rumble into the clearing without a care.

I think we can correctly assume this is how the Lord of Glory thinks of you when the valley people mention your breasts are like two fawns. You are secure in your Beloved's love. And this makes you carefree. Your breasts also indicate nourishment. The young roes weren't concerned about their wellbeing. Their mom was there, and they knew she would feed them. You are as gleeful, rambunctious, and carefree as these young roes. You possess the good life, and you know it, and furthermore, you know the Holy Spirit will nourish you.

Are you worried about your future? No, you are playing games! You are enjoying life to the fullest. You can do this because you trust Beloved has your best interest in mind. Even in the hard times, you do not worry, because either Beloved has a ministry purpose for allowing the difficulty or He is working out a solution that is yet to be revealed.

Those twin romping roes were pursuing life to the fullest. In the King James, these are mentioned as "roes." Why are they roes instead of does? We all know boys (and roes) are the more rough-and-tumble candidates than little girls are, so the vignette records them as boys rather than girls. Therefore, you are not only carefree, you are as carefree as these young gents.

Enjoy living, Bride of Christ.

Beloved wants you to enjoy every day to the fullest extent.

The lily people acknowledge the Lord has blessed your life. You have won His favor, and you have the best blessed life possible.

Be carefree today.

Beloved believes in you, and so do the people whom you teach. Thrust off the worries of life, because Beloved has a plan, and He will make sure you will see it fulfilled. He's got this. Trust His unseen hand.

THE BRIDE'S NECK

Next, the valley people describe your neck as being *like an ivory tower* (Song 7:4b). John writes, *"He who overcomes, I will I make him a pillar in the temple of My God"* (Revelation 3:12a). Your neck is as stately as this strong ivory pillar, just like Beloved's legs are! Your head is upright, and your gaze is upon the Lord. Your head is not downcast from shame or guilt or any other sorrow. Your countenance is blessed and, consequently, your posture is upright.

Ivory is luminous and white. This indicates you, blessed Bride, are glorious and pure. In the first scene, you were riddled with regret and battling shame. But here, Beloved has glorified and purified you, His blessed Bride.

Don't allow past failures to define you. Remind the enemy any time he tries to attack you that, to Beloved, you are pure as white ivory and luminous throughout with the radiance of your Groom's glory.

THE BRIDE'S GAZE

Let's examine your eyes. We already know they are Spirit-filled, but there's more. Here, the people say, *Your eyes* like *the pools in Heshbon, by the gates of Bath Rabbim* (Song 7:4b). It takes a little digging to know what the lily people are saying about you. Heshbon was a city known for its many pools of peaceful water, and, by definition, it means, "stronghold."[196] This peaceful city was bordered on all sides by enemy lands. It was assigned to the Levites, who were the priestly tribe of the Jews. Bath Rabbim is one of the gates of Heshbon, and it means, "daughter of multitudes" or "daughter of many."[197]

You have eyes that resemble these peaceful pools of Heshbon. This means that even when enemies border you on all sides as they did Heshbon, you can reflect Beloved's peace. You are not rattled by the presence of the enemy. You are a Queen of multitudes, and you lead people spiritually, whether they are peaceful or angry. You can do this because you have tapped into the Lord of Glory and He protects you. You teach as many "daughters" as the Lord entrusts you with. You influence multitudes with the peace of Beloved. Just like the En Gedi oasis of Scene Three, you are at rest, regardless of circumstances.

THE BRIDE'S NOSE

The valley people describe your nose. They say, *Your nose is like the tower of Lebanon which looks toward Damascus* (Song 7:4b). The word "Damascus" means "alertness."[198] It may derive its name according to the silk of butterfly cocoons that lived at the foot of the mountain. Damask, a Danish cloth, derives its name from this, and Damascus was a merchant city that, among other wares, sold silk, as well as other fine clothing materials and outfits.

Your gaze is as Damascus. You are alert spiritually, waiting for Beloved's instructions and

---

[196] Blue Letter Bible; word search on Heshbon
[197] Blue Letter Bible; word search on Batharabbin
[198] Blue Letter Bible; word search on Damascus

obeying Him, and you are looking toward the mountain. This indicates you are bent on praying. Lebanon's mountain range is your abiding place. This makes your stature upright and your nose lifted, because you are praying to Beloved, whether He is with you spiritually and even when He is not with you physically. Lebanon's whiteness—with its glorious luminosity—is your reward. Because you have eyes only for your Beloved, His glory rests upon you, His alert, sanctified Bride.

THE BRIDE'S ATTIRE

You are clothed in the best silk as was the virtuous woman of Proverbs 31. You have purchased soft purple silk on your Damascus visits where you have been attentive to your Groom. The lily people see the beauty that you have because of your prayer life, and they describe your prayers as resembling a gorgeous silk dress, a silk fabric that has most likely been made from butterfly cocoons. Your dress is a word picture of attentiveness to prayer. This damask tapestry is woven so tightly it looks luminous! So, the glory that is within you as His Bride is again featured.

Picture a migration of butterflies soaring upward, leaving their silk cocoons behind. This will help us remember this metaphor of attentive prayer and fine silk clothing as your royal attire. You look out for the spiritual welfare of the people by being in tune with your Beloved.

The people had said in the previous scene, *Who is she who looks forth as the morning, fair as the moon, clear as the sun, awesome as* an army *with banners* (Song 6:10)? You are a formidable foe to the enemy. You are as pure and fiery as the sun and waving Beloved's army banner. Here again, you look to Beloved, which presents the same concept.

You look toward Damascus, the merchant city that is the source for the Virtuous Woman's provisions. Your stature and royal clothing reflect a Bride who is attentive to her Husband-King. Again, you are seen as a prayer warrior, fighting for the security of your people. They appreciate your attentiveness, and they feel secure because you keep watchful eye for their safety. You have the mountaintop perspective of Beloved, and you guide them into all truth.

THE BRIDE AND GROOM'S DISCOURSE

After the people speak, you and Beloved speak. Let's discuss your conversation.

THE BRIDE'S HEADDRESS

Let's evaluate your hair. It's as purple as the mountains of Carmel, which translates as "fruitful land."[199] Mt. Carmel was noted for its beauty. Your life is so fruitful that you've captured Beloved's glances. The New King James reads, *A king is held captive by your tresses* (Song 7:5b). The King James renders this passage as, *The king is held in the galleries* (Song 7:5b KJV). The tresses, or curls, speak of your covenantal relationship. Beloved is held captive and held in the galleries by the majesty of you, His Bride because you look at and to Him and you're completed only by Him. Although even kings are held by your spiritual beauty, only Beloved's matters to you. And He adores you. Glory!

Beloved recognizes your solidarity, mentioning your veil of purple-as-Carmel locks that represent strength and majesty, as His locks do. Beloved knows you have responded to His calling to climb ever higher with your King of Majesty.

Imagine this—our King is apprehended by our spiritual beauty! Beloved speaks of your countenance, saying, *How fair and how pleasant you are, O Love, with your delights* (Song 7:6)! The maidens spoke this into your spirit long ago. Now, this has become your reality. You have attained the destiny they foretold. The *dowd* of Beloved has remade you into a virtuous Bride capable of capturing your Lover's gaze.

THE PALM TREE

---

[199] Strong. OT #3760; *Karmel*

First, you and Beloved mention the stately palm tree. There's nothing crooked or puny about how a palm tree grows. It rises straight up! You arise, too, right into Beloved's arms. Your humility came first; and so, now, He exalts you.

In order to fully appreciate this metaphor, we must know about the date palm's growth habits. The date palm has two sexes—a male and a female tree. The female tree will lie close to the ground in a humble posture. However, as soon as a male date palm is growing in the region, the female date palm will begin to lean toward the male tree, and she will rise up. This interaction is never independent; it is a response to the presence of her counterpart.

The female date palm rises underneath her male complement, and there she becomes fruitful as the pollen falls upon her date flowers. You have been as this female date palm, humble and now rising underneath your Groom, fruitful and satisfied with His love.

Let's look at the palm branches in relation to your Beloved. The people celebrated with palm branches as He entered Jerusalem. John recorded this celebration, penning, *The next day a great multitude that had come to the feast, when they heard that Jesus was coming to Jerusalem, took branches of palm trees, and went out to meet Him, and cried out, "Hosannah! 'Blessed is He who comes in the name of the LORD!' The King of Israel!"* (John 12:12-13). In the vignette, when you take hold of these palm boughs, you celebrate your Lord prophetically as those who welcomed Beloved's entrance into Jerusalem. Glory!

THE VINEYARD

Coupled with this description of the stately palm tree is the vineyard, which also represents your spiritual walk. Beloved describes the Bride's breasts *like clusters* (Song 7:8b) of the vine. If we recognize the prophetic significance here, we will notice the meaning right away. Let's crack the code.

Beloved says, *"I am the vine, you* are *the branches. He who abides in Me, and I in him, bears much fruit: for without Me, you can do nothing"* (John 15:5). Because you abide in your Beloved—and, in fact, you delight in doing so—you abound in spiritual fruitfulness. Your Spirit fruits are nourishment to the peoples, and a foretelling of Messiah to come is woven into this same description.

THE BREATH OF THE BRIDE AND GROOM

Let's look at the next piece of imagery. You and Beloved abide so closely that the fragrance emanating from your nose is as the breath of Beloved's Spirit! This perfume of *apples* (Song 7:8b) is reminiscent of the Holy Spirit, and the Communion table that holds the apple as one of its bounties. This reminds us of the Communion of Scene Seven. We discussed this apple as being the citron, which is probably an orange or other citrus fruit, but the point is the scent wafting from your breath is reminiscent of Beloved's own breath. As you fellowshipped with Beloved in a Communion embrace and He fed you apples, raisin cakes, and other delicacies, you plucked the fruit from the tree you rested underneath and you ate it.

Contrast this apple to the apple in The Garden of Eden. You eat this apple; you could not touch Eden's apple. You can touch it because you've matured, abiding in Beloved's love and uniting with Him so you are ready. This tree in the vignette you recline under represents nourishment and wisdom from the Holy Spirit, and you were raised up underneath this glorious tree, eating its fruits, being filled further with the Holy Spirit. The overflow from these spirit to Spirit exchanges results in ministry opportunities.

As you rest in Beloved's arms you breathe the same Holy Spirit, and this is the breath that awakens the people. You have a rhythm, even of breath, that is in sync like a dance. You are this unified with your Beloved. Truly, you are as *a company of* two armies (Song 6:13 KJV) or *the dance of two camps* (Song 6:13).

Both metaphors—the fruitful vineyard and the palm tree—show the dependence of the Bride on her Bridegroom. This dependency has created spiritual beauty, maturity, and an effective witness.

THE HOLY SPIRIT INFILLING

The next portion of imagery is of the wine's and apple's joyous effect. You say, The wine goes down smoothly *for my beloved, moving gently the lips of sleepers. I am my beloved's and his desire is toward me* (Song 7:10). You and Beloved cause a spiritual awakening of the people. The result is upon the lips of the believers, as they gently move their lips and are spiritually awakened.

Let's look at this same concept in the New Testament. Paul records in Ephesians, *Be filled with the Spirit; speaking to one another in psalms and hymns and spiritual songs, singing and making melody in your heart to the Lord* (Ephesians 5:18b-19). In the vignette, when you describe how the wine represents Beloved's blood atonement, this creates life for the people. The sleeping people arise to commune with Beloved, spirit to Spirit, and their mouths reflect this change as they speak in new languages — *glossia* — tongues that are inspired by Beloved Himself.

Are you seeking to receive your spiritual language? Focus on Beloved rather than the spiritual language. The key to receiving is in this passage of the vignette and repeated in Ephesians and elsewhere. The valley people are not laboring to speak in a heavenly dialect, nor are you. Rather, by acknowledging Beloved's blood atonement and His majesty, this results in a spiritual infilling and a joyous overflow. Our spiritual language emerges from worship. As we acknowledge the sacrifice Beloved gave for us as we tarry in this place of remembrance, and then, as we press just a little bit further, the Holy Spirit starts speaking to and through us. What we hear is the Spirit's dialect. So, my friend, don't seek tongues, seek Him.

There are spiritual gifts that come along with this heavenly language. But our focus should never be on collecting giftings or anointings. Rather, our adoration of Beloved should result in the spiritual awakening pictured here in the vignette. Our Bridegroom and His blood atonement should be our focus.

THE BRIDE'S GIFTS

Look at the gifts you bring to Beloved. You say, *Let us get up early to the vineyards; let us see if the vine has budded,* whether *the grape blossoms are open,* and *the pomegranates are in bloom. There will I give you my love* (Song 7:12b). Here, the word, "love," is plural, and in the King James it is rendered *loves* (Song 7:12b KJV). This is important in our understanding of the meaning of this passage. Although bridal love has been a theme throughout, here you are referring to the people as "loves."

The gifts you bring your Groom are souls. Each soul you have evangelized or discipled is a precious gift you present to your Husband-King. So here, we see the love we have as Bride has a purpose — that of multiplication — as we present souls to our Groom.

Here, you are checking the vineyards, looking for spiritual fruit in the people, examining their welfare to see if their spiritual vines are budding, because if they are, then they need protection from the little foxes that would nip their spiritual buds off! You, as Bride, prune the vines and protect them from harm, disciple them, and cherish their development so that their fruit can develop.

THE MANDRAKES

You say, *The mandrakes give off a fragrance, and at our gates* are *pleasant fruits, all manner, new and old, which I have laid up for you, my beloved* (Song 7:13). This indicates you are winning new disciples as well as discipling those who already know Him. You spend time on both activities.

Evangelism is vital, but do a motive check before you go. Let me share a story to drive this point home. I once went on an evangelism trip that I thought was pathetic. The man I was witnessing with went scripted and carried check-off cards so he could tally the number of people he "evangelized." As soon as the sprinter would read his pre-determined speech, he would ask the individual to recite a canned prayer and check the box on one of his cards. Then he would race to the next individual, trying to persuade the person to repeat the prayer and check the box. I honestly wondered if there would soon be a word-of-mouth chain, "Check the guy's box so he'll leave you alone."

I was supposed to learn from this man, but I abandoned him. I ended up sitting with a lady at a bus station, and I fought tears as I listened to her story. Finally, I offered to pray with her, and she gladly accepted. The lady was already saved; she had just slipped back due to the situation she had found herself in. I had determined that within seconds. She did not need to get saved, but she had deep spiritual hurts and she needed love that day and a reassurance that Jesus was still with her. Beloved had sent me to deliver that message, along with a hug and a prayer, and I did so.

The sprinter found me and showed me his card collection of individuals he had "won" for Christ. When he asked me how many I had won, I said "None." He was horrified, but I wasn't, and I don't think the Lord was either. Even though I didn't have a check on a ministry card, I had accepted the Holy Spirit's assignment to reach one individual. I hope the encouragement I gave her made an impact.

Beloved had sent me to one soul that day.

One soul.

And to my Bridegroom, this one soul needed a timely rescue.

At other times, I've ministered to many more than one soul, but that day reminds me to always do a motive check. If I'm in ministry to generate numbers, I'm doing it for the wrong reasons.

I did not feel the need to prove to the soul winner guy my worth by collecting evangelism cards as trophies that I'd done a good job. I simply needed to respond to the Holy Spirit's assignment. I said goodbye to the sprinter because I felt his methods were both ineffective and uncaring. I never again ministered with him. That type of ministry can be a turn-off for individuals who could have otherwise been won. Love should be our motivation, and pride should have nothing to do with our ministry.

According to this vignette scene, discipling is equally important. If soul winning is not followed up with discipleship, what have we really accomplished? I had posed this question to the sprinter and he passed it off as "the church's responsibility," but seeing as he was not offering them a way to get there, that point was mute. If we are going to give Beloved souls, let's make sure we are willing to walk with them throughout their spiritual journey, or at the very least, point them to a person equipped to disciple them through their next step.

Discipleship is usually messier than soul winning, and that's why we often shy away from it, but we shouldn't. Discipling new believers requires patience, being there, and encouraging spiritual growth.

It has taken me a whole year of discipling one individual I'm working with and she is finally ready to attend church. Sometimes I felt like I was spinning my wheels, but the Lord would remind me how patient those who discipled me in my early years were. It takes time to see results, so when discipling, be in it for the long haul.

CONCLUSION

Throughout this scene you desire to minister. Your shoes are sparkling, white with glory, and ready to travel. You begin to make the ministry requests of your own. You call to Beloved early in the morning and you say, "Hello, my Beloved, can we work the harvest fields today? I think I see a sparkle in my friend's eyes." You call again and you say, "I want to go check the grapevines. Can we go?" Beloved does not have to keep you motivated. Your shoes are on, and you're ready to go!

Oh, look at those darling shoes you're wearing this very moment! They are glorious, with sparkles of beryl all the way to the joints of your thighs! It must be you have touched the beryl-set nail prints as you held your Groom's hand during your morning worship. While you rested with Him last evening, He must have brushed your lips with the kisses of His peace.

Because you love Beloved deeply, your harvest field will be full, my friend. Speak forth your witness with boldness. Care about each individual as you harvest souls, for this is the best gift you can present to your Bridegroom-King.

Before we read the concluding scene, let's bow and reverence our Beloved:

My Towering Palm Tree,

I treasure Your kisses of peace as I treasure You. Sing Your love songs through me, for I yearn to work the harvest fields of white. Help me to bring forth Your anointed message.

You are my all-in-all, and I desire for You to keep our romance fresh. Keep me humble, for as the date palm tree only rises under the shadow of her mate, so must I, likewise, be dependent upon You at all times.

Help me to commune with You and recline under the Holy Spirit tree that is ripe with spiritual fruits. Make these Communion embraces, where I first rested in Your presence, an ongoing experience.

Anoint my shoes, so they will sparkle bright and pure with Your holy glory. Make my thighs jeweled as I travel the path You have ordained for me. Let my witness be of Your beryl-set hands, which were once pierced for me. Because of the price You paid to redeem me, help me to be Your soul-winning Bride. And those I win for You, help me to disciple.

And now, I mean every one of these three closing words of this prayer: I love You.

Your Harvesting Bride,
Love

BRIDAL REFLECTION

1) Describe your shoe collection. In the vignette, how does this relate to your witness?

2) When you witness, does this affect one person or is there a chain reaction? Justify your answer by mentioning a biblical example (i.e.: Esther, Rahab, Ruth, Daniel).

3) Describe your mid-section, as Beloved does, and how this represents the Communion of the Bride.

4) Compare Proverbs 31 with the Damask cloth of this chapter. What does this represent?

5) Discuss the covenantal relationship in relation to the Bride's thigh.

6) What does "Heshbon" represent? How does this apply to your gaze?

7) How does the female palm tree become fruitful? How does this apply to you as Bride?

Chapter Twelve
Kept by Love
*Make haste, my beloved, and be like a gazelle
or a young stag on the mountains of spices.*
~Song of Solomon 8:14

Surely, I come quickly.
~Revelation 22:21b

Periodically, I ask my husband to pull our wedding album from the closet. This is the joy of having a six-foot husband. He can reach almost everything! As we turn the yellowed pages of this album, we treasure memories of our wedding day. We thought we were grown-ups when we tied the knot. But as we look back, one of our fondest memories is recognizing we were kids — barely out of our teens — but serious about everything, including the life we planned on making with each other and with the Lord.

Anyone desiring to photograph the bride and groom on our special day was supposed to wait until after the ceremony. That's a good rule. It helped us to focus on the moment. But one amateur photographer captured Phil's spur of the moment wedding embrace on the sly. I am glad this gentleman felt the need to snap this photo. It is the lousiest photo we have of the event — the lighting is non-existent, the focus is blurred, an uncle's arm is in the way, and it's off-centered — but this is the photo we cherish the most. This makeshift photographer captured "our moment" as my fiancé swept me off my feet and into his arms to kiss me. Glory!

One simple photograph of two teenagers caught up in a spontaneous embrace tells our love story. When I stand face-to-face with my Beloved Jesus, I will tell Him He chose the best earthly groom for this imperfect bride. I will also thank Him for the renegade photographer who captured the moment our love found expression by my husband's kiss that sealed our vow and wrote our story.

After the wedding album comes off the shelf, we inevitably look at albums of our children, followed by our vacation adventures, and an album of our daughter's dog, Izzy, who has one all her own. Shoeboxes filled to the tippy-top find their way onto the coffee table and we delight in the memories of relatives — some of whom we have never met — but we know their stories from family who do.

We treasure photos of Grandma Joyce, who adopted the neighborhood through her love. There's Phil's brother David, the romantic who when courting his love, Lisa, put a rose on her windshield. There's Phil's sister, Beverly, the person I admire most because she loves deeply, and her family of adopted children. We look at photos of her son Justin, who died too young, and the children and wife he left behind. We shed a tear and continue, looking at photos of Phil's dad, who welcomed me as a daughter. We look at pictures of my mom and dad on their trip to England… The treasure hunt continues until we have littered the couch and table with album after album, and box after box of loose photos as well.

Oh, the stories we tell as we look through those photos. Some are unbelievable but true — like the time Phil's brother jumped an abandoned bus with his bicycle — and how all three siblings managed to keep the secret until they were young adults. Or the times my husband played "bowling" with our then toddler-aged children — they were the "pins" and a beanbag chair was the "bowling ball." Phil always chose to play "bowling-with-kids" when I was occupied in the kitchen. Humm… I wonder why? We share secrets, future plans, to-do items on our bucket list. But most of all, we share love.

How do these photos relate to the final scene of the vignette? Scene Seventeen is a portrait of memory snippets of your life as the Bride of Christ. If it's all right with you, I'd like to portray this scene as seven "photos." This is your life in review. You and Beloved have memories to share, and these are your favorites. In each memory, you learn how Beloved's kiss of peace has kept you secure, and maturing, no matter the circumstance—the first "photo" outlining your need to yield fully to Beloved, whereas your final "photo" portrays you as a mature Bride who is pleading her Bridegroom's quick return.

As you enter this final scene, Love, ready yourself to receive Beloved's kisses of peace as never before. Ponder not only what is written in this scene, but how your own life story and these snapshots relate. Beloved is present in every one of these flashback segments, and He continues to be your peace today.

Come into the arms of grace, and rest.

Receive each of the seven kisses…

Revel in divine love…

You have never walked alone—ever—and you never will. Your *Dowd Sheloma*—your Beloved Peacemaker—is here with you, and He will be with you into eternity. His kiss of peace has been, and always will be, your reality.

Enter in, Bride of Christ:

*****

SONG OF SOLOMON 8:1-14
Scene Seventeen—Kept By Love

SETTING:	Flashback segments, like photographs, of LOVE's life. Each memory is called a "PHOTO."
AT RISE:	Center Stage: LOVE and BELOVED.
	As BELOVED and LOVE speak the dialogue, stagehands carry props of each "photo" onto Stage Right, and then Stage Left, alternating. Spotlight follows BELOVED and LOVE as they stroll hand-in-hand to Stage Right, then Stage Left, alternating.
	(Cables have been attached to BELOVED and LOVE for their ascent scene.)

PHOTO ONE: ROMANCING/COMMUNING COUPLE
(Stage Right: BELOVED approaches LOVE as a courtier. They hold hands, facing each other. The couple leans in, heads touching.)

LOVE
[1]Oh that You were like my brother, who nursed at my mother's breasts! *If* I should find You outside, I would kiss You; I would not be despised. [2]I would lead You, *and* bring you into the house of my mother, she *who* used to instruct me. I would cause You to drink of spiced wine of the juice of my pomegranate.

PHOTO TWO: MINISTRY AS A MARRIED COUPLE
(Stage Left: LOVE reclines under an apple tree of the Sharon Valley. BELOVED steps toward LOVE. They recline together. They wear their lily and Rose of Sharon wedding garlands.)

178

LOVE

³His left hand *is* under my head, and His right hand embraces me. ⁴I charge you, O daughters of Jerusalem, do not stir not up, nor awaken love, until it pleases.

PHOTO THREE: LEANING/HARVESTING SOULS

(Stage Right: LOVE is witnessing to VALLEY PEOPLE. Two DAMSELS play tug-of-war. BELOVED approaches LOVE; she leans on Him; they walk together. He picks a fruit. LOVE and BELOVED recline under the tree, embracing.)

MAIDEN

⁵ᵃWho *is* this coming up from the wilderness, leaning upon her Beloved?

BELOVED

(Addressing LOVE)

⁵ᵇI awakened you under the apple tree. There your mother brought you forth; there she *who* bore you brought *you* forth.

PHOTO FOUR: KEPT BY LOVE

(Stage Left: BELOVED and LOVE embrace.)

LOVE

⁶Set me as a seal upon Your heart, as a seal upon your arm; for love *is* as strong as death; jealousy *as* cruel as the grave; its flames *are* flames of fire, a most vehement flame. ⁷Many waters cannot quench love, nor can the floods drown it. If a man would give for love all the wealth of his house, it would be utterly despised.

PHOTO FIVE: THE BRIDE'S WITNESS; AN INNER FIRE

VALLEY PERSON

(Stage Right: VALLEY PERSON pointing toward two YOUNG VALLEY PEOPLE; shrugs; questions LOVE.)

⁸We have a little sister, and she has no breasts. What shall we do for our sister in the day when she is spoken for?

LOVE

(Looks at BELOVED; then answers)

⁹If she *is* a wall, we will build upon her a battlement of silver: and if she *is* a door, we will enclose her with boards of cedar.

PHOTO SIX: THE CONSECRATED BRIDE

(Stage Left: BELOVED and LOVE hold hands, adoring each other.)

LOVE

¹⁰I *am* a wall, and my breasts like towers; then I became in His eyes as one who found peace.

MAIDEN

¹¹Solomon had a vineyard at Baal Hamon; He leased the vineyard to keepers; everyone was to bring for its fruit a thousand silver *coins*.

LOVE

[12]My own vineyard, *is* before me. You, O Solomon, *may have* a thousand, and those who tend its fruit two hundred.

PHOTO SEVEN: THE ROMANCE CONTINUES
(Stage Right: BELOVED and LOVE dance.)

BELOVED
(Addresses all Brides; represented by the AUDIENCE; offers hand to LOVE.)
[13]You who dwell in the gardens, the companions listen for your voice—let Me hear *it*!
(Center Stage: BELOVED and LOVE exit.)

LOVE
(Center Stage: LOVE enters and addresses her unseen BELOVED.)
[14]Make haste, my Beloved, and be like a gazelle or a young stag on the mountains of spices.
(Spotlight increases; glitter falls from the ceiling.)
(BELOVED descends [suspended from the cable] and embraces LOVE. BELOVED and LOVE arise, arms raised, clasping hands, dancing still.)
(Curtain closes.)

NARRATOR
The Bride and Groom's love story has only begun. Love and Beloved will be romancing beyond the end of time…This is only the beginning, for with Beloved, there is no end.

THE BEGINNING
*****

What is happening in this scene? Your Groom is showing you a synopsis of your life from its conception to the present day. Beloved shows you His favorite memories. Beloved has loved you at all times, and He will come again to take you to His heavenly home.

Oh, what a reunion that will be! Of necessity, you must wait, so you harvest souls, but you yearn for the glorious day when you will meet your Beloved Jesus Christ face-to-face in all of His majesty.

Let's look at each of these "photographs" of your life's album:

PHOTO ONE: ROMANCING/COMMUNING COUPLE
BABY JESUS

In Photo One, you say, *O that you were as my brother…* (Song 8:1). Beloved is not a distant, far-away God—rather, He is like a brother to you—He is closer than a friend and familiar with your likes, dislikes, and desires. You continue, …*who nursed at my mother's breast* (Song 8:1b)*!* Beloved is to you as innocent as a nursing baby. Jesus in the manger is a remembrance we may go to when reading this.

THE KISS

From here you move into your desire to court Beloved, saying, If *I should find you outside, I would kiss you; I would not be despised. I would lead you* and *bring you into the house of my mother, she who used to instruct me* (Song 8:1b-2a). You mention your desire to kiss Beloved and not be despised, thus you need to bring Him to your family's home for approval.

Notice your mother's instruction is something that used to happen—because you are a mature Bride, you now have biblical knowledge that you readily follow of your own accord, without needing basic instruction to do so. The Word of God is deep within your heart.

This memory represents Scene One, as you and Beloved shared the private Communion cup and marital intimacy. Neither you nor Beloved are ashamed of the ardent love you have as a married couple. But keep in mind, this is an allegory, so this represents only your spiritual union.

POMEGRANATE WINE

You drink pomegranate wine while inviting Beloved to your mother's chamber, *I would cause you to drink of spiced wine, of the juice of my pomegranate* (Song 8:1b). This represents the nurturing Holy Spirit causing intimacy.

Notice this is your desire, and your pomegranate. Beloved has waited for you to be ready for divine love. As aforementioned, pomegranate juice is an aphrodisiac, and you desire Beloved to impart His wisdom, as also represented by the pomegranate juice. You desire a covenantal marriage relationship represented by this wine of Communion.

This is no ordinary pomegranate wine. The juice has been mixed with spices. In your marital stroll through the Lebanon mountain range, you found these spices growing in abundance in the secluded prayer garden retreat of Mt. Hermon, which represents the Holy of Holies. Divine love becomes yours, and sometimes, within the garden of spices, with the wisdom of your Romancer, you exude pure, holy *dowd.* You carry this God-love as a spiritual gifting.

In the marriage-bed scene, we saw the spices representative of different aspects of intimacy. So, the spiced pomegranate wine represents passion. You go beyond an "I got saved, I'm satisfied" attitude, to an ardent desire to romance your Groom. You don't want to be satisfied; you want to be satiated.

Let's look at the Communion cup in this scene, which we also saw in Scene One. As you partake of His cup, you renew your marriage vows. With this cup of atonement, you are saved through and through, and this creates *shalom* within you. Beloved's lips are like wine as He kisses you with His peace.

SPICES

The spices include the anointing apothecary, so this represents your spiritual romance and subsequent marriage. They also represent your respect for Beloved's sacrificial love, and your commitment to be sacrificial in the love you share with others.

You desire prayer intimacy, as also represented by some of the various spices. You desire the most fragrant, rich, and invigorating marital relationship with Beloved that you can have. You invite Beloved to examine your life from its conception to your wedding and beyond. He is to be your Lord of your past, present, and future.

Let's sum up what we've ascertained from Photo One: In one photo, it encapsulates your life's story, and Beloved's, from the start to the conclusion. The vignette does a good job of showing divine love and peace in this one snippet.

PHOTO TWO: THE EMBRACE THAT LEADS TO MINISTRY

In Photo Two, it is not enough for you to know Beloved's love; you are compelled to witness because of His love. You say, *His left hand is under my head, and His right hand embraces me. I charge you, O daughters of Jerusalem, do not stir not up, nor awaken love, until it pleases* (Song 8:3).

Remember, the "it" in this verse is plural, so this represents you and Beloved both being able to choose the duration of the prayer time. Until both you and He are satisfied with the prayer embrace, neither you nor He should leave this place of intimacy. This is why we should plan our prayer times and have extra time to spare. If we are going to have the throne room experience, it takes time. There is no shortcut.

We know the conclusion that is reached. As you learn to lean into Beloved's embrace and stay there until the anointing lifts, He transforms you, and from the abundance of His prayer embrace, you minister to the people, speaking to both maidens and gents, damsels, and lost souls, as you impart divine love to them.

Tarrying in Beloved's embrace always preceded ministry. You teach your maidens to lean into Beloved's love before they minister. You show them Beloved as the source of the anointing. They can only effectively witness and disciple from the overflow of this anointing they experience during their tarry times.

Witnessing and discipling souls is now a delightful activity to you. Your relationship did not begin that way—you wanted nothing to do with your family and your acquaintances because they picked on you. But now, you seek them out to share the love and peace you have found in your Beloved. Their snarls, back-stabbings, and disapproving glances do not rattle you as they once did; rather, you ache for them, eager for them to find the same divine love you have found in your Beloved's embrace.

You've experienced a paradigm change. Beloved's love compels you to witness, so this is no longer a difficult task. Your gift to Beloved is souls. You bring Him Loves (Song 7:12b); these are "Brides." Thus, you win as many souls as possible; not just one or two. But you do this through loving and discipling them rather than trying to perform and check boxes off a numbers chart.

The quick conclusion of your marriage is this—love breeds love—and the type of love it breeds is the divine *dowd* of boiling-hot passion that is indescribable outside of an allegory.

PHOTO THREE: LEANING WHILE HARVESTING SOULS

In Photo Three, you are pictured as leaning on your Beloved as you walk together through the harvest fields. A maiden says, *Who is this coming up from the wilderness, leaning upon her Beloved?* (Song 8:5a). and your Groom answers, *I awakened you under the apple tree. There your mother brought you forth; there she who bore you brought you forth* (Song 8:5b).

This is a flashback of you leaning into Beloved's embrace that started on your wedding day. The action of leaning represents your receptivity to Beloved's love. The action of walking represents your willingness to rely on His direction. Not only are you leaning while coming aside to eat of the Holy Spirit fruits, as represented here by the *apples* (Song2:3, 5, 8:5b)[200] on the tree, but you are also leaning while you walk the harvest fields with Beloved. Notice your Groom is always present when you witness or disciple souls. You do not do this on your own; you co-partner with Him.

Remember the previous discussion of walking. There are two aspects: we walk with Him and we obey His lead. The phrase *come away* (Song 2:10-13) that we saw in Scene Eight translates as two inseparable words: "Come," *yalak,* meaning "to walk," and "away," *halak,* meaning to "behave while walking." Beloved wants to shape our character on our strolls with Him, and it is obvious because you are leaning into Beloved in this scene, you have learned this lesson well. Therefore, He is able to form within you the spiritual fruit He desires to impart. Holiness has become a process you are learning to incorporate into your bridal experience.

How can we lean and witness at the same time? We cannot. We would eventually tip over. So, the metaphorical meaning is this: There are times when it is vital for us to come aside into our prayer garden to focus exclusively on our Beloved in unfettered seclusion. Equally, there are times where we are called to witness and disciple souls, for out of the overflow of anointing we are compelled to share. We need to listen closely to Beloved to discern the times. Even when we do minister, we need to be listening, and promptly obeying His instructions.

The metaphor of leaning while walking is shown as one. You walk and lean at the same time because both are of equal importance. Beloved kisses you with His peace because He loves you, but there is an expectation that you will show love for others from the overflow of peace His kiss creates. The kiss multiplies our desire to love like He does.

---

[200] *Citron*; tropical citrus fruit such as an orange

Beloved Jesus sums this up, saying, *The first of all the commandments is: 'Hear, O Israel, the LORD our God, the LORD is one. And you shall love the LORD your God with all your heart, with all your soul, with all your mind, and with all your strength.' This is the first commandment. And the second like it, is this"* 'You shall love your neighbor as yourself.' *There is no other commandment greater than these* (Mark 12:29b-31). This is the love we must have for God and for others, and in order to attain this, we must lean into Beloved's embrace.

Beloved Jesus also tells us, *"Go into all the world and preach the gospel to every creature"* (Mark 16:15b). This confirms that the only way we will be able to accomplish Beloved's mission is to be filled with Him; therefore, we must stroll with Him in the prayer garden, permitting Him to shape our character there, and these strolls result in a vibrant, public ministry.

PHOTO FOUR: KEPT BY LOVE

In Photo Four, you speak about of the strength of love. You say, *Set me as a seal upon your heart, as a seal upon your arm; for love* [ahabah] *is as strong as death; jealousy as cruel as the grave; its flames are flames of fire, a most vehement flame. Many waters cannot quench love* [ahabah], *nor can the floods drown it. If a man would give for love* [ahabah] *all the wealth of his house, it would be utterly despised* (Song 8:6).

The love you describe here is of Beloved as a seal upon your heart that is stronger than death itself. This love is jealous and as passionate as a consuming flame. Therefore, as previously mentioned, we would guess the word used for *love* (Song 8:6) is *dowd*, divine love, but this is not the case. Remarkably, the word used in this passage is *ahabah,* which is sometimes used to describe God-love, but is usually used to describe natural or romantic love, and it is commonplace for *ahabah* to represent the romantic love expressed in a marriage.

What do we learn from this puzzling word usage? We learn this: If in the vignette, natural human love has as much passion associated with it as a jealous and vehement flame, then the strength of Beloved's divine love—*dowd*—is infinitely stronger than this, the starting point of describing love. Beloved's *dowd* truly does go beyond human love, and we, therefore, see why Song of Solomon is an allegory. God's love truly is indescribable in human languages, divine love [*dowd*] being as dynamic as a boiling pot.

Furthermore, if Beloved is the personification of divine love—*dowd*—then He displays a depth of love unfathomable to the human mind. If human love is stronger than death, stronger than the most vehement flame, better than passion, and more intense than a flame that cannot be quenched by a torrent of water, then the divine *dowd* love our Beloved Groom personifies is majestic—far beyond what words can describe.

We can easily conclude that if Beloved is the personification of the most passionate indescribable love, then we can conclude that our expressions of human love—*ahabah*—can only be perfected through maintaining a covenantal relationship with Him.

Can we succeed at this? The answer is "Yes!" As the Bride of Christ, we are kept by Beloved's divine love. The love Beloved keeps us with is beyond our most focused imagination of natural love. Therefore, at times we can express His divine love—*dowd*. While we are in communion with Him, especially through our Communion experiences, we are graced with His divine love called *dowd*.

Your name is inscribed upon Beloved's very heart as a seal. When I first got saved, my Lord gave me a Scripture that has become my life-verse. Beloved says, *"Fear not; for I have redeemed you, I have called you by your name; you are Mine"* (Isaiah 43:1b). Beloved has redeemed and sanctified you, as well, taken you as His Bride, inscribed you upon His heart, and given you a bridal name. You are Beloved's wife—your name is "Love"—for you are chosen by Him and kept safe by His divine kisses of peace.

You and Beloved are inseparable because of the depth of His love for you. For Beloved to leave you, He would have to depart from His own beating heart. He won't leave you, so rest secure that He has you secured by His love, even during your weak moments. Let me express that again—

especially during your weak times, Beloved secures you by His divine kisses of peace.

Beloved already knew your weaknesses and mine when He chose us to become His Bride. He paid Calvary's price because in His estimation, and in Father's and Holy Spirit's, the Bride is worth this high bridal cost. Beloved loves you, Love, and He has chosen you.

You and your Husband-King have one purpose. What is it? Beloved says, *"I chose you, and appointed you, that you should go and bear fruit, and that your fruit should remain"* (John 15:16b). You have been born to align with the Spirit fruits of Beloved's choosing. You are *appointed* (John 15:16b) — which translates as "ordained" in the King James — and you have Spirit fruits to share.

Thus, your life's purpose is to love Beloved and to share Him with others. He makes sure you succeed. In fact, He keeps you as an inscription upon His beating heart.

PHOTO FIVE: THE BRIDE'S WITNESS; AN INNER FIRE

In Photo Five, we see two kinds of people you minister to, and instructions on how you can reach both kinds. They are represented by two adolescents. Each damsel has come to *the day when she shall be spoken for* (Song 8:8b). In other words, these individuals are at their point of decision, here represented by a marriage day. Will they say "Yes!" to Beloved's marriage proposal as you once did?

Your witness to them is crucial…

I AM A WALL

The first adolescent is *a wall* (Song 8:9a) She accepts salvation, and she is careful to walk a holy life. What you share with this believer is redemption, which is represented by the silver palace. This is her primary need — she knows redemption is available all throughout her lifetime — not as a one-time event. Because she is aware of her sinful nature, she can readily accept the marriage proposal.

This is when you also were pliable — your understanding of your need for Beloved to transform you, which we saw in Scenes Two and Three, resulted in Beloved being able to take *my filly among Pharaoh's chariots* (Song 1:9b), who was unknowingly serving the enemy, and transforming you into the Bride of Ammi Nadib (Song 6:12b KJV), the nobles' representative of the earthly and heavenly armies aligning forces.

Redemption is not a one-time event; it is ongoing. Most of us don't realize this; therefore, we live a life of guilt. You can help this Bride-to-be by showing her the silver palace of redemption that is available throughout our lifetimes.

We've all heard the saying that the church is a hospital, but we rarely act like this is true. Beloved knows it is true and He shows you here in this photo that redemption is a vital message to share. Beloved knows we are imperfect. He says, *"Those who are well have no need of a physician, but those who are sick"* (Matthew 9:12b). Redemption is available to each believer, whether the person needing this fresh start is the pastor, deacon, member, attendee, new convert, or unchurched believer. Let's get this message shared!

I AM A DOOR

The other adolescent is *a door* (Song 8:9b). In other words, this individual just lets in all sorts of beliefs without discerning truth from fiction. She has come to a point of decision, but confusion reigns within.

To this person, you share the message of the cross, enclosing this individual with the strong cedar boards of salvation. You help her become a believer in Jesus Christ and explain the Gospel message clearly over and over until she believes without hesitation.

You answer all her "silly" questions, because they aren't really silly — we probably had the same ones — and you disciple her over time as the Maidens once did for you. You share the benefits of salvation, but also the consequences of unbelief. This is the truth she needs to hear.

Discipleship is important during this step so she doesn't slip away. Once we witness to a person, we need to have steps set in motion to help the individual keep their decision for Christ intact. The enemy lurks, trying to steal away the new convert. We must care enough to help the person get acclimated to her new life in Christ, perhaps helping her attend a new converts class or secure counseling for felt needs, inviting her to fellowships so she builds relationships with Christians, or finding other ways we can help the newcomer succeed.

PHOTO SIX: THE CONSECRATED BRIDE

In Photo Six you declare your solidarity by saying, *I am a wall, and my breasts like towers; then I became as one who found peace* (Song 8:10). In the King James, *peace* (Song 8:10b) translates as "favor." You know you have won Beloved's favor because you are enclosed within His love, and this does indeed bring peace to your heart.

By saying you have *breasts like towers* (Song 8:10a), you indicate that people are nourished by your spirit. You are tapped into Beloved's love, so you have something to share. He favors and equips you. By your breasts having previously been as *twins* (Song7:3b), you are indicating you have a doubly secured and favored position within Beloved's love. You have favor and then some! Beloved cannot keep from looking at you! You have captured His attention because your loving glances demonstrate you are fully committed to your Groom. He means everything to you. You've held back nothing from Him. You love your Romancer with every ounce of your being.

And He notices that you love Him…

No matter the frailty of human love, He is perfecting it because you are expressing it.

Your spiritual works are represented by the vineyard. You say, *My own vineyard, is before me* (Song 8:12a). By this you acknowledge your responsibility to maintain your spiritual life. In Scene Two, you neglected this; but now, it is the most important activity you do. In fact, you feel it is profitable to do so, because then you can break ground and plant more vines. You are a garden dweller, having learned the art of living in Beloved's clefts.

Notice the location of the vineyard: you are once again pictured as enclosed within Mt. Hermon's prayer garden. You minister in the Valley, but you abide in the prayer garden retreat—Mt. Hermon—the Holy of Holies.

Both metaphors—the twin breasts and the well-tended vineyard—indicate you have attained strength through solitude. Tarrying in Beloved's love is once again featured.

When you come down to the people from your garden abode, you have something to say because of the time you have spent in the heights. Beloved says to all of you, *The companions listen for your voice – Let me hear it* (Song 8:13)! Why does Beloved want to hear your voice, and other Brides as you? You have won His favor through your worship, so He wants to instruct you. When you worship, He can fill your mind and inflame your spirit with nourishing messages for the people. There is an urgency in His dialogue here, because He knows Father will send Him to redeem His Brides soon.

Beloved wants all to be ready for His soon return. Are we committed to win souls and make them His Brides?

PHOTO SEVEN: THE ROMANCE CONTINUES

At last, we come to Photo Seven. This final photo is of you and Beloved romancing until the end of time and into eternity until He raptures you into His final—and eternal—embrace. You say with passion, *Make haste, my beloved, and be like a gazelle or a young stag on the mountains of spices* (Song 8:14). You await Beloved's quick and sudden return, when you will step into His chariot and ascend with Him into the heavenlies. You want Him to come quickly!

Your closing sentiments here in Song of Solomon echo the final lines of Revelation, *He who testifies to these things says, "Surely I am coming quickly." Amen. Come Lord Jesus! The grace of our Lord Jesus Christ be with you all. Amen* (Revelation 22:20). You can add your double *Amen* to this sentiment.

The last verses of Song of Solomon end with the same sentiment as the last verses of the Bible.

You miss your Groom, and you desire the day, with great anticipation, when you will be face-to-face and cheek-to-cheek with your Beloved Jesus Christ. It is then He will whisk you into eternity, ride you through Heaven's streets, and perfectly impart to you His divine kiss of peace. What we see through a glass darkly will become a romance you can fully embrace. The Lord of the dance will be with you, in full measure, forever.

Love, what are you doing when Beloved's chariot arrives? You are His spotless, harvesting Bride when He comes! He expects you to be in the harvest fields, which glisten white with the souls of expectant Brides-to-be, and you do so, willingly sharing the gospel message.

How has your life changed? Once, you did not tend to your spiritual life. You had a crumbling fortress of vines that were tangled and fallen due to neglect, over-commitment, and shame that even your closest relatives — the mother, father, stepfather, and siblings — imposed on you. This was your lot.

But now, you have a vineyard that is abundant, and it is producing a thousand pieces of silver redemption for your Beloved, with two hundred for your listeners. Notice this is a metaphor, because vines produce grapes, not silver. Notice also the connection between the Communion cup of wine and the silver cup of redemption.

Your vineyard is as productive as the *vineyard at Baal Hamon* (Song 8:11a). This begs the question: Who is "Baal Hamon?" This name means "possessor of abundance."[201] So, as you mention this name, you are making the spiritual connection that you are abundantly blessed. You are not blessed with a measure — rather, you are blessed beyond measure.

Once, you had traversed *the mountain of Bether* (Song 2:17b) — Division Mountain — now, you traverse *the mountains of spices* (Song 8:14b) — Romance Mountain. Once, you were like a horse needing to be bridled (see Song 1:9a). Now, you are leaning into Beloved's voice, and sharing the same wisdom that He whispers into your heart (see Song 8:13). Once, you possessed natural love — *ahabah* (see Song 8:6). Now, in increasing measure you possess the divine love — *dowd* and peace of your Husband-King (see Song 8:10). Truly, your life is abundant, for you are a reflection of Beloved's own persona. You are His and He is yours. You and Beloved are passionate lovers who are united in *dowd*, co-laborers in the harvest field and in constant communication.

You are the well-pruned vine Beloved mentions in John 15:1a, 5, "*I am the true vine… I am the vine, you are the branches. He who abides in Me, and I in him, bears much fruit; for without Me you can do nothing.*" The assumption here is that when we partner with our Groom, we can do everything! We are the Bride of Christ, and our name is "Love." We are married to the Groom of all grooms, whose love and peace hem us in. Beloved's divine kisses of peace are ours, and everything we do, we do for Him.

You are the Bride, kissed with peace…

CONCLUSION

Does this romance ever end? Let me answer with a personal experience. While writing *The Kiss of Peace*, I got to this final scene and I simply did not want to conclude the study. It is then that I heard my Beloved Jesus Christ whisper into my heart a truth that is applicable to you as well, so I would be honored if you remember this as your truth, not just mine.

Beloved spoke into my spirit, "Your love story has only just begun." At first, I did not understand His message. I said, "But Beloved, I've researched and prayed, and pondered Song of Solomon for years, and I've been obedient to write about this bridal experience. Are You saying I don't understand? Did I fail?" What I then realized, as He cradled me into His arms and reassured me I had indeed been obedient to His will, was that even a lifetime of study will never exhaust the depths

---

[201] Strong OT #1174; possessor of a multitude. From OT #1167; master, husband, possessor.

of our bridal experience with Beloved Jesus Christ. The treasures hidden within Song of Solomon will only grow sweeter as time goes by. Even in eternity, we will be swept into a glorious romance.

And so, I say to you with all confidence, your love story has only begun. Beloved will be romancing you, His Bride, until the end of time, and after that, we await Heaven. There we will step into our glorious Romancer's arms of grace, dance with Him, and kiss Him, face-to-face.

With these final lines, I say to you, Love, continue the romance. Live your life from the abundance of your Romancer's embrace. Receive every one of Beloved's divine kisses of peace. Enjoy each stage of your romance, and share your *Dowd Shelomah*, your Beloved Solomon, your Beloved Peacemaker Jesus Christ, with all who will listen.

Let's pray one more time. I'm glad you've practiced going off script, because your Beloved Romancer is ready to tarry you, and meet the longing of His heart, which is to impart to you His divine kiss of peace:

My Beloved Jesus,

Thank You, my Bridegroom, that our romance has only begun. When the last scene here on earth is written for me, I will be romancing You still, yet ever more completely. Thank You for Your divine kiss of peace.

Come, my glorious Romancer. As the Hart upon Mt. Hermon's prayer garden, I desire to commune with You in a glorious dance. Set my spirit ablaze by Your glorious embrace. I await the day when I will receive Your divine kisses of peace face-to-face.

Shalom,
Love

BRIDAL REFLECTION

1) In Photo One, why is the pomegranate wine spiced? What do the pomegranate, the spices, and the wine represent?

2) In Photo Two, Beloved is embracing you. Describe this in detail.

3) When you harvest souls in Photo Three, what is the significance of your bridal walk, in relation to how successful you will be?

4) In Photo Five, you witness to two types of people. Which kinds are these and how do you effectively witness to each?

5) Are you the Bride who is the "wall" of Photo Six?

6) Has this study helped you become a consecrated Bride?

7) Write a prayer of thanksgiving to your Beloved Jesus Christ.

Leader's Guide for
The Kiss of Peace: A Contemporary Exploration into Song of Solomon

INTRODUCTION

This Bible study is designed as a twelve-week study through Song of Solomon. The objective is fourfold:

1. This Bible study draws the contemporary reader into the knowledge that Jesus Christ is the Beloved Romancer of Song of Solomon and that His divine love is personally available.
2. It offers the modern-day reader edification and, as the book title suggests, the divine love and peace of the Bridegroom, Jesus Christ.
3. To help the student recognize this book as an allegory of divine love, which is far too spectacular to be able to be conveyed outside of allegorical form.
4. It restores to the Bride of Christ the message originally intended in Song of Solomon — that it is an allegorical rather than a literal romance, and it counters viewpoints that present erroneous teachings.

This is a journey into the divine love and peace of the Bridegroom. As your students realize they are each, indeed, the Bride of Christ as portrayed in the vignette and that her Bridegroom is none other than her Lord and Savior Jesus Christ, she will be able to internalize the divine truths this vignette conveys. Don't worry about the scholarly acumen of each student. Each is on a different spiritual level. You, however, are well-advised to study so you can give your students the best experience possible. With that in mind, let's look at the background of Song of Solomon.

LITERARY CONSTRUCTION

VIGNETTE/SONG

Song of Solomon is a vignette sung by the Bride and Groom. As your student participates in vignette dialogue, she is able to mature in stages rather than instantaneously. We no longer have the song; only the dialogue remains. Nonetheless, your student will tend to personalize the vignette as her own story as she reads and imagines the vignette scenes. At various stages of growth, she will internalize a new truth. Jesus Christ used parables in a similar manner.

ALLEGORICAL LANGUAGE

It is vital that your students recognize this vignette is not to be taken literally; rather, the physical expressions allegorize the spiritual dimension of her Beloved Bridegroom Jesus Christ, who invites His Bride to explore divine love. Redirect any student that tries to interpret this as literal, pointing out it is an allegory that conveys spiritual truths.

This spiritual realm is indescribable, having no equivalent human language. Therefore, since our Groom is limited to the human dimension, He uses man's most passionate expression — a romance within the bounds of marriage — to approximate His divine love for His Bride, the church.

The strength of the Groom's divine love for His Bride is His signature of authorship. It is as if He is saying, "Get this first: I love you with a limitless love that is boiling in intensity, and I am not ashamed of my zeal for you, My cherished Bride."

SCENE ONE

Scene One is a flashback of the Bride's consummation within the veil, the blessed marriage chamber, and represents the Holy of Holies, where the Bride comes face-to-face with her Bridegroom Jesus Christ. Every other scene in the vignette relates back to this first scene, so pay particular attention as you teach this, to do it well. Avoid making it appear sexual—rather give full credence to this as being an allegory of divine love.

Scene One details how the Bride receives her Bridegroom's divine love. It's all about Communion and communing—in a word, relationship. Your goal in teaching this first scene is to get your students interested in having a relationship with Jesus Christ rather than being happy with rote religious dogma. The best way to do this is to stress who they are. "Love" is their stage name, and they are loved by the Bridegroom, "Beloved," who is divine love personified. These stage names are ripe with relationship motivation. You might also decide to share other names used for the Bride and Groom, but stress the stage names Love and Beloved. This is plenty for your students to set to memory.

The final scene of the vignette references Scene One as the Bride's motivation to evangelize. Because she has become secure, having experienced a divine love and peace only her Bridegroom can fully possess, she is ready to reach out to the lost and dying, broken, and scarred world around her. She embraces this mission with a passion. Knowing this will help you encourage your students to follow this study with any outreach class your church may provide.

NAMES

Here's a helpful chart you can refer to in order to teach your students the names of the Bridegroom and His Bride. It's not necessary that they memorize these, but it is useful to share these:

BELOVED

The Groom's character is encoded in His Hebrew name, Beloved Solomon:
- Beloved, *Dowd*, (Strong. OT #1730) means divine love personified.
- Solomon, *Sheloma*, (from *shalom*) (Strong. OT #8010) means completeness or peace.
- Therefore, allegorically, *Dowd Shelomah* means the Beloved Peacemaker. This is a perfect description of the Lord Jesus Christ, for He indeed is our Beloved Peacemaker.

LOVE

The Bride's character is revealed through the names her Groom calls her:
- Love, *Rayah*, (Strong. OT #7474) is the Groom's most used reference for the Bride. This name implies a marital relationship. It translates as "wife" with the emphasis on the Groom's unconditional love.
- Sister/Spouse, *Achowth/Kallah*, (Strong. OT #269/ OT #3618) These terms are used in conjunction to approximate the closest marital relationship possible, where both partners are considered as equally important, particularly in the area of communication. Sister means, "sister." Spouse means, "perfected bride" or "wife." A covenantal relationship is implied.
- My Fair One, *Yapah*, (Strong. OT #3303) means "bright, comely, or fair" and indicates the glory of the Groom illuminated in His Bride. This reveals the Bride's completion as she partners with her Groom.

POINT OF VIEW

It is important for your student to appreciate from whose point of view the vignette is written. We would think Beloved Solomon (Jesus Christ in this allegory) would write Song of Solomon from His point of view, but this is not the case. The Bridegroom pens the Bride's recollections. Though Beloved is superior in every way, He invites, rather than forces, a relationship with His Bride. Therefore, He is delighted to pen her story.

The reason for this point of view is simple:

- This vignette is for all times, and it never goes stale. It is as relevant in our contemporary day as it was when it was first written.
- The Bride's story in the vignette is the reader's story. The vignette is designed to be personalized.
- Written as a personal journey through the eyes of the Bride, this vignette gives the reader time to explore divine love, where nothing is forced and where the Bride knows she is accepted at every stage of her journey.
- She can grow in love as she lives out this vignette in her real-life journey. As she reads and re-reads vignette scenes, working through them, her relationship with her Bridegroom strengthens.

By the close of the vignette, the Bride has received her Bridegroom's message and His love and peace envelopes her. Scene One, the anchor of the vignette, is actualized, and her heart's desire to share her Groom's love with every person she encounters is strong.

You have been entrusted by the Bridegroom Jesus Christ to shepherd your students through their journey into divine love. I am certain He will bless your efforts as you help them tap into the divine love and peace of the Bridegroom.

PROTOTYPES

You may choose to share some of the below Scripture parallels as you teach each lesson, to help your students focus on various aspects of their Bridegroom. This can be used as bonus material as time permits. Have one of these aspects of the Bridegroom handy so you can share it if you have extra time at the end of the lesson.

The Groom, Beloved Solomon, is a prototype of Jesus Christ. New Testament parallels support the following conclusions about His character:

HE HAS ACCESS INTO THE HOLY OF HOLIES
- Song of Solomon 1:4
- Matthew 27:51

HE SHARES THE COMMUNION ELEMENTS
- Song of Solomon 2:5
- Luke 22:15

HE SHARES MYRRH AND FRANKINCENSE OINTMENTS
- Song of Solomon 5:2-5
- Matthew 2:11; Luke 23:55-56

HIS HANDS ARE PIERCED, THEN GEM-SET
- Song of Solomon 5:14
- Mark 15:24

HIS RETURN IS IMMINENT
- Song of Solomon 8:14
- Revelation 22:20

HISTORY OF SONG OF SOLOMON

The canonicity of Song of Solomon has been debated since its inception due to misconceptions regarding its sexual content. Rabbi Akiba argued for the book's inclusion in the Bible and won at the council of Jamnia in 90AD.[202] He correctly presented Song of Solomon as an allegory. Akiba explained that the romance represented the divine love God had for Israel, and the wedding chamber

---

[202] https://www.bible.ca/b-canon-council-of-jamnia.htm

represented the Holy of Holies. He stated, "The whole world attained its supreme value only on the day when the Song of Songs was given to Israel."[203] He strongly believed this message, and he was willing to be martyred rather than deny his Lord.

Other ancient biblical commentators concurred, such as Origen of the third century and Theodore of Cyr of the fifth century. However, these scholars went a step further, noting the messianic interplay between the Groom Jesus Christ and His Bride, the church.

In biblical times, Jewish leaders permitted a person to read Song of Solomon only after the age of thirty in order to guard against viewing the vignette as sexual. It is not this. Song of Solomon is an allegorical representation of the Lord Jesus Christ and His Bride, the Church.

When we look at the role of the Groom, it becomes evident Song of Solomon is an allegory. It is impossible for a human groom to fulfill every character trait of the Groom of Song of Solomon. Jesus Christ is the only groom capable of embracing the Bride with divine love so magnificent it is indescribable outside of an allegorical rendering. He also is the only groom who fulfills the prophetic references in the vignette.

WHO WILL BENEFIT FROM THIS BIBLE STUDY?

Students who will most benefit from this Bible study are Christian women who desire an intimate relationship with the Lord Jesus Christ. Although this Bible study assumes a female student, either gender can relate to being the "Bride" of Beloved, so these classes can be taught as co-ed, or to married couples, or as a ladies' study.

Please do not invite young teens or children to this Bible study. The material is not suitable for a young audience as they may not have the capacity to think along allegorical terms. Also, each lady needs the focus this class will provide. You, as teacher, provide a refuge for them to grow spiritually.

Today's society is in desperate need of this message. Every day, love is taken away, as is peace. People scramble to and fro, aimlessly searching, and this includes church people. People are angry, confused, uncentered, unchurched, and falling away in record numbers. Where is love? Where is peace?

Taught well, *The Kiss of Peace* will heal society's brokenness, and become a soul anchor. Make it your burning passion to restore the Bride of Christ to her Groom, Jesus Christ, as allegorically revealed in the vignette, Song of Solomon, in which divine love and peace can be found.

BOOK SECTIONS
Each chapter in *The Kiss of Peace* has four sections:
- **LEAD-IN**
  This allows your student to relate a modern-day example with biblical truths. From there she explores the vignette scene(s).
- **VIGNETTE SCENES**
  Through role-play, your student internalizes biblical truths of her Groom's message, rather than figuring out the logistics of speakers, settings, customs, and other nuances. These are all identified for her.
- **CHRISTIAN LIVING**
  Exposition follows each vignette portion. Your student is addressed as "Love." Her Groom is referenced as "Beloved Solomon." This serves as a constant reminder that this is her love story; she *is* the Bride of Song of Solomon. It will be helpful for you to call your students by their vignette name as well. When she hears herself referred to as "Love," it will strengthen her understanding that she truly is the Bride of Christ.
- **PRAYER**

---

[203] Wright, J. Robert. *Introduction to Proverbs, Ecclesiastes, and Song of Solomon.* New York: Intervarsity Press, 2004.

The student incorporates these short prayers into her experience; thus, she receives the biblical truths she has discovered. Encourage your students to not skip over these prayers — they serve as anchors of the truths she has learned in each chapter. Also encourage your students to personalize these prayers to suit her heart's desire.

THE ERRONEOUS BOOKSHELF

Your student will at some point most likely notice books on Song of Solomon that have opposing viewpoints to *The Kiss of Peace*. These erroneous books abound. They crowd the bookshelf, leaving this study looking like the oddball.

The Kiss of Peace is intentionally different from most studies, with the mission to restore the original understanding of Song of Solomon as an allegory of divine love between the Bride and the Bridegroom Jesus Christ. The early writer, Rabbi Akiba, identified the Bridegroom as the Messiah, although not yet able to know He was Jesus Christ. Encourage your students who are looking for books with similar content to *The Kiss of Peace* to check earlier writings, like Akiba's or other early-day scholars.

Although we could spend hours showing erroneous books about Song of Solomon, I have included three of the worst offenders, so you can see the relevancy of your mission:

BOOKS WITH OPPOSING CONTENT TO *THE KISS OF PEACE* INCLUDE:

- ISBN#1939622220: 2015: Idleman, Kyle and Desirae: *Awaken Love: A Couple's Devotional Inspired by Song of Solomon.*

  This six-week devotional focuses on marital restoration, using Song of Solomon as its text. Couples learn how to "fight fair, increase intimacy, and cultivate commitment." Nowhere in Song of Solomon do we see the Bride and Groom fighting. Therefore, it is incongruent with sound doctrine to think the vignette can be misconstrued as a text to learn to "fight fair" with their spouse.

- ISBN# 9781615214693: 2014: Dillow, Linda, and Pintus, Lorraine: *Intimacy Ignited: Conversations Couple to Couple: Fire Up Your Sex Life with the Song of Solomon.*

  Dillow quotes, "the Bible's very own manual on sex and intimacy — the Song of Solomon." She continues, "Discover the freedom, holiness, and beauty of the marriage bed, as well as creative lovemaking ideas." It is not surprising, due to Dillow's gross misuse of Scripture, that not a single reviewer on Christian Book Distributors was willing to write a review thus far.

- ISBN# 1892112167: 2010: Pearl, Michael: *Holy Sex: Song of Solomon.*

  This author writes, "Take a refreshing journey through biblical texts showing that God designed marriage to be the context of erotic pleasure." The word "erotic" does not exist in the Hebrew language. This book is an absurd and gross misrepresentation of Song of Solomon. Not only does Pearl's view counter Scripture; it may draw the reader into a satanic lure.

YOUR MISSION AS TEACHER

The biblical viewpoint of Song of Solomon as an allegorical representation of the Holy of Holies, as Rabbi Akiba, Origen, Theodore of Cyr, Estes, and other ancient scholars believed, and a few modern-day writers, must be restored! There is a dire need for *The Kiss of Peace* to be taught in order to counter these modern-day misrepresentations of Song of Solomon. What was known to the ancients, and consequentially canonized, must be restored. Make this your mission.

LESSON PLAN, WEEK BY WEEK

Let's explore possible lesson plans for the twelve weeks you will teach your students. Use this as a guide, but listen to the Holy Spirit and be open to the ways He will creatively instruct you. God has chosen you and will equip you with many ideas. Utilize them. For answers to the Bible Reflection Questions, go to the end of this teacher's guide.

Recognize that people remember best what they experience, so your classes should include the tactile fun activities suggested in the weekly studies. They may ask, "Are we really going to sip tea and chew gum, etc.?" to which you can confidently affirm the validity of the exercise. They can opt-out, but why would they miss the fun?

Educators recognize the validity of involving the five senses, as well as kinetic learning. Do the same. We are basing these activities from how Song of Solomon is written—as a vignette—which uses song, play acting, and other forms of experiential learning to impress on the reader God's message through Song of Solomon.

Make the assumption your students have read the chapter you will be teaching. Spend an equal amount of time teaching and dialoguing with your students. With that said, here are suggestions:

WEEK ONE
Chapter One: The Kiss
Preview

The reader learns Song of Solomon is an allegory and a vignette. She discovers the meanings of the Bride and Bridegroom's stage names, "Love" and "Beloved," as well as other names they possess. She experiences the depth of her Groom's divine love as a "boiling pot" in its intensity as she encounters Him in the wedding chamber, representative of the Holy of Holies.

Opening Prayer

Fun Activity
Supplies: Dry erase marker for each student; dry erase board.

As each student enters, hand her a dry erase marker and invite her to draw on the board her vignette name and her Bridegroom's vignette name. Encourage her to use her fanciest writing. You might have to clue her into her name, "Love," and her Bridegroom's name, "Beloved." After the first student gets this, others will follow, and they will help other students to know the answer to this object lesson.

NOTE: If any of your students write other names for the Bride, such as My Sister/Spouse or My Fair One, thank them for their scholarly observation. Although you are looking for your students to answer with "Love," the Bride's most frequently referenced name, these are not wrong answers; your most studied students may respond with these, so prepare for this.

Question/Answer Time

Choose three of the seven questions, found at the chapter's end, for your students to discuss.

Closing Prayer

WEEK TWO
Chapter Two: Kedar's Scar
Preview

Love's Israelite family calls her "dark" and they reject her because her birth father, Kedar, is of Arabian descent. When she embarks on a spiritual pilgrimage, she realizes she has been predestined to offer reconciliation to both nations through her redeemer, the Beloved.

Opening Prayer

Fun Activity
Supplies: Bubble gum and two sheets of unlined paper for each student.

As each student enters the classroom, hand her a stick of gum and ask her to start chewing it. Also give her the two sheets of paper.

When everyone gets there, ask the students to place their clewed gum on one sheet of paper. Next, ask them to remove the gum without ripping the paper. (They won't be able to.)

Discuss how the labels placed on Love felt like gum on a sidewalk — the harder she tried to counter the false labels, the stickier they were.

Next, ask your students to write in large letters, the opposite of a false label they have been called. Stress they are to write the opposite, not the label. Ask students to volunteer their answers. (Please don't force responses as some might be reluctant to share theirs. That is fine.)

This should be a tear-jerker.

It also inevitably addresses the ridiculous nature of prejudices, whether they result from ethnicity, physical or mental abilities, or the like. Their answers should indicate Beloved Jesus' viewpoint, to counter the false labels we, as humans, give to each other. They are like the gum on the sidewalk — once given, they are not easily reversed.

Share the importance that, as the Bride of Christ, we both know who we are in Him and that we serve as the bridge between broken human thinking and the divine love-message Beloved Jesus has entrusted us to share with the world.

We are Christ's ambassadors, and we are on a mission to remove some sticky false labels by showing others who they are or whom they can become when they reside in Beloved Jesus' love. The divine love of the Bridegroom counters every false label!

Question/Answer Time

Choose three of the seven questions for your students to discuss.

Closing Prayer
Preparation for next week: Ask each student to bring a teacup.

WEEK THREE
Chapter Three: The Oasis
Preview

Love learns seven oasis keys: 1) Acceptance, 2) Beloved's Lordship, 3) Mind Renewal, 4) Focused Time, 5) Obedience, 6) Communion, 7) Ongoing Spiritual Growth. These are the elements necessary to maintain the oasis way of life, and they bring her into an understanding of Beloved's divine peace.

Opening Prayer

Fun Activity
Preparation: Write on the dry erase board the seven oasis keys, numbered.
Supplies: Tea bags of various flavors, honey or sugar, stir sticks, a thermos or pot of hot water. (Inevitably a student will have forgotten her teacup, so you might want to have some extra cups on hand.)

Today it is teatime! It may be helpful to refresh your student's minds by sharing Betty's mother's story from the beginning of this chapter.

Pour tea for each student.

Ask three students to share a brief story of how Beloved Jesus has shown her His love. Then ask how this has brought her into an oasis experience. Point to the board and ask her to share which of the oasis keys this experience has strengthened her in.

Question/Answer Time

Choose three of the seven questions for your students to discuss.

Closing Prayer

WEEK FOUR
Chapter Four: The Banqueting Table
Preview

There is a celebratory atmosphere to this Communion/wedding day scene. Love ascends, taking her place of authority beside her Husband-King. Key words and phrases are connected (in the construct state), which emphasizes unity. Even so, Beloved remains Lord of His Bride.

Opening Prayer

Fun Activity
Preparation: Ask permission from your pastor for you to share Communion with your class or invite him to distribute the elements for you.
Supplies: The Communion elements, a Dixie cup, and a fancy wineglass.

Serve Communion.

Ask students to share how this experience draws them closer to their Beloved Bridegroom and strengthens their understanding that they are the Bride of Christ, deeply loved by the Groom who sacrificed His all at Calvary so they could live.

Hold up the Dixie cup and the wineglass. Discuss how the attitude of our heart is more important in receiving Communion than fancy cups or dishes and how we are receiving Jesus Christ as our suffering Savior and soon-coming Groom. We are to reverence Him and commune with Him.

Question/Answer Time

Choose three of the seven questions for your students to discuss.

Closing Prayer

WEEK FIVE
Chapter Five: Shadowboxing in Bether
Preview

Love climbs Bether ("Division") Mountain. As she begins her ascent, she is vulnerable to enemy attack. She learns Beloved is with her at all times. Only as she listens to His subtle promptings is she able to ascend. She realizes her greatest weapon is the decision to worship and to reveal every secret to Beloved's loving inspection.

Opening Prayer

Fun Activity
Supplies: Flashlights. Enough for half of your students. Markerboard.

As they enter, hand every other student a flashlight.

Ask your students to partner up with someone who has a flashlight. (If odd number, the last group consists of three students instead of two.)

Ask your students to make shadowy shapes on the marker board. The student with the flashlights, light up the hands of the student without the flashlight.

After five minutes, ask your students to return to their seats. Ask how this relates to Beloved Jesus Christ taking away the shadowy, distorted lies we may believe outside of His influence. Stress the timing—that the shadows are apparent each time the Bride ascends and that her awareness of Beloved Jesus' guidance should be looked at as strength rather than weakness. Ask how they felt about this experience and what they thought of the modern-day King David story.

Question/Answer Time

Choose three of the seven questions for your students to discuss.

Closing Prayer

Preparation for Next Week: Ask your students to dress fancy and bring an appetite for an after-church luncheon. Gowns are not necessary, but if they have one, invite them to feel free to wear it.

WEEK SIX
Chapter Six: The Chariot Rider
Preview

Love role-plays the Hebrew customs of ancient biblical times as if she is a Jewish Bride readying herself for her Groom, such as: 1) The *Huppah*—the marriage chamber, representative of the Holy of Holies. 2) The *Ketubah*—this written marriage contract represents the Bible, a love letter written by Jesus, and every word of His contract is true. 3) The *Mohar*—the high purchase price the Groom gave to redeem His Bride, fulfilled by the blood Jesus shed on Calvary.

Opening Prayer

Fun Activity
Preparation: If at all possible, prepare a limousine to pick up your class after church. Eat at a fancy restaurant. Discuss on the ride over how this limousine represents Beloved Jesus' extravagant chariot ride they will someday experience.
Supplies: An assortment of fancy pens and unlined paper.

Hold up your Bible. Ask them to share what it represents in the Hebrew wedding (our *Ketubah*—marriage contract.) Choose two more of the seven questions for your students to discuss.

Pass out fancy pens and paper. Ask your students to write their favorite Bible verse. Ask three volunteers to share theirs and to tell why this is Beloved's favorite promise. Remind your students again of the connection between the verse they just wrote and the *Ketubah*. Suggest to your students that they display this verse in a prominent place in their home.

Question/Answer Time

Spend the remainder of the Q/A time fielding questions. By this time, it is likely they will have some.

Closing Prayer

WEEK SEVEN
Chapter Seven: The Marriage Bed
Preview

Love journeys with Beloved to six mountains and a hill. She learns each location has spiritual significance. In order of her ascent, they are: 1) Mt. Bether, 2) Mt. Myrrh, 3) Frankincense Hill, 4) Mt. Lebanon, 5) Mt. Amana, 6) Mt. Senir, 7) Mt. Hermon.

Opening Prayer

Fun Activity
Preparation: Write on the marker board the names of the six mountains and the hill, numbered.
Needed: Fabric, preferably sparkly; a rectangle for each student.

Ask your students to pretend they are behind the veil of the Holy of Holies (represented by the fabric rectangle.) Which of the mountains do they visit most with Beloved at this spiritual juncture in their lives? Why?

Ask for three students to volunteer their answers. Applaud their willingness to share. For some, this will be a tear-jerker. No matter which mountain they most relate to, Beloved is pleased with them.

Share that this exercise emphasizes the relational journey of the Bride of Christ with the Bridegroom.

Question/Answer Time
Choose three of the seven questions for your students to discuss.

Closing Prayer

WEEK EIGHT
Chapter Eight: Night Visitors
Preview
Ministry is crucial, but it is often inconvenient. Beloved's fingers, brow, and locks are drenched with the fragrant oil of sacrificial love—myrrh. When she hesitates to respond to His knockings, Beloved departs. Love searches for Him and finds Him in the Sharon Valley, teaching the people. Her King invites her to minister alongside Him.

Opening Prayer

Fun Activity
Preparation: Be prayed up. If your church has a prayer team, you may choose to invite them to pray for the students with you, but remain in the lead. It is your class.
Supplies: Anointing oil of frankincense and myrrh.

This entire activity will be a prayer. Ask for the class to form a circle of joined hands. One by one, each willing student may step into the center of the circle. The student shares a blessing she desires to receive. You (and trusted elders, if they are available) may anoint the student and pray a blessing upon her. Take your time, and permit the Holy Spirit to lead your response.

Pray only blessings—nothing discouraging is to be spoken over the Bride of Christ you are blessing. If you are in a charismatic church, you might want to have a spotter or a chair for her to sit in.

Avoid being the push-over minister, bowling them over by finger pressure to a student's forehead. To avoid this, touch the sides of the head rather than her forehead, and, by all means, permit the Holy Spirit to lead. You want to be open to Beloved's leading, while showing respect, gentleness, and not drawing attention to yourself.

Make sure to have your teeth brushed and mints available, as you'll be in close contact with your students.

Question/Answer Time
Choose three of the seven questions for your students to discuss.
Closing Prayer

WEEK NINE
Chapter Nine: My Beloved
Preview
Love's remembrances of her Groom's earthly and heavenly character traits become the cornerstone of her faith. Prophetic significance flows throughout her entire recollection. She describes Beloved's pierced hands set with the beryl stone and His anointed locks dripping with sacrificial oils of love. She remembers His tender words, and the sweet kisses of peace He gives her within the holy wedding chamber.

Opening Prayer

Fun Activity
Supplies: Lined paper, one sheet per student. Candy Valentine hearts.

Ask your students to write their Beloved Valentine Jesus Christ a valentine message. Ask volunteers to share their responses. Distribute the candy hearts.

Question/Answer Time
Choose three of the seven questions for your students to discuss.

Closing Prayer

WEEK TEN
Chapter Ten: My Love
Preview
The people of Sharon Valley long for Love's return. They recognize her authority as they describe her purity, passion, unity with the Lord. and authority. Love learns to recognize when she sees a glint of glory in a seeker's eyes, shining white like the white wheat that gleams in the sunshine, indicating the person is ready to receive her witness.

Opening Prayer

Fun Activity
Preparation: In marker, in bold letters, write the name of each student on construction paper hearts. Place these hearts at the front of the class, on a table.
Supplies: A stack of index cards. Lots of them! Valentine candy hearts.
This activity will demonstrate to your students they are each uniquely loved by the Bridegroom and by each other. Ask your students to write 1) the name of their classmate and 2) one character trait they have observed them to possess but not their name. These are anonymous notes (although some will have fun guessing by handwriting analysis).

Tell your students that instead of writing Beloved Jesus a Valentine card, they are writing one for each of their classmates, and a one-word or a one-liner response is sufficient. As they write these, they are to give them to you to place on their name hearts.

Inevitably, students will notice similar traits for their classmates. This affirms them. (If in the unlikely scenario an unflattering card is written, pocket it rather than putting it on their name badge.) Ask your class to make sure every person gets several, so if they see a short stack, ask them to write one for that person.

Discuss how the Bridegroom loves them even more than these compliments they've received. Permit the students to take these name hearts with their index cards home, to treasure. You also should have prepared some to add to each name. Don't add yours until the class gets started so they are not influenced by your cards.

Distribute Valentine candy hearts again.

Question/Answer Time

Choose three of the seven questions for your students to discuss.

Closing Prayer

Preparation for Next Week: Invite the students to wear fancy shoes, especially sparkly ones.

WEEK ELEVEN
Chapter Eleven: A Search for Lilies
Preview

The people describe Love's shoes, symbolic of her witness. They describe other parts, such as her belly, symbolic of the Communion cup. She learns the female date palm rises and bears fruit only when under the shadow of her mate. In order to bear spiritual fruit, Love must remain in her Husband's shadow. As the bowing date palm, she also must model Beloved's humility and love.

Opening Prayer

Fun Activity
Supplies: A vase of stemmed flowers, preferably white lilies, if available. One flower per student.

As each student enters, hand her a flower.

Ask three students to share the traits of the lily and how this applies to those they share the message of the Bridegroom with. (Examples: bent over — humble, important to Beloved — fragrant, holy — white, etc.)

Permit the students to keep their flowers and to pray for the Lord to reveal one person this week they are to evangelize, disciple, or pray for.

Ask your students the meaning of the fancy shoes according to the vignette. (They represent the Bride's evangelistic desire.)

Question/Answer Time

Choose three of the seven questions for your students to discuss.

Closing Prayer

Preparation for the Final Week — students are to bring a picture they are willing to give you that you can keep and not return.

WEEK TWELVE
Chapter Twelve: Kept by Love
Preview

This chapter summarizes Love's life. Key scenes are noted, such as her wedding, Communion under the apple tree, and her eagerness to witness to the people. Love guards her once-neglected spiritual vineyard, and while she waits for her Groom's imminent return, she disciples others. Her Groom has conquered every "Bether" within her. The Bride is complete and has fully received her Groom's kisses of divine love and peace.

Opening Prayer

Fun Activity
Preparation: A large posterboard, decorated ahead of time with any accoutrements you want to use to make it pretty. You might want to have the name of the Bible study and the date and also the date of the next Bible study somewhere on the poster.
Supplies: Rubber Cement.
　　Ask your students to come to the front, put rubber cement on their picture, and place it on the poster board at a location of their choosing.
　　After everyone has had an opportunity to put their picture on the poster board, ask for volunteers to share how the person they prayed for has been blessed. Inevitably, you will have testimonies of answered prayers.

Question/Answer Time
　　Choose three of the seven questions for your students to discuss.

Closing Prayer
　　Thank your students for their participation in the class, and ask them to give you the name(s) of one or more person(s) who might benefit from taking the study next time. You may desire to give them a certificate of completion.

BRIDAL REFLECTION — QUESTIONS/ANSWERS

CHAPTER ONE — THE KISS

1) Think of a kiss that caused remembrance. Why is a groom's kiss more intimate than any natural kiss? How does Beloved's divine kiss of peace compare/differ to a groom's kiss? (Subjective: Beloved's is the most intimate because it represents the spiritual realm.)

2) Why is Song of Solomon written as a vignette (play)? How does this format help you to experience Beloved Jesus Christ's divine message? (Song of Solomon is in play format to encourage participation.)

3) Who are the two main actors in Song of Solomon, and who do they represent? (The two main actors are the Bride and Bridegroom, the Church, including myself, and Jesus Christ.)

4) Why is it important to keep Rabbi Akiba's wisdom alive regarding the vignette, Song of Solomon? Discuss the canonization of Song of Solomon. (Rabbi Akiba acknowledged the Bridegroom, and the Holy of Holies, allegorically represented in the vignette. Future messianic commentators recognized the Bridegroom as Jesus Christ. It is important that with Akiba's work Song of Solomon was canonized because it was almost left out of our Bibles. Akiba's stamp of approval helped it to be canonized, preserving the writing for us to read.)

5) Why is Beloved's divine love—*dowd*—like a boiling pot? (His love is intense.)

6) You, as Bride, say to Beloved Jesus Christ, "Draw me away!" How does this statement help to create marital intimacy in the spiritual realm? (Beloved is a gentleman; He wants to be involved in my life but He waits for my invitation.)

7) In the vignette, what is the bridal name your Groom Beloved Solomon, allegorically Jesus Christ, calls you most often? In your fanciest writing, write your bridal name in the blank: _____ (My bridal name is "Love.")

CHAPTER TWO — KEDAR'S SCAR

1) In the vignette, who is Kedar? Describe his way of life, his religion, country of origin, and other facts about him. How does this absence of father and Kedar's bend toward enmity affect his life and yours? (In the vignette, Kedar represents my birthfather. Kedar is a murderer worse than Cain, entrenched in enmity, and this represents the enemy's work in my modern-day family tree.)

2) Discuss the lives of Adam and Eve, Cain, Abraham and Sarah, Hagar, Isaac, and Ishmael. Why was it important for these characters to choose peace over enmity and faith over self-will? Which of these people succeeded? (Subjective. The student is to distinguish the difference between self-will and the enmity this choice produces, versus dependence upon God through faith, and the divine love and peace this choice produces.)

3) What is your choice today? Do you choose love and peace or self-will and enmity? Write a brief one- or two-sentence prayer expressing your personal choice. (Subjective)

4) In the vignette, you are an ambassador of God's love and peace to your birthfather, Kedar. In the world today, are you the Bride of Christ still called to be Beloved's ambassador or has this calling subsided? (This calling remains sure.)

5) True or False: God has a destiny for all nations. (True.)
6) We all have "dark," false labels that have been imposed upon us. The way to overcome these is to reflect on Beloved's true labels for His Bride, that of "Love" (all three forms), "fairest amongst women," "vinedresser," "shepherd," and "lovely." Of these, share the label you relate to the most at this juncture of your journey. Share why this is so. (Subjective)
7) Describe the "inner curtain." What does this represent? How would you rate your inner curtain (of worship) at present: A) frail but pliable, B) lukewarm, C) on fire for God, D) other? Discuss this, and end by praying a blessing upon each person in your small group. If you are doing this study independently, pray a blessing upon yourself. (The inner curtain represents my inner self where my spirit meets God's Spirit.; Second answer is subjective; third answer is an activity.)

CHAPTER THREE—THE OASIS

1) Name the seven Oasis Keys of this chapter. Which do you most relate to? (Acceptance; Lordship; Mind Renewal; Focused Time; Obedience; Union through Communion; Spiritual Growth. The second question is subjective.)
2) Compare Song 2:7, 3:5, and 8:4. Which stage of development best describes your current relationship with Beloved? (Subjective)
3) King David found an oasis at En Gedi that made him unreachable by enemy attacks. He was sheltered in this refuge, so every attempt Saul made to injure him, failed. Compare this to your bridal relationship with Jesus Christ. (Beloved hems me in because I belong to Him.)
4) Read Isaiah 54:17. Declare over your life that no weapon the enemy forms against you will prosper because as the Bride of Christ you abide in the refuge of Beloved's divine love. Write the verse and decorate your paper. (Activity)
5) Moses' face shone during times of worship. Can you, as Beloved's Bride, also expect to experience the glory, even if your face doesn't shine in the natural realm? (Yes. Absolutely!)
6) What shape is the Communion table? Discuss why this is so. (The Communion table is round, emphasizing the unity I gain with Beloved while I partake.)
7) In the vignette, your skin exudes the fragrant oil of spikenard, expressing your desires to have a perfect marriage. Relate this to today. Share the desires you have to deepen your relationship with Beloved Jesus Christ. (Subjective)

CHAPTER FOUR—THE BANQUETING TABLE

1) Share your salvation experience. If you have not yet gotten saved, would you like to do so today? If so, ask a saved friend, leader, or pastor to pray a salvation prayer with you. (Testimonial)
2) True or False: The literary structure of Scene Seven, where phrases and/or words are paired, shows the unity of the Bride to her Groom Jesus Christ. (True.)
3) What does the raisin cake represent? Why is it one single element, while expressing the bread and wine of Communion? (The raisin cake represents Communion, and the unity it produces between me as Bride and my Bridegroom Jesus Christ. This also represents the unity of believers with each other through Jesus Christ.)
4) Compare and contrast the Rose of Sharon with the lilies of the valleys. (Answers may include the rare, sweet, trail-blazing Rose of Sharon, versus the common white lilies, pure and varied. Both lilies have the five-pointed star of David in their design, the trumpet shape representing the Bride as ambassador heralding Jesus's messages, and the flower is downward facing,

respectively representing humility.)

5) Share a Communion experience that was special to you. (Testimonial)

6) What is written on Beloved's banner that flies at Father's house. What does this mean? Reflect on this. (She said "yes." This indicates I must personally say "yes" to my Beloved Bridegroom's marriage proposal. He does not force a bridal relationship on me.)

7) Have you said "yes!" to Beloved Jesus Christ's Communion invitation to be His Bride? If so, ask a friend, leader, or pastor to pray a prayer of commitment with you. (Activity)

CHAPTER FIVE—SHADOWBOXING IN BETHER

1) In the modern-day example of King David, we saw he had position, title, and a developing anointing when he transgressed. You, as Bride, have these same characteristics. What must you do to shepherd the anointing carefully? (I must make sure I prioritize Beloved's Word, time with Him, and obedience to all He tells me, being watchful to avoid enticing schemes of the enemy.)

2) King David repented and wrote Psalm 51. Read this Psalm and pray its principles for your own life. How can you be watchful for enemy traps? (Prayer activity; subjective)

3) Why is it important to conquer the "little foxes" in your bridal experience? (If I am watchful, committed to conquering little sins, transgressions aren't able to set in.)

4) Read Song of Solomon 2:11 NKJV. What does the phrase, "over *and* gone" emphasize about your old life versus your new life as Bride of Beloved? (The repetition emphasizes I am Beloved's and my past has no hold on me. I am completely forgiven.)

5) In Song of Solomon 2:9, Beloved comes to you, "gazing" through the garden lattice. The word, "gazing," means "twinkling," and this indicates He is revealing His glory to you, enticing you to come beyond the known and into a deeper relationship with Him. Describe a time you felt He was doing this in today's times. How did your communion with Him strengthen as He revealed Himself to you? (Testimonial)

6) Do you have a prayer garden retreat, whether it is in a garden or in a room, closet, chair, or other location? How does having a specific place to pray strengthen your relationship with Beloved Jesus? (Subjective)

7) What did you think of the idea of writing on our day timers, "Meeting with the King," as a way to remind ourselves Beloved Jesus Christ is the most important person we will meet with all day? (Subjective)

CHAPTER SIX—THE CHARIOT RIDER

1) Describe how the differences between the Jewish marriage of ancient biblical times contrast with today's bridal customs. (Answers may include prearranged marriages of ancient biblical times verses the dating scene common to American households.)

2) Your Bible equates today to your *ketubah* of the Jewish wedding. What is a *ketubah*? Share your favorite verse in your Bible that your Groom writes to you. (A *ketubah* is the Jewish marriage contract. My Bible is Jesus' marriage contract to me, His Bride.)

3) How does the high bridal price—the *mohar*—of Beloved, who was willing to go to Calvary to redeem you as His Bride, make you feel about the depth of love your Groom has for you? (Subjective)

4) Your love story is embroidered on the "tapestry seat" of Beloved's chariot. Who embroiders this seat? Share your testimony and aspects of your relationship with Beloved Jesus Christ that are most important to you. (Testimonial)

5) What do the crossbeams of the chariot represent? Why are they made of silver? Why is the floor of the chariot covered with gold dust? Where does this gold dust originate? (The crossbeams represent the cross, silver indicating redemption. The floor of the chariot is covered with gold

dust representative of Heaven's glory.)

6) What did Rabbi Akiba believe about Song of Solomon in relation to the Holy of Holies? What happens in the *huppah,* and how does this spiritually represent the Holy of Holies? How many days do the bride and groom spend in the *huppah*? (Rabbi Akiba believed the veiled wedding chamber, and the Holy of Holies represent bridal intimacy, and spiritually are one in the same. In the *huppa* I gain full access to my Bridegroom. Jewish couples spent seven days in the *huppa,* or bridal chamber, representing the Holy of Holies.)

7) Describe how Beloved's chariot is like a limousine ride. How does this assure you He has your best interests at heart? Celebrate reading this chapter by making a fancy dinner or going out to eat. Invite friends! (Beloved lavishes divine love upon me, His Bride. Second part of the question is an activity.)

CHAPTER SEVEN—BEHIND THE VEIL

1) Describe a wedding that you witnessed. How does the bridal veil of today's marriages relate to the bridal veil of the vignette? Does knowing Beloved desires an eternal marriage covenant with you, His Bride, bring you security in the strength of His love and the depth of His commitment? (Testimonial; The bridal veil equates to today's wedding ring; subjective)

2) The Lebanon Mountain Range equates to Prayer Mountain. You, as Bride, visit the seven the locations therein: 1) Mt. Gilead 2) Mt. Bether 3) Mt. Myrrh 4) Frankincense Hill 5) Mt. Hermon 6) Mt. Amana 7) Mt. Senir/Mt Hermon. What is your favorite location? (Subjective)

3) Have you ever experienced a healing or miracle as Mt. Bether alludes to that was and still is available to us as Beloved's Bride? If so, share your healing/miracle testimony. Read Hebrews 13:8 from several translations of the Bible. What do you conclude? (Testimonial)

4) Describe Mt. Amana. Why is it important to be in agreement with Beloved's Word in order to be in agreement with Him? (Mt. Amana represents prayer agreement with Beloved's Word. I don't decide what truth is; Beloved does that through His Word. I cannot just accept some of the promises in the Bible and reject the ones I don't like.)

5) In Song 4:7, Beloved says you are "all fair," therefore beautiful to Him in spirit. Have you received His forgiveness for past, present, and future sins? How does this strengthen your relationship with Beloved Jesus Christ? (Forgiveness is freeing. I am forgiven and made new.)

6) Describe the enclosed garden found in Mt. Hermon. What does this location equate to in the spiritual realm? (Hint: Rabbi Akiba drew the same conclusion) (The Holy of Holies equates to Mt. Hermon. It is here that I experience the greatest spiritual intimacy with my Beloved. But I must be watchful, because Mt. Senir is in close proximity. Therefore, with every spiritual ascent, I must be prepared to wage spiritual warfare.)

7) How has your view of Beloved Solomon in the vignette, who allegorically equates to Jesus Christ, changed so far during this study? Share the ways you have experienced spiritual growth. (Subjective)

CHAPTER EIGHT—NIGHT VISITORS

1) Did you relate to Ted Williams' salvation story? How can you help the "Teds" in your sphere of influence maintain a relationship with Beloved Jesus Christ? (Subjective)

2) Describe Beloved's myrrh-drenched, ductal, oil-infused, raven-black curls. What do each of these mean as they relate to Beloved's character? (Beloved's ductal curls ooze from the inside-out. Myrrh represents His priestly role, which He emphasizes here in the vignette. Thus, He is showing His willingness to be the Suffering Servant.)

3) Beloved wears the oil of myrrh, as well as the oil of frankincense. Why does He only deposit the oil of myrrh on the latch of the door? What role is He trying to emphasize—High Priest or Suffering Savior? How does this relate to your calling to minister alongside Him? (I need

forgiveness, and Beloved as my High Priest can impart that to me fully. Beloved deposits the myrrh on the latch of the door because He is a gentleman and respects my decision to accept or reject His ministry calling. In order to minister effectively, I must be ready the moment Beloved calls me.)

4) Are you willing to get your feet "dirty" in order to respond to Beloved's ministry calling? What are ways you can minister and not resent the messy task this presents? (Yes! Subjective)

5) Have you had a "night visitation" where Beloved called you to witness at an inopportune time? Did you respond quickly enough? How does knowing Beloved leaves the myrrh help you to know you are still called? (Subjective. Beloved is quick to forgive so I know I am still called.)

6) Why must your robe remain on and you never take it off? What does the robe represent? (I must guard the anointing, so I must never take off my robe, which represents the anointing.)

7) If Beloved were visible, what would you say to Him first? Write a prayer to Him, envisioning Him as your Bridegroom who loves you in all seasons. (Activity)

CHAPTER NINE – MY BELOVED

1) Fill in the blank: My Beloved Jesus is _____. (Subjective)

2) Are you still "lovesick" for your Groom Jesus Christ? Describe your relationship with Him. Give Him praise for being in your life. (Subjective)

3) Describe Beloved's earthly and His heavenly characteristics that you most admire. (Subjective)

4) Define the term, *kenosis*. How does this relate to Beloved Jesus Christ? (Kenosis is an emptying of oneself of pride; it's a humbling of oneself. Beloved Jesus is the humblest person ever, demonstrating through Calvary's cross, and many other actions, that He loves humanity and is the Savior, spotless and humble. He is Son of God, and He is equally Son of Man.)

5) Has Beloved Jesus Christ ever sinned? Read Hebrews 4:15 to check your answer. How does being sinless relate to Beloved's ability to redeem you, His Bride? (Jesus Christ has never sinned. He is and always will be sinless. Therefore, He was able to pay the price of death for sins, in order to redeem mankind.)

6) Describe Beloved's eyes, cheeks, hands, and His divine kiss of peace. (Subjective; any of the things discussed in the chapter are viable answers, as well as personal observations the student may have)

7) Do you feel you can describe your relationship with Beloved as a friendship? Explain. (Subjective)

CHAPTER TEN – MY LOVE

1) Describe a Valentine gift you have received or sent. How does this relate to the power of love? (Subjective)

2) Discuss Saint Valentine and his commitment to honor love. How does Beloved Jesus' love surpass these expressions? (Saint Valentine honored love so much he laid down his life to heal a girl and to marry soldiers in the army. As a result of his defiance of Claudius 11, the king sentenced Saint Valentine to death on February 14, 270 AD. My Beloved Jesus Christ laid down His life on Calvary's cross to redeem me because He loves me.)

3) Who is Tirzah? Where is she mentioned in Song of Solomon? What correlation does Tirzah's life have regarding your spiritual inheritance as the Bride of Christ? (Tirzah and her sisters were the daughters of Zelophehad who had no sons. Tirzah and her sisters wondered what would happen to their father's family name when they reached the Promised Land as it was customary for men to inherit the lands. Tirzah asked Moses to give them their father's inheritance. Moses prayed, and passed the inheritance to Zelophehad's daughters. Tizrah went on to be a ruler of a land, with great authority. In Song of Solomon 6:4, Beloved equates the Bride of Christ as having spiritual authority equivalent to the fame and authority Tizrah had.)

4) When Beloved Jesus says you are "awesome" (KJV "terrible"), who are you frightening by your spiritual authority as the Bride of Christ? (My love and allegiance to Beloved frightens Satan. The enemy is terrified of me because of my marriage to Beloved Jesus Christ.)

5) Why does Beloved say your eyes are like doves? How is it they have overcome your Groom? (When I press into my relationship with my Bridegroom Jesus Christ, the Holy Spirit embodies my spirit. These are like dove's eyes to Beloved, and He notices the presence of His Holy Spirit within me, reflected through my eyes.)

6) How do you know when someone is ready to receive a witness? (Hint: "white.") (Someone who is ready to receive the Holy Spirit will look glorious, sparkling inside.)

7) Write a prayer to your Beloved Valentine. (Subjective)

CHAPTER ELEVEN – A SEARCH FOR LILIES

1) Describe your shoe collection. In the vignette, how does this relate to your witness? (Subjective)

2) When you witness, does this affect one person or is there a chain reaction? Justify your answer by mentioning a biblical example (i.e.: Esther, Rahab, Ruth, Daniel). (Yes; Subjective)

3) Describe your mid-section, as Beloved does, and how this represents the Communion of the Bride. (My mid-section represents the bread and wine of Communion, and the people we reach for Christ. I lack nothing, being nourished by the bread and wine of Communion. This is the basis of my marriage covenant with Beloved Jesus Christ.)

4) Compare Proverbs 31 with the Damask cloth of this chapter. What does this represent? (The Damask cloth, of the silk worm, is expensive; this represents my high value to my Beloved. Because Beloved values me, I am a formidable enemy to the enemy.)

5) Discuss the covenantal relationship in relation to the Bride's thigh. (The thigh represented covenant in Old Testament times.)

6) What does "Heshbon" represent? How does this apply to your gaze? (My eyes reflect peace like the peaceful pools located in Heshbon.)

7) How does the female palm tree become fruitful? How does this apply to you as Bride? (As the female palm tree leans beneath her mate, she rises with Him, becoming fruitful.)

CHAPTER TWELVE – KEPT BY LOVE

1) In Photo One, why is the pomegranate wine spiced? What do the pomegranate, the spices, and the wine represent? (The pomegranate wine is an aphrodisiac, and contains the apothecary spices used on Jesus Christ at burial. The spices may also include any of those we saw in the secluded garden of Song 4:12-15, and represent completion. I as Bride am satiated.)

2) In Photo Two, Beloved is embracing you. Describe this in detail. (Subjective)

3) When you harvest souls in Photo Three, what is the significance of your bridal walk, in relation to how successful you will be? (I will be successful as I permit Beloved to shape my character.)

4) In Photo Five, you witness to two types of people. Which kinds are these and how do you effectively witness to each? (To the individual who resembles a door, I offer salvation through my Beloved. To the walled off individual, I offer the silver of redemption's forgiveness through Beloved, which is continually available.)

5) Are you the Bride who is the "wall" of Photo Six? (Subjective)

6) Has this study helped you become a consecrated Bride? (Subjective)

7) Write a prayer of thanksgiving to your Beloved Jesus Christ. (Subjective)

THANK YOU!

Students, thank you for completing this Bible study! Teachers, thank you for teaching this! May your Beloved Bridegroom bless you for your time, commitment, and for following His leading.

About the Author

Diane Virginia (Cunio) is an award-winning author, the founder/director of VineWords: Devotions and More, and the co-editor, co-compiler, and contributing author to *Love-Knots: Stories of Faith, Family, and Friendships* (VineWords Publishing), the first of a series of devotionals VineWords will release.

Her book, *The Kiss of Peace: A Contemporary Exploration into Song of Solomon* (Mount Zion Ridge Press), reveals Song of Solomon to be an allegory of Christ's divine love for His Bride, the Church. In this book, Diane takes the reader on a journey into her Beloved Jesus Christ's divine love. *The Kiss of Peace* placed third in the Sparrow Awards at the 2020 Asheville Christian Writer's Conference.

The sequel, *Behind the Veil: Becoming the Ascended Bride of Song of Solomon*, is a study/devotional geared towards deepening the reader's spiritual intimacy with her Beloved Bridegroom Jesus Christ, as she understands the significance of the seven mountain locations He takes her to.

To complement these books on Song of Solomon, Diane has developed the model for motion-activated musical prayer centers for use at the church or home garden retreat. She envisions these prayer gardens to be themed to the seven mountain locations of Song of Solomon. She hopes these will serve as refuges for seekers and believers alike where they can tarry, worship, and find or deepen their relationships with Jesus Christ.

Diane is published at Answers2Prayer, Christian Broadcasting Network, Christian Devotions Ministries, Faith Beyond Fear, Inspire a Fire, Pentecostal Publishing House, PresbyCan Daily Devotional, The Secret Place, VineWords, and other ministries.

Contact Diane if you'd like her to speak to your ladies' group or church on any theme related to Song of Solomon.

You can find her online:

https://www.vinewords.net

Email@vinewords.net

CPSIA information can be obtained
at www.ICGtesting.com
Printed in the USA
BVHW090742021021
617991BV00013B/428